F.W.I.C.
Education
028

GW00586797

King's College Lond

Information Services Centre
Franklin-Wilkins Building
150 Stamford Street
London SE1 8WA

Telephone: 020 7848 4378

This book may be recalled at any time and must be returned or
renewed by the date shown.

New Perspectives on Conceptual Change

ADVANCES IN LEARNING AND INSTRUCTION SERIES

Series Editors:
Neville Bennett, Erik DeCorte, Stella Vosniadou and Heinz Mandl

Published

BLISS, SÄLJÖ & LIGHT
Learning Sites: Social and Technological Resources for Learning

DILLENBOURG
Collaborative Learning: Cognitive and Computational Approaches

KAYSER & VOSNIADOU
Modelling Changes in Understanding: Case Studies in Physical Reasoning

VAN SOMEREN, REIMANN, BOSHUIZEN & DE JONG
Learning with Multiple Representations

Forthcoming titles

COWIE, AALSVOORT & MERCER
Social Interaction in Learning and Instruction

KOZULIN & RAND
Experience of Meditated Learning: An Impact of Feuerstein's Theory in Education and Psychology

ROUET
Using Complex Information Systems

WOOD & THOMAS
Learning to Teach to Learn

Other titles of interest

REIMANN & SPADA
Learning in Humans and Machines: Towards an Interdisciplinary Learning Science
Computer Assisted Learning: Proceedings of the CAL series of Biennial Symposia 1989, 1991, 1993, 1995 and 1997 (five volumes)

Related journals—sample copies available on request

Learning and Instruction
International Journal of Educational Research
Computers and Education
Computers in Human Behavior

New Perspectives on Conceptual Change

edited by

Wolfgang Schnotz
Stella Vosniadou
and Mario Carretero

Earli

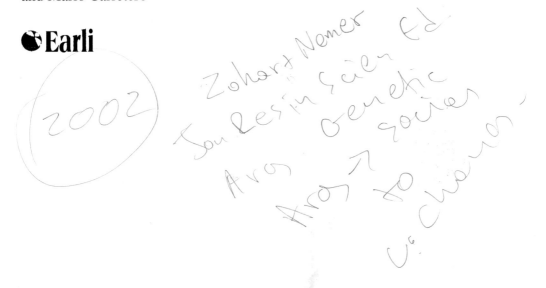

Pergamon
An imprint of Elsevier Science
Amsterdam – Lausanne – New York – Oxford – Shannon – Singapore – Tokyo

ELSEVIER SCIENCE Ltd
The Boulevard, Langford Lane
Kidlington, Oxford OX5 1GB, UK

First edition 1999 by Pergamon (an imprint of Elsevier Science Ltd) in association with the European Association for Research on Learning and Instruction (EARLI)

Library of Congress Cataloging in Publication Data

New perspectives on conceptual change / edited by Wolfgang Schnotz,
   Stella Vosniadou, and Mario Carretero.
        p.   cm. -- (Advances in learning and instruction series)
    Includes bibliographical references.
    ISBN 0-08-043455-X
    1. Concept learning. 2. Learning, Psychology of. 3. Knowledge,
Theory of.   I. Schnotz, Wolfgang, 1946-   . II. Vosniadou, Stella.
III. Carretero, Mario.   IV. Series.
    LB1062.N49 1999
    370.15'23--dc21
                                                            99-36628
                                                            CIP
British Library Cataloguing in Publication Data
A catalogue record from the British Library has been applied for.

ISBN: 0 08 043455 X

Typeset by The Midlands Book Typesetting Company, United Kingdom

∞ The paper used in this publication meets the requirements of ANSI/NISO Z39.48-1992 (Permanence of Paper).
Printed in The Netherlands.

Table of Contents

Acknowledgements

The editors want to thank the Deutsche Forschungsgemeinschaft [German Research Foundation] who supported the preparation of this book by sponsoring an International Symposium on Conceptual Change at the Friedrich-Schiller-University of Jena, Germany, from 1–3 September, 1994. The exchange of theoretical perspectives and research findings during this symposium was the starting point of a discussion that finally resulted in the set of papers presented in this volume.

The editors also would like to express their thanks to a number of persons who have helped with this volume. We thank Harriet Grzondziel, Claudia Petruch, Achim Preuß and Thomas Zink for their assistance in preparing and organizing the symposium. Furthermore, we thank Petra Entzminger and Birgit Penniger for their help in preparing the manuscripts, and we thank Wolfgang Edel for his work on the subject index.

Contributors

Anna E. Berti
Universita' degli studi Padova
Dip. Psicologia dello Sviluppo
via Beato Pellegrino 26
35137 Padova
ITALY

Harm J. A. Biemans
University of Nijmegen
Department of Educational Sciences
P.O. Box 9103
6500 HD Nijmegen
THE NETHERLANDS

Mario Carretero
Universidad Autonoma de Madrid
Facultad de Psicologia
Cantoblanco
E-28049 Madrid
SPAIN

Erik De Corte
Catholic University of Leuven
CIP & T
Vesaliusstraat 2
B-3000 Leuven
BELGIUM

Reinders Duit
Universität Kiel
IPN, Abt. Physikdidaktik
Olshausenstraße 62
24098 Kiel
GERMANY

Miguel Angel Gómez
Universidad Autonoma de Madrid
Facultad de Psicologia
28049 Madrid
SPAIN

Ola Halldén
Stockholm University
Department of Education
Frescati Hagväg 24
S-10691 Stockholm
SWEDEN

Devorah Kalekin-Fishman
University of Haifa
School of Education
Mt Carmel
31905 Haifa
ISRAEL

Sabien Lasure
Catholic University of Leuven
CIP & T
Vesaliusstraat 2
B-3000 Leuven
BELGIUM

Margarita Limón
Universidad Autonoma de Madrid
Facultad de Psicologia
Cantoblanco
E-28049 Madrid
SPAIN

Richard Lowe
Curtin University of Technology
Faculty of Education
GPO Box U 1987
6845 Perth
AUSTRALIA

Terezinha Nunes
University of London
Institute of Education
20 Bedford Way
WC1H 0AL London
UK

Sabina Pauen
Psychologisches Institut
der Universität Tübingen
Friedrichstraße 21
72072 Tübingen
GERMANY

Paul Pintrich
University of Michigan
School of Education
610 E. University, 1225 SEB
Ann Arbor, Michigan 48109-1259
USA

Juan-Ignacio Pozo
Universidad Autonoma de Madrid
Facultad de Psicologia
28049 Madrid
SPAIN

Achim Preuß
Universität Jena
Am Steiger 3/Haus 1
07743 Jena
GERMANY

Roger Säljö
University of Göteborg
Dep. of Education
Box 300
SE-40530 Göteborg
SWEDEN

Angeles Sanz
Universidad Autonoma de Madrid
Facultad de Psicologia
28049 Madrid
SPAIN

Wolfgang Schnotz
University of Koblenz-Landau
Dept. of General and Educational Psychology
Im Fort 7
D-76829 Landau
GERMANY

Robert-Jan Simons
Katholieke Universiteit Nijmegen
Faculty of Social Sciences
P.O. Box 9104
6500 HE Nijmegen
THE NETHERLANDS

Lieven Verschaffel
Catholic University of Leuven
CIP & T
Vesaliusstraat 2
B-3000 Leuven
BELGIUM

Stella Vosniadou
University of Athens
Department of History
and Philosophy of Science
8, Chersonos
Gr-16121 Athens
GREECE

Preface

Most researchers in the field of learning and instruction agree that individuals are not passive recipients of information, but rather active constructors of their own knowledge. Even young babies actively explore their environment according to epistemological principles that seem to be genetically implemented in the cognitive system (Baillargeon, 1994; Spelke, 1990). When children enter school, they are, therefore, not "empty vessels", but have already acquired a common-sense understanding of their natural and social environment based on experiences in everyday life. Unfortunately, this common-sense understanding frequently does not correspond to or is incompatible with the knowledge taught in school. Obviously, learning requires not only enrichment of knowledge and integration of new information, but also reorganization of existing knowledge, usually referred to as conceptual change.

Traditional Research on Conceptual Change

The investigation of conceptual change is rooted in developmental psychology as well as in research on science education. For many years, developmental psychology was dominated by the ideas of Piaget (1950), who tried to explain cognitive development by a general tendency of the individual to achieve a mental equilibrium, i.e. to free itself from cognitive conflicts. Conceptual change was described as a domain-general modification of cognitive structures that affect the knowledge acquisition process in all subject-matter areas. This view has received severe criticism during the last decade. Recent research has demonstrated that children show, much earlier, much higher performances than should be expected according to Piaget's theory (Carey & Gelman, 1991). Instead of searching for global changes of knowledge structures, developmental psychologists today focus on domain-specific processes of conceptual change caused by an increase in domain-specific knowledge rather than an increase in general logical capabilities (Carey, 1985).

An approach to cognitive development and conceptual change that is fundamentally different from Piaget has been held by Vygotski (1962). He considered the human cognitive development as a process of enculturation, of growing into a community with a shared practice, common tools and a common language. According to this view, concepts are cognitive tools for orientation, which grasp relevant regularities within the natural and social environment, originate in the human practice and are applied in human practice. Vygotski argued that the concepts acquired spontaneously in everyday life and the scientific concepts acquired from school belong to qualitatively different conceptual systems. He assumed that the concepts acquired from everyday experiences are closely related to real phenomena, but are not part of a coherent system. On the contrary, the scientific concepts taught in school were supposed to form coherent systems, but not to be sufficiently related to the phenomena of everyday experience. He suggested that schooling should help the different conceptual systems grow together: learners should integrate their spontaneously acquired everyday concepts into coherent systems and should apply the concepts acquired in school to their everyday experience. In practice, however, an integration of the different conceptual systems frequently turns out to be impossible, because the respective conceptual systems are not compatible.

Another line of research on conceptual change has its roots in science education. Studies in this area have produced a rich body of knowledge about learners' naive concepts in the fields of physics, chemistry, astronomy, biology, social sciences, history and mathematics. These naive concepts have been frequently referred to as misconceptions or, less derogatorily, as "alternative frameworks of reference". A very influential approach on conceptual change in science education has been developed by Posner et al. (Strike & Posner, 1982). According to their theoretical framework, conceptual change is considered a replacement of old conceptions for new. This process requires that the following conditions are fulfilled: (i) there must be dissatisfaction with existing conceptions; (ii) there must be a new alternative conception that is intelligible; (iii) the new conception must appear initially plausible; and (iv) the new conception should be fruitful. This framework has provided a theoretical justification for the instructional use of "cognitive conflict" and has become the leading paradigm to guide research and instructional practice in science education.

Empirical research has shown, however, that cognitive conflicts frequently do not result in conceptual change. If concepts are considered as cognitive tools, one has to admit that the so-called naive concepts are rather useful in everyday life. As learners often feel no dissatisfaction with these ideas, it seems rather unrealistic to expect that they would give up their well-functioning cognitive tools in favour of a new, so-called scientific knowledge. Even if there is some dissatisfaction, but no alternative and intelligible idea available to the learner, there is no reason for conceptual change. Finally, it is possible that there is an intelligible alternative, which is, however, not plausible. In this case, there is no conceptual change, because learners are able to understand a new theory without believing it.

Contrary to the view of children as "intuitive scientists", learners do not usually differentiate clearly between theoretical hypotheses and empirical evidence (Kuhn, 1989), and they apply various ad-hoc strategies to cope with situations in which the two sides conflict with each other (Chinn & Brewer, 1993). Learners frequently lack metaconceptual awareness about the epistemological status of their own knowledge: they do not understand that their view is not necessarily true, but consists of hypotheses that might be evaluated and perhaps falsified (Vosniadou, 1994). Instead of being replaced, the naive conceptions frequently stay alive and co-exist besides the new conceptions. Students learn to master the scientific vocabulary, learn to reproduce the knowledge taught in school and to answer the teacher's questions. Outside school, however, they continue to use their old conceptions, while their new knowledge remains "inert" (Collins et al., 1989).

New Approaches

The criticism against the traditional views has led to the development of new theoretical approaches that help to draw a more differentiated picture of conceptual change. These views differ from each other with respect to the following questions: What is the nature of the learner's preconceptions? What are the mechanisms that bring about conceptual change? What makes conceptual change difficult? What can we do to foster conceptual change? With regard to the nature of individual preconceptions, di Sessa (1988, 1993) has argued that children's naive knowledge consists of isolated pieces, so-called phenomenological principles. Accordingly, conceptual change is primarily an integration of phenomenological principles into more comprehensive conceptual structures. The initially low coherence of naive knowledge is considered to result from children's metacognitive deficits and inadequate comprehension standards.

A quite different view has been adopted by Vosniadou and Brewer (1992, 1994). They argue that misconceptions are not caused by a lack of coherence or by metacognitive deficits but, rather, are the result of active and creative efforts to establish mental coherence. According to Vosniadou and Brewer, children construct mental models based on their everyday experience. In order to reconcile new information with old assumptions about the subject matter, the children's initial models are transformed into so-called synthetic models. These models result from active attempts of the learner to take old and new information into account as far as possible; therefore, they include a mixture of previous naive knowledge and new, culturally conveyed knowledge. Conceptual change is, according to this view, a gradual process that leads from initial mental models via synthetic models to scientifically correct models.

An essential point in the approach of Vosniadou and Brewer is their distinction between different levels of conceptual knowledge. As concepts are embedded into more comprehensive theoretical structures, a distinction is made between framework theories and specific theories. A framework theory consists of entrenched ontological and epistemological beliefs about the target domain that are acquired early in the individual's learning history and that are repeatedly confirmed by everyday experience. A specific theory includes specific explanations of phenomena from the target domain. Specific theories are constrained by framework theories. According to this view, conceptual change is difficult, not because of the preconceptions *per se*, but because the ontological and epistemological assumptions of the respective framework theory are difficult to modify. First, learners are not aware of their implicit ontological and epistemological assumptions. Second, the ontological and epistemological assumptions are deeply entrenched because of continuous confirmation by everyday experience. Third, a modification of a framework theory has consequences for all specific theories based on it. According to Vosniadou and Brewer, conceptual change requires a gradual revision of the assumptions of framework theory combined with a reinterpretation of previous experience.

Further theory on the nature of individual preconceptions has been developed by Chi et al. (1994). These authors assume that an individual, during its cognitive development, acquires specific ontological categories such as "matter", "processes" and "mental states". The basic hypothesis of this view is that misconceptions arise when the individual assigns a concept to a wrong ontological category. For example, individuals frequently subsume the concept "heat" under the category "matter" instead of the category "processes". As a result, "heat" is considered an attribute that can be transferred from one object to another by direct contact. Besides the arbitrary distinction of ontological categories, this approach has difficulties in explaining why conceptual change across category-borders is more difficult than within a category.

The strong focus of conceptual change research on the quality of conceptual structures has been recently criticized by scholars who consider learning and cognitive development, in line with Vygotski (1962), as a process of enculturation. They emphasize that knowledge is always situated, i.e. embedded in human practice, and argue that the so-called conceptual change does not require a modification of conceptual structures, but rather a change in the embedding of these structures. In other words, it is not the knowledge itself that has to be changed, but rather the situatedness of this knowledge (Caravita & Halldén, 1994). So-called naive knowledge should, therefore, not be replaced by scientific knowledge. Instead, individuals should learn to distinguish between different contexts and learn which concepts are useful in which situation (Spada, 1994). Finally, the traditional approaches have been criticized for analysing conceptual change only from the perspective of "cold cognition". Pintrich et al. (1993) have emphasized that these processes are also influenced by affective, motivational and social factors. Accordingly, conceptual change can be promoted by goal orientations, interests, motivational beliefs about self-efficacy and by individual control beliefs.

The different theoretical views on conceptual change result in different suggestions on how to foster conceptual change. For example, if one considers naive knowledge as incoherent, the practical consequence is to promote mental coherence formation. If one assumes that misconceptions are caused by metacognitive deficits, the practical consequence is to foster metacognitive skills and the learner's awareness about the epistemological status of his or her own knowledge. Quite different instructional consequences emerge if one assumes that naive knowledge is coherent and that misconceptions derive from the construction of synthetic mental models influenced by implicit framework theories. In this case, the practical consequence is to exempt the learner's mental model construction from inadequate constraints, by a revision of her or his ontological and epistemological assumptions. Finally, if one considers conceptual change not as a reorganization of existing knowledge, but as a change in the contextualization of knowledge, learners should be taught how to distinguish between contexts and learn which knowledge structures are useful in which situations.

The research situation described above was the background for organizing an International Symposium on Conceptual Change, which was held from 1–3 September 1994, at the Friedrich-Schiller-University of Jena in Germany. The purpose of this symposium was to provide an opportunity for scientists from different countries to exchange theoretical concepts and empirical findings on conceptual change with the aim of attaining further integration and intensifying scientific exchange between different lines of research. The participants came from Australia, Belgium, Finland, Germany, Greece, Great Britain, Israel, Italy, Spain, Sweden, South Africa and Cyprus. The symposium was organized by the first editor and financed by the Deutsche Forschungsgemeinschaft. The conference was the starting point of an ongoing discussion among a number of researchers. This discussion finally resulted in a set of papers that analyse problems of conceptual change from different perspectives and these are presented in this volume. The papers are grouped into four sections representing the main topics of the discussion: (1) cognitive, developmental and motivational aspects, (2) situational aspects, (3) domain-specific aspects, and (4) instructional aspects.

Cognitive, Developmental and Motivational Aspects

The chapters in Part 1 deal with basic issues of conceptual change from the perspective of cognitive, developmental and motivational psychology. In Chapter 1, Vosniadou provides an overview of conceptual change research. She first describes the impact of science education on this research area and discusses problems of knowledge coherence and incoherence, the use of cognitive conflict as an instructional strategy, the idea of replacing old conceptions by new ones, the assumption of multiple representations and the notion of knowledge contextualization. Vosniadou then analyses the influence of developmental psychology on conceptual change research. She describes the function of knowledge acquisition mechanisms in infancy that lead to domain-specific framework theories and constrain further learning; she addresses problems of domain-generality versus domain-specificity and points out alternative views of so-called misconceptions. She argues that these conceptions result from the construction of synthetic mental models that try to reconcile new information with old framework assumptions. Vosniadou then suggests possible directions for further research on conceptual change. She proposes a synthesis of science education and developmental research, which takes into account that concepts are always embedded into contexts associated with specific social and cultural practices, and that conceptual change may be different in different subject-matter areas. Finally, she critically discusses the position of radical situationism and investigates the relationship between conceptual enrichment, restructuring and cognitive flexibility.

In Chapter 2, Pauen investigates the principles of ontological categorizations of living and non-living things, animate and inanimate things, natural things and artefacts used by young children. Pauen first analyses the views of Piaget, Carey and Keil concerning children's categorizations. Whereas Piaget argues that young children are unable to operate with abstract concepts and will focus on single attributes in order to categorize things, Carey explains children's ontological categorizations by a lack of domain-specific knowledge that forces them to look for perceptual similarities or analogies. Whereas Carey assumes that biological knowledge emerges from naive knowledge about humans through thinking by analogy, Keil argues that biological knowledge develops as an autonomous knowledge domain because of an innate knowledge acquisition device that helps to distinguish humans, animals, plants and non-living things.

Pauen shows that none of these approaches takes into account the inconsistencies in the categorizations made by children and suggests an alternative approach. In her cause-and-effect-of-changes model, she assumes three general dimensions that become integrated into conceptual structures according to the context. The dimensions are (i) causality (i.e. changes of living objects are caused by internal factors, artefacts are caused by human beings), (ii) functionality (i.e. movements of a living object are goal-oriented and its properties have an internal purpose; artefacts have higher functionality than natural non-living things), and (iii) predictability (i.e. the behaviour of living objects is less predictable than those of non-living objects). According to Pauen, children use these dimensions in different ways depending on their background knowledge and the salience of the dimensions in the present situation. Inconsistencies are not caused by cognitive incompetence, but result from an adaptive cognitive mechanism that forms conceptual structures according to the situational context and the task at hand. As concepts are viewed as variable context-dependent constructions on the basis of stable dimensions, conceptual change does not follow a fixed sequence. Instead, it is based on a continuous enrichment of knowledge about basic dimensions and the ability to integrate this knowledge into flexible conceptual structures.

In Chapter 3, Pintrich describes, from a constructivist and sociocultural viewpoint, the influence of motivational beliefs on conceptual change and analyses how this influence is modified by situational factors. Pintrich first analyses the impact of different goal orientations, epistemological beliefs, personal interests, self-efficacy and the influence of control beliefs on conceptual change. He argues that intrinsically motivated learners with a mastery orientation, who focus on understanding and mastering the subject matter, are more likely to be engaged in deeper cognitive processing and, thus, show more conceptual change than extrinsically motivated learners with a performance orientation, who focus on external rewards, good grades and besting others. He also points out that learners who believe in fixed abilities, who think that knowledge is simple and that materials can be learned quickly without much effort, who have no doubts about the correctness of the taught knowledge and who believe in knowledge authorities, are usually less cognitively engaged and show less conceptual change than learners with a constructivist view that is characterized by the opposite assumptions. Furthermore, learning contexts that activate personal interests will result in more learning, higher willingness to persist and, therefore, will make conceptual change more likely.

Pintrich emphasizes that self-efficacy can have a double function for conceptual change. Self-efficacy, as confidence in one's own capabilities to use effective learning strategies and to modify one's ideas, can foster conceptual change, whereas self-efficacy as confidence in one's own ideas might have the opposite effect. Furthermore, beliefs in personal control have a supporting effect on intentional learning and are supposed to foster conceptual change. Finally, a challenging, authentic and meaningful situational context can facilitate the adoption of a mastery goal orientation and of a constructivist view of learning, which supports deeper cognitive processing and, thus, results in greater conceptual change than a context that ignores personal meanings and is characterized by rigid authority structures.

Situational Aspects

The chapters in Part 2 investigate the impact of contextual and situational factors on the process of conceptual change. In Chapter 4, Halldén critically analyses previous theoretical approaches that consider conceptual change as a replacement of incorrect for correct ideas. He emphasizes that concepts are always embedded in cognitive, situational and linguistic contexts. They are embedded in specific theoretical frameworks and in specific situational contexts of shared social practices. Furthermore, they are communicated among individuals who use specific speech genres as cultural forms of speaking and thinking. Halldén argues that the problems of learners in applying scientific concepts correctly are primarily problems of contextualization. The so-called misconceptions result from difficulties of the learner in identifying the adequate context for specific concepts. If there are no hints available on adequate contextualization, learners are biased towards those contextualizations that are most familiar to them, but these are sometimes not adequate. Teaching new concepts should, therefore, focus explicitly on adequate contextualizations, when these concepts are applied.

In Chapter 5, Nunes analyses the role of sign systems in knowledge acquisition and thinking. She emphasizes that specific aspects of a situation can take over the function of an external sign system and that these systems allow extension of the human cognitive system. Referring to examples from the field of mathematics, Nunes demonstrates that external sign systems both enable and constrain our thinking and communication about subject matter. She compares different forms of representing numbers with regard to their operating advantages and disadvantages: finger arithmetic, oral arithmetic, written arithmetic and abacus-arithmetic. She also demonstrates that different ways of constructing geometric figures result in different figural concepts. The characteristics of a sign system as a cultural product and the cultural practices of operating with it, influence the strengths and weaknesses of our thinking and communication. As Nunes points out, external sign systems do not fully determine our thinking. Individuals can use different sign systems that complement each other, and that allow representation of a problem in different ways according to specific situational requirements. Instruction should, therefore, aim at extending the individual repertoire of sign systems and foster the learner's capability to use these systems flexibly according to the situation.

A provoking socio-constructivist view on conceptual change research is presented by Säljö in Chapter 6. He accuses cognitive research of considering concepts as isolated, stable and ready-made structures that exist independently from human social practice. Säljö argues that concepts are not internal structures in the mind of the individual and that cognitive constructs should be omitted from the discussion about conceptual change. He assumes that the nature of concepts can be found in the discursive practices of individuals who communicate with each other in social activities. When individuals are growing into a social community, they adopt specific kinds of viewing, thinking and communicating that is associated with specific settings. According to Säljö, a learner's insufficient capability to apply scientific concepts is not caused by misconceptions, but results from insufficient access to authentic discursive practices in which scientific concepts are functional. It will require further discussion to clarify whether cognitive research is adequately described here, and whether the suggestion to omit cognitive constructs from research on conceptual change will be fruitful or lead back to crypto-behaviouristic methodology.

In Chapter 7, Kalekin-Fishman analyses the situational aspects of conceptual change from a sociological viewpoint. Her considerations are based on the assumption that the formation and modification of concepts is part of a social process and that what is defined as knowledge is basically a social product. Starting from a survey of classical theoretical views on social development, which range from Comte via Spencer, Durkheim, Parsons, Weber, Marx, Mead, Goffman and Garfinkel, Kalekin-Fishman argues that the creation of a common culture is correlated with the development of concepts and shared symbols. Concepts and symbols function as a mental backbone to socio-cultural formations that support the coordination of activities within and between different social subsystems. Kalekin-Fishman considers the field of systematic instruction and learning as a social domain that allows individuals to adapt their activities to different social systems through the successive acquisition of internal representations. Both maintenance of concepts and conceptual change can, therefore, have an impact on the distribution of power among different social groups. Accordingly, the probability of conceptual change can be considered as a function of a social group's gains and losses with regard to its social fitness and influence. Viewing concepts as a product of a social negotiation can be seen as a specific aspect of metaconceptual awareness, which might be useful in supporting conceptual change in schools and other social institutions.

Domain-Specific Aspects

Part 3 presents a number of studies that demonstrate the necessity in conceptual change research to take into account the constraints of specific knowledge domains. In Chapter 8, Berti investigates conceptual change in the domain of economy. Her basic assumption is that conceptual change is less difficult in the field of economy because the framework theories that constrain the acquisition of knowledge in this domain are based on experiences that differ fundamentally from those in the natural sciences. The framework theories of economic knowledge consist of assumptions about the motives of human actions and about the equivalence and reciprocity of transactional processes. These assumptions do not hinder the acquisition of correct concepts, and the respective framework theories are less entrenched than those in natural sciences.

Berti describes empirical studies that she performed to evaluate her assumptions. One study demonstrated that 8- to 9-year-old children without prior knowledge, after receiving only a 2-hour lesson, could attain the knowledge of 10- to 11-year-old children. A 3-month intervention resulted in almost all children developing a full understanding of deposits and loans, and of deposit interests and loan interests. Another study showed that, with only a 2-hour lesson, most 10- to 11-year-old children could develop a knowledge level that is usually only found in children who are 5 years older. Finally, Berti found that an 18-hour lesson enabled most 9- to 10-year-old children to eliminate misconceptions and to acquire a well-founded knowledge of deposits, loans and interests in banking operations, and that this knowledge remained stable for at least 8 months. The author considers that these results support her view that misconceptions about the function of economic institutions are not deeply entrenched, that economic concepts can be modified relatively easily, and that these modifications are relatively permanent.

In Chapter 9, Limón and Carretero analyse conceptual change in the field of history. This domain is generally ill-defined and allows an interpretation of events from different perspectives. The authors assume that historical knowledge is strongly influenced by ideologies and emotions, which results in higher resistance to conceptual change than is usually found in the natural sciences. Limón and Carretero report two empirical studies in which they investigated the interaction between individual learning strategies and domain-specific knowledge with regard to the selection and interpretation of historical documents. In the first study, the authors compared undergraduate students of history with professors of history with regard to their reaction to documents about the expulsion of the Moors from Spain; this included data that contradicted the learners' previous hypotheses. In a second study, a similar group of subjects were instructed to re-read previously studied documents and to analyse them carefully with regard to the advantages and disadvantages of the expulsion for different social groups, but they did not receive the documents with conflicting data. In both studies, half of the subjects did not change their previous hypotheses. Some subjects performed a peripheral change of their theory, and some subjects differentiated between short-, medium- and long-term advantages and disadvantages of historical events for a social group. Subjects who changed their views during knowledge acquisition, frequently reinterpreted the data or considered conflicting data as an extension of their prior hypotheses. Although subjects were generally aware of cognitive conflicts, they either ignored or excluded the conflicting data from further analysis. The instruction to re-analyse the documents was as effective in promoting conceptual change as was presenting conflicting data. Undergraduate students and professors did not differ significantly from each other in this respect. Limón and Carretero consider that their data support their assumption that conceptual change in the field of history knowledge is quite difficult. They suggest further studies with longer instruction periods, with presentations of more extensive sets of historical documents and with higher differences in the learners' prior knowledge.

In Chapter 10, Pozo, Sanz and Gómez analyse problems of conceptual change in the domain of chemistry. Chemical phenomena are spontaneously interpreted by learners in a macroscopic view, which considers chemical substances as continuous and dense without a vacuum between its parts. Scientific analyses, on the contrary, uses a microscopic view, which considers chemical substances as discontinuous and consisting of particles with a vacuum between them. Novices frequently mix up these different views by associating attributes of the macroscopic view with particles of the microscopic view. The authors describe an empirical study that demonstrated that individuals learn to discriminate more, and more correctly, between different representation levels, but do not give up the macroscopic view of chemical phenomena. Even experts continue to use this knowledge in well-defined contexts and show high metacognitive awareness of their different theoretical concepts. Pozo, Sanz and Gómez argue that instruction should, therefore, not aim at replacing everyday concepts by scientific ones. Instead, individuals should attain multiple views on phenomena, use multiple mental representations according to the requirements of the specific context and integrate these different views into a comprehensive framework.

In Chapter 11, Verschaffel, De Corte and Lasure investigate the change in views of learners on their prior knowledge of solving mathematical problems. Students tend to exclude prior knowledge and context-related considerations when solving arithmetic word problems because of an impoverished diet of artificial arithmetic problems that can be solved in a stereotyped way through standard routines. Usually, this practice results in a number of mathematical misconceptions, such as that multiplication always results in a larger amount, and that division always results in a smaller amount. The authors describe an empirical study of simple scaffolding, which aimed to activate prior knowledge in solving arithmetic text problems; but resulted in very little improvement. Obviously, scaffolding is not effective if it is not sufficiently tuned to the learner's zone of proximal development. In another study, Verschaffel et al. attempted to modify the learner's concepts of the role of world knowledge in solving arithmetic problems by creating a new, more authentic learning culture. The students received tasks that could not be solved by standard routines, that required inferences and that did not explicitly mention the relevant conditions for solving the problem. Discussions took place concerning the nature of the mathematical problems and the methods needed to solve them. The authors found that students modified their view after modelling and solving the arithmetic text problems, that they referred more to their prior world knowledge, took more context-bound considerations into account, and attained qualitatively better results, which could also be transferred to other types of tasks. Students with higher learning prerequisites seemed to profit more from such a learning culture than students with lower learning prerequisites.

Instructional Aspects

The chapters in Part 4 deal with instructional implications of conceptual change research. In Chapter 12, Schnotz and Preuß study conceptual change within short-term processes of learning and instruction from the perspective of cognitive psychology. They adopt a Vygotskian view of conceptual knowledge as a general cognitive tool for a task-oriented construction of more specific mental representations, such as propositional structures and mental models. Mental models are not considered to be permanently stored in long-term memory, but are temporary mental representations in working memory. This view has implications for knowledge consistency and for the assumed mechanisms that drive conceptual change. Conceptual change is assumed to occur within a task-oriented interaction between different mental representations. Therefore, it can be fostered by learning tasks that stimulate individuals to construct mental models and the use of these models in a sufficiently variable way that enables learners to detect their conceptual deficits.

The empirical study reported here supported these claims, but also showed considerable individual differences on how learners react to learning tasks that should support conceptual change. Learners with lower capabilities for mental model construction seemed to profit more than learners with high capabilities, whereas learners with high skills in propositional encoding could, paradoxically, be hindered in their process of conceptual change, as they invested less cognitive effort in the construction and use of a mental model. Accordingly, the increased coherence and consistency of conceptual knowledge is considered a result of the sufficiently broad use of mental models. There is never a total replacement of old concepts for new, but, rather, competition between alternative concepts that have different likelihoods of being activated according to their previous usefulness under their respective context conditions.

In Chapter 13, Lowe analyses instructional possibilities that foster conceptual change in the field of meteorology, and compares experts with novices with regard to their use of weather maps. Whereas experts consider a weather map as a section of a more comprehensive system and interpret it as snapshot of a continuous flow of gas masses, novices focus on local aspects and consider the map as a depiction of discrete, rigid and solid objects. Lowe considers the conceptual changes in becoming an expert of meteorology as a progression of mental models; this can result in problems for several reasons. Individuals' everyday experience does not provide access to meteorologically relevant information about the behaviour of an atmospheric system, but is dominated by discrete solid objects. Because of a lack of specific meteorological knowledge, the subject's mental model construction is constrained by framework theories based on everyday experience with discrete and solid objects instead of continuously flowing gas masses. Furthermore, the visuo-spatial information of a weather map is too abstract to result in cognitive conflict with the subject's own everyday experience.

Lowe suggests that, in order to support conceptual change in knowledge acquisition about meteorology, learners should be given the opportunity to have new experiences in the behaviour of complex atmospheric systems. Such experiences can be provided with animated, manipulative maps that allow simulation of the behaviour of systems. These maps add a temporal context to the visuo-spatial context and allow individuals to construct, evaluate and revise their mental models on a larger information base. In this way, learners should be better enabled to revise their meteorological assumptions and to interpret weather maps from the perspective of a conceptual system that applies to flowing gaseous objects instead of discrete and rigid ones.

In Chapter 14, Biemans and Simons analyse how conceptual change can be fostered by computer-based instruction. Learners frequently have difficulty in activating the relevant parts of prior knowledge, in relating this knowledge systematically to new information, in detecting cognitive conflicts and in adequately processing unexpected data. The authors describe a computer-based strategy program that aimed to stimulate learners to search actively in their prior knowledge for relevant concepts, to relate these concepts to new information, to construct new concepts and to evaluate these concepts with regard to new tasks. Learners were expected to detect inconsistencies by themselves and to integrate old and new information into a coherent framework. Biemans and Simons report on two empirical studies that used fifth and sixth graders, and aimed to evaluate whether such a strategy could effectively support conceptual change. The first study showed that the strategy program resulted in too strong a focus on certain central concepts of the learning content, whereas other concepts were disregarded. Therefore, the authors developed a second version of the strategy with additional strategical information that aimed to help learners focus their attention not only on a few central concepts, but allowed a more flexible application of the strategy program. The second version resulted in concepts of higher quality that could be effectively applied to new problem situations, even after long periods of time. Biemans and Simons emphasize that instruction should make learners more independent, and that individuals should internalize such strategies and gradually learn to apply them without external support.

In Chapter 15, Duit provides a final overview of conceptual change research from an instructional perspective. He describes and analyses traditional views of conceptual change as well as alternative phenographic and socio-constructivist approaches that consider conceptual change not as a modification of cognitive structures, but as a modification of an individual's relationship to its environment. Duit points out that conceptual structures are embedded in a conceptual ecology, which includes the learner's preconceptions about the nature of science, as well as the process of teaching and learning. Furthermore, he emphasizes that conceptual change is influenced not only by cognitive, but also by affective, contextual and social factors. As the so-called naive concepts are usually not replaced by instruction, but co-exist with new concepts and can be applied in specific contexts, Duit argues for a stronger emphasis on the situatedness of concepts both in conceptual change research and in instructional practice. Individuals should learn which concepts are better suited for specific purposes in specific contexts. Furthermore, Duit proposes a careful application of cognitive conflicts, and suggests that instruction should not aim at a sudden radical restructuring of existing knowledge, but rather a gradual reinterpretation of available information towards scientific concepts. He argues that besides inducing cognitive conflicts, analogies or meta-phors provide an efficient way to enhance conceptual change. Finally, Duit emphasizes that the learning content and the objectives of learning should be meaningful for the individual and he points out that the climate in a learning group can be an important supportive condition for promoting conceptual change.

The chapters of this volume cover a broad spectrum of theoretical views on conceptual change and help to clarify various essential topics in this field. Nevertheless, there exists an abundance of questions that require further research. We lack, for example, the specific knowledge of how situational factors interact with domain-specific preconceptions, motiva-tional beliefs and the strategies used by learners in the process of knowledge acquisition. Further studies are needed that investigate the interplay between domain-general and domain-specific constraints during the process of conceptual change in specific subject-matter areas and that explore how a context-sensitive usage of multiple representations can be enhanced by instructional strategies and appropriate learning environments.

These questions cannot be answered by a single discipline. They require cooperation between developmental psychology, cognitive psychology, psychology of motivation, educational psychology and science education. Cooperative, multidisciplinary research in this field will help to attain not only a deeper understanding of human learning and cogni-tive development, but also a more differentiated view of the instructional process. It will help to create learning environments that foster conceptual change under different perspec-tives and enable learners to cope better with the complexity of a rapidly changing world. We hope that this book will help to intensify the dialogue among researchers from different disciplines and stimulate further research, which could lead to a comprehensive theory of human learning and development.

Wolfgang Schnotz
Stella Vosniadou
Mario Carretero

PART 1

Cognitive, Developmental and Motivational Aspects

1

Conceptual Change Research: State of the Art and Future Directions

Stella Vosniadou

Introduction

This chapter provides a general introduction to the theoretical approach that has come to be known as "conceptual change", addresses some current criticisms of this approach, and makes suggestions for the directions conceptual change research can take in the future.

The conceptual change approach has its roots in at least two relatively independent research traditions: the cognitive-developmental and the science education traditions. In developmental psychology, conceptual change research can be traced to the efforts of developmental psychologists to provide an alternative to the Piagetian explanation of cognitive development (e.g. Carey, 1985; Gelman, 1990; Wellman & Gelman, 1992). The last 20 years or so of cognitive and developmental research have reinforced Piaget's claims that the child is an active, constructive agent in the knowledge acquisition process, but have also challenged his stage theory and emphasis on the development of context-independent logical operations. In science education, the term conceptual change is related to the theoretical framework developed by a group of science educators at the University of Cornell (Posner et al., 1982; Strike & Posner, 1985). The science education approach to conceptual change is much more closely connected with instructional theory than the developmental approach; it is a theory about how to teach science in order to promote conceptual change.

My purpose in this chapter is to clarify the contributions of these two approaches to the problem of understanding conceptual change. The chapter starts with a discussion of science education approaches to conceptual change and their instructional applications. It continues with a discussion of developmental approaches, focussing more specifically on the aspects of this research that try to describe children's initial conceptual structures in specific subject-matter areas and how they develop. It concludes with a discussion on how the conceptual change approach could be modified as a theoretical framework to lead us to further advances in understanding development, learning, and instruction.

Science Education Approaches to Conceptual Change

Since the 1970s science educators such as Viennot (1979) and Driver and Easley (1978) realized that students bring to the science learning task, alternative frameworks or misconceptions that are robust and difficult to extinguish through teaching. Although most of these researchers had been influenced by Piaget's constructivist epistemology they realized the need to pay more attention to "the actual content of the pupil's ideas and less on the supposed underlying logical structures" (Driver & Easley, 1978, p. 76). According to

Novak (1977a) it was time to shift from a stage-dependent view of cognitive development to a the view that cognitive development is dependent "on the framework of specific concepts and integrations between these concepts acquired during the active lifespan of the individual" (p. 473).

In their search for a theoretical framework to conceptualize the learning of science some science educators turned to the philosophy and history of science as a major source of hypotheses concerning how concepts change (Posner et al., 1982). These researchers drew an analogy between Piaget's concepts of assimilation and accommodation, and the concepts of "normal science" and "scientific revolution" offered by philosophers of science such as Kuhn (1970) and Lakatos (1970) to explain theory change in the history of science, and derived from this analogy an instructional theory to promote "accommodation" in students learning science.

According to Posner et al. (1982), there are four fundamental conditions that need to be fulfilled before conceptual change can happen: (i) there must be dissatisfaction with existing conceptions, (ii) a new conception must be intelligible, (iii) a new conception must appear initially plausible, and (iv) a new concept should suggest the possibility of a fruitful programme. This theoretical framework became the leading paradigm that guided research and instructional practices in the science education profession for many years, but also became subject to a number of criticisms, some of which are discussed below.

How Robust, Coherent and Resistant to Instruction are Students' Naive Conceptions?

Conceptual change theory is based on the idea that students possess alternative conceptions that are internally coherent, robust and difficult to extinguish. The most well-formulated challenge to this notion comes from di Sessa (1993) who argues that students' alternative ideas or misconceptions do not constitute a coherent and internally consistent theoretical framework but are fragmented, "knowledge in pieces". The pieces are certain primitive schemata called "p-prims" (phenomenological primitives), which are superficial interpretations of physical reality and serve important roles in explaining physical phenomena. In this system, conceptual change occurs through the reorganization of p-prims or through increases in the internal coherence and systematicity of the collections of p-prims that serve as explanations.

Is Cognitive Conflict a Good Strategy for Producing Conceptual Change?

If students' beliefs are fragmented, then instructional interventions aimed at producing cognitive conflict do not make much sense. di Sessa proposes looking at the student as an architect and helping him or her better synthesize the necessary p-prims to construct appropriate explanations. Dissatisfaction from the use of cognitive conflict as an instructional strategy has also been voiced by other science educators who have observed that, in situations of cognitive conflict, students usually patch-up local inconsistencies in a superficial way and do not undergo the more radical kinds of conceptual changes often necessary to understand a complex scientific concept.

Replacement of Alternative Ideas or Multiple Representations?

Another related criticism of the conceptual change approach is that it assumes that science learning requires the replacement of alternative ideas with scientific theories, rather than that different kinds of representations can co-exist and can be used in different ways by the subject, according to the context (Pozo et al., this volume; Spada, 1994). According to this position, conceptual change does not mean replacement of "incorrect" with "correct" conceptions, but different contextual activation of alternative representations. In this case, the purpose of instruction could be seen as that of promoting the use of multiple representations in the appropriate contexts (Spada, 1994).

How Productive is the Analogy Between Students and Scientists and How Much Do We Need to Reframe the Problem of Conceptual Change?

According to Caravita and Halldén (1994), the analogy between children and scientists "constrains rather than empowers the inquiry and the interpretation of the learning processes occurring in the classroom" and that what is needed is to "re-frame" the problem of conceptual change. The dissatisfaction with the analogy between children and scientists has at least two branches. One is the general dissatisfaction with the rational and neglect of the affective, social and motivational influences on conceptual change (see, for example, Pintrich, this volume). The other is related to the emphasis on "contextualization" (e.g. Halldén, this volume). Many science educators point out that the context in which a scientific problem or a question is embedded plays an important role on how the problem is interpreted and, therefore, on the particular explanation that is offered. Some explanations that may seem very natural in one context but not in another. To the same student some explanations can appear to be "scientific" in some contexts and not in others. It is probable that new information is first acquired in restricted contexts and then is applied to a greater variety of situations.

Conclusions

The conceptual change framework developed in the science education research tradition has served as the dominant approach for guiding instructional practices for many years. Recent criticisms have made apparent a number of limitations of this approach that deserve closer examination.

Developmental Descriptions of Conceptual Change

In developmental research, the conceptual change approach emerged as an attempt to reconcile Piagetian constructivism with experimental findings that show, on the one hand, that young children are much more cognitively capable than Piaget had originally thought and, on the other, that initial conceptual structures undergo radical changes with development. The beginnings of this approach can be traced to Carey's (1985) suggestion that cognitive development could be thought of as domain-specific restructuring. Until then, developmental psychologists, who were influenced by Piaget's stage theory, conceptualized cognitive development in terms of "global restructurings", that is, changes in the structure of thought brought about by growth in the child's logical capabilities. These changes were supposed to constrain children's ability to reason and acquire knowledge in all domains.

Carey argued for a type of developmental change that was domain-specific theory change. According to this view children begin with a few theory-like conceptual structures (e.g. a naive psychology and a naive physics) that, through restructuring, give rise to new theories (e.g. biology, economics, a theory of mechanics, of heat, etc.). This type of restructuring is conceptualized as a product of the child's increased knowledge of a domain (brought about by the child's experience and/or by instruction), rather than as the result of the child's logical capabilities *per se*.

The emphasis on domain-specificity is consistent with recent accounts of the human mind as a modular system rather than as a general information processor. During many years of evolution this system has developed specialized cognitive mechanisms to deal with different kinds of information (see Hirschfeld & Gelman, 1994). Domain-specificity is also consistent with the results of research investigating the expert/novice shift showing that experts in physics, medicine or chess differ from novices mainly in the content and organization of information in the knowledge base, rather than on the use of more powerful general processing strategies (Chi et al., 1981; Larkin, 1983). Finally, such results agree with science educators' observations that the learning of science is dependent on the framework of specific concepts, and integrations between these concepts acquired during the active lifespan of the individual (Novak, 1977b, p. 473).

Developmental research on conceptual change has taken different directions. Some developmental psychologists have focused on investigations of the conceptual knowledge of infants and young children trying to determine how it is organized and whether it can be said that it has the status of a "theory". Others have tried to understand how conceptual structures change in the process of development and with the acquisition of expertise. I will focus here on the last line of developmental research.

Most developmental psychologists agree that the knowledge acquisition process starts early in infancy and that it is guided by some general principles or constraints. Recent research has shown that infants that are only a few months old understand certain general characteristics of physical objects, such as, for example, that they are solid, that they do not move by themselves, and that they fall down when not supported (e.g. Spelke 1991). By the time they enter elementary school and before they have been exposed to any systematic instruction, children have already acquired substantial information about the physical world based on their everyday experiences. In earlier work (Vosniadou, 1994), I have argued that children's initial conceptual knowledge about the physical world can be thought to be organized in a framework theory of physics that provides the foundation upon which further knowledge is constructed, without being available to conscious aware-ness and hypothesis testing.

While this naive framework theory facilitates the knowledge acquisition process, it can also hinder later learning, particularly in the case of science. This can happen because the currently accepted, scientific explanations of natural phenomena are often quite different from the ones children have constructed on the basis of their everyday experience. For example, research findings show that many students operate on the basis of an initial concept of heat that is based on the experiential distinction between felt hotness and cold-ness. Hotness and coldness are thought to be two distinct properties of physical objects that can be transferred to other objects by direct contact. Because children think of heat as a transferable property of physical objects, they are likely to confuse the amount of a given substance with the intensity of its hotness or coldness (Vosniadou & Kempner, 1993). This initial concept of heat stands in the way of understanding the scientific concept of heat and of making the differentiation between heat and temperature (Wiser & Carey, 1983)

Some of the ways in which framework theories constrain further learning can be seen in Vosniadou and Brewer's (1992) explanation of children's misconceptions about the shape of Earth. Young children start with a concept of the earth as a physical (rather than an astronomical) object, which is shaped like a flat rectangle or a disc, supported by ground below and covered by the sky above its top. This initial concept of the earth is embedded within a framework theory of physics according to which physical objects exist in three-dimensional space organized in terms of the directions of up and down.

This initial concept of the Earth influences the way children interpret the information they receive (usually from instruction) about the spherical shape of the Earth. Some children interpret this information to mean that the Earth is a sphere but that people live on flat ground deep inside it. Some other children believe that the Earth is spherical but flat on the top where the people live. Others thinks that there are two Earths: a flat one on which people live and a spherical one which is a planet up in the sky. Children construct these misrepresentations of the Earth in order to reconcile the information they receive from the culture that the Earth is a sphere with their presuppositions and beliefs that the ground is flat, that space is organized in terms of the directions of up and down and that unsupported physical objects fall in a downward direction.

These misconceptions are, in other words, synthetic models, attempts on the part of the children to synthesize two fundamentally inconsistent and conflicting pieces of information: the information they receive through instruction according to which the Earth is a sphere and their existing beliefs and presuppositions (based on interpretations of everyday experience) that the Earth is flat.

There are other explanations of misconceptions that are not necessarily inconsistent with the above-mentioned explanation provided by Vosniadou and Brewer (1992). According to Chi et al. (1994), for example, misconceptions are formed because students assign science concepts to an ontological category to which they do not belong. For example, students may assign the concept of "heat" to the ontological category "matter", when in fact, it belongs to the category "process".

There is no doubt that changes in categorization are one type of change that happens during the knowledge acquisition process and, in this respect, Chi et al. (1994) are correct. We have also noticed that children's initial concept of the earth is assigned to the category "physical object" rather than the category "astronomical object"[1].

One of the problems of the Chi et al. explanation is that some of the ontological categories that they propose seem rather arbitrary. Why should, for example, "process" be an ontological category? Also, they do not explain why children "assign concepts to an ontological category to which they do not belong" or why the reassignment of a concept

---

[1]A similar, in some respects, reassignment of categories to the concept of the Earth is also observed in the move from the Ptolemaic system of classification of celestial bodies, where the Earth is seen to belong to a different category from the Planets, to the Copernican system, where the Earth is seen to belong to the category of Planets.

from one ontological category to another is so difficult in some cases as compared with others.

We believe that the explanation for the difficulty of understanding science concepts and the creation of misconceptions is to be found in the inconsistencies that exist between the fundamentally contradictory systems of presuppositions and beliefs that lie behind different ontological categories. A second, important factor that needs to be taken into consideration are the mechanisms whereby the two systems are reconciled or synthesized during the knowledge acquisition process.

In order to explain why science concepts are difficult to learn and misconceptions happen, we must assume that initial conceptual structures are supported by a system of interrelated observations, beliefs and presuppositions that form a relatively coherent and systematic explanatory system, which works relatively well in the everyday world and is rather difficult to change. This is the point where the Vosniadou and Brewer (1992; Vosniadou, 1994) view also differs from di Sessa's (1993) proposal that intuitive knowledge is composed of a collection of p-prims (phenomenological primitives). Misconceptions are explained by di Sessa as being triggered by particular p-prims, all of which have the same status in the theory. For example, the impetus misconception in mechanics (the idea that force is imparted into an object and becomes the cause of its movement until it dissipates in the environment causing the object to stop), is traced to a class of p-prims, such as "force is a mover", "dying away", "dynamic balance", etc., which are associated to describe a small set of situations but do not constitute a coherent and systematic theory.

The notion of phenomenological primitives that capture aspects of the physical reality is analogous in many respects to the beliefs and presuppositions that Vosniadou and Brewer (1992, 1994; Vosniadou, 1994) have proposed. Nevertheless, there are important differences between the two theoretical frameworks. Vosniadou and Brewer distinguish between "beliefs" that are based on superficial observations and that are relatively easy to change (such as, the belief that hotness can transfer to other objects only by direct contact) as compared with "presuppositions" that are deeper theoretical constructs, and more difficult to change (such as, the presupposition that heat is a property of objects). This distinction is crucial in order to explain such an empirical finding that in the process of knowledge acquisition, some children's knowledge about the physical world is more difficult to change than others.

Unlike di Sessa (1993), Vosniadou and Brewer (1992, 1994) and Vosniadou (1994), for example, argue that the presuppositions of the framework theory do not operate "in pieces" but form a relatively coherent explanatory structure. As a result, the main difference between novices and experts is not that novices lack an explanatory framework for their knowledge in pieces, but that the explanatory framework they have is tied to ontological and epistemological presuppositions that are fundamentally different from the principles and laws of physics.

On the other hand, di Sessa (1993) is correct in pointing out that the concepts novices use lack the systematicity and coherence of the theory of physics used by experts. We would also like to add to this the lack of metaconceptual awareness in novices as compared with experts. In other words, novices are not aware of the hypothetical nature of their beliefs and presuppositions but, rather, they treat them as facts about the way the physical world operates, facts that are not subject to hypothesis testing and have the possibility of being falsified.

To conclude, developmental research has produced certain important findings about the nature and process of conceptual change. One is the finding that by the time they enter elementary school children have already constructed initial conceptual structures about the physical and social world that are in many ways different from the scientific concepts to which they will be exposed through instruction. These initial conceptual structures facilitate but may also hinder later learning. Finally, conceptual change appears to be a gradual process during which information that comes through instruction is synthesized with information in the initial conceptual structures producing synthetic models or misconceptions.

On the Future of Conceptual Change Research: Towards a Synthesis of Science Education and Developmental Approaches

The conceptual change approach developed by science educators was an approach designed to support instruction that would bring about conceptual change. This approach was based on a number of assumptions about the process of learning and conceptual change that have not always been supported by empirical evidence. On the other hand, cognitive developmental research has provided rich descriptions of the knowledge of children at different ages that help us make better hypotheses about the knowledge acquisition process. However, cognitive developmental psychologists usually focus on descriptions of the cognitive performance of subjects at different ages and at different levels of expertise rather than on explanations of this cognitive performance. Furthermore, they are primarily interested in understanding the cognitive, mental processes that are assumed to go on inside the head during intellectual activity. This research does not provide information about the external, environmental variables that can be manipulated to facilitate cognitive performance and conceptual change. It is knowledge of these variables that is needed to guide instructional research and practice.

As we look at the future of conceptual change research, it becomes apparent that what is needed is a bridge between cognitive developmental and science education research, a bridge that can only be provided by a theory of learning: a theory of learning that specifies the mechanisms that can take an individual from one level of cognitive performance to the next, and shows how these mechanisms are related to external, environmental factors. This is exactly what has started to happen in conceptual change research during the last few years, and it is indeed an exciting change with great promise for educational research.

Cognitive developmental psychologists can of course be concerned with internal, cognitive states in their descriptions of performance during problem solving, language comprehension, etc. However, changes in internal states cannot be attributed solely to mental, cognitive mechanisms, ignoring the role of the environment. The results of the instructional experiments and interventions of the last years have clearly shown that concepts are embedded in rich situational contexts, in the tools and artefacts of the culture, and in the nature of the symbolic systems used during cognitive performance. Conceptual change can be, and in fact most often is, initiated, facilitated and consolidated by social and cultural processes. As conceptual change research moves ahead towards not only a description of the performance of subjects at different ages and level of expertise, but also of the mechanisms that can bring about this change, the roles of the situational context and of culture start to become much more important. Future research on how to promote conceptual change should certainly take the turn of understanding and describing these processes in greater detail.

In doing so it is important to pay attention to certain critical issues that have the potential to lead future conceptual change research in different directions. The remaining pages of this paper will be devoted to this discussion.

Radical Situativity Theory and the Abolishment of Mental Representations

Moving towards consideration of situational and cultural variables does not necessarily mean the abandonment of the level of mental representations and its replacement with discourse analysis as suggested by some radical situationists (e.g. Säljö, this volume). Uneasiness with the construct of mental representations may have been understood in the days of behaviourism, when psychologists lacked appropriate methods for the investigation of internal cognitive processes, but it is not justified now. As Gardner (1985) argues, one of the most significant accomplishments of cognitive psychology has been the clear demonstration of the validity of positing a level of mental representation. "The triumph of cognitivism has been to place talk of representation on essential equal footing with these entrenched nodes of discourse — with the neuronal level, on the one hand, and with the socio-cultural level, on the other. Whoever wishes to banish the representational level from scientific discourse would be compelled to explain language, problem solving, classification and the like strictly in terms of neurological and cultural analysis. The discoveries of the last 30 years make such an alternative most unpalatable" (p. 283).

A linguistically- and anthropologically-based discourse analysis cannot provide a satisfactory account of meaning. Linguists and anthropologists themselves have found it necessary to introduce in their theories the notion of "cultural models" to make sense of their data[2]. According to Quinn and Holland (1987) there is a convergence between anthropologists and linguists on the importance of cultural models, and a shift from previous work on semantic analysis toward greater reliance on cultural models with subsequent testing of the adequacy of these models on different kinds of data and the analysis of natural discourse.

> But the different questions which draw linguists and anthropologists should not obscure the common insight ... that culturally shared knowledge is organized into prototypical event sequences enacted in

---

[2]A cultural model is defined by Roy G. d'Andrade (1994) as "a cognitive schema that is intersubjectively shared by a social group. Because cultural models are intersubjectively shared, interpretations made about the world on the basis of a cultural model are experienced as obvious facts of the world" (p. 810).

simplified worlds. That much of such cultural knowledge is presumed by language use is as significant a realization to anthropologists as to linguists. For the latter, these cultural models promise the key to linguistic use, while for the former, linguistic usage provides the best available data for reconstruction of cultural models (Quinn & Holland, 1987, p. 24).

A theory of conceptual change needs to provide a description of the internal representations and processes that go on during cognitive activity, but should also try to relate these internal representations to external, situational variables that influence them. Furthermore, special attention should be paid to an understanding of how external symbolic systems, products of our culture, are internalized and exert their own influence on thinking processes. A great deal of conceptual change can be attributed to the internalization and use of complex systems of symbolic expressions in different symbolic media (see, for example, the chapter by Nunes, this volume, as well as Glaser et al., 1996; and, of course, Vygotsky, 1978). This system could be easily expanded to include motivational beliefs, beliefs about the self, goals and other variables that need to be brought into the picture as we move away from "cold" cognition. Pintrich's paper in this volume is an excellent example of how some of these factors can start to be taken into consideration in a conceptual change theoretical framework.

Conceptual Change Versus Conceptual Enrichment

The term conceptual change has been proposed to denote that conceptual development involves not just the enrichment of existing structures but their substantial reorganization or restructuring (see Carey, 1985; Vosniadou & Brewer, 1992). Some researchers are now challenging the notion of restructuring, particularly because conceptual change appears to be a slow and gradual affair rather than a sudden shift of theory.

It is true that the classical conceptual change theoretical approach implied that conceptual change involves a sudden shift, and it is in the context of this implication that cognitive conflict makes sense as an instructional strategy. This assumption has not, however, been supported by the empirical evidence. In trying to understand what is going on it is important to make a distinction between the process of conceptual change and the end result of conceptual change.

The notion of restructuring is clear when one compares, let us say, the conceptual system of a young child to that of an expert scientist in areas such as physics and biology. Expert physicists, regardless of the influence of contextual, task or situational variables, are operating on the basis of a different theory of physics than that of an elementary school student. However, the process whereby a novice becomes an expert is not a sudden and radical theory shift but a gradual and slow one. In the section on developmental approaches to conceptual change we have tried to describe some aspects of this process. Future research needs to further address the problem of how small and gradual changes in conceptual organizations can bring about radical restructurings in the long run, as well as the implications of all these for instruction.

Nevertheless it is important not to overlook the fact that, with increases in age and with expertise, we not only have a restructured system, in the sense of developing radical different representations of reality that were not available before, but, as the proponents of the multiple representations view would argue, also a more flexible system, a system that makes it easier to take different perspectives and different points of view. One of the limitations of conceptual change research is that it has paid little attention to the development of cognitive flexibility and metaconceptual awareness. There is no doubt that adults, and particularly those literate in science, have a different conceptual organization of science concepts than elementary school students, but they also have a more flexible organization, one that allows them to take different points of view.

What brings about this cognitive flexibility is, in my opinion, and again this is an interesting area for future research, the development of metaconceptual awareness. It is difficult to understand other points of view if you do not even recognize what your own point of view is. As has been mentioned in earlier work (Vosniadou, 1994) one of the limitations of children's thinking is the lack of metaconceptual awareness of their entrenched presuppositions and beliefs. In other words, children do not realize the hypothetical status of many of their beliefs about the nature of the physical world. Increased awareness of one's own beliefs and presuppositions and of the fact that they represent interpretations of physical reality that can be subjected to empirical test, is a necessary stop in the process of conceptual change.

Knowledge Acquisition and Domain-Specificity

The knowledge acquisition process may be different in different subject matter areas: in the physical sciences, in mathematics, in the social sciences, etc. We need more research that details the nature of the system, the symbolic languages that are involved and the nature of the conceptual changes that are going on. Again, we need to move from a focus on internal, cognitive processes to understanding the interaction that exists between internal representations and the external, symbolic cultural representations that are different in different domains as a result of our biological and cultural evolution. A great deal more research is needed before we can say what are really the similarities and differences, and whether they involve changes in conceptual structures, in reasoning process, or in both.

Concluding Remarks

It has been argued that conceptual change research has its roots in the efforts of science educators to provide a theoretical framework that can capture the learning of science concepts and can be used to guide instructional interventions. Cognitive developmental research has also provided rich descriptions of the kinds of conceptual change that happen during the knowledge acquisition process and explanations of the formation of synthetic models or misconceptions. Further developments will come by bridging the two types of research. We need to better understand the external, environmental variables that are related to internal, conceptual changes, as well as the tools, artefacts and symbolic languages that have developed through social and cultural processes. Such understanding will result in the development of better instructional interventions and the design of more successful learning environments.

key for essay

2

The Development of Ontological Categories: Stable Dimensions and Changing Concepts

Sabina Pauen

Introduction

It seems characteristic of human thinking that we organize our knowledge about the world by forming concepts and categories on various levels of abstraction. This chapter deals with conceptual changes on the ontological level. It focuses primarily on the following two questions: How do children come to group objects in categories such as animate versus inanimate objects, living versus non-living things, or natural versus unnatural kinds? and what causes them to change such abstract concepts? To study these issues, the term "concept" needs to be clarified first.

Recently published definitions of the term "concept" reveal controversial positions. Based on empirical studies indicating high context-specificity in adults' use of conceptual knowledge, Barsalou defined concepts as temporary representations of categories in working memory (Barsalou, 1987, 1989, 1993). Similarly, Jones and Smith (1993) suggested that concepts have no constant structure, but are instead continually created (see also Smith & Heise, 1992). Others warn that care has to be taken not to equate instability in outputs or behaviour with underlying or internal instability (Medin & Ortony, 1989). Based on their own experimental findings, which show that conceptual beliefs are coherently structured, Murphy and Medin (1985) concluded that concepts have stable cores (see also Keil, 1989, 1991; Medin & Shoben, 1988).

Another point of disagreement concerns the content of concepts: Whereas the first group of authors maintains that perceptual structure is what conceptual beliefs are all about (Barsalou, 1993; Jones & Smith, 1993; Smith & Heise, 1992), the second group underlines that conceptual knowledge includes an interconnected set of causal beliefs about the nature of a given object. According to the latter view, causal beliefs enable children as well as adults to disregard irrelevant perceptual information and to focus on relevant structural properties when making inductive judgements (e.g. Gelman & Markman, 1987; Gelman & Wellman, 1991; Keil, 1989).

These two different views about the stability and content of concepts have important implications for the interpretation of conceptual changes: If concepts are defined as temporary products of perceptual analysis, conceptual changes should occur on a frequent basis, and accompanying each change in the perception of a given object. Moreover, they may also result from shifts in weighting different feature dimensions (Smith & Heise, 1992) because of changes in contextual variables or actual goals of the perceiver (Barsalou, 1993). By contrast, if concepts are interpreted as stable knowledge structures that include a coherent set of causal beliefs, conceptual changes should occur less often and result from changes in our naive theories about the nature of a given object (e.g. Carey, 1985, 1991).

One way to explain why categorization processes vary with the task at hand without accepting the argument that concepts have no stable structure would be to assume that we learn about material entities with respect to perceptual as well as causal aspects (see also Keil, 1991). We then integrate this information into our stable concept structure, while the situational context specifies which aspects of this knowledge will be actualized in a given situation. According to this view, conceptual changes only refer to changes in our stable concept structure; they may either involve perceptual or causal aspects of knowledge about a given object.

Whereas the term "concept" refers to the meaning of a given noun, the term "category" refers to its empirical application (Schwartz, 1979). It follows that changes concerning the meaning of a noun should go along with changes concerning the basis on which objects are grouped together and vice versa (Chi, 1992). By studying differences between children's and adults' category systems, we thus hope to learn more about fundamental conceptual changes as they may occur in the course of cognitive development.

Taxonomies of human knowledge organization have been proposed by philosophers (e.g. Sommers, 1971) as well as psychologists (Carey, 1985; Chi, 1992; Gelman, 1988; Keil, 1989). According to these authors, category systems are hierarchically structured. On the highest level, ontology divides the diversity of existing entities into only a few general classes, such as "matter", "events" and "abstractions" (Chi, 1992). Members of each ontological category are governed by a distinct set of potential properties (Sommers, 1971). Material entities, for example, may or may not have a specific colour, but a description of events or abstractions in terms of their colours makes no sense. Each of the three mentioned categories generates a "tree" of subcategories. Any two given subcategories may still be ontologically distinct if one is not a superordinate of the other. In the case of matter, philosophers and psychologists typically interpret natural and unnatural kinds to be ontologically distinct. The natural kind category is further subdivided into living and non-living things. Within the category of living things, plants and animals can be distinguished (Figure 1). Below the ontological level, further subcategories can be formed on the superordinate, the basic and the subordinate level (see Rosch et al., 1976). As one proceeds downwards within this hierarchy, exemplars of the same category become more and more similar to each other on a perceptual level. As one proceeds upwards, similarities between exemplars of the same category become more and more defined in abstract terms. According to traditional theories of cognitive development, young children are unable to think in abstract terms. Their concepts are assumed to be primarily perceptually-bound (Flavell, 1970) and closely tied to concrete experiences (Vygotsky, 1934). This implies that development proceeds from perceptual to causal understanding and that low-level categories should be formed earlier than high-level categories. Following this line of argument, young children should not yet be able to make distinctions on the ontological level because ontological meanings are usually defined in non-perceptual terms. This view has recently been challenged by new experimental findings indicating that children may form categories on highly abstract levels before they develop distinctions on the basic level (Mandler & McDonough, 1993). Furthermore, it has been shown that pre-schoolers base their inductive thinking on knowledge about category membership rather than on perceptual similarity (Gelman, 1988; Gelman & Coley, 1990; Gelman & Markman, 1987; Keil, 1989). Some authors have thus concluded that the traditional "Concrete to Abstract view" concerning concept and category development needs to be revised. Based on their own experimental work, Simon and Keil

(1995) recently suggested an "Abstract to Concrete shift", assuming that children may first develop the ontological distinction between natural and unnatural kinds, and later come to differentiate categories on lower levels of abstraction. Pointing in the same direction, others have argued that a distinction between animate and inanimate objects may already be present in infants (Gelman, 1990; Mandler, 1992; Premack, 1990) and could serve as the first basis for developing the physical and social domain of causality (Gelman & Spelke, 1981).

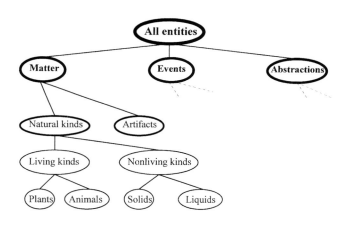

Figure 1: Segment of an idealized ontology (after Chi, 1992)

Whether our organization of knowledge develops from concrete to abstract, or from abstract to concrete categories, has different implications for our understanding of conceptual changes in the context of development theories. In the first case, conceptual change should mainly result from the attainment of new knowledge about hidden object properties or invisible causal structures (abstract information), followed by the process of restructuring that combine familiar concepts on the next higher level. In the latter case, conceptual change should mainly consist of enrichment or differentiation of existing knowledge structures. Research on concept and category formation during childhood seems to provide evidence for both kinds of conceptual changes. Accordingly, one might also take a third view, assuming that there is neither a general developmental trend in one or the other direction. Rather, it may be the case that children of all ages develop concepts and categories on concrete as well as on abstract levels at the same time, using multiple different sources of information in order to group material entities in ways that serve them best in dealing efficiently with their environment.

As already mentioned above, this chapter deals with the question of how children group objects on the ontological level. In the following paragraphs, I will first give a brief summary on existing theories about children's understanding of ontological categories of matter such as natural and unnatural, living and non-living, or animate and inanimate kinds. Based on recent empirical findings, a new theoretical framework, referred to as "Causes and Effects of Changes (CEC) Model" will be introduced to describe the formation of ontological categories. The role of conceptual change within the model presented will be discussed at the end of this chapter.

The Development of Ontological Categories of Matter: Existing Theories

Traditional theories assume that young children have false beliefs about the categorical status of material entities. Research on this issue has mainly focused on the distinction between living and non-living kinds: Piaget (1979) observed that children younger than 6 years of age identify all objects that perform a certain function and show some kind of activity as living kinds. Later, the term "alive" is applied to objects that show some kind of movement (age 7–8), followed by a stage when only self-starters are judged to be alive (age 8–12). This tendency of young children to attribute life to non-biological functional or moving things is referred to as *childhood animism*[1]. According to Piaget, children won't develop a correct concept of living and non-living kinds before they reach formal operational level.

The hypothesis that movement is highly relevant for young children's concept of living kinds has been confirmed by many authors. More specifically, the causation of movement seems to play a key role in this context (Bullock, 1985; Massey & Gelman, 1988; Richards & Siegler, 1986). Objects that appear to show self-initiated movement are more likely to be misclassified as living kinds than others. Studies conducted by Berzonsky (1971), Laurandeau and Pinard (1962), Looft (1974) and Madsen (1982) further indicate that unfamiliar moving objects (e.g. the sun) are judged to be alive more often than familiar ones (e.g. a bicycle), thus suggesting that the "self-starters rule" may serve as a heuristic strategy or as a fall back option when sufficient other information about the life-status of a given object is not available. Experiments conducted by Richards and Siegler (1986) point in the same direction. The authors have shown that people of all ages use movement as an indicator for life when reasoning about unknown objects on another planet, but this does not imply that they are completely unaware of other differences between living and non-living kinds. Although Piaget may have been correct in highlighting the relevance of movement for children's judgements, his theory contradicts other findings indicating that children use biological properties to distinguish animals and plants from artefacts long before they have reached formal operational level.

A more recent approach describing the development of the distinction between biological and non-biological entities has been proposed by Carey (1985). The author conducted a series of studies using the induction paradigm. In this paradigm, children of various age-groups were asked whether unfamiliar animals, which varied in the degree of perceptual

---

[1]In the psychological literature, the terms "animate" and "inanimate" often refer to the distinction between self-starters and non-self-starters, thus implying a distinction between people and animals on the one hand (animate things) and plants, other natural kinds, or artefacts on the other (inanimate). Even though this understanding of the term "animate" differs substantially from philosophical definitions, it will also be applied in the given context.

similarity to humans (e.g. dogs and worms), have the same properties (internal organs) or show the same kind of behaviours (e.g. sleeping, eating, having babies) as humans. Carey found that pre-schoolers' number of "yes"-answers decreased with the decrease in perceptual similarity of a given test-item to humans, whereas older subjects showed no difference in their reactions to similar and dissimilar animals. The author concluded that young children have not yet developed a clear concept of "animal" or "living kind" but rather induce an unknown object's properties on the basis of an analogy to humans. Carey suggests that children first develop a psychological framework of causal reasoning based on their experiences with people. As soon as they come to realize that people and animals have things in common, they make an induction from people to animals, based on the perceptual similarity of a given animal to humans (e.g. they make fewer inductions from people to worms than to dogs). According to Carey, young children are largely ignorant of the life-status of plants. Only at about 10 or 11 years of age do they begin to understand that all animals and plants share biological properties with people, such as reproduction or growth, and that these properties define the category of living kinds.

Even though some of Carey's own findings support the person analogy hypothesis, other studies show that young children's reasoning about objects is not always based on a comparison with humans. For example, Inagaki (1990) has shown that children who once kept a goldfish as a pet made use of this experience when asked to think about potential behaviours and properties of an unfamiliar water animal. Despite the fact that analogical thinking certainly provides a powerful tool for inductive reasoning about biological properties of unknown objects, it does not seem to be the only strategy used by young children: 2- to 4-year-olds have been found to prefer information about category membership rather than information about perceptual similarities between objects whenever the former kind of information is available (Gelman & Coley, 1990; Gelman & Markman, 1987). Inagaki and Hatano (1991) further demonstrate that 6-year-olds use the person-analogy in a constrained way, making wrong inductions only when other biological knowledge is still lacking. In sum, the reported findings suggest that analogical comparisons to people may primarily be involved when children are asked about properties or behaviours that are typical for humans (e.g. eating, sleeping, having babies), and when information about category membership of the target object is not available.

A third theory about the development of ontological categories has recently been proposed by Keil (1992). He hypothesizes that some "knowledge acquisition devices (KAD's)" for highly abstract domain-specific knowledge may be innate. According to the author, children are predisposed to learn certain facts about the biological world that help them distinguish people, animals and plants from non-living kinds. Among these facts are the following seven aspects: (i) biological things reproduce, (ii) they have a complex heterogeneous internal structure, (iii) they grow and undergo canonical and usually irreversible patterns of change that are highly specific for different biological kinds, (iv) something intrinsic to biological kinds produces most of their phenomenal properties, (v) typical phenomenal properties are usually diagnostic of underlying non-phenomenal ones, (vi) properties have purposes for biological kinds, and (vii) biological entities regulate resources so as to maintain various patterns of homeostasis.

Keil's theory predicts that a rudimentary theoretical distinction between ontological categories of matter can already be found in very young children and that learning experience helps children to further shape this basic categorical structure. His theory offers an explanation for the presence of biological knowledge in pre-schoolers. However, it does not explain why young children often associate life with the ability to produce motion or why they make other kinds of systematic mistakes. If our cognitive system were actually tuned to detect specific relational structures in the real world that distinguish living from non-living kinds on the basis of biological features, why then should children use inappropriate distinctions such as the distinction between self-starters and non-self-starters? Keil concedes that an object's movement behaviour could be so salient to young children that it works against an early understanding of the term "living thing", but he does not suggest how this idea could be integrated within the KAD account.

All three theories assume that children start with some naive understanding of the concept "living kind", which then undergoes multiple revisions during the elementary school years. The development of ontological distinctions is thus interpreted as a product of conceptual changes. Different opinions exist concerning the reason for this development. Whereas Piaget claims that young children's egocentrism and their general inability to think in causal or abstract terms is responsible for the late development of a correct understanding of the term "alive", Carey and Keil both argue that a lack of world knowledge explains age differences concerning our conceptual understanding of living and non-living kinds. Carey and Keil disagree on other points, however: while Carey proposes that biological knowledge develops out of a naive psychology, Keil claims that biology develops as an autonomous knowledge domain. Another difference concerns prerequisites for the development of ontological distinctions: Carey assumes that this development is primarily based on our ability to reason by analogy. In contrast, Keil argues that it is supported by innate knowledge acquisition devices. Although each of the presented theories offers a powerful explanatory framework for the interpretation of certain findings, each also seems to contradict other evidence at the same time. Existing evidence appears to allow no final decision concerning the question whether young children first make an animate/inanimate distinction, as suggested by Piaget, a people/other distinction, as indicated by Carey's findings, or whether they show early awareness of the fact that people, animals and plants belong to the same ontological category, as hypothesized by Keil. Their actual behaviour in various experimental settings produces a mixed impression of early competencies, on the one hand, and lack of understanding, on the other. This raises the question of whether the development of ontological distinctions shows any systematic pattern at all and, if so, which aspects might guide the process of categorization.

In this chapter, I will argue that our perception of changes may provide an important tool for understanding why humans make certain basic distinctions between general classes of material entities and not others. Starting with the first day of life, new-borns pay special attention to changes in their environment. Objects are not only perceived in terms of their static perceptual properties (e.g. shape or colour) but more so in terms of their activities. In order to deal efficiently with the material world, children need to find out which classes of objects cause what kind of activity under what circumstances; they need to predict changes, to understand what causes them and to evaluate the usefulness of certain activities for specific purposes.

The following paragraphs will describe three dimensions that carry information crucial for human survival and may thus be of central importance for children's early learning of ontological distinctions. These three dimensions are: (i) causality, (ii) functionality, and (iii) predictability. Given that they all somehow deal with information about changes involving a given object and that causality seems to play a key role in the given context, the theoretical framework that unifies them will be referred to as the "Causes and Effects of Changes (CEC) Model".

Dimensions of the CEC-Model

Causality

Recent studies indicate that children's ability to reason about causal events develops during the first months of life (e.g. Baillargeon, 1994; Spelke, 1991) and serves to distinguish between different kinds of objects based on their activity (Gelman, 1990; Mandler, 1992; Premack, 1990). How may information about Causes of Changes allow us to distinguish ontological categories of matter?

Living and non-living kinds can be categorized based on the information whether or not internal causes are needed to explain changes performed by a specific object. An object with the ability to perform internally induced or self-initiated changes is usually assumed to be animate or alive, an object without this ability is assumed to be inanimate or non-living. It should be noted, however, that purely self-initiated or externally-induced changes do not exist. Rather, the use of this attribute seems to help us reduce the complexity of multiple causal interactions between properties of a given object and the environment. Accordingly, our understanding about the causation of different changes involving the object in question should influence our judgement of whether or not this object is able to perform self-initiated changes. Self-initiated changes may involve one of the following aspects: (i) a given object's external and/or internal features, (ii) its state of existence, or (iii) its location in space.

Self-initiated changes of external and/or internal features. Such changes refer to changes of the object's physical appearance and/or its internal state. Growth and ageing are prominent examples of changes that involve both aspects. Experiments conducted by Backenscheider et al. (1993) show that pre-schoolers expect only living things, and not artefacts, to grow back parts that have been cut off. They also know that artefacts do not get larger with age whereas animals and plants usually do (Rosengren et al., 1991). At pre-school age, children consider colour and shape to be features that change in growing animals (Rosengren et al., 1991). According to Keil (1992), children of this age know that any biological entity develops in a characteristic way and that this development reveals more about its category membership than does the object's final appearance, whereas this is not the case for artefacts. Gelman and Wellman (1991) further report that pre-schoolers expect baby animals to have specific intrinsic potentials that are not visible early in their development but will become manifest over time. In sum, all these studies suggest that young children use knowledge about self-initiated changes of internal or external features to distinguish living from non-living kinds.

Self-initiated changes of an object's state of existence. Changes of this kind are only performed by living kinds. Unlike artefacts and non-living natural kinds, animals and plants reproduce. In addition to offspring, they often generate parts or new entities (e.g. feathers in the case of birds, or leaves and fruit in the case of trees). Knowledge about such self-initiated changes in an object's state of existence or the state of existence of parts belonging to that object may help children to learn the difference between living and non-living kinds, as already pointed out by Keil (1992). Within the group of living kinds that are capable of changing another object's state of existence, humans give themselves a special status. Objects that exist because of human intervention are called artefacts or unnatural kinds. Whereas Piaget (1979) originally claimed that young children expect all things to be created by humans — a phenomenon called *artificialism* — newer studies reveal that even 4-year-olds do understand that some things are made by people and that others can be found in nature (e.g. Gelman & Kremer, 1991). Again, it is information on the Causality dimension that appears to be crucial for categorization — this time for the distinction between natural and unnatural kinds: Humans provide causes for the existence of artefacts, whereas nature provides causes for the existence of natural kinds.

Self-initiated changes in location. In addition to knowledge about self-initiated changes concerning specific features or the state of existence of a given object, self-initiated changes in location carry valid information for categorization. In our everyday understanding, only animals and humans can move without the help of external forces. They have their own energy system and a specifically developed movement apparatus that enables them to change places. Plants, other natural kinds, and artefacts remain stationary unless set in motion by an external agent. The role movement plays in learning the distinction between general categories was first recognized by Piaget. New research on this issue shows that adults, pre-schoolers, and maybe even infants, focus on the causation of movement in order to make inductions about an object's ontological status (Bullock, 1985; Gelman & Spelke, 1981; Massey & Gelman, 1988; Premack, 1990; Richards & Siegler, 1984, 1986;).

Seeking the cause of a given change and identifying it as either being self-initiated or externally induced thus seems to provide children with knowledge that fosters their conceptual understanding of the differences between living and non-living, natural and unnatural, or animate and inanimate kinds. One might speculate that we tend to explain a given change as being self-initiated as long as we lack knowledge about potential external causes. Following this hypothesis, a child who does not yet understand what makes the sun move, rise in the morning, change its colour in the evening, or disappear at night may conclude that the sun is capable of self-initiated changes and probably belongs to the category of living kinds. Piaget's finding that young children attribute life to inanimate moving objects (especially to remote objects such as celestial bodies), may thus reveal limited causal knowledge rather than a general lack of cognitive capacities used for causal reasoning.

This analysis underlines the high relevance of information about different causes of changes for the development of the distinction between ontological categories of matter. Another potentially useful source of information is functionality. Whereas knowledge about Causes of Changes deals with "why?" or "how?" questions, knowledge about functionality deals with the question "what for?"

Functionality

Humans manipulate aspects of their environment in order to pursue their own goals. We evaluate activities as well as properties of material entities according to their function. This kind of evaluation seems to be a core component of object representation, even in infants (Nelson, 1974). By at least 14 months of age, children are able to categorize objects according to functional properties (Madole, 1992; Madole et al., 1993). Furthermore, 9- to 12-month-olds have been shown to infer the presence of functional properties across objects that differ in colour or surface pattern (Baldwin et al., 1993).

Given children's early competence in encoding aspects of functionality, one might ask how this kind of information helps us to categorize objects on the ontological level. Concerning the distinction between natural and unnatural kinds, the answer seems rather simple: Artefacts differ from natural kinds in that they usually have a much higher functional value for humans. Further suggestions concern the animate/inanimate distinction: Gelman and Spelke (1981) have pointed out that animate movement differs from inanimate movement in that the former is usually goal oriented (e.g. an animal approaches food in order to eat) whereas the latter does not have any function or purpose for the moving object itself. Concerning the distinction between living and non-living kinds, philosophers (e.g. Dennett, 1987) as well as developmental psychologists (Keil, 1992) have pointed out that certain properties of living kinds have an internal purpose, namely to guarantee their survival, whereas the properties of non-living kinds only serve an external agent. Experiments conducted by Keil (1992) indicate that what he calls the "teleological/functional" stance is closely associated with the concept of living kinds. In one study about invisible disease agents, the author told second and fourth graders about a "thing" that either "rubs around inside your body causing abrasion" (mechanical description), "has been made by people" (human designed description), "wants to get inside you and make you sick" (intentional description), or that "has to get inside people's bodies and use parts of their bodies, or it won't last long" (teleological/functional description). Keil found that children of both age groups attributed life and other biological properties about twice as often to the teleological/functional and intentional entities than to the mechanical and human designed entities. The author concludes that "Describing something as having a functional role leads to a conviction that it is a biological kind … unless you specifically flag it as an artefact" (Keil, 1992, p. 126).

Although they focus on distinct aspects of object representation, the two dimensions of causality and functionality seem closely related. Functional thinking often guides our search for causal explanations. Causal knowledge, on the other hand, can produce new insights into the functionality of an object's parts or properties. The third dimension to be considered in the CEC-Model is predictability. Information about the predictability of an object's behaviour is crucial for human survival: in order to interact successfully with our material environment, it is not sufficient to merely know the range of possible changes that various classes of objects perform and to explain the causes as well as the purposes of these changes — we also need to build expectations concerning the likelihood of their occurrence. How such expectations may help us to differentiate ontological categories will be discussed next.

Predictability

The range of possible changes that can be perceived in any given artefact or non-living natural kind is usually limited, and the occurrence of such changes is typically dependent on the presence of specific external causes. Both aspects lead to a rather high degree of behavioural predictability. Animals and plants, on the other hand, can both change in various ways, and these changes are produced by a complex interplay between external and internal processes. This complex interplay usually makes it much harder to predict precisely when and how a living thing, in comparison to a non-living thing, will undergo a specific change (e.g. move, change shape, produce sounds, grow a fruit). Within the category of living kinds, self-initiated changes performed by animals seem less predictable than self-initiated changes performed by plants. Again, this appears to be a consequence of differences in the complexity of both classes of organisms. Even though young children may not yet know much about the internal complexity of a given system, it seems likely that they are already able to perceive differences in the predictability of the object's behaviour. This information could help them group objects based on perceptual abstractions and motivate them to explore why such differences exist.

Empirical studies exploring the role of predictability for categorization are still rare. The only context in which this aspect has gained some attention thus far is the identification of animate movement. Mandler (1992) suggests that young children recognize animate motion as self-initiated and following an irregular path. Predictability is the psychological correlate to regularity. When something is irregular it is less predictable than something regular. The decision whether a given object moves along a regular or an irregular path may thus result from an analysis of the predictability of the object's movement behaviour. Some of my own studies on animal and machine movement (Lamsfuss, 1995) provide evidence in support for this hypothesis: 4- and 5-year-olds as well as adults were shown different pairs of "tracks" (depicted as simple dot patterns; see Figure 2 for some examples). Tracks were used in order to avoid giving additional perceptual information about the object that produced the motion. The studies differed with respect to the specific dot patterns being used but one of two tracks on each test-picture was always comparably more regular than the other. Irregularity not only resulted from changes in the direction of the movement path, but also from variations of the distance between the patterns that belonged to one track and between the dots forming each single pattern. This means that the relevance of information about the predictability/regularity of motion for categorization was tested in a broader sense than originally suggested by Mandler (1992).

When asked which of two tracks looked more like it could have been left by a machine, children as well as adults chose the regular track more often than when asked the same question about animals. Similar results were obtained with biology experts. For animals, participants in each group sometimes chose the perfectly regular and sometimes picked out the irregular track, indicating that they did not have a general idea that animal movement is irregular or follows an irregular path. Rather, they expected that animals can move in various alternative ways (regular as well as irregular) and thus show low predictability in their behaviour whereas machines typically produce regular movement and are highly predictable. No significant developmental trend was found concerning the strength of the association between regular tracks and machines, and irregular tracks and animals. Neither age nor expertise influenced the results (see Figure 3). These findings suggest that information about behavioural predictability can be used to distinguish animals from machines by children as well as by adults.

Follow-up studies will test whether the reported findings can be extended to other behavioural measures and classes of objects. In a first study along these lines, different pairs of tone sequences were presented to pre-schoolers as well as adults, one with and one without

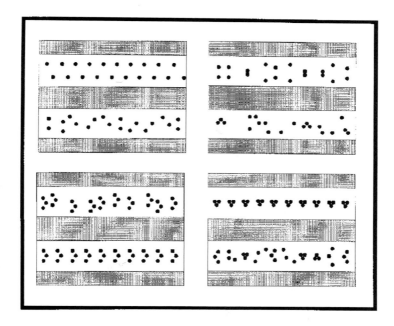

These test-items have been used in different studies. Left top: two-dot patterns; perfectly regular track versus track with variations on the dimensions: vertical distance between patterns and orientation of patterns. Left bottom: three-dot patterns; track with variations on the dimensions: vertical and horizontal distance between patterns versus perfectly regular track. Right top: two-dot patterns; track with variations on the dimensions: horizontal distance between patterns and distance between dots within each pattern versus random dots. Right bottom: three-dot patterns; perfectly regular track versus track with variations on the dimensions: orientation of patterns and distance between dots within each pattern.

Figure 2: Examples for test-items used in studies by Lamsfuss (1995)

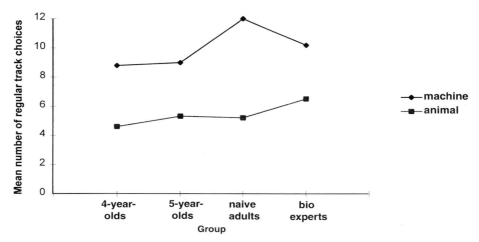

Figure 3: Track choices under machine/animal instruction

modulation of each tone. Again, half of the participants in each group were asked which of both sequences sounded more like it could have been produced by an animal, and the others were asked which sequence sounded more like it could have been produced by an animal. The basic findings replicated those obtained in the motion study: whereas no specific kind of sequence was preferred for animals, both pre-schoolers as well as adults chose the monotonous sequence more often for machines than would be expected by chance. These findings suggest that the dimension Predictability of Changes (and not simply changes concerning the object's location in space) contains relevant information for categorization on the ontological level.

In summary, the previous analysis reveals that pre-school children already know a great deal about the distinction between animate and inanimate, living and non-living, and natural and unnatural kinds. Domain-specificity may result from the fact that information about causality, functionality and predictability is usually correlated in nature. For example, some objects behave in mostly unpredictable ways: they perform changes in the absence of external agents, and such changes occur independently of human intentions. Other objects perform changes that are highly dependent on human intentions, follow well-known rules and are comparably easy to predict. It is because these kinds of correlative structures exist in the real world and because our cognitive system extracts information about those aspects that we construct ontological categories the way we do (see also Keil, 1991).

Which information is used to categorize objects or to make living/non-living judgements in a specific situation may depend on a given individual's background knowledge as well as on the demands of the task at hand. Whereas knowledge about specific aspects of changes may be highly relevant in one context, knowledge about different aspects may be more important in others. Varying performance in different situations should thus be interpreted as a sign of "adaptive conceptualization" rather than concept instability or cognitive incompetence.

A Comparison Between Existing Theories and the CEC-Model

Piaget emphasizes the role of motion for young children's concept of living kinds. A comparison between Piaget's approach and the CEC-Model reveals that categorization by movement behaviour is closely linked to the CEC-dimension *Causality*, or more specifically: to the aspect *causes of changes concerning an object's location in space*. The two accounts differ, however, in their evaluation of this aspect. In contradiction to Piaget, who assumes that movement is the only criterion used by young children to make life-status judgements, the CEC-Model treats knowledge about the causation of movement as just one of many aspects that children may refer to when they learn to classify people, animals, plants, non-living natural kinds and artefacts (even though this aspect may indeed be more salient for younger than for older children).

Carey postulates a shift in the development of children's concepts from a concrete people concept to a broader animal concept to a general living kind concept, whereas the CEC-Model assumes that children are able to simultaneously identify concrete as well as abstract similarities and differences between various classes of objects, and that rather abstract perceptual and conceptual differences provide the basis for learning the distinction between ontological categories. According to the CEC-Model, the development of ontological distinctions does not necessarily have to be preceded by the formation of a general animal-concept, as suggested by Carey.

Keil's view shows the most similarities with the CEC-Model: Facts about the biological world that Keil believes young children are predisposed to learn can be related to the CEC-Model — many of them to the dimension Causes of Changes: e.g. "biological things reproduce" (self-initiated change in existence), or "they grow and undergo canonical and usually irreversible patterns of change that are highly specific for different biological kinds" (self-initiated change in appearance). The fact that "properties have purposes for biological kinds" and that "typical phenomenal properties are usually diagnostic of underlying non-phenomenal ones" relate to the functionality dimension. In addition, the belief that biological things "have a complex heterogeneous internal structure" may partly be derived from the experience that their behaviour is usually hard to predict. Both models expect young children to seek causal explanations and to be able to learn about objects on a conceptual level (see also Carey, 1985). Furthermore, domain specificity is assumed to result from the fact that certain properties of objects are usually correlated in nature. Nevertheless, one important difference between Keil's account and the CEC-Model remains: The biases called KAD's within Keil's theory are more concrete than the dimensions of the CEC-Model. For example, when Keil mentions the "teleological stance" as an example of a KAD bias, he is referring to a highly specific aspect of functional knowledge (properties have purposes for living kinds), whereas the CEC-Model assumes that various different aspects of functional knowledge may simultaneously influence the process of categorization on the ontological level.

Conceptual Change on the Ontological Level and Cognitive Development

As has been pointed out in the introduction, conceptual changes are closely related to changes in categorical structure. According to Chi (1992), conceptual changes within an ontological category should be distinguished from conceptual changes across ontological categories. The former kind of conceptual change involves processes of restructuring knowledge within an ontological tree, such as the migration of concepts, which may either result from the acquisition of new facts or changes in the salience of specific attributes associated with a given concept. By contrast, radical conceptual change involves the reassignment of a given concept to a new ontological tree without allowing for an isomorphic mapping between the old and the new meaning. In this case, the old and new concept no longer share the same core meaning — they are considered to be incommensurable (see also Kuhn, 1982). In accordance with Chi, Carey (1991) argues that conceptual changes can be placed on a continuum from the enrichment of concepts that maintain their core to the evolution of one set of concepts into another that is incommensurable with the original. Whereas processes of enrichment represent weak forms of restructuring knowledge, the development of new concepts incommensurable with old concepts represents the strongest form.

What kind of conceptual changes occur in the development of ontological categories of matter? Each of the presented models suggests a different answer: Piaget's theory predicts that movement plays a key role for categorization in young children, whereas adults categorize objects according to biological properties. If a child actually changes her or his concept of living kinds from moving things to biological things, such a change would imply strong restructuring of existing knowledge. This is because the movers/non-movers "life"-concept of the 4- to 6-year-old would be incommensurable with the biological/non-biological life concept of an adult.

Carey's people-analogy hypothesis assumes that young children regard people and animals as distinct categories. Later, they come to realize that people are just one subcategory of animals and that plants should also be assigned to the category of living kinds. Chi (1992) interprets these kinds of changes as revisions of part–whole relations — changes concerning the level at which a given concept is located within the same ontological tree (here: "living things"). According to the author, revisions of part–whole relations do not imply radical conceptual change.

Piaget's and Carey's models both assume a specific sequence in which people, animals, plants and artefacts will be grouped together in the course of cognitive development. Keil's KAD theory makes no such assumption. If children are equipped with special knowledge acquisition devices to learn the biological/non-biological distinction, then there is no reason to expect the development of wrong groupings before a full understanding of true ontological distinctions has been attained. At least, no prediction concerning the kind of mistakes that might occur can be derived from this theory. Conceptual change should thus mainly result from processes of enrichment and consist of a gradual increase of causal knowledge supporting the living–non-living, or natural–unnatural kind distinction.

According to the CEC-Model, people of all ages learn about qualitatively different but closely related sources of information simultaneously. How much a given child knows about causes of specific changes, the functionality of an object's activities and properties, or about the predictability of its behaviour depends on his/her particular learning experiences. The evidence reported in this chapter contradicts the idea that children come to understand ontological categories in a clearly fixed sequence. Rather, they seem to develop different kinds of distinctions in parallel (e.g. people/other; animals/other; animals and plants/other; artefacts/other) and apply their ontological knowledge flexibly depending on the special demands of a given situation. This tendency to apply multiple classification systems at the same time can still be observed in adults. Existing descriptions concerning the organizational structure of ontological categories suggest that the natural/unnatural and the living/non-living kind distinction can be integrated in a hierarchical system (see Figure 1). A closer look reveals that this idea is misleading: the natural/unnatural kind distinction is not clearly superior to the living/non-living kind distinction; instead, both reflect alternative groupings of the same classes of objects (see Figure 4) and differ mainly with respect to the specific combination of criteria used in order to classify objects.

Not only do adults use multiple systems for classification on the ontological level, they also seem to use the same concept with different meanings, depending on the given concrete situational context. Carey illustrates this point by referring to the concept "animal":

> The English word "animal" is ambiguous among three dominant uses. Sometimes it contrasts with plants and with inanimate objects, as in "the animal kingdom" ... Sometimes it contrasts with people, as in "Don't eat

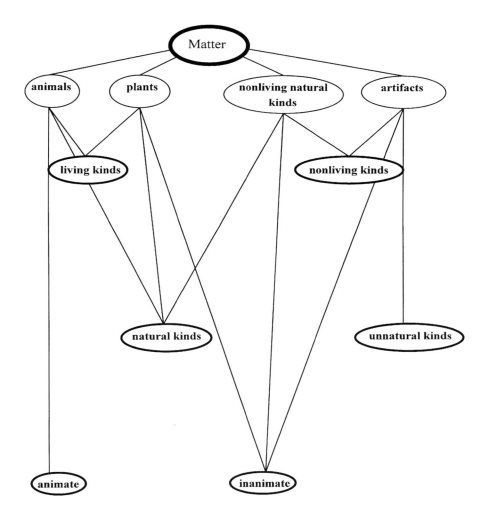

Figure 4: Multiple classifications on the ontological level

like an animal". And sometimes it means roughly "mammal", as in
"birds, bugs, snakes, and animals" (Carey, 1985, p.73).

The assumption that children and adults learn about different ontological distinctions simultaneously and that they use multiple classification systems in their everyday reasoning does not imply that each ontological distinction will be fully understood at the same age, or that systematic mistakes in classifying objects won't occur. Besides the fact that children certainly know quantitatively less about material objects and about the "correct" (conventional) use of concepts in specific task contexts, they may also treat information concerning causality, functionality and predictability differently from adults; the salience of information about certain aspects within one dimension may shift in the course of cognitive development, thus leading to a reorganization of existing knowledge structures.

For example, it may well be that the causation of movement is highly relevant for categorization in young infants (Mandler, 1992; Premack, 1990). This seems plausible as humans are predisposed to pay special attention to motion, and our natural environment contains numerous moving objects, and because the difference between objects that do and those that do not need physical contact with external agents in order to start moving can be perceived early in life. Insight into other causes of changes (e.g. changes that have to do with growth, ageing, reproduction) requires careful exploration of an object's behaviour over a longer period of time, or obtaining explanations from adults. The young child who may have more difficulties acquiring this kind of knowledge as compared with knowledge about movement may therefore base categorization on a limited selection of information about Causes of Changes. This would explain why non-living moving objects are sometimes judged to be alive in the absence of visible external forces causing this movement. It should be noted, however, that Causes of Changes concerning an object's location in space is not the only information that helps children learn the distinction between ontological categories. Changes in the salience of specific aspects may also occur on the functionality dimension: For example, it seems rather easy to differentiate objects with a high and a low functional value for humans or to understand the functionality of a certain property within a given system, but it may be comparably difficult to learn that some properties have relatively more inward than outward directed purposes. This insight not only requires knowledge about specific functional properties, but also the ability to combine various aspects of functional knowledge and to make integrated judgements. Accordingly, it may be easier for young children to grasp the natural/unnatural kind distinction than the living/non-living kind distinction when considering information on the functionality dimension.

Concerning the predictability dimension, it can be assumed that children gradually learn to detect more and more complex or abstract regularities in the real world and that they continuously get better at predicting specific kinds of object changes. It follows that more objects should perform unpredictable changes from the point of view of a young child than from the point of view of an adult.

This analysis reveals that the animate/inanimate distinction should be comparably easy for young children to learn because most information necessary to make this kind of distinction (information about the causation and predictability of movement) can be attained through direct perceptual analysis (Gelman, 1990; Mandler, 1992; Premack, 1990). To distinguish natural from unnatural kinds seems to be a little bit more difficult: in order to understand this kind of distinction, children need to know that some things in the world have been made by people and that they have a high functional value for humans whereas others exist independently of human actions and goals. The living/non-living kind distinction seems even harder to grasp as children need to use multiple sources of knowledge about Causes and Effects of Changes in order to classify objects correctly. In addition, the status of plants seems somewhat arbitrary: the self-initiated changes that plants perform are typically too slow to be perceived directly, and the existence of many plants appears to be partly caused by humans (e.g. farmers putting seeds in the ground). Furthermore, many plants have a high functional value for humans, and their changes seem less difficult to predict than those of animals.

Even though certain basic categorical distinctions may be understood more easily than others, it is not necessary to assume that one kind of distinction develops out of the other (e.g. an abstract animal concept out of a concrete people/animal distinction), or replace the other (e.g. the living/non-living kind distinction replaces the self-starters/non self-starters distinction). In the present context, conceptual change is interpreted as a continuous process of enriching knowledge about different classes of objects and re-evaluating the importance of specific aspects for determining category membership in a given situation. Concepts may gradually change their meaning each time newly discovered facts are integrated into existing knowledge structures. What remains stable, however, are the dimensions that are relevant for making basic cuts in the world.

Concluding Remarks

The current version of the CEC-Model focuses primarily on highly abstract dimensions of knowledge. It places special emphasis on behavioural aspects and does not deal with questions concerning the role of perceptual features (e.g. shape, form, colour, parts), or of the language used for categorization. Although perceptual similarities and word use are both known to be important for processes of categorization, these aspects alone cannot explain why humans make certain basic cuts in the world and not others. Accordingly, we need to think about more abstract forms of knowledge that also contribute to the development of ontological distinctions. The dimensions presented in this chapter may provide examples of such abstract knowledge.

The CEC-Model assumes that concepts are stable in the sense that the dimensions to which humans refer when distinguishing ontological kinds remain stable. Furthermore, information about the object's appearance, behaviour and its relations to other objects is assumed to be stored in long-term memory. Concepts are flexible in that the specific demands of a given situation determine which information will be focused. Concept development and conceptual changes result from the acquisition of new knowledge concerning relevant dimensions and attempts to integrate this knowledge into existing structures. This process may sometimes lead to shifts in the salience of specific aspects that are part of a child's object representation. The occurrence of conceptual changes is not restricted to childhood, however. If we look at new technical developments (the computer revolution, genetic engineering, etc.) we cannot be entirely sure that what adults currently consider to be essential features of natural and living kinds or animate things will always keep the same informative value. The identification of animate movement provides a good example: About 200 years ago, one could easily determine whether a given object's change in location was self-initiated and use this information to distinguish people and other animals from inanimate objects. In the age of robots and other machines that are set in motion by computers or by remote control, information about the presence or absence of external forces is not always immediately apparent and thus does not provide a sufficient basis for making this distinction. Accordingly, information about the predictability and functionality of changes gains diagnostic value. In order to account for these developments, we need to assume a flexible cognitive mechanism that guides processes of categorization. Dimensional accounts such as the one presented in this chapter allow for this flexibility without accepting the idea that concepts have no stable structure at all.

3

Motivational Beliefs as Resources for and Constraints on Conceptual Change

Paul R. Pintrich

Introduction

Recent models of conceptual change have stressed the role that ontological and epistemological beliefs play in the process of conceptual change. For example, Vosniadou and Brewer (1994) have proposed a model of conceptual change that involves changes in a person's mental model for phenomena as they acquire conceptual knowledge. Their model suggests that both ontological and epistemological presuppositions serve to constrain the types of beliefs and inferences a person may hold in their mental model. This model assumes that students make observations about phenomena based on their experience in a cultural context. This experience gives rise to certain inferences, beliefs and conceptual knowledge about the phenomena. However, these beliefs and conceptual knowledge are constrained by the epistemological and ontological presuppositions that individuals hold. For example, epistemological presuppositions include the criteria individuals use to judge what constitutes a phenomenon, the assumption that phenomena require an explanation, and that causal explanations can be used to explain physical phenomena. Ontological presuppositions include the basic beliefs about the nature of objects such as physical objects are solid, stable and, if not supported, will fall down (Vosniadou & Brewer, 1994). In this model these presuppositions constrain the specific beliefs and conceptual knowledge that individuals may acquire from their observations and experience in the cultural context by limiting the inferences individuals make about their observations.

This model provides a good description of how epistemological and ontological assumptions can facilitate or constrain conceptual change. The purpose of this chapter is to extend the logic of this model to suggest that motivational beliefs about the self and learning can play the same role in terms of being a resource to support conceptual change or a constraint that can hinder conceptual change (see Duit, this volume; Pintrich et al., 1993a). This is a step in the direction of extending models of conceptual change to include a variety of cognitive, motivational and social/contextual factors. As Strike and Posner (1992) have recently noted:

> A wider range of factors needs to be taken into account in attempting to describe a learner's conceptual ecology. *Motives and goals and the institutional and social sources of them need to be considered* (italics added). The idea of a conceptual ecology thus needs to be larger than the epistemological factors suggested by the history and philosophy of science (p. 162).

Given this gap, there is a need to incorporate motivational beliefs and goals into our models of conceptual change. At the same time, this integration can be attempted more easily given that motivational models have moved away from traditional personality and trait models of motivation to social cognitive models of motivation (Pintrich & Schunk, 1996).

The general conceptual model used in this paper attempts to add to the basic model presented by Vosniadou and Brewer (1994) by suggesting that various motivational beliefs about the self and learning also can act as "presuppositions" that can facilitate or constrain conceptual change. For example, as Pintrich et al. (1993a) have pointed out, when making observations about a phenomenon, individuals must attend to the information being presented to them, they must encode it in some way using various cognitive strategies, and they also must regulate their awareness and cognition through metacognitive and volitional control strategies. The use of these strategies should result in a deeper processing of the material to be learned. Chinn and Brewer (1993) also have suggested that engagement in deeper processing of the content to be learned will help in the process of conceptual change. The various cognitive operations that result in deeper processing are often dependent on various motivational beliefs about the self as a learner (Pintrich & Schrauben, 1992). Accordingly, motivational beliefs may not have a direct influence on conceptual change, but, as "presuppositions" or theories about the self and learning, they may influence the types of inferences and belief formation that take place as students acquire knowledge and build their mental models. For example, certain types of motivational beliefs may inhibit certain types of cognitive processes from occurring, whereas other motivational beliefs may facilitate cognitive engagement (Duit, this volume; Pintrich, et al., 1993a; Pintrich & Schrauben, 1992).

These motivational beliefs and various cognitive and metacognitive strategies are assumed to be "resources" that students can bring to bear on the task at hand to help them learn. In this way, the model parallels Smith et al.'s (1993) call for a constructivist model of misconceptions that takes into account the "the cognitive resources that can support the bootstrapping of more advanced cognitive structures" (p. 124). Smith et al. (1993) focus on the features of the cognitive system, in particular the students' existing understandings or prior knowledge and mental models. In the model of Smith et al. (1993), these prior mental models are very useful resources that students can use to develop deeper understanding, thereby facilitating conceptual change. In the Vosniadou and Brewer (1994) model, the prior mental models and ontological and epistemological presuppositions are generally seen as constraints that inhibit or hinder conceptual change. The model discussed in this paper assumes that prior knowledge can both facilitate and constrain conceptual change. More importantly, the model discussed here adds various motivational beliefs to the cognitive system and assumes that these beliefs can be drawn on by the individual to both support and constrain conceptual change.

At the same time, these motivational beliefs are embedded in various classroom contexts that can support the development of positive motivational beliefs or activate motivational beliefs that are less conducive to learning. Accordingly, it is important to consider the role of different classroom contextual factors in the process of conceptual change (Pintrich et al., 1993a). The proposed model focuses on the individual's constructions and beliefs, which is in line with constructivist models that focus on the individual student, but by including classroom context factors it also attempts to integrate ideas from more sociocultural models of learning. In this way, the model attempts to be informed by both constructivist and sociocultural models as suggested by Cobb (1994). In particular, by including both individual and contextual factors, the model attempts to avoid problems associated with decontextual-ized views of the learner when there is too much focus on the individual, as well as problems of ignoring individual variation and construction when there is too much concern with just the contexts of learning (see Cobb, 1994; Confrey, 1995).

Following Pintrich et al. (1993a), this chapter is organized around general motivational beliefs including goal orientation, epistemological beliefs, interest/value, efficacy and control beliefs. In the five sections on each of these beliefs, a general proposition is presented with regard to how the motivational belief might facilitate conceptual change, followed by a discussion of how the belief might influence learning and how the classroom context might condition the relations between motivational beliefs and cognition. This chapter does not attempt to provide a literature review of all related studies, but rather build an argument for the inclusion of both motivational and classroom contextual factors in models of conceptual change.

Proposition 1: Adoption of a Mastery Goal Orientation Should Facilitate Conceptual Change

Goals are cognitive representations of the different purposes students may adopt in different achievement situations. Like general intentions and purposes, in motivational theory goal orientations are assumed to guide students' behaviour, cognition and affect as they engage in an academic task (Dweck & Elliott, 1983). These goal orientations are self-constructed "theories" about what it means to learn and what it means to succeed in a context. In this way, these goal orientations help students make meaning of their own learning in the context. They provide the overall interpretative frame by which the students set proximal goals, decide how to approach a task, and evaluate their progress. In this way, they function as a resource that can facilitate or constrain learning. In addition, most of the current models of goal orientation assume that individuals construct these goal orientations in the imme-diate situation, they are not assumed to be stable individual differences. Accordingly, the development and activation of different goal orientations is assumed to be situated in the classroom context and influenced by the features of the context.

There are a variety of different conceptualizations of goal orientations, but the main distinction is between an intrinsic, mastery and task-involved orientation and an extrinsic, performance and ego-involved orientation (cf. Ames, 1992; Dweck & Leggett, 1988; Harter, 1981; Nicholls, 1984). Students who adopt a mastery orientation are assumed to focus on learning, understanding and mastering the task whereas those who adopt a performance orientation are assumed to focus on obtaining a good grade, a reward or besting others. There have been a number of studies that have shown that these two different types of goal orientation can lead to different patterns of cognitive engagement (Pintrich & Schrauben, 1992).

For example, Pintrich and his colleagues, in a series of correlational classroom studies (e.g. Pintrich, 1989; Pintrich & De Groot, 1990a, b; Pintrich & Garcia, 1991), have shown that junior high and college students who adopt an intrinsic goal for learning focused on understanding are more likely to report using deeper processing strategies, such as elabora-tion, as well as more metacognitive and self-regulatory strategies (e.g. planning, comprehension monitoring, regulating). Meece et al. (1988) in a correlational study of elementary science classrooms found that students who adopted a general intrinsic orientation to learning as well as task specific mastery goals were more likely to report using more cognitive and metacognitive strategies. Nolen (1988), in a laboratory study of text comprehension, found that junior high school students who adopted a task orientation focused on learning and understanding were more likely to use both deeper and surface processing strategies, whereas those with an ego orientation (a focus on the self and besting others) were more likely to use surface processing strategies. Graham and Golan (1991), in another experimental study of elementary students' memory and depth of processing, found that an induced motivational state (task or ego-focused) did not differentiate students' memory performance when shallow processing was required by the memory task (recall of rhyming words), but when required by the task to remember meaningful words from sentences, students who were more task focused performed significantly better. More recently, Hammer (1994), in a case study of six physics students, found that students who had a goal of understanding the physics material were more likely to question the material and think deeply about the meaning of the material as they studied. In addition, these students seemed to have a more coherent and systematic perspective on the nature of physics and performed well in the course.

Taken together, these results suggest that when students have a mastery orientation activated, they will be more likely to process the information in a deeper manner that increases the probability that conceptual change will occur. This complements Chinn and Brewer's (1993) suggestion that deeper processing will increase the probability of conceptual change by noting that mastery goals increase the likelihood that deeper processing will occur. As Reif and Larkin (1991) and others (Cole, 1992; Thagard, 1992) have pointed out, scientists may have a number of goals operating as they engage in research, but they almost always have a goal of mastery and understanding the phenomena under study. In a parallel fashion, students who adopt a mastery goal orientation focused on learning and mastery should be more likely to engage in the type of cognitive processing necessary for conceptual change to occur (Chinn & Brewer, 1993; Pintrich et al., 1993a).

This same set of studies also shows that the adoption of a more extrinsic goal orientation results in lower probability of deeper levels of cognitive engagement. Students that are focused on just getting a good grade or receiving an extrinsic reward are more likely to just attempt to complete the classwork, rather than engage the material in a meaningful way (Pintrich & Schrauben, 1992). In this way, an extrinsic goal orientation could serve to constrain conceptual change by limiting the level of deeper cognitive engagement. Of course, it is still possible that at least having an extrinsic orientation in the absence of a mastery orientation provides some incentive for cognitive engagement (see Pintrich & Garcia, 1991), but it does appear that having a mastery orientation will facilitate deeper cognitive engagement, whereas an extrinsic orientation can constrain engagement.

Although the link between students' goal orientation and their cognitive engagement seems to be relatively robust, it is important to note that most goal theorists assume that individuals' goal orientations are dependent on and situated within a classroom context (Ames, 1992; Blumenfeld, 1992). There seem to be several important dimensions of classrooms that can influence the adoption of a mastery goal orientation. First, the nature of the tasks that students are asked to accomplish can have an impact on students' goals. It appears that tasks that are more challenging, meaningful and "authentic" in terms of actual activities that might be relevant to life outside school can facilitate the adoption of a mastery goal

(Ames, 1992; Brophy, 1983; Lepper & Hodell, 1989; Meece, 1991). However, many, if not most classrooms, do not offer students the opportunity to work on authentic tasks (Gardner, 1991), thereby decreasing motivation and the opportunities for transfer of knowledge learned in school to other contexts. At the same time, the authority structures in classrooms often do not allow students much choice or control over their activities, which decreases the probability of a mastery orientation being developed in students (Ames, 1992; Ryan et al., 1985). Finally, evaluation procedures that focus on competition, social comparison and external rewards can foster a performance goal orientation where the learner focuses on besting others rather than conceptual understanding of the content (Ames, 1992; Elliott & Dweck, 1988; Grolnick & Ryan, 1987).

This research supports the assumption that the classroom context can influence the adoption of a mastery goal orientation, which in turn can influence the nature of students' cognitive processing and potential for conceptual change. These linkages between context, motivational goal orientation and cognition suggest that it may not be enough for teachers to present new information in a conceptual change instructional format that creates disequilibrium or dissatisfaction on the students' part (see Osborne & Freyberg, 1985). It appears that teachers must consider how the instruction is embedded in the task, authority and evaluation structures of their classrooms. If teachers use a conceptual change instructional model without changing the traditional task, authority and evaluation structures of the classroom, then students still might adopt a performance or extrinsic goal orientation to the new instructional method. In turn, this extrinsic goal orientation would tend to undermine the teacher's attempts to have the students engage the material in a deep and thoughtful manner. Accordingly, teachers may have to change not just their general instructional strategies for teaching for conceptual change, but also their task, authority and evaluation structures to focus the students on mastery and understanding goals (Blumenfeld et al., 1992).

Proposition 2: Adoption of More "Constructivist" Epistemological Beliefs Should Facilitate Conceptual Change

Vosniadou and Brewer (1994) include epistemological presuppositions in their model of conceptual change. In this model, which is based on research on conceptions of the day/night cycle, these presuppositions include the criteria by which to decide what constitutes a phenomenon, an idea that these different phenomena need to be explained, and a general preference for causal explanations of these phenomena. Although these beliefs are important, there are other more general epistemological beliefs that may play a role in conceptual change. There has been research on broadly defined epistemological beliefs, but most of this research has focused almost exclusively on the development of these beliefs, not on how these beliefs are related to other aspects of cognition and learning (Hofer & Pintrich, 1997). In addition, some of the research on epistemological beliefs (e.g. Schommer's program of research, see below) has proposed dimensions of epistemological beliefs, such as a belief in fixed ability, that are related to goal orientation models of motivation (i.e. Dweck & Leggett, 1988). Accordingly, the epistemological beliefs discussed here are given their relationship to goal orientation beliefs, but certain dimensions of epistemological beliefs are probably distinct from other more traditional motivational beliefs.

The research that is most directly related to the argument presented here is the research of Schommer and her colleagues (Schommer, 1990; 1993; Schommer et al., 1992; Schommer & Walker, 1995). In this research, Schommer has proposed that there are four independent factors or dimensions of epistemological beliefs including: (i) fixed ability, (ii) quick learning, (iii) simple knowledge, and (iv) certain knowledge. She also proposes a fifth dimension, source of knowledge, although this dimension has not always emerged as a separate dimension in all her factor analytic studies (see Schommer, 1990, 1993). Beliefs about fixed ability are derived from Dweck and Leggett's (1988) theory of motivation and basically represent their entity-incremental theory of intelligence, whereby individuals who endorse an entity or fixed ability view of intelligence believe that their intelligence is set and can't be changed by learning, whereas those with an incremental view of intelligence (or in Schommer's work, less endorsement of fixed ability) believe that their intelligence is malleable and can be developed over time with experience. In Schommer's model, the general assumption is that students with a fixed ability or entity view of intelligence will not be as likely to be cognitively engaged in contrast to students who have an incremental view. Although there is some support for this prediction in Schommer's research in terms of zero-order correlations (Schommer, 1990, 1993; Schommer et al., 1992), fixed ability beliefs are usually not the strongest predictors of learning when considered along with the other dimensions in regression analyses (see also Qian & Alvermann, 1995). In general, the effects of fixed ability beliefs are most likely mediated by motivational goal orientation as proposed by Dweck and Leggett (1988), so it may not be surprising that they do not have a direct effect on learning and comprehension. Accordingly, fixed ability beliefs may not have a direct effect on conceptual change, except through their link to goal orientation, and the links between goal orientation and conceptual change were explained in the previous section.

The second dimension proposed in Schommer's model is quick learning, or the belief that material can be learned quickly without much cognitive or behavioural effort. Although this belief is probably not conceptually a belief about knowledge or how knowledge is judged (see Hofer & Pintrich, 1997), it seems likely that students who endorse a view that learning is (and should be) quick and not involve much time or effort, will be less likely to be cognitively engaged. Schommer and her colleagues (Schommer 1990, 1993; Schommer et al., 1992) have found that students who endorse a belief in quick learning are more likely to draw simplified conclusions from text material and to have lower performance on comprehension tasks. In the same fashion, students who believe that learning should be quick may not be willing to engage in the lengthy and involved process of conceptual change. Given that conceptual change seems to take a fairly long time, a belief in quick learning would then be a constraint on conceptual change learning.

The third, fourth and fifth dimensions are more directly related to beliefs about the nature of knowledge, such as where knowledge comes from, how it is generated or constructed, and the criteria used to evaluate knowledge claims (Hofer & Pintrich, 1997). The third dimension, simple knowledge, reflects the belief that the knowledge in the domain is fairly simple or that the answer to a problem is clear, simple and straightforward. A belief in simple knowledge also reflects a belief that there should be general principles that apply across all situations, rather than a more complex perspective on how knowledge and principles might have to be applied differently depending on the context. In this sense, a belief in simple knowledge is in opposition to a more constructivist view of knowledge.

A belief in simple knowledge seems to be related to less comprehension and learning in Schommer's work (Schommer, 1990, 1993; Schommer et al., 1992), thereby representing a potential constraint on conceptual change. In addition, Qian and Alvermann (1995), in a study that examined conceptual change in physics, found that a belief in simple and certain knowledge was negatively related to amount of conceptual change. In contrast, adopting a belief that knowledge in an area is more complex and contextualized should be a resource for conceptual change. If students believe that knowledge in a domain is complex, then they should be less likely to foreclose their thinking early in the learning process and instead be open to continual thinking about the domain, which should increase the probability of conceptual change. This issue of early foreclosure versus continued thinking parallels Kruglanski's (1989) views on epistemic cognition (see Pintrich et al., 1993).

The fourth and fifth dimensions in Schommer's model also concern the constructivist nature of knowledge and epistemology. Certain knowledge refers to the belief that individuals can be very sure of the correctness of their answers or very confident in the certainty of their knowledge base. Again, endorsement of this belief seems to lead to less engagement and lower performance in Schommer's research and others (Qian & Alvermann, 1995; Schommer, 1990, 1993; Schommer et al., 1992). Source of knowledge, although it has not been identified as a separate dimension in all of Schommer's research, is an important aspect of epistemological beliefs (Hofer & Pintrich, 1997). Basically, the source of knowledge dimension refers to the perceived locus of knowledge and knowledge generation. The dimension can be characterized from the endpoint of knowledge being seen as given by authorities, such as the teacher, textbook, or experts in the field, or the other endpoint of knowledge as something that individuals can generate and construct on their own (Hofer & Pintrich, 1997). Students that adopt the view that knowledge is given by authorities, particularly teachers, may just accept the "answers" from their teachers without much reflection, but this knowledge may just become inert knowledge because of the lack of cognitive construction and reflection. Accordingly, these students may endorse the correct scientific answer regarding natural phenomena on a test or in class, but they do not integrate this knowledge with their experiential knowledge of the phenomena, thereby maintaining their misconceptions. On the other hand, students that adopt a more constructivist view that knowledge can be generated and constructed through their own efforts may be more likely to interrogate their own knowledge and beliefs, and eventually construct a more scientifically acceptable answer.

Taken together, the results from this programme of research suggest that an adoption of a more constructivist view of knowledge should be linked to deeper levels of cognition and conceptual change. Of course, more research is needed like that of Qian and Alvermann's (1995) that actually examines the relations between epistemological beliefs and the process of conceptual change, but the results so far do support the general argument being proposed here. In addition, the more general developmental research on epistemological beliefs (see Hofer & Pintrich, 1997; King & Kitchener, 1994) suggests that the adoption of a constructivist perspective is relatively late developing, not occurring until adolescence or adulthood. This implies that it may be difficult to foster the development of constructivist epistemologies in young children. However, there is research emerging from various constructivist research programmes (see Steffe & Gale, 1995) that suggests that dramatically changing the nature of classroom instruction to bring it more in line with constructivist views of learning can foster a classroom environment where children will not believe that learning is quick, simple or certain (Ball, 1993). In these types of classrooms, the children may develop more constructivist views of learning and then be more inclined to engage in deeper cognitive processing and eventually conceptual change.

Proposition 3: Embracing Higher Levels of Personal Importance, Value and Interest Should Facilitate Conceptual Change

In a previous section, goal orientation beliefs were related to the quality of students' cognitive engagement, but there are other motivational constructs that also are related to students' reasons for engaging in tasks. These constructs are not the same as goals and goal orientations, albeit they also are related to the quality of students' engagement in tasks. These constructs include students' interest and value beliefs, which are somewhat more affective or attitudinal in nature and may be more stable and personal in comparison to the more cognitive and situational representations of goals.

It is important to note that interest and value beliefs are assumed to be personal characteristics of the students that they bring to different tasks, not features of the task itself. In contrast, concepts such as situational interest refer to environmental features (e.g. text features that make a text interesting) that induce interest in almost all students who experience the task (Hidi, 1990). We will focus on the individual difference and personal variables that are activated in the situation. Eccles (1983) has proposed that there are three general interest or value beliefs. Interest simply refers to the student's general attitude or preference for the content or task (e.g. some students just like and are interested in science). Utility value concerns students' instrumental judgements about the potential usefulness of the content or task for helping them achieve some goal (e.g. getting into college, getting a job). Finally, the importance of the task refers to the student's perception of the salience or significance of the content or task to the individual. In particular, the importance of a task seems to be related to the individual's self-worth or self-schema. If a student sees herself as becoming a scientist, that is, a scientist is one of his or her possible selves (Markus & Nurius, 1986; Markus & Wurf, 1987), then science content and tasks may be perceived as being more important to her, regardless of her mastery or performance orientation to learning.

Hidi (1990) has discussed issues related to the role of interest and its influence on learning. She summarizes the research on interest by concluding that both personal interest and situational interest have a "profound effect on cognitive functioning and the facilitation of learning" (Hidi, 1990, p. 565). In particular, she suggests that personal interest influences students' selective attention, effort and willingness to persist at the task, and their activation and acquisition of knowledge. In addition, Hidi (1990) notes that interest may not necessarily result in more time spent processing information, rather, depending on the nature of the task (complex versus simple), students may take more or less time to perform the task. The difference lies in the quality of the processing, not the quantity of processing or time spent on the task (Hidi et al., 1992). Similarly, using both experimental and correlational designs, Schiefele (1991, 1992) has shown that interest is related to a variety of cognitive measures. For example, college students' ratings of their interest in their course material were positively related to measures of the quality of their cognitive engagement, including their self-reported use of elaboration strategies, the seeking of information and their engagement in critical thinking. Also, interest was negatively related to the use of rehearsal strategies (a surface processing strategy). In an experimental study where interest was manipulated, and reading and strategy behaviour were observed, interest was correlated with underlining and note-taking, and strongly related to the use of elaborative strategies. Pintrich and his colleagues (Pintrich, 1989; Pintrich & Garcia, 1991) also have shown that college students who report that their course material is more interesting, important and useful to them are more likely to use deeper processing strategies such as elaboration and metacognitive control strategies. Other studies with elementary and high school students have also shown that interest and value beliefs are positively related to cognition. For example, Renninger and Wozniak (1985) demonstrated the positive effects of interest on the processes of attention, recognition and recall for very young children. More recently, Renninger (1992) has shown that fifth and sixth graders' reading and math performance were influenced by individual interest. Tasks that included high interest or value contexts (e.g. interesting reading passages or math word problems) resulted in more competent performance. It is important to note that this study showed that the high value context did not necessarily result in students' use of the prerequisite cognitive skills, but it did result in longer persistence at a task. In another study that assessed students' beliefs about value, Pokay and Blumenfeld (1990) found that high school students' beliefs about the value of geometry did not directly predict performance on tests, but value was predictive of use of general cognitive strategies, specific geometry strategies, metacognitive strategies and effort management strategies. These findings for task value support the view that perceptions of the value of a task do not have a direct influence on academic performance, but they do relate to students "choice" of becoming cognitively engaged in a task or course and their willingness to persist at the task. Taken together, these studies suggest that personal interest and value beliefs are aspects of a "self-generated" context or resource that interacts with the task features to support learning by increasing attention, persistence and the activation of appropriate knowledge and strategies (cf. Renninger, 1992). To the extent that conceptual change requires students to maintain their cognitive engagement in trying to understand alternative views in order to accommodate to new, conflicting information, these value beliefs provide a resource that may facilitate the process, whereas lack of interest and value may constrain conceptual change.

Most of these studies have focused on the students' personal beliefs and interest that they bring with them to the task. Situational interest is more influenced by classroom, task and text features, and is, therefore, more amenable to teacher control. At the classroom and task level there are a number of features that could increase students' situational interest such as challenge, choice, novelty, fantasy and surprise (Malone & Lepper, 1987). In the text-processing literature, many of these same features have been shown to influence situational interest and students' cognitive engagement (Garner et al., 1992; Hidi, 1990; Hidi & Anderson, 1992; Wade, 1992). To the extent that classrooms, tasks or text materials have these features, we would expect students to be more or less interested in the content of the lesson with concomitant levels of cognitive activity. For example, Roth and Roychoudhury (1994) found that physics students' interest in their text material and physics classroom was related to their motivation to learn, their use of learning strategies, and their epistemological beliefs about science.

Again, the features of the classroom context seem to be important moderators of the relationship between student motivation and cognition. Classrooms that stress conceptual change and disequilibrium-inducing material, but do not have some of these other moti-vating features, may undermine the conceptual change process because students will not be interested enough to attend to the new information. In addition, most of the work on challenge and intrinsic motivation (see Malone & Lepper, 1987) stresses the importance of optimal levels of challenge, keeping novelty, difficulty and surprise within the capabilities of the student. Instruction that is designed to foster conceptual change but that goes beyond the students' range of knowledge and capability (or alternatively, zone of proximal development) will probably short circuit the change process. In such a situation, assimilation processes are more likely to operate than will accommodation processes, thus limiting the possibility that conceptual change will take place.

Proposition 4: Adoption of Higher Levels of Self-Efficacy for Learning Should Facilitate Conceptual Change

Goals, interest and value beliefs concern students' reasons for why they might engage in different tasks. However, another important aspect of motivation is students' beliefs about their capability to accomplish the task. Self-efficacy beliefs have been defined as individuals' beliefs about their performance capabilities in a particular domain (Bandura, 1986). In an educational context, self-efficacy beliefs refer to students' judgements about their cognitive capabilities to accomplish a specific academic task or obtain specific goals (Schunk, 1985). Self-efficacy beliefs are assumed to be relatively situation-specific, not global personality traits or general self-concepts. In a conceptual change model of learning, self-efficacy beliefs could be construed in two ways. First, in the bulk of the research on self-efficacy, the construct is used to represent students' confidence in their ability to do a particular task. In applying this construct to conceptual change, this could translate into students' confidence in their own ideas, prior conceptions, and epistemological and ontological presuppositions. In this case, higher levels of self-efficacy or confidence in one's own beliefs would be a hindrance or constraint on conceptual change. That is, the more confidence students have in their own beliefs, the more resistant they would be to new ideas and conceptions. In fact, much of the conceptual change literature is based on the notion of destabilizing students' confidence in their beliefs through the introduction of conflicting data, ideas or theories.

A second way to conceive of self-efficacy relating to a conceptual change model is the confidence students have in their capabilities to change their ideas, and to learn to use the "cognitive tools" necessary to integrate and synthesize divergent ideas. Following the scientific paradigm and scientist metaphor of conceptual change, self-efficacy would be the students' confidence in using the "research methods" of thinking (hypothesis testing, gathering evidence, considering alternative arguments, etc.) to effect a change in their own conceptions. In this sense, self-efficacy would refer to students' confidence in their own learning and thinking strategies.

There has been very little research on students' self-efficacy for thinking and using sophisticated strategies for problem solving. In one of the few studies, Strike and Posner (1992) reported that high school students' learning attitudes (a single factor that was composed of three constructs, which we have keep separate in our model: self-efficacy, mastery goal orientation and deeper processing strategies) were positively correlated with conceptual change in physics. However, there have been a variety of other studies linking students' self-efficacy beliefs for an academic task to their cognitive engagement in those tasks. For example, Schunk (see reviews in 1985, 1989, 1991) has consistently shown in experimental studies that changing self-efficacy beliefs can lead to better use of cognitive strategies and higher levels of academic achievement for math, reading and writing tasks. Other correlational studies have supported this view. Paris and Oka (1986) found that elementary school students' perceptions of competence were positively related to performance on a reading comprehension task, metacognitive knowledge about reading, and actual reading achievement. Pintrich and De Groot (1990a) also found that junior high school students' use of cognitive and metacognitive strategies was positively correlated with self-efficacy judgements. Shell et al. (1989) found that college students' self-efficacy beliefs about their reading and writing skills were related to their performance on a reading comprehension task and an essay writing task. Pintrich and his colleagues (Pintrich & Garcia, 1991; Pintrich et al., 1993b) have found that college students' self-efficacy beliefs about their performance in a college course are strongly related to their use of cognitive and metacognitive strategies in the course, as well as their actual performance as measured by course grades. The use of these cognitive and metacognitive strategies should result in deeper processing of course material and should increase the probability of conceptual change. As Strike and Posner (1992) suggest in their revised "interactionist" model of conceptual change, students that have confidence in their ability to understand science, value science, and approach science learning with a focus on understanding, should show more conceptual change.

This suggests that instructional strategies must be developed that increase students'efficacy in their capability to accomplish the tasks as well as their efficacy for using the appropriate cognitive and metacognitive strategies to facilitate understanding. In this sense, it is not useful for teachers to create tasks that increase the opportunities for cognitive conflict and then leave students entirely to their own devices to resolve the conflict. Students must be assisted in their learning of how to resolve cognitive conflict through both modelling and scaffolding. In his work on how to increase students' self-efficacy as well as cognitive skill, Schunk (1989) has suggested a number of instructional strategies that may be useful. Verbalization and modelling of appropriate strategies by both the teacher or other students seems to be helpful for students' efficacy and learning. In addition, there is experimental evidence that students observing a "coping" model, who initially have difficulty with a task and then eventually master it, increase their efficacy and learning more than students who see a mastery-only model (Schunk & Hanson, 1985). In scaffolded instruction, or other classroom instructional models that rely on a great deal of in-depth interaction between teachers and students, the possibility that students will see other students having difficulty is increased. This should then have positive effects on the observers' efficacy and learning. Of course, this presupposes that the task is eventually mastered by some of the students in the instructional group. The complexity of classroom instruction and, in particular, the role of peer models as representations of successful learners, highlights the need for conceptual change instruction to introduce tasks that may induce cognitive conflict, but not at a level that is beyond the students' actual capabilities to master the task or beyond their efficacy beliefs about what they can master.

Proposition 5: Adoption of a Belief in Personal Control of Learning Should Facilitate Conceptual Change

Most social cognitive theories of motivation include some construct that refers to an individual's belief about how much control they have over their behaviour or the outcome of their performance. Self-efficacy theory distinguishes between an individual's perceptions of their capability to perform a task (self-efficacy) from their outcome expectations, which refer to their beliefs that the environment is responsive to their actions on that task. For example, a student may have a relatively strong belief in their efficacy to do chemistry problems, but a low outcome expectation for their grade on a chemistry exam because the grading curve in the class is set at a very difficult level. Intrinsic motivation theorists also have proposed that control beliefs are an essential aspect of an intrinsically motivated learner. For example, Connell (1985) has proposed that there are three general control beliefs: internal control, external control and unknown control. He has shown that students who believe that they have internal control over their own learning and performance in contrast to students high in external control or unknown control perform better in school. Skinner and her colleagues (e.g. Chapman et al., 1990; Skinner et al., 1988a, b, 1990) also have proposed that students' beliefs about perceived control have important implications for motivation and academic performance. They make a distinction between three types of perceived control beliefs: agency beliefs refer to students' perception that they can perform the appropriate behaviour for the task (this is congruent with self-efficacy from social cognitive theory, e.g. "I can use this strategy."), means-ends beliefs that parallel the outcome-expectancy belief construct from social cognitive theory and involves the belief that there is a contingent relation between performing a behaviour and the outcome (e.g. "If I use this strategy, I will learn better") and control beliefs, which is a generalized expectancy for a relation between the agent and the outcome (e.g. "I can learn, I can get good grades").

Although there is an overwhelmingly large number of studies on the relations between control beliefs and just about any behaviour of interest (e.g. Baltes & Baltes, 1986; Lefcourt, 1976), including academic achievement (e.g. Findley & Cooper, 1983; Stipek & Weisz, 1981), research on its relation to students' cognitive engagement is fairly recent. For example, Pintrich (1989) found that internal control beliefs were positively related to college students' use of deep processing and metacognitive strategies and their actual performance on class exams, lab reports, papers and final grade in the course. Fabricius and Hagen (1984) found that early elementary students' memory performance and use of memory strategies was positively related to attributions to internal ability. Kurtz and Borkowski (1984) also found that attributing memory performance to controllable factors had a positive relation to the subsequent use of memory strategies on transfer and generalization tasks. In studies with upper elementary and junior high students, there is evidence that beliefs regarding the importance of effort (an internal and controllable attribution) are related to metacognitive knowledge, actual memory strategy use and performance (Borkowski et al., 1990; Schneider et al., 1986). In contrast, some studies have not found positive relations between control beliefs and memory performance (Chapman et al., 1990; Weed et al., 1990), general engagement (Skinner et al., 1990), or general academic performance (cf. Findley & Cooper, 1983; Stipek & Weisz, 1981). Qian and Alvermann (1995) found that learned helplessness or a belief in a lack of control was negatively correlated with conceptual change, but it was not a strong predictor in contrast to epistemo-logical beliefs. It appears that these relationships may vary depending on the age of the student, the definition of the construct, the types of measures employed, and the timing of the assessments of the motivational beliefs. It is unclear at this time what psychological mechanisms might underlie these empirical irregularities. However, the theoretical mecha-nisms thought to be central to conceptual change are good candidates for exploration.

The idea that students' perceptions of how much control they have over their own learning may have implications for the process of conceptual change. Bereiter (1990) has recently argued for a more global construct for the development of learning theory, which he labelled the intentional learner. This construct includes the idea that individuals assemble into modules the knowledge, skills, goals and affect (for both task and self-related factors), which are then used in a specific context for guiding and directing learning. In a conceptual change model, self-related beliefs about control over learning could direct the level of accommodation or assimilation to new information. If a student did not see her- or himself as an intentional learner with some control over her or his learning, they might be less willing to try actively to resolve discrepancies between her or his prior knowledge and the new information. Instead, she or he might regard the discrepancies as something beyond her or his understanding, something that takes place in the classroom but not under her or his control. In contrast, an intentional learner who believes she or he does have some control over her or his learning may actively try to resolve the discrepancy in some fashion. This does not mean that it will be resolved in favour of the scientifically acceptable answer, only that the student may have the cognitive and motivational resources to be more willing to engage in thinking through some of the issues. Accordingly, control beliefs may be more related to the initiation of cognitive engagement, but not specifically influence the direction of thinking.

Instruction designed to foster conceptual change is likely to take place over larger units of time than more conventional didactic instruction, thereby providing somewhat different opportunities for control. For example, project-based learning in science is often designed so that students investigate a significant problem with a specific question that serves to organize and drive activities. The pursuit of these activities results in variety of products, such as analyses of water quality in the local watershed, that eventuate in a final product to answer the driving question of the project (Blumenfeld et al., 1991). Conceptual change instruction, such as is implied by project-based learning, involves at least two venues for opportunities for student control.

First, students can exercise some control over what to work on, how to work, and what products to create in project-based learning. These features of project-based learning should increase students' perceptions of control. Given their choice over activities and how to do them, they should come to believe that they have some control over their own learning in project-based classrooms as suggested by intrinsic motivation researchers (Deci & Ryan, 1985; Malone & Lepper, 1987). This increase in control beliefs may lead to deeper levels of cognitive engagement. However, many research and instructional questions remain regarding the optimal degree of choice and control to be shared by teachers and students so that novices are not overwhelmed by the opportunities before they attain the requisite competence to use choice and control productively.

Second, a central feature of student control is over the learning strategies they use to accomplish academic tasks. Control over learning strategies requires students to be metacognitive and self-regulating. Two aspects of metacognitive control are relevant to conceptual change instruction. One is tactical, relating to the moment-to-moment control of cognition; the other is strategic and pertains to more molar levels of control over larger units of thought. These two features of metacognitive control refer to different strategies for accomplishing academic tasks. Tactical control represents students' ability to monitor and fine tune thought as they work through the details of particular tasks. This type of cognitive control enables students to remain focused on the goals of the activity while they struggle through the hard work required in conceptual change instruction. Learners with inadequate tactical control are likely to have difficulty sustaining mental effort in the moment-to-moment work of generating products in project-based learning. Strategic control represents the student's ability to engage in purposeful thought over what might seem to be disconnected elements of learning as the students engage in a variety of different activities in project-based learning. Students need to be responsible for guiding and controlling their own activities and focusing their work over a long period of time in this type of instruction. The capability of students to organize their mental effort in the service of these more long-term purposes depends on strategic metacognitive control. In this sense, both tactical and strategic control beliefs are necessary for successful project-based learning and, at the same time, should be fostered by project-based instruction.

Conclusions and Future Directions for Research

Motivational beliefs seem to be important resources and constraints on the process of conceptual change given the argument and research discussed in this chapter. In addition, various classroom contextual factors can facilitate or constrain the development of adaptive motivational beliefs and cognition that will increase the probability of conceptual change. One of the important next steps is the development of a research agenda that actually examines the empirical relations among motivational beliefs, classroom context and conceptual change. There are a number of directions for future research, but only a few of the most pressing concerns are discussed in this concluding section.

Need for Theoretical Clarity in Conceptualizing Motivational Beliefs

There are a number of different theories of motivation and a number of different motivational belief constructs proposed by these theories. Researchers need to be very clear conceptually about which motivational beliefs they are investigating, how they are hypothesized to be related to conceptual change, and how they are measured. For example, Strike and Posner (1992) seem to place efficacy, value and a mastery goal orientation into one global variable and link that to conceptual change. Schommer in her research programme (Schommer, 1990, 1993) includes both motivational beliefs, such as fixed ability, which is related to a mastery goal orientation, as well as other more epistemological beliefs about knowledge, into her general framework. To her credit, however, she does keep these dimensions separate in her analyses. In any event, researchers need to be clear that all motivational variables are not the "same thing"; interest and utility value are different from one another and are even less similar to self-efficacy beliefs. There are large differences conceptually in these different beliefs and there should be empirical differences in the links to conceptual change between goal orientation, self-efficacy, interest and value beliefs. More attention, both theoretically and methodologically, to these distinctions are important for progress in research.

Need for Research to Clarify Directional Relations in Propositions

In the propositions developed earlier, it was proposed that higher levels of self-efficacy, interest and value will be a resource for conceptual change. However, there may be occasions when higher levels of these beliefs might act to constrain conceptual change. For example, future research will need to examine both students' confidence in their pre-existing beliefs, and misconceptions and their perceptions of efficacy to learn science, as they might interact in the process of conceptual change. In addition, there needs to be research on students' perceptions of efficacy for using the various cognitive, metacognitive and self-regulatory strategies often used by scientists and how these beliefs interact with other self-efficacy beliefs. It may be that students do not have confidence in their actual beliefs, but at the same time they do not feel efficacious in using the tools of thinking and hence will be less likely to become cognitive engaged in the task. On the other hand, they may feel very strongly about their pre-existing beliefs and do not feel any need to change them, even if they do have confidence in their ability to use the tools of science and think scientifically.

In the same fashion, high levels of personal interest should facilitate conceptual change given that interest usually fosters more cognitive engagement in terms of attention, time, effort and the use of deeper processing strategies. However, high levels of personal interest are often correlated with high levels of prior knowledge about a topic (Tobias, 1994). That is, individuals that have high levels of personal interest in a topic often spend more time learning about that topic, for example, reading material on it outside of school or watching television shows about the topic. In fact, some researchers have proposed that personal interest is only defined by high levels of knowledge and high personal value (Renninger, 1992). However, it may be that students' high level of knowledge about the topic could still involve misconceptions, and given the strength and depth of their knowledge, these misconceptions would be harder to change. In the case of high personal interest and high knowledge, albeit misconceptions, personal interest would be correlated with less conceptual change. This is similar to the argument made for self-efficacy as a constraint on conceptual change, if self-efficacy is defined as confidence in one's knowledge and beliefs. Accordingly, there is evidence that suggests that high levels of efficacy and interest would be positively related to conceptual change, but there is a need for research that examines the countering propositions regarding their potential constraints on conceptual change.

Need for More Empirical Research on the Mechanisms by Which Motivational Beliefs Influence Conceptual Change

This chapter has suggested that motivational beliefs are related to cognitive processes that can influence conceptual change. However, the research has only been descriptive and has proposed *how* motivational beliefs may be related, not *why* they are related theoretically.

For example, the research marshalled in this chapter in favour of the view that motivational beliefs can influence conceptual change has been mainly concerned with how motivation is linked to deeper processing of information. Certainly, deeper processing of information seems to be a reasonable mechanism to facilitate conceptual change (Chinn & Brewer, 1993). However, there are other possibilities, including the simple mechanism of more time spent on the material because of positive motivational beliefs, regardless of the nature of cognition. This possibility has to be examined in studies that attempt to separate out the mechanism of simple quantity of time spent on learning the material in contrast to the quality of cognition.

In addition, other potential cognitive mechanisms need to be examined. Chinn and Brewer (1993) have suggested that different types of prior knowledge, including discipli-nary knowledge, ontological beliefs and epistemological commitment, have different roles to play in conceptual change. Accordingly, there is a need for studies that examine how motivational beliefs may lead to the differential activation of prior knowledge or ontolog-ical beliefs. For example, does adopting a mastery goal orientation lead to different types of prior disciplinary knowledge or ontological beliefs being activated in the situation, or are these knowledge and beliefs tied more directly to the task and content and not to motiva-tional beliefs? Does a mastery goal orientation foster more accommodation processes in knowledge acquisition than assimilation processes? The research to date has not really examined how motivational beliefs are linked to the knowledge base because it has focused more on strategy use.

Besides the knowledge base, other mechanisms that still need to be examined in more detail include self-reflection and epistemological commitments. Although there is work on the links between motivation, self-regulated learning and metacognition, there is not as much on general self-reflection with regard to knowledge, and more generally on thinking and problem solving. For example, do certain motivational beliefs lead to more questioning and reflection on the appropriateness of the knowledge base? Do motivational beliefs lead to the questioning of epistemological commitments? Do certain types of motivational beliefs lead to different definitions of the problem space or the use of different problem solving heuristics? These possibilities have not been examined in the current research on motivation and cognition and there is a clear need for more research in these areas.

Need for Methodological Rigour in Assessing Motivational Beliefs

At the same time, there also needs to be more methodological rigour in the measurement and assessment of the motivational beliefs in all this research. Much of the research discussed in this chapter has used self-report questionnaires to assess students' motivational beliefs. This is not as problematic as the use of self-report measures in the assessment of cognition (see Pintrich et al., forthcoming) given that motivational beliefs are assumed to be constructions of the individual student. This phenomenological perspective proposes that it is more important to assess what the individual thinks and believes subjectively, rather than just the "objective" reality. Accordingly, self-report measures that tap into students' percep-tions of themselves and the classroom context can be used to assess motivational beliefs (Pintrich & Schunk, 1996). Nevertheless, this does not mean that researchers can develop self-report items quickly or easily and rely on face validity of their self-report items to justify their use. It takes a concerted development effort with much pilot testing and revision to develop reliable and valid self-report instruments. Researchers can't just sit down and write out a few items and give them to students and assume on the basis of face validity that they are appropriate measures. Accordingly, there is a need for much more construct validity research on these self-report measures that follow the usual psychometric procedures for determining construct validity.

In addition, other measures of motivational beliefs such as interviews, think-alouds and observations can be used to provide other data on not only students' motivational beliefs but also their knowledge, strategy use and thinking. There is a technology in place that uses concept mapping to assess students' conceptions and misconceptions in the conceptual change literature. This research can provide detailed maps of students' thinking about a topic. Similar kinds of methods need to be developed to generate detailed maps of students' self-schemas and motivational beliefs. This type of data can provide more in-depth and richer pictures of students' motivational beliefs that are not provided by self-report questionnaires. Although there are no simple procedures for linking these more detailed and qualitative data on individuals' motivational beliefs to their disciplinary conceptions and knowledge base, attempts to do so could provide some interesting insights into how an individual's theory of self and motivation is related to their theory of the content area, better illustrating the interpenetration of self-beliefs with disciplinary knowledge.

Need for More Studies That Include Classroom Contextual Factors

Moreover, as suggested in all the sections above, there is a need for classroom research on how different patterns of classroom and instructional constructs influence both motivation and cognition. For example, it may be that increasing students' control beliefs through various instructional changes, such as allowing for choice in topics or tasks, leads them to spend more time on topics where they have more prior knowledge and interest, which could lead to more confidence in their own pre-existing beliefs and a discounting of new, more scientifically correct, information. Accordingly, research needs to look for both the potentially positive motivational effects of changing classrooms to give students more control, but also the possibility that there could potentially be some subtle negative effects. It may be that it is important to have instruction that encourages students' control over their learning and the various cognitive and self-regulatory strategies, but not relinquish control over the content of the instruction, at least in conceptual change instructional models. Clearly, there is a need for more research on these various possibilities.

Need for More Long-Term Studies

In most of the conceptual change research it is pointed out that conceptual change learning can be difficult and take a fair amount of time (Pintrich et al., 1993a). However, most of the studies that have been discussed in this chapter that have linked motivation to cognition have been short-term studies with only one or two data collection points. These designs limit our ability to detect and observe conceptual change. Accordingly, there is a need for research designs that examine students' motivation and cognition over longer periods of time, as well as use multiple waves of data collection and continual assessment. These studies could involve more traditional longitudinal designs where data collection is carried out over fairly long periods of time such as months or years. However, these studies may miss crucial time periods when actual change is taking place, thereby obscuring the mechanisms of conceptual change and the dynamic interplay of motivation and cognition. Microgenetic designs where multiple assessments are taken from the same individuals over shorter time periods, when students are actually engaged in learning the material, may provide a better window through which to view conceptual change.

Taken together, these suggestions for future research should help us understand more clearly how motivational beliefs can act as resources to facilitate, or act as constraints on, the process of conceptual change. There is a clear need to develop models of conceptual change that are not just based on assumptions of "cold" rational cognition, but include "hot" components of motivational beliefs and also involve the situated nature of learning in classroom contexts. The ideas presented in this chapter should provide some suggestions for both theoretical development and empirical research, which will result in the generation and testing of these admittedly more complex, but simultaneously more realistic, models of conceptual change.

PART 2

Situational Aspects

4

Conceptual Change and Contextualization

Ola Halldén

Introduction

A common way of understanding the difficulties students encounter in trying to understand a scientific concept is to regard the problem as being one of *conceptual change* (e.g. Posner et al., 1982; Strike & Posner, 1992; for a review of the field see Duit this volume). According to this view, understanding the scientific way of describing the world is associated with relinquishing old, naive, inconsistent and vague conceptions about the surrounding world and adopting instead precise, potent and otherwise scientifically accepted ways of conceptualizing the world. In this respect, this line of reasoning is similar to that of Piaget or of science historians who, having knowledge of the end result, attempt to describe the pathway that would lead to that result.

Quite another way of conceptualizing the problem is offered by Säljö (this volume) and within the research area of socially shared cognition (Resnick, 1987, 1991). Within this area of thought the problem is not how to bring about a conceptual change, but rather to know what characterizes the situation in which the students entertain their common-sense descriptions and explanations; consequently, the educational problem is how to create a situation where the appropriate scientific ideas will come into play. If concepts "create objects" that are discursive in nature (Säljö), then we are no longer able to say that students hold conceptions and that these conceptions can be changed; there are only situations that can be arranged in such a way that students act in accordance with certain principles, for example, the scientifically accepted rules for investigating and discussing a specific phenomenon.

However, if we retain the propositions that students act within the medium of language and that these actions are context dependent, then we need not abandon the claim that students do in fact hold conceptions, and that context is a central factor in explaining why they tend to maintain their conceptions. To show this I will use an intentionalist model of action suggested by von Wright. The questions von Wright addresses when talking about intentionality relate to classic philosophical problems concerning the meaningfulness of behaviour, the explanation of action, and problems regarding reasons and causes. However, the model is also interesting in a pedagogical context because it relates cognitive factors to behaviour and the individual to his or her culture. In that sense the intentional perspective can be regarded as a pedagogical perspective.

An Intentional Perspective

In his analysis of action, von Wright (1971, 1979) distinguishes among different aspects and different antecedents of action. To begin with, one aspect of action is its intentionality. In order to understand a sequence of behaviour as an action, and not merely as a reflex or a series of muscular movements, we have to ascribe meaning to the behaviour. We do this, according to von Wright, by looking upon the behaviour as having been performed intentionally. The intention gives meaning to the behaviour. The intention is what the agent means by doing something, or what an outside observer understands that action to mean.

The intentionalist model of action conforms, according to von Wright, to a practical syllogism. The syllogism can be formulated in different ways; the following can serve as an illustration:

> A person *P* intends to do *x* (where *x* is a verb or a verb-phrase).
>
> *P* believes that he cannot do *x* unless he does *y* (where *y* is a verb or a verb-phrase).
>
> Thus, *P* does *y*.

Thus, to construe an intentional explanation is to look upon behavioural sequences as forming intentional actions or to look upon a single action as being one in a sequence of actions forming a larger whole, and this larger whole is an action in itself.

> Behaviour gets its intentional character from being *seen* by the agent himself or by an outside observer in a wider perspective, from being *set* in a context of aims and cognitions. This is what happens when we construe a practical inference to match it, as premises match a given conclusion. (von Wright, 1971, p. 115)

Von Wright's notion of intentionality is similar in some respects to Searle's concept of *intention in action* as opposed to *prior intention* (Searle, 1983). Intention (in action) in this sense is part of the action itself (or "the action utterance", to use Searle's term), whereas prior intentions stand in a causal relationship to actions. As for the notion of causal antecedents, von Wright differentiates between internal determinants, such as wants, beliefs and abilities, and external determinants that constitute duties and opportunities for acting. These determinants of action are illustrated in Figure 1.

Using this model of action and its determinants, I propose an alternative way to conceptualize students' difficulties in acquiring new conceptions, and that is to regard the problem as one of contextualization. As indicated by Figure 1, there are different kinds of contexts. Broadly speaking, there is the *cognitive context*, which comprises cognitive abilities and cognitive structure and, leaving aside theories of moral and value, the cognitive aspects of wants. Then there is the actual setting for an action that forms the *cultural context*, which refers to aspects of the interaction between the individual and the situation, and to norms and patterns of behaviour in the society. It goes without saying that these different kinds of contexts are in play simultaneously or, to put it another way, they constitute separate aspects of the context as a whole.

Here, I will talk about contextualization in three respects: first, the contextualization of explanations, i.e. as pertaining to the relevance of different forms of explanation in different situations; second, the contextualization of a concept within a more embracing conceptual framework; and third, the contextualization of descriptions or explanations within a given speech genre. I will talk about this by drawing on three empirical examples, each of which highlights the different kinds of contextualizations. This does not mean that each example contains only one kind of contextualization. As already pointed out, the different kinds of contextualizations should be regarded as being in play simultaneously, but, in the examples presented here, they have different explanatory value.

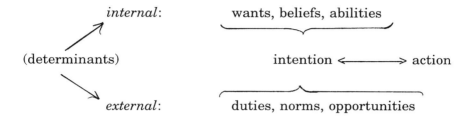

Figure 1: Determinants of action based on von Wright (1971, 1979)

When talking about conceptual change, Strike and Posner (1982) postulated four conditions for conceptual change to occur, i.e. "dissatisfaction with existing conceptions"; "intelligibility of the new conception"; "plausibility of the new conception"; and "fruitfulness of the new conception". Since then, most of the discussion has concerned the condition of dissatisfaction with existing conceptions and, related to this, the establishment of a cognitive conflict in order to bring about a conceptual *change*, whereas the role of "intelligibility" and "plausibility" has not been accorded similar interest. With reference to the three kinds of contextualizations outlined above, we can say that not enough attention has been paid to the contextualization of new concepts in the act of explaining something, i.e. the applied or semantic side of the matter; the contextualization of new concepts within the framework of more embracing ideas, i.e. the psychological or cognitive side of the matter; and the contextualization of new concepts in the narrative forms used in different communicative settings, i.e. the cultural side of the matter. Thus, the composite character of the concept of conceptual change has not been seriously taken into account.

Forms of Conceptual Change

The concentration on conceptual change can perhaps be explained by a failure to distinguish between the various ways an individual can incorporate new conceptions. In a learning setting, conceptual change can signify at least three different processes. First, in some contexts the process is in fact one of abandoning an old conception and replacing it with a new one, as in cognitive development. A case in point is the child who, up to the age of 5–6 years, believes that the sun and the moon follow him, but who, at about the age of 11, knows that they only *appear* to do so (Piaget, 1973). Second, in other contexts, the process is one of acquiring an entirely new conception, in which case there is in fact no conceptual change at all, but rather the emergence of a quite new conception. This was exemplified in a study by Silvia Caravita on how pupils in elementary school organize the concept of organism. A reasonable conclusion from the study was that both the concept of organism and a conceptual framework for this concept were created during the course of the instruction (Caravita & Halldén, 1994, with references). Third, in still other contexts, conceptual change may entail acquiring a new way of conceptualizing the world, not in order to replace the conceptions one already entertains, but rather to enrich one's repertoire of conceptualizations of a particular phenomenon (e.g. Caravita & Halldén, 1994; Wistedt, 1994).

These different processes in the acquisition of new conceptions actualize different kinds of questions. First of all, there is the *normative* question of what kinds of acquisitions we want our students to make. It is not always the case that we want our students to abandon their old conceptions and replace them with new ones, or, to quote Joan Solomon, "It would indeed be a poor return for our science lessons if they /the pupils/ could no longer comprehend remarks like 'wool is warm' or 'we are using up all our energy'" (Solomon, 1983, p. 50). Then, there is the *logical* question of what kinds of acquisitions *can* in fact take place: Is there already an alternative conception that can be altered or are we trying to get the students to construct an entirely new framework? And then there is the *empirical* question of what is actually taking place: How do students cope with conceptions introduced in the instruction and what is the end result of the instruction?

My remarks here on contextualization relate primarily to this last question. By drawing on some examples I will try to point at some of the difficulties students encounter in coping with scientific conceptions and explanations, and show that these difficulties need not be regarded as arising from the failure to bring about a conceptual change, but rather can be regarded as difficulties students encounter in finding adequate contexts in which to put the questions that confront them. In the concluding discussion I will then relate this question of contextualization to the problem of learning something entirely new.

The Applicability of Scientific Theories and Models to Everyday Problems

If we ask students direct questions pertaining to theoretical principles, we risk getting responses that mirror verbatim learning only. If, on the other hand, we ask real-world questions, we are in fact testing much more than the students' knowledge of theoretical principles. We are also testing their ability to contextualize problems in the realm of the appropriate scientific field as well as their ability to identify a problem as a case in which a specific scientific principle is to be applied. Kahneman and Tversky (1982), in studying how judgements are made under conditions of uncertainty, speak about *errors of comprehension* and *errors of application*. This dichotomy makes it difficult to know at first glance the reason for a student's failure in problem solving. It may be that the student has not acquired the particular concept or scientific rule necessary to solve the problem or, that having acquired the concept or rule, has failed to apply it correctly.

In their investigation of statistical intuition, Kahneman and Tversky (1982) presented subjects in one of their studies with the following personality sketch:

> Linda is 31 years old, single, outspoken, and very bright. She majored in
> philosophy. As a student, she was deeply concerned with issues of

discrimination and social justice, and also participated in anti-nuclear demonstrations (Kahneman & Tversky 1982, p. 496).

Respondents were then asked which of the following two statements about Linda was the more probable one: (i) Linda is a bank teller; or (ii) Linda is a bank teller who is active in the feminist movement. In terms of probability theory, of course, statement (i) is the correct answer; the conjunction rule states that the probability of a conjunction A and B cannot exceed the probability of either A or B alone. This means that the more predicates we attribute to an entity, the greater is the risk of fallacy. However, Kahneman and Tversky found that 86% of the undergraduate students and 50% of the graduate students in psychology chose statement (ii), i.e. that Linda is a bank teller who is active in the feminist movement, as being the more probable one.

Even after extensive discussion, the "statistically naive" students, i.e. those who had not had former training in statistics, stuck to their initial choice. Kahneman and Tversky concluded that these students did not have a solid grasp of the conjunction rule, resorting to a heuristic of representativeness instead; that is to say, the students based their judgements on the extent to which the characteristics of an element, in this case Linda, matched archetypical characteristics of a particular class, in this case the class of anti-nuclear demonstrators who majored in philosophy.

But do we in fact know anything about how the students who chose statement (ii) understood the conjunction rule? I have amused myself by presenting a group of about 50 of my students, most of them women, with the same personality sketch as that used by Kahneman and Tversky, with the addition that I also asked them to give their reasons for their choice. Then, after giving the students the correct answer according to probability theory, I asked them to comment once again on their initial answer, after which we had an open discussion. The results of the exercise were very similar to those of Kahneman and Tversky with regard to the quantitative distribution of responses between the two alternatives. The interesting result, however, was to be found in the students' comments regarding their choices.

One student gave an apt description of the dilemma in choosing an alternative:

> First I thought (i), according to the rules for determining the probability of a true statement, but then I thought that I was supposed to draw *conclusions* from the text describing Linda and thus I chose (ii). Now, however, I realize I was wrong!

This student is talking about two different methods for solving the problem: one is to apply probability theory and the other is to "draw conclusions". What is meant here by "drawing conclusions" is not entirely clear, however. A possible interpretation is that it refers to a kind of causal reasoning or to the construction of a good reason assay: if certain characteristics can be attributed to a person, or if it can be assumed that he or she embraces certain beliefs and attitudes, then that person can be expected to behave in a particular way. This kind of reasoning is illustrated in the comment made by another student:

> Since Linda had been involved so much in issues of discrimination and social equality while at school, I thought she'd be inclined to carry on the "struggle" later on in her working life.

Still another student chose statement (ii) on the basis of "social grounds": Linda "... shows commitment to a variety of social issues and, besides, she has a lot of time because she's single".

One of the students who chose statement (i) seems to have done so on the basis of a deliberate choice of method with respect to the nature of task confronting the student:

> I chose (i) because that way I'm neither assuming too much nor too little. A safer judgement. The risk of being prejudiced or making generalizations determined my choice of (i). ... Maybe it wouldn't have been wrong to say that she belonged to the feminist movement, but it might not have been right either, so I left it out.

Here, the student seems to have made a deliberate effort to avoid using causal reasoning or a good reason assay analysis in solving the problem. The reluctance to make what could be a prejudiced judgement in the face of insufficient information led this student to use probability theory instead.

In the first comment presented above, the student concluded by saying that she realized she was wrong. This conclusion can be compared with the initial comment made by another student:

> An academic grade in philosophy does not land you a job in a bank, the feminist movement speaks for (ii).

After being presented with the statistical solution, this student continued:

> From now on I'll have to take everything's probability into account, but in this case I don't intend to change my mind.

This cursory dispatching of the method of statistical analysis was also exemplified in the open discussions carried out at the conclusion of the exercise. Some of the students said that they were quite clear about the principles of probability theory, but that they nevertheless were of the opinion that alternative (ii), i.e. that Linda was both a bank teller and active in the feminist movement, was the more probable one.

I will argue that these students can make a good case for their standpoint. If my analysis here is correct, the students were in fact choosing between two quite different methods for solving the problem: one method entails applying causal reasoning or making a good reason assay analysis, the other method entails applying the principles of probability theory. Furthermore, we cannot in fact know with any degree of certainty that the students who chose statement (ii) failed to grasp the conjunction rule and thus had committed an error of comprehension, nor can we know that they had committed an error of application. In order to know if either case applied, we would have to be able to argue that the information given in the task clearly indicates the superiority of the one method over the other, which means that we will have weighed that information in the face of what we know about human behaviour. This information would also have to be weighed in relation to the goal for the activity, in this case to arrive at a decision about Linda. That is, what is the reason for deciding whether Linda is a bank teller and/or active in the feminist movement? If Paul Cobb is right in saying that the overall goal of everyday reasoning is "to act so that the individual can achieve his or her particular goals in a specific situation" (Cobb, 1986, p. 3), it may well be the case that the students who rejected the use of probability theory as a means for solving the problem in the exercise were quite right to do so.

It may be that how we function in everyday life is facilitated by the guesses we make about causal relationships and stereotypes. Thus, a good reason assay analysis may be a more functional approach in handling our relations with other people than the statistical analysis of human actions and characteristics. It is only when situated in the context of academic reasoning about judgement under uncertainty that this kind of reasoning is disregarded; in fact, the students simply "failed to play the academic reasoning game", as Cobb phrased it (1986, p. 3).

To conclude so far, the outcome of this exercise supports the view that students tend to perceive problem-solving tasks in the context of everyday life and consequently apply the kinds of problem-solving strategies that they use in everyday life (cf. also Wistedt, 1994). In our example here, this means that many of the students chose not to use the methods of probability theory to solve the problem, preferring instead a kind of causal reasoning or good reason assay analysis, not because they did not understand or were unable to apply probability theory, but because they did not find it meaningful to do so in this particular case.

Against this conclusion it could be argued that the students who did not make this explicit choice in their written commentaries, and they were the vast majority, perhaps failed to do so because they lacked knowledge of the principles of probability theory and the conjunction rule. A counter-argument to this objection is, in the first place, that there is a methodological problem in all this. That a student did not explicitly discuss a problem in a written commentary does not imply that the student was unaware of the problem. There are a number of other reasons that could account for the student not having done so: perhaps the problem was regarded as irrelevant in this particular context, or it was too time-consuming to write everything down, or too laborious, or the student had an attitude of "I don't really care", etc. It is only when a person responds to our efforts that we can classify his or her responses; it is quite another thing to deal with omitted responses. The interesting thing here, however, is that some of the students actually did comment on their choice of method for solving the problem and thus provided examples of other kinds of explanations besides the one of having failed to make a conceptual change. But of course, from this alone, we cannot say anything about the frequency of these cases; we do not know if other students had made the same sort of choice, but for some reason or other did not comment on it, or if the students who had commented on their choice of method were the only ones to have made such a choice.

In the second place, this says nothing about the students who perhaps did not have any knowledge of the scientific conception of probability. In such case, the choice of method we have been describing so far was certainly not available to them and, thus, it does not seem that the question of contextualization applies to them at all; what does apply to them is the question of concept acquisition. However, I will argue that contextualization is an important issue even in concept acquisition and will return to this in the concluding discussion.

Contextualization Within More Embracing Ideas

To contextualize a problem can mean to relate it to a specific physical situation, but it can also mean to relate the problem to other ideas. In the former case we are talking about situational contexts, and in the latter about cognitive contexts. "Concepts are embedded within larger theoretical structures that constrain them", as Vosniadou has phrased it (1994, p. 63); and Tiberghien (1994) has argued that "in physics, interpretation and prediction imply a modelling process which consists of three levels: theory, model and experimental field of reference" (p. 74), and that there is continual interaction between these levels. Theory is concerned with questions about explanation, paradigms, laws, etc.; the level of model is concerned with relations between physical quantities and qualitative aspects associated with observable phenomena; and the experimental field of reference is concerned with measurement, facts and experimental devices.

Tiberghien restricts her discussion to the field of physics. However, this kind of reasoning is applicable to most academic subjects, even though it may not always be possible to make such clear distinctions between these different levels as it is possible to do in physics. In relation to learning in history I have differentiated between alternative frameworks at different levels, the empirical, the conceptual and the theoretical (Halldén, 1993), and I have used the same distinctions in studies on learning biology (Halldén, 1990) and further, together with Caravita, in a discussion of conceptual change (Caravita & Halldén, 1994).

Examples of difficulties with this kind of contextualization can be found when students are presented with a problem whose solution is counterintuitive. A colleague of mine, Lars-Johan Norrby, at that time associated with Stockholm University, presented the following problem to freshmen in chemistry as a diagnostic test (Norrby, 1982): a pad of commercial steel wool was suspended in an old-fashioned two-armed balance and then tarred. The students were asked what they thought would happen if a lighted match were held under the pad of steel wool. What does happen is that a coating of Fe_3O_4 is formed, making the sample heavier. Before carrying out the experiment, about half of the students believed that the steel wool would become lighter and the other half that it would become heavier. After the heat was applied, all the students were able to see that the steel wool had indeed become heavier, the problem now was to explain why. Some of the students gave fully acceptable explanations, others gave no explanation at all to what they had seen, or they made no mention of weight in their explanations; still others, according to Lars-Johan Norrby (personal communication), quite simply denied that the steel wool had become heavier.

This appears to be a case in which the embracing conceptual structure in which the problem is contextualized is one of common sense. The students know that in everyday life we consume energy, judging at least from the information on our electricity bills; we also burn things, whether it be wood burned in the fireplace or rubbish thrown into the incinerator.

But it is not only that we sometimes contextualize problems in terms of a common sense framework even though they were intended to be put into a scientific framework, it is also that we cannot always be sure of which scientific framework a problem actually belongs (cf. Linder, 1993). In an ongoing study on conceptions of evolution in biology at the university level, we asked students a question previously used by Margaret Brumby (1984). The question was intended to actualize evolutionary reasoning.

> Scientists have warned doctors of the danger of their increasing use of antibiotics (e.g. penicillin) for treating minor infections. What is the main reason for their concern?

Comparable groups of students answered the question before and after a 5-week introductory course in biology (Halldén et al., 1994). The results were somewhat puzzling in some respects. There was an increase in answers mentioning the adaptation of bacteria to antibiotics after the course compared with before the course. But, although there were good Darwinistic descriptions in the answers the students gave to another question that referred more directly to natural selection, there was a predominance of answers mentioning only "adaptation" in the explanations the students gave to the antibiotics question. About half of the students who appeared to have a profound grasp of the concept of evolution, judging from their answers to the direct question on natural selection, gave strictly adaptational answers to the antibiotics question.

One interpretation of this result is, of course, that the students had probably learned the formula of natural selection verbatim but that they were unable to apply it in a practical case, and this would thus be an example of an error of application. However, there was some evidence against such an interpretation. Most of the students in this group also referred in their answers to recent findings in biology pertaining to heredity in bacteria, such as the existence of mobile segments of the DNA, i.e. transposons, and the possibility of genes moving from one chromosome to another and even from one species to another. With that knowledge in mind it is no longer obvious that the neo-Darwinian principles of evolution can be used to explain adaptation with regard to bacteria; that is, the theoretical context for the problem is no longer self-evident. In passing, it can be mentioned that when the results from this study were presented before an audience in which several of those present had an extensive academic background in biology, an animated debate broke out concerning the evolution of bacteria and the relevance of Darwinian reasoning in relation to this. For the debaters, the theoretical framework in which the problem ought to be contextualized did not seem to be self-evident.

After completing the introductory course in biology, several of the students in our study went on to specialize in molecular biology, geosciences or chemistry. Preliminary results from additional testing indicated that the ability of these students to use evolutionary reasoning when presented with a question pertaining to natural selection tended to decline, despite additional study in related fields. That is to say, the answers they gave to questions on evolution directly after the introductory course in biology were more profound than the answers they gave further on in their academic career when their studies had become more specialized. In particular, the mention of the factor "struggle for life" in these students' explanations of natural selection occurred much less frequently. The inclusion of this factor was regarded as one of the most significant learning results of the introductory course. But further on in their studies the students seemed inclined to try their hand at applying models from the molecular level in biology, from chemistry, and so on, in solving problems of natural selection. Assuming these results hold after closer inspection we can see how students contextualize problems within other theoretical frameworks than those that were intended.

The discussion so far has concerned the contextualization of a problem in everyday contexts and within various theoretical frameworks. I have referred to these as situational contexts and cognitive contexts, respectively. But there is still another kind of context that can be mentioned here, the cultural context or speech genre.

Speech Genre as a Form of Contextualization

In our study of students' conceptions in biology, a group of students were given the following question on a written examination. The question was formulated by the examining lecturer.

> The elm tree disease can wipe out the whole elm tree species (*Ulmus glabra*). How does this happen? And what can be done to protect the *Ceratosystis* fungus which carries the disease?

This question can be regarded as having to do with natural selection and the survival of the fittest — perhaps not so closely as one might think at first glance, but that need not concern us here. Actually, the question consists of two parts: first, there is the question of why the fungus can eradicate elm trees; and second, there is the question of how to save the fungus from extinction. It is the second question that is of interest here.

It is, of course, a provocative question. Why save the *Ceratosystis* fungus if it destroys the beautiful elms? But the question the students were to answer was how to save the fungus from extinction; if the fungus wipes out the elm tree and the elm tree is its only possible host, the fungus will as a consequence destroy itself.

The analysis of the study is still in progress, so the following figures are preliminary. However, they are accurate enough for the point I want to make here. Of the 49 students taking the examination, four made no attempt to answer the question at all. Of the remaining 45 students, 34 gave some sort of answer to the question while the other 11 tried by one means or another to circumvent the question. It is these 11 students who are our concern here. Several of the 11 students simply restated the problem: it was now a question of saving the elms, not in order to save the fungus, but as a goal in itself.

> The fungus is sensitive to pollutants, and so its life conditions have deteriorated. The fungus dies and as a consequence the ability of the elm tree to take up nutrition is impaired. ... Maybe there is a fungus that is more resistant than *Ceratosystis* and could be made to coexist with the elm tree.

Here the fungus does not constitute a threat to itself. It is threatened by other factors, which in turn constitutes a threat to the elm. For this student, the only reason for saving the fungus seems to be in order to save the elms, and to reach that goal the student is prepared to replace the *Ceratosystis*, i.e. the species that was to be saved from extinction, with another fungus.

Other students did not seem to realize the nature of the problem confronting them. They concerned themselves with the problem of saving the fungus without relating this goal to the problem of the extinction of the elms. One student suggested that:

... you can make sure poisonous chemicals (to the fungus) are not spread around. You can take better care of the elm tree forests so that there are always new trees to replenish the old. If the trees grow closer together and are not spread out, the life conditions of the fungus will also be improved.

Apparently, this student's only concern was how to take care of the *Ceratosystis*. Then there were students who did not accept the project of saving the fungus as being worthwhile:

I must have missed something here altogether. What do you mean elm tree disease? Why would anyone want to protect a fungus that causes the disease?

A common characteristic of the answers given by these 11 students is that the conflict actualized by the question — how to save one species without bringing about the extinction of the other — is circumvented in one way or another. The fact that there is a conflict here is either disregarded by the students altogether or made short work of because of their main concern is the preservation of the elm.

The failure to realize the nature of the problem or simply reinterpreting the problem as one of how to save the elms can be understood as a contextualization of the problem in terms of popular ways of talking about nature today: pollution, saving the whales and the koala bear, and so forth. In this sense it can be regarded as an example of a speech genre or an orchestrated dialogue where the non-biological society has the louder voice (Bakhtin, 1986). The question, as it was formulated on the written examination, lay outside the framework of popular ways of describing problems pertaining to the extinction of endangered species and environmental pollution common to the age in which we live.

The answers given by the 34 students who addressed the question of how to save the fungus indicated that the students were aware of the conflict between the fungus and elm trees. In the case of 23 of the students, the nature of the conflict was explicitly stated. The students not only tried to answer the question, they also clearly stated what was the nature of the conflict. This can perhaps be regarded as one means of drowning out the public voice so that the voice of biology can be heard; that is, to find the appropriate disciplinary context.

Concluding Discussion

According to Goodwin and Duranti (1992), a context is a frame "that surrounds the event being examined and provides resources for its appropriate interpretation" (p. 3). Thus, embedded in a context is a focal event and this focal event acquires meaning from the context. Here, I have tried to show how different kinds of problems can be understood as focal events seen from a variety of contexts, and how this can explain the students' ways of solving the problems.

First, we looked at contextualization in everyday settings, or the *situational context*. When scientific concepts compete with common-sense thinking in explaining everyday problems, it is not self-evident that the scientific concepts will prevail. This means that the students are not always on the wrong track when they apply everyday thinking rather than the conceptions accepted in the sciences. As I have tried to show, many of the students who used everyday reasoning in answering the probability question, did so as a deliberate choice. Furthermore, in my view, in many instances the kind of reasoning that is the most fruitful is an open question. Perhaps this is often the form of contextualization confronting us when students give "wrong" answers to applied everyday problems, from which we conclude that "conceptual change" has not occurred. The students have situated the problem in an everyday setting and there they find the scientific explanation inappropriate.

Second, we looked at contextualization within more embracing ideas, or the *cognitive context*. In disputes among scholars, the question of how a phenomenon ought to be contextualized can be a vitally important one, as the example on the adaptation of bacteria shows. In such discourses, however, the problem of context is often explicitly stated and discussed. In learning situations, on the other hand, contextualization is often tacit or implicit; it is not immediately apparent to which conceptual framework a student relates a focal event. However, in learning situations, this kind of contextualization is probably the most important one and the most difficult one to deal with (cf. Wistedt, 1999). The problem relates to the so-called learning paradox. Plato formulated it in the dialogue *Menon*, where Menon says to Socrates that if we know what virtue is we need not make any study of it but, on the other hand, if we do not know what virtue is, how do we know when we have found it? Thus, in order to understand lower order concepts it is necessary to already possess a higher order concept that forms the context for the lower order concepts, and a condition for possessing that higher order concept is that the lower order concepts are already understood. It is this paradox we are trying to solve when we introduce our students to a new subject matter field.

Third and lastly, we looked at contextualization in a speech genre, or the *cultural context*. Perhaps it is in this direction we should look for a solution to the learning paradox. To become an expert in a field can be regarded as becoming socialized into a specific view of the world. Fred Davis (1974) talked about how to go about recognizing a good sociological story. He said that, even if many students can tell good and quite truthful stories about the data they have acquired, often the data belong to genres other than sociology, often ideological, psychological, or religious genres. It is not always easy to distinguish a good sociological story from other kinds of stories. In order to be able to make that distinction, the novice sociologist must acquire "a sound knowledge of and abiding love for his discipline" (p. 316). Further, in *Towards a Theory of Instruction*, Bruner (1966) argued that when students are to study a particular discipline, they should be introduced into the way of talking and joking — with the jargon — common to that discipline. These recommendations seem to me to be a plea for introducing the students into a specific speech genre. Such a speech genre might then become part of a higher order conception that could help students to structure focal events, even if only vaguely.

If I am right so far, contextualization also plays an important role when we are trying to learn something entirely new. This, what we are trying to learn, becomes intelligible when put in context and it is the context that can make the interpretation of the focal event plausible. This line of reasoning suggests that learning is not to be looked upon as a linear process, where we at first learn "facts", i.e. about the empirical level or the level of the experimental field of reference, and then try to understand these facts, i.e. relate the empirical level to the conceptual or model level, and then, in turn, to the theoretical level. Rather, learning is to be regarded as a simultaneously processing of these levels where the learner is constantly oscillating between these levels. After all, this is only to say that accommodation and assimilation, in the Piagetian sense, are both constantly in play. In the beginning of a learning process both the understanding of the meaning of facts and the theoretical understanding are vague, as for example the understanding of the concept of adaptation and its empirical manifestations within the Darwinian theory. When we are trying to learn something entirely new, our point of departure can perhaps only be constituted by a common speech genre. However, when knowledge grows, the theoretical understanding as well as the ability to interpret empirical evidence become more articulated, as was suggested in the antibiotics example. If instruction is linearly organized, or if the theoretical context is not made explicit as in the Linda example above, the learner has to invent higher order structures. For the novice, these could of course not be other than a commonsense view of the world, but as was seen in the probability example this could also be the case for the experienced person when the demanded theoretical context was not made explicit.

The overall aim of this chapter has been to question the fruitfulness of looking upon the difficulty students encounter in understanding scientific concepts solely as a problem of conceptual change. The problem might be better understood as a problem of contextualization. The implications of this view for both research and instruction then, are that more attention should be given to the various forms of contextualization that are in play when students make an effort to understand a particular phenomenon, concept, situation or event.

5

Systems of Signs and Conceptual Change

Terezinha Nunes

Introduction

Concepts have most often been discussed on the basis of underlying structures. This idea is pivotal in Piagetian theory of logico-mathematical development and also is central in other theories of conceptual development. Consequently, conceptual development and change has been viewed as a process of structural change. In Piagetian theory, for example, conceptual change is obtained when existing structures are challenged by new observations or other viewpoints that cannot be dealt with by the existing structures. Disequilibrium follows conflict and the process of equilibration, which re-establishes the equilibrium between the organism and the environment, becomes activated, resulting in changes in the logical structures of assimilation already developed by the subject (Piaget, 1950). Vygotsky's work (1978) on spontaneous and scientific concepts, although less explicitly concerned with structures, also rests on the idea that conceptual changes involve the reorganization of structures of meaning; whereas, spontaneous concepts involve functional categories, based on experiential relations (for example, an axe is classified with a log because you need an axe to chop the log and the log is quite useless if you don't have anything to chop it with), and scientific concepts are taxonomic-based categories (for example, an axe is classified with a hammer because they are both tools). Because underlying structures have constituted the basis for definitions of concepts, current theories of conceptual change also have tried to define conceptual change in structural terms. Within the Alternative Framework Movement, the terms "structures", "mental models", and "frameworks of reference" are often used interchangeably (e.g. Vosniadou, 1994, p. 61, where the conceptual structure underlying different mental models of force are explicitly discussed). Chi et al. (1994) allow for conceptual changes that don't involve a change in structure but, rather, the reassignment of a concept to another category within the pre-existing structure.

Recently, Vergnaud (1985) has suggested a broader approach to the definition of concepts, which allows for new ways of analysing conceptual change. According to Vergnaud, concepts cannot be defined solely by their structure: a comprehensive analysis of concepts requires that we consider the properties of the concepts (which constitute the structural aspects), the situations in which the concept is used, and the systems of signs that subjects use to think and talk about the concept. Thus conceptual change might involve not only structural change, as already pointed out in the different theories of conceptual change, but also a shift in the boundaries to include or exclude situations in which it can be used and the acquisition of new systems of signs, which allow for different manipulations in the use of the concept.

The need to consider the situations in which concepts are used has been pointed out rather often in the last decade or so (see, for example, Carpenter & Moser, 1982; Cheng & Holyoak, 1985; Lave, 1988; Nunes et al., 1993). In most of this work, the same people are shown to be more successful in solving problems that involve the same concepts in some types of situations rather than others. Recently, we (Nunes & Bryant, 1995) have also shown that these situational differences do not only apply to success in problem solving but also to recognizing whether a particular property of a concept can be applied: children understand that the commutativity of multiplication can be applied in some situations more readily than in others.

In this chapter, I will focus on the third aspect of concepts: the systems of signs used in thinking and communication. I will not be concerned with concepts in a static manner (i.e. what kind of concept does the subject *have*?) but in a dynamic manner (i.e. what conceptually based *activities* does the subject carry out?). I wish to suggest that systems of signs used in thinking and communication play a major role in conceptual development and change. They enable, direct and constrained reasoning through their mediating function; but further, they play a structuring role in concept formation and influence the sort of concept developed during learning experiences.

The conception of systems of signs I will use is a broad one. I will include, as a system of signs, different resources that subjects can draw on during problem solving and will concentrate particularly on the use of resources that can be observed and described in some detail. The evidence that I will draw from is in the domain of mathematics education, where Vergnaud's theory of conceptual fields has already been used to develop and interpret much evidence. However, it is likely that it is well-worth exploring the role of systems of signs in the realm of scientific concepts, and I will explore some of the possibilities in the concluding section.

The Enabling Role of Systems of Signs

According to Luria (1973), all higher mental functions are mediated by systems of signs. Without such mediation, we would be basically restricted to the here and now. The enabling function of systems of signs in the domain of mathematical concepts is so obvious that only two examples of very elementary mathematical activities will be mentioned here.

First, consider the activity of counting. In order to count adequately, as Gelman and Gallistel (1978) have pointed out, we need to: (i) establish a one-to-one correspondence between unique counting words and the objects that are being counted; (ii) maintain the counting words in a fixed order; and (iii) use the last word to represent the number of objects in the set. As simple as this activity may seem, it cannot be carried out without the mediation of counting words. A system must be used if we wish to keep the words in a fixed order. Most 7- to 8-year-olds in many cultures could easily count to 1000, if they chose to, and produce 1000 counting labels in a fixed order. This marvellous accomplishment, which we take for granted, is only possible because they rely on a system whereby they generate, rather than memorize, the words in a fixed order. Once the structure of the oral counting words is understood, the user of the system can produce counting labels he/she has never heard. In this case, the structure of the system enables the user to go beyond the limits of her/his natural memory.

The highest number that can be produced by a subject who has mastered the counting system in his/her environment is not determined by the counter's memory skills but by the system. Non-base systems, such as those described by Lancy (1983) in Papua-New Guinea, use the names of body parts taken in a systematic order as an *aide memoire*, and enable their users to count sometimes up to 68 or so. However, because the system does not have a base and is not recursive, the system is finite and so is also the counting ability of the user. In the case of counting, over the course of history cultures have developed numeration systems that enable their users to surpass their natural memory limitations.

A second example can be found in the case of measurement systems. Our perception of length, for example, is subject to all sorts of illusions. In the case of the widely known Muller–Lyer illusion, for example, we fail in comparing two line segments that are presented in close proximity. Our perception is subjected also to a size constancy illusion, whereby we overestimate the size of objects at a distance, and to the well-known illusion of the size of the moon, which we perceive as having varying sizes as the evening goes on. Our memory of length is also limited and we could hardly hope to look at a window and go to a shop to buy the right amount of material to make a curtain for it. And further, perception of length is subjective in the sense that different people may not agree in their judgements of length in the same situation. For example, in the case of the Muller–Lyer illusion, different subjects show different levels of the illusion, and no agreement would be observed across subjects were they to be asked to estimate the size of the difference between the line segments. Throughout the course of history, cultures have developed measurement systems that allow their users to overcome their perceptual, mnemonic and also intersubjective limitations. Although our vision is not improved, we can measure the line segments in the Muller–Lyer illusion and verify that the line segments have the same length.

The enabling role of counting and measurement systems is clearly fundamental to our ability to carry out many mathematical activities in our everyday life in and out of school.

The Directing and Constraining Role of Systems of Signs

The enabling role of systems of signs is quite easily demonstrated. It is much more difficult to demonstrate the directing and constraining roles of systems of signs on reasoning because this issue involves the interaction between the reasoning processes of subjects and the external system. In this section, several examples of how people calculate with different systems of signs will be briefly presented to demonstrate that the process of calculation is both directed and constrained by the system of sign. Four different sorts of representation used in calculation will be contrasted: fingers, oral numbers, written numbers and abacus.

Finger Arithmetic

Marton and Neuman (1990) observed young children's (7 years old) calculating abilities when they had to solve problems where the problem situation was additive but one addend was unknown, for example, "Your teacher has 4 pencils and 10 children want to draw; how many more pencils does she need to get from the cupboard?". For young children, this situations is additive because the teacher needs more pencils and not subtractive because nothing is taken away. But how do you add a number when you do not know what the number is? Marton and Neuman observed that the successful children had developed a way to represent the situation with their fingers that allowed for success. They would lift up all 10 fingers and move four away from the others. When they did this, most children did not even need to count the fingers in the other set: they recognized the visual pattern for six. This procedure led to success even if the children did not know which arithmetic operation to perform and most children at this age did not know which operation to perform to solve this problem. However, the use of "finger numbers", as Marton and Neuman call them, is restricted to problems in which at least one of the numbers is not greater than 10. The same problem given to the same children with larger numbers leads to failure. Thus "finger numbers" are restricted to small values as a consequence of the number of visual patterns that can be recognized.

A different use of fingers in calculation has been described recently by Nunes and Moreno (1995). We observed young children with hearing problems using a finger algorithm for performing addition and subtraction. In the addition algorithm, for example, the sign for one of the addends is executed with one hand while the sign for the other addend is executed with the other hand. As the child gradually moves up the numbers signed for the addends in one hand, he/she moves down the numbers in the other hand, as if transferring the value from one hand to the other, until there are no more numbers to be added. The algorithm is useful for children with hearing problems because it frees them from the need to try to remember verbal addition facts (such as $8 + 5 = 13$). Children with hearing problems who know this algorithm are better at answering addition and subtraction questions (such as "what is $8 + 3$?" or "what is $14 - 5$?") than a cohort group of children with hearing problems that does not know the algorithm. The algorithm plays an enabling role. However, there are limitations in their performance that can be clearly traced to the use of the algorithm. When the number 8, for example, is signed, three fingers are lifted up: the index, the middle-finger and the ring-finger. If 8 is being added onto another number, these three fingers need to be retracted as each unit is added on to the number signed with the other hand. When the three fingers are retracted, all the fingers are now down but the child needs to remember that there are still 5 units to be added. It is not uncommon that young children learning this algorithm will forget the remaining 5 units and obtain, for example, 8 as the result of the addition $5 + 8$. This error can be traced directly to the system; the same children will not make this error if they solve the same computation using blocks to represent the addends. Thus the signing algorithm simultaneously enables the children, by freeing them from the need to memorize verbal addition facts, which are difficult for them, and constrains their practice of calculation in particular ways.

Oral and Written Arithmetic

Nunes et al. (1993) have described in detail the use of oral and written numbers during calculation and the effects of these systems of signs on the process of calculation. The studies were carried out in Brazil, where children from working class families were exposed to two forms of arithmetic test: oral and written.

Written arithmetic is taught in school. Although the children need to produce the addition facts (either from memory or through finger counting) themselves, the arithmetic practice they use is characterized as written because of the directing and constraining role that is played by the written symbols during calculation. When addition is carried out, i.e.

once the numbers are written down, the user of the system seems to stop thinking of the values as a whole. Digits are added from right to left. Calculation can be performed in this fashion because the relative value of the digit has been "off-loaded" (to use Hatano's, 1995, terminology) onto the paper. It will be recovered later when the result is read, this time from left to right. Paper-and-pencil calculation exploits the spatial characteristics of the system: addition is carried out by columns that must be properly aligned for the result to be correct. This is actually one source of difficulty for children in initial stages of learning because children may not respect a column arrangement or may arrange the column from left to right, using the direction in which numbers are written down as a guide. A further characteristic of the written algorithm is that all digits are treated in the same way, regardless of their place in the number, and partial results are written down, allowing for memory restrictions to be quickly overcome.

The consequences of these characteristics lead to the prediction of strengths and weaknesses in calculation performance as a consequence of the use of written algorithms. The strength resides in the fact that very large numbers, as well as long lists of numbers, can be operated on in a relatively effortless way. Using this algorithm we can, for example, add lists of numbers that we could not memorize. The weakness is in the types of errors expected in written arithmetic. Calculation from right to left means that the value of an error is magnified as calculation proceeds. Calculation on the basis of digits, without regard for the quantity the number represents, also leads to a weakening in the control of partial results during calculation. In contrast to written arithmetic, oral arithmetic is not systematically taught in Brazilian schools but rather learned in everyday situations such as in shopping. Oral arithmetic favours the process of control of results because reference to the quantities remains explicit throughout the process of calculation. Calculation is carried out from larger to smaller values and continuously monitored throughout the process.

To illustrate, a typical solution of an addition problem such as 230 + 150 in oral arithmetic would be: 230 + 100 = 330, and then 330 + 50 = 380. Similarly, in a subtraction such as 200 – 35, a typical solution is: 200 – 30 = 170 and then 170 – 5 = 165. A final example will be given, from a division problem where a child was solving the problem of distributing 75 marbles equally among five boys: Give 10 marbles to each one, that's 50 marbles. 25 left over, to give to 5 boys. (...) . That's 5 more each, that's 15 each (Nunes et al., 1993).

Oral arithmetic, like the written practice, has strengths and weaknesses. It is difficult to use oral arithmetic with very large numbers and with long lists, and this is a major weakness. However, the fact that meaning is preserved during calculations strengthens the process of control of calculation. When errors are made, they are expected to be smaller.

The weakness of written arithmetic in contrast to oral arithmetic was observed in studies that used a within-subjects design, when the same children solved problems using either oral or written arithmetic on different occasions, and an across-subjects design, when subjects who are users of oral arithmetic and have little formal instruction (small rural producers, foremen in construction sites, fishermen) were compared with students who rely more on written arithmetic practices. The use of oral practices led to significantly fewer errors for any of the four operations. When errors were observed, those resulting from oral arithmetic were relatively smaller than those resulting from written arithmetic, as demonstrated by a significant association between type of arithmetic procedure used and relative size of error (Nunes et al., 1993).

Another study that contrasted oral and written arithmetic was carried out by Nunes (1993) with directed number problems, where calculation played a minor role, but monitoring the process of problem solving by keeping its meaning in mind was very important. The values used were all simple tens (e.g. 40, 30, 20); the important question for the problem solver was whether to add or subtract the numbers. In written arithmetic, problem solvers have to deal with the fact that -20 and -30 need to be added together although they are preceded by the minus sign, which under other circumstances would indicate subtraction. In oral arithmetic, where the numbers and operations are not represented in written form, the choice of operation should not be influenced by difficulties stemming from the written notation.

In this study, children and adolescents from three grade levels were assigned either to an oral or to a written condition of testing and presented orally with the same directed number problems. All problems related to gains and losses of a hypothetical farmer in his different types of harvest, a situation that was familiar to all subjects. Those assigned to the written condition were asked to write the numbers down before solving the problem and those assigned to the oral condition did not have paper and pencil available in the testing situation.

Subjects in the oral condition performed significantly better than those assigned to the written condition. An analysis of the errors displayed in the written condition indicated that they resulted from a conflict of two written arithmetic practices that subjects had learned in school. This conflict involves (at least) two major rules. First, in written arithmetic taught before directed numbers, signs stand for operations and children are taught that they need to carry out different operations separately. They should not, for example, add and subtract using a single algorithm. When directed numbers are introduced, signs no longer stand for operations because two negative numbers can be added or a positive number can be subtracted from a negative one. Second, when subjects use the plus and minus signs to represent an operation, they cannot write down the sign for the operation after the presentation of the first figure in the problem, but only after the second figure has been presented. At such an early stage in problem presentation, the subjects cannot yet know which operation they will need to carry out and must wait for further information to know what the sign ought to be.

Typical errors in directed number problem solutions are therefore expected to be of two kinds. In the first type of error, subjects in the written condition are expected to fail to write down whether the first figure in the problem is positive or negative. The operation will depend on whether the second figure indicates a profit or a debt and they wait until they have obtained this information to write a sign. A second type of error involves carrying out the operation indicated by the sign regardless of whether two debts are presented consecutively. This would result, for example, in subtracting a negative number from another rather than adding them. These were the types of errors observed by Nunes (1993).

The subjects' difficulties with written arithmetic in solving directed number problems could not be simply attributed to a lack of understanding of directed number problems, for the following reasons. First, it must be recalled that subjects were randomly assigned either to the oral or to the written condition and subjects in the oral condition performed almost at ceiling level. The random assignment is assumed to control for subjects' abilities. Second, subjects in the written condition often were able to realize that they had made a mistake when asked to explain how they arrived at the result. They would then self-correct during this oral explanation and conclude by saying "I can't do it on paper, I can only do it in my head". For example, the following problem was given to J.C.: "Seu Severino (the farmer's name) started the season with a debt of 10 cruzados (the Brazilian currency at the time). He planted manioc and beans. He had a profit of 20 on the manioc and a profit of 10 on the beans. What was his situation at the end of the year?" J.C. wrote down 10 without a sign (an error of the first type), plus 20 underneath (a profit requires a plus sign), and then 10 in a third row below the 20 without a new sign. He added all the numbers and wrote 40 for the answer. However, when asked whether this 40 was a profit or a loss, a question routinely asked when subjects did not indicate the direction of the value, J.C. answered: "No, it's not that. I can't do it on paper. He took his profit from the beans, paid the 10 he owed, and he still has the 20 from the manioc."

In short, the contrast between oral and written arithmetic illustrates how the systems of signs and the cultural practices that belong with them direct and constrain the subjects' reasoning during their execution. When the subject is able to step outside one system and use the other one, a different reasoning process can be observed. These changes in reasoning cannot be accounted for without attributing a directing and constraining role to the systems of signs used in mediating reasoning.

Abacus Arithmetic

Hatano (1997) recently reviewed the literature on abacus arithmetic and described the characteristics of its use by the grandmasters. Grandmasters appear to develop a mental, spatial representation of the abacus that works like a "mental abacus". Research indicates that this internal representation is spatial (and thus preserves the characteristics of the external system of signs) for different reasons. First, grandmasters can carry out calculations while answering simple questions, a finding that indicates that verbal interference is not significant. However, if asked to look at a picture, their performance is disrupted, a result that indicates that spatial interference is significant. Another indication that the internal abacus preserves the spatial characteristics of the external system is that grandmasters can remember numbers with 15/16 digits and say the digits backwards and forwards with the same ease, a task that cannot be carried out easily when we use verbal codes to remember digits. Finally, although they show such marvellous memory for digits, which can be registered in their mental abacus and thus supported by the system of signs, their memory for other lists such as names of flowers is no better than anyone else's.

The characteristics of operation with the abacus are in some sense similar to written arithmetic: operations are carried out on digits and use spatial representation as a support. Like written arithmetic, control of the values during calculation is not part of the cultural practice. It is quicker to calculate twice to see whether the same result is obtained than to include control of values during calculation. Obviously grandmasters do not make mistakes when calculating, as young Brazilian children do when using written arithmetic. However, their lack of monitoring of calculation when they use the abacus is observed in two ways. Firstly, if given the same list of numbers to add twice in a row with a slight modification (such as moving the first number to the last position in the list), they do not recognize that they have just added the numbers. Secondly, they do not simplify the calculation by using related facts. For example, if asked to multiply a number by 99, they do not multiply it by

100 and then subtract the number. This latter technique is used when consideration of the value is part of the calculation process.

Thus, abacus arithmetic, even if carried out on a mental abacus, preserves the spatial aspects of the abacus plus the strengths and weaknesses of this cultural practice.

Taken together, the analysis of these different forms of arithmetic indicates that the systems of signs used during calculation, either externally represented (fingers, written digits, oral productions) or internalized (the mental abacus) seem to become objects on which we operate. While we interact with these objects, our reasoning process is a product of this interaction; the systems of signs both direct and constrain what we can achieve with them.

The Structuring Role of Signs in Concept Formation

When we think about problem situations, we necessarily use systems of signs that mediate our interactions. When a system of signs is used as mediator in a learning situation, it influences our interaction in the situation and the type of concept that will emerge from these interactions. This can be illustrated when the use of different systems in the same situation can lead to diverse conceptual schemas. I want to draw here on two lines of investigation: a series of studies on the concept of area (Nunes et al., 1993, 1994) and some of the work carried out in the context of learning mathematics in computer environments (Noss, 1986).

Alternative Ways of Representing the Concept of Area

There are (at least) two ways in which the area of a plane figure can be calculated. The first one is the most common in our society and is formally transmitted in school. It involves taking the measurement of the height and of the width of the figure and using these measures in a formula that gives the area. The area of the rectangle, for example, is height times width. This way of calculating the area corresponds to the schema of *product of measures* (see Vergnaud, 1983). In this type of conception of area, two elementary measures, height and width, obtained, for example, in centimetres, are multiplied to yield a third and new measure, the area, in square centimetres. The second schema of area involves starting out from area units, e.g. square centimetres. If these area units are arranged in rows and columns on the figure, the area is calculated through multiplying the number of units in a row by the number of rows. This approach is equivalent to a schema in multiplication termed (see Vergnaud, 1983) isomorphism of measures. In this conception of area, there is a one-to-many correspondence between the number of rows and the number of area units in each row. The two conceptions differ in a very basic way: the product of measures conception involves three variables whereas the isomorphism of measures conception involves only two.

This analysis led us to hypothesize that children would develop different schemas for area depending on whether they were given learning experiences in which they used either linear or area units. In a series of studies about area (Nunes et al. 1993, 1994) investigated whether children could explain how they obtained the area of figures such as rectangles and parallelograms in different ways that corresponded to the type of measuring tool they were given. The measuring tools were, in this case, systems of signs that would mediate their attempts to quantify area.

We asked pairs of English children (aged 8–10 years) to solve some area problems. The pairs of pupils were randomly allocated to one of two conditions. In the first condition, they were given rulers as their measurement tool. In the second condition, they were given 1-cm^2 bricks but not enough bricks to fully cover the figures so that a solution by simply covering the figure and counting the number of bricks was not possible.

The children were presented with two figures, the area of which could not be visually compared with certainty — for example, two rectangles one of which was longer whereas the second one had a bigger height. The children were told that the two figures were the drawings of two walls that had been painted by two friends, each one having painted one wall. The friends were then paid for the paint job together. Before dividing the money, they wanted to know whether they had done the same amount of work and needed to compare the surface of the two walls. There was, therefore, no doubt that surface covered was what mattered in the comparison. The pupils received feedback in the successive trials by observing the experimenter cover each figure with previously cut coloured paper that could be rearranged so as to perfectly cover both figures, when they had the same area, but covered only one of them exactly, when the areas differed. This procedure was understood as a good test of the equality by all the children.

Although all children had been taught about area in school, we could reasonably expect that they would have to develop their understanding of area further during our studies because it has already been documented (see Dickson, 1989, for example) that English children at this age level have not mastered the area of rectangles despite teaching. The children in our study had been initially taught to cover figures with area units and count them. After this practice, they had a formalization lesson, in which they were taught the height-times-width formula. We expected that the children who had assimilated the formula would have no difficulty with the initial problems in our study, which involved the comparison of rectangles, but would still have to adjust their procedures when dealing with a U-shaped figure that could be decomposed into rectangles and also when comparing a rectangle with a parallelogram.

The performance of the pupils in these problems differed as a function of the systems of signs they had available in the experimental situation: rulers versus area units. The differences were observed both in terms of the number of correct responses and the type of conception used during problem solving. The children who had area units available performed significantly better than those who had rulers.

The pupils who had the ruler as their measuring instrument were more likely to add the measures than to multiply them. They either calculated the perimeter or the half-perimeter. Some pupils then proceeded to make a decision about the relative size of the figures on the basis of this information; other pupils did not consider this information adequate but didn't know what to do next; they felt they could not decide whether the two children had or not done the same amount of work. These subjects' responses seem to indicate that they conceive of linear measures as appropriate for linear evaluations. Previous teaching did not help them very much because the measuring tool had not been appropriate to mediate their interactions with the objects from their viewpoint. A third group of children displayed a problem-solving strategy that seems quite significant. They attempted to use the ruler as an area unit, placing it against one of the edges of the figure and moving it to the other side as they counted how many rulers fit into the figure. The ruler as a conventional, linear measuring tool was disregarded and treated as a non-conventional area unit. The analysis of these children's performance shows that their difficulties with the concept of area were related to the system of signs that they had to mediate their interactions. A system that yields linear measures did not seem a good means for their end. Even the children who could successfully solve the problems of comparing rectangles using the height-times-width problem had difficulty in comparing a rectangle and a parallelogram. They did not figure out that the height and the side of the parallelogram are not the same. They used a side-times-side conception, which, when applied to the parallelogram, produces an incorrect solution.

The pupils who had the area units as measuring instrument often discovered a formula to solve the problem, number of bricks in a row times number of rows, and used it success-fully to overcome the shortage of bricks. This formula was more easily modified to solve the problem of the area of the parallelogram than the height-times-width formula they had been taught. The height of the parallelogram and the number of rows are the same measure. These pupils' relative success in comparison with those who had the rulers cannot be explained by a better understanding of area because they had been randomly assigned to their groups. We are led to conclude that their success was possible because the measuring tool that mediates their interactions in the problem situation had an effect on these interac-tions, which resulted in a different operational conception of area.

To sum up, children's schema of area in this series of problems was clearly influenced by the measuring tool they had been given. The children who received area units invented a formula "number of bricks in a row times number of rows". The children who had been given rulers may have used a previously learned or developed "side-times-side" formula for calculating the area of parallelograms. Each system of signs seemed to throw light on particular aspects of the concept rather than others.

It must be stressed, however, that the structuring role of systems of signs in concept formation cannot be viewed in a deterministic way. Subjects have their own ideas about what they wish to achieve in the situation and may make use of a tool in an unexpected manner when the mediating system itself is considered. In these experiments, children who wanted to rely on area units used the ruler as an area unit rather than an instrument for obtaining linear measures. Thus systems of signs play a structuring role in the subject's interactions as mediators of reasoning but do not determine the outcome of learning without our taking into account the subject's own role in the situation.

Concepts Developed in Computer Environments

The next illustration of the structuring role of signs in concept development relates to chil-dren's mathematical learning in computer environments. I will pursue only one example here (for further examples, see Noss, 1997).

In order to work in computer environments, children need to learn systems of signs that, I believe, structure the type of understanding they develop in the situation. This structuring role can be seen, for example, in the context of drawing figures with LOGO[1] in two ways. First, the activities of drawing a figure with paper and pencil and with LOGO are very

[1]LOGO is a computer environment where children can manipulate the movements of the cursor — represented by a turtle on the screen — by typing in commands. The commands may be simple directions, such as FORWARD 10 (which maks the turtle move forward 10 units) or small programmes containing a series of commands where vari-able inputs can be entered.

different. When drawing with paper and pencil, certain characteristics of the figure need to become salient for the figure to look right at the end. For example, when we draw a parallelogram with a ruler and paper and pencil, we need to use procedures that will ensure that the opposing sides are parallel and of the same length. Little or no attention is given to angles (especially in the most common situation where we draw using a ruler but not a protractor). The equality of opposing angles is a result of the procedure, which may not have been intentional and of which the subject may have been unaware. In contrast, when drawing a parallelogram with LOGO, the fact that the opposing sides are parallel is a product of the procedure that may have received little attention. The procedure specifies the value of the angles and the length of the sides, but not the relationship between the sides. Thus the two activities stress different aspects of the same figure and are likely to result in different views of what a parallelogram is.

Second, drawing a figure with LOGO can be done through general procedures, which leave particular values without specification, although a place-holder needs to be entered in the procedure indicating that some value will later be specified. For example, the size of an angle or a side in a figure may not be identified, but a name, such as ANGLE1 or SIDE1, will be entered in the procedure. This way of drawing figures is likely to have two effects: (i) it may allow pupils to come to see as similar, or belonging to the same family, figures that were previously thought of as very different, if the figures can be produced by the same procedure by entering different values for ANGLE1 or SIDE1; and (ii) it seems to afford direct experience with the concept of variable, whereby variables are given a name in a procedure and values are filled in later on.

Noss (1995) reports a study in which 11-year-old pupils were involved in working with LOGO to devise a general procedure for drawing parallelograms. According to him, a number of the pupils started out with the notion that a parallelogram is a "lopsided rectangle". This notion, according to Noss, precludes a rectangle from being a parallelogram. However, in the course of drawing figures with LOGO, these 11-year-olds were led to develop general procedures for drawing parallelograms, such as the one below:

TO SHAPE :SIDE1 :SIDE2 :ANGLE

REPEAT 2 [FD :SIDE1 RT :ANGLE FD :SIDE2

RT 180 : ANGLE]

END

When thinking of parallelograms in terms of this formulation, within a system of signs such as LOGO, where figures are represented by the procedures used to draw them, some pupils could come to the realization that a rectangle is actually a special case of parallelograms, where ANGLE = 90. According to Noss, this is what in fact was observed; some (though not all) pupils came to see parallelograms as including the special case of the rectangle.

Another result observed by Noss (1986) was that pupils working in the LOGO environment developed their understanding of "variable" and showed positive gains in an independent evaluation of this understanding carried out on a computer. An example of the type of item included in this test involves giving the formula for the perimeter of an irregular figure with many sides, all of the same length. However, the exact number of sides of the figure could not be seen because an ink blot partially covered the figure. The expected solution is to use a letter to represent the number of sides, indicating that, whatever the number of sides, this is the value that goes into the formula. This solution was observed among Noss's subjects more often in a post-test, given after they had worked with LOGO, than in a pre-test, before the work with LOGO. Moreover, the notation used by LOGO learners in solving the problems in the post-test reflected the system of signs that they had used in the LOGO environment rather than the traditional literal notation for variables used in algebra (for example, they might have used the word SIDE to indicate number of sides rather than the letter n).

In short, systems of signs provide the users with the opportunity of approaching problems in particular ways that relate to how situations can be represented. Because signs mediate the subjects' thinking and often also their actions in a learning situation, they become part of the elements that structure the subjects' interactions and the emerging concept. Different systems of signs may highlight different aspects of a concept, and the coordination of these different aspects is not a simple and straightforward matter.

Conclusion

The influence of systems of signs on the development of the mind is not a new topic. Whorf (1956), for example, suggested that thinking was so influenced by language that we were led to see the world in ways that were determined by our language. This hypothesis was (inadequately perhaps) simplified into testing whether people saw colour differently as a function of the colour vocabulary in their language. And this particular hypothesis turns out to be wrong (Berlin & Kay, 1969): People who only use two colour terms still see many different colours and demonstrate the variety of colours they perceive when asked to make colour discriminations.

Vygotsky (1978) and Luria (1973) also stressed the influence of systems of signs on our thinking. One of their hypotheses was that systems of signs were mental tools that allowed humans to surpass their natural limits of perception and memory, for example. They stressed, however, that contrary to manual work tools, which do not radically change the anatomy of our hand, signs as mental tools changed the mind of the user. Written language, they suggested, makes language into an object and thereby allows people to develop an objective approach to language, to surpass their immediate experience and reason about linguistically created realities. From this, they expected literate and illiterate people to differ radically in their ability to think logically and use language to structure their reasoning. Scribner and Cole (1981) put this hypothesis to the empirical test by examining three groups of literates and one group of non-literates in Liberia. Two of their literate groups acquired literacy outside school, either in a religious setting, learning to read the Q'ran, or informally, learning to read and write in an indigenous script informally transmitted outside school. If literacy had the effects predicted by Vygotsky and Luria, all three groups of literates should perform better than the illiterate subjects in logical (syllogistic reasoning), metalinguistic (concepts of word and syllable, for example) and memory tasks. All tasks were presented orally and subjects also responded in the oral mode. Scribner and Cole's results were quite unambiguous, and the hypothesis of a transformation of the mind through literacy acquisition was not confirmed: in none of the tasks was observed a clear separation between literates, on the one hand, and illiterates, on the other. Literacy did not seem to radically alter the minds of people.

The lack of success of these earlier analyses of the impact of signs on thinking seems to me to result from expecting too much from a single system of signs. Natural language and literacy, although potent, do not do all the jobs for the mind. We still need other systems, even for everyday life. The capacity for the use of multiple systems is likely to be an important factor in overcoming the rigidity of the mind, which is in a certain sense part of both Whorf's view of language, and Vygotsky's and Luria's view of literacy. If we had only one system of signs, we could hardly tell the nature of the system from the nature of the mind and the nature of the object.

A new way of looking at systems of signs is to look at the variety of signs, and to assume that signs influence reasoning processes *in the course of a subject's activity*, but not when they are not in use. We can then ask questions such as: What do the same people accomplish with different signs? What opportunities does the use of different mental tools afford the learner during learning? What does the tool enable or constrain? And when is it a good time to change to another tool?

There is already some evidence — although it is clearly scant — that systems of signs influence children's reasoning about science concepts. Erickson and Tiberghien (1985) asked pupils between the ages of 7 and 11 to predict the temperature of the water resulting from pouring water from two containers, A and B, into a larger one, C. The temperature of the water was either presented in words (hot, cold) or in numbers (80°, 20°). A large percentage of children at all age levels made mistakes in these predictions: they seemed to think in additive terms, predicting that two lots of water at 80° would have the final temperature of 160°, and two lots of hot water put together would yield water that was even hotter. However, fewer children made this mistake when the problem was presented in words. This finding has been recently replicated by Desli (1999).

Thus similarly to what is observed in mathematics, in the science classroom pupils come into contact with a variety of systems of signs. Yet, we know very little about how these signs affect their learning and reasoning about science. When studying genetics, for example, diagrams seem to be a very useful way of systematically generating the genotype of the offspring in order to analyse what sorts of phenotype (and in what proportion) might be observed. However, we know relatively little about the effect of mastering this system of signs on the ability to solve genetics problems in school.

Similarly, it is possible that graphs might play a role in learning physics. In a pilot experiment I carried out several years ago about the concept of density (Carraher, 1988), the pupils were asked to plot the volume of some containers (measured in cm³) against the weight of the container (in grams) when filled with marbles just up to the point where the container neither floated nor sank completely. Because of errors of measurement, which are reasonably expected in such an experiment, the students did not realize when obtaining the measures that the weight divided by the volume would be approximately 1 for all the containers, regardless of shape and material. However, as they plotted the graph, the linearity of the relationship became clear, and students were able to ask themselves why that should be so. In a post-test about density, these students performed significantly better than their classmates who had only attended the regular instruction about density offered in the classroom. Although it is not possible from this study to discuss the role of the graphic representation on their learning, because so many other aspects of the experience in the two groups differed, the example illustrates the sort of question one might want to pursue in analysing the role of different systems of signs in learning physics.

To sum up, there is much evidence to suggest that systems of signs play a major role in concept development and use in mathematical reasoning. They act as mediators or mental objects we reason with. However, there is no need to make them into the hardware of thinking. They can be used and set aside in different circumstances and for different purposes. This flexibility in the relationship between thinking and the use of different systems of signs is likely to play an important role in the development of mathematical concepts because different systems highlight different aspects of the same concept. It might be the case that the same sorts of effects can be observed when studying scientific concepts and that using a new system of signs to work with a familiar concept might end up by bringing into focus a new aspect of the concept and bring about conceptual change.

6

Concepts, Cognition and Discourse: From Mental Structures to Discursive Tools

Roger Säljö[1]

Introduction

Human knowledge is largely conceptual in nature. Concepts are the resources through which human beings render intelligible events that are open to many different interpretations. They are also the means by which we escape the paralysis that would occur if our perceptions were mere registrations of sense data in a camera-like fashion. We are clearly not prisoners of perceptual impressions. Instead, we have an amazing ability to identify and contextualize what we see in a flexible manner by means of our conceptual resources. We can construe objects that are very different as similar because they share certain features that are contextually relevant. But we can also discover variation and uniqueness in what to many would appear as identical objects. The development of expertise is largely a matter of being able to utilise conceptual resources to make fine-grained distinctions that are not apparent to everyone. The specialist in reading radiography pictures relies on conceptual distinctions when making a picture meaningful. Although the novice may look at the same picture, and thus be exposed to identical stimuli, she may in effect not be able to see anything without access to concepts that are contextually relevant and that have to be put to work. But concepts do more than help us categorize; they are the tools that enable us to perform concrete actions in social settings. As Harré and Gillett (1994) put it, "applying a concept to something enables me to act in ways that otherwise I could not" (p. 41). In some fundamental sense, concepts are repositories of human sense-making capacities and activities, they are sediments of human experiences and simultaneously tools for action.

Basic to my argument is the assumption that concepts are linguistic, or, rather, discursive phenomena that do concrete work in concrete settings. They are devices by means of which an event or a phenomenon is construed as something — as a member of a class. This, I think, is largely in line with what most theoretical positions of present-day psychology would argue. However, when saying that something that we perceive is a member of a class, this should not be interpreted in terms of class inclusion in the sense of formal logic. What constitutes a class and what determines membership of that particular class will vary between human practices. As students of human thinking and communication we therefore have to be aware of the variations in social practices that people participate in modern society, and the likelihood that events will be categorized differently as we move from one activity to the next. In scientific classifications, whales are considered to be mammals, but in what is nowadays referred to as "naive theories" or "lay misconceptions" (cf. below), we

[1] The research reported was financed by the National Board of Education and by the Swedish Council for Research in the Humanities and Social Sciences.

will not be surprised to hear people refer to these animals as fish to take one of the favourite examples in text books on concept formation.

Categorization in most theorizing within cognitive psychology has been construed as an essentially passive and mechanical phenomenon. This would be true even of many positions that have emphasized the constructive or ecological nature of human cognition, such as the one suggested by Neisser (1967, 1976), as has been argued recently by Harré and Gillett (1994) and Edwards and Potter (1992). The conceptual classification is something we read off the world when it is presented to us. Concepts are abstractions and symbols that "stand in correspondence to entities and categories in the real world (or in possible worlds)." (Lakoff, 1987, p. 163), as is the dominant assumption of the role and nature of language. However, concepts are by no means simply pictures of the world. If they were, and if meanings were in the objects themselves or in our brain or neurological system, we would indeed be slaves to our perceptual apparatus. We would respond to sense data as perceptual and cognitive automata rather than think or reason.

What constitutes a relevant categorization is often conflictual and, on some occasions, it will not even be enough to appeal to science for the establishment of a true definition. Let me take an amusing and recent example that concerns the concept of banana. One would hope that in this enlightened time, the definition of what counts as a banana and what does not count as a banana would be fairly easy to establish. If one asks a botanist with expertise in such matters, one will learn that there are many different kinds of bananas and that there is essentially no difficulty in establishing what qualifies as a banana. That could be the end of the story. However, if we take the banana into a very different kind of discourse and practice — a socio-political one — we will soon discover that the matter is not so easily settled. Within the European Union (and the associated EES countries) there has been an intense conflict over the past few years over what counts as a banana. Politicians, even prime ministers, bureaucrats, businessmen, consumer organizations, ship owners and freight companies, and experts of different kinds have been involved in trying to establish what counts as a banana and what does not. The background of this interest is a social practice that is very different from the abstract and allegedly neutral commitment of the botanist to classifying bananas according to scientific criteria. Since bananas are grown in one region in the southern parts of the European Union, producers have been interested in making use of union rules that protect domestic production and allow for an import tax to be put on bananas imported from other parts of the world, primarily Central and South America. Consumers in some countries that have a high consumption of bananas, such as Germany and Sweden, have protested loudly. Their argument has been that the small, green and not very tasty fruits that come from within the union, and that do not even have the appropriate shape of a banana, cannot be considered as bananas. They clearly cannot be considered to be equivalent to the yellow, rich and delicious fruits that come from across the Atlantic. Thus, we have an interesting case in point where bananas as botanical objects have one classification (which would include both these fruits), and an alternative one where consumers claim that as objects to eat, these two products are not the same.

This example illustrates that conceptual classification is something that has to be argued for, and that is sustained not by static characteristics that reside *in* objects but by discursive practices *about* objects. Objects are not just identified and recognized by means of concepts, they are constituted in manners that fit different communicative and practical purposes. The example also illustrates the other element that I mentioned above; concepts are tools for action. In this case, the decision of whether to classify these objects as according to one or other of these sides will have implications for socio-economic activities of thousands of people involved not only in the growing of bananas on plantations, but also in the administration of the goods, transport and shipping, and so on.

Mentalist Notions of Concepts and Conceptual Knowledge

In the tradition of modern cognitive psychology, concepts have been conceived as abstract constructs that intervene between the biological substrate — the brain — and behaviour. As part and parcel of this construction of human cognition, a series of assumptions has followed regarding how individuals perceive events, how they process information, and how they act in concrete settings. There has been an individualist bias in the sense that thinking "by past consensus and implicit definition [has been construed as] an individual act bounded by the physical facts of brain and body" (Resnick et al., 1991, p. 1). There has also been a mentalist bias with several implications. Concepts (and other mental entities, cf. below) that make up the "structures and mechanisms of mind" have been conceived as located within individuals rather than between them. Cognition and conceptual knowledge are not construed as something that extends over time and space, and keeps people together in coordinated activities, but rather as mental phenomena that somehow cause behaviour. Jean Lave (1988) has referred to this view as a claustrophobic interpretation of human thinking. There is also a tradition in research and theorizing of disconnecting conceptual knowledge from its use in practical settings, and to study it as if the meaning of concepts can be established and understood outside social practices. Thus, concepts have been treated as non-situated phenomena that can be defined and understood without reference to the human practices in which they have been produced, and in which they do some concrete work. To learn a concept is to be able to define it rather than to use it. This tradition, in my interpretation, represents a very powerful assumption that exerts considerable influence on how formal teaching of conceptual knowledge is organized.

The recent attempts to bridge the gap between the abstractions of psychological theorizing and human concrete practices by considering the situated nature of human knowledge and thinking (cf., e.g. Chaiklin & Lave, 1993; Resnick et al., 1997; Rogoff, 1990) have illustrated how concepts and conceptual knowledge are intimately linked to practical action and physical skills. In fact, practical action in activities, such as building a house, navigating, mending a car engine, playing chess or baking and cooking, to mention just a few examples, is heavily dependent on insight and resources of a conceptual nature. The concrete steps involved in repairing the electric system of a car engine that does not ignite properly or in the making of a soufflé in the kitchen are charged with conceptual knowledge. Expertise in such activities presupposes conceptual and practical sophistication rather than one or the other. Even in a supposedly manual activity such as blacksmithing, the linking of the intellectual and the practical is essential, as has been described by Keller and Keller (1993) in their analysis of the work of a smith producing a certain kind of artefact — a skimmer handle. As these authors write, "rather than an exclusive emphasis on either the mental or the material, [one has to focus on] the inherent integration of internal representations and external actions and objects in the accomplishment of a task" (p. 141) in order to understand how the smith operates. Conceptual knowledge about the quality of the raw material (iron), how hot it should be when forging and hammering out, how the particular artefact produced is to be used in a range of practices when cooking, what makes the product functional (for instance, making sure that the proportions of the handle are such that it can be used with very hot liquids) as well as aesthetic criteria that will satisfy the demands of customers, are all part of the smith's activity of producing the object. His concrete actions can be seen as the nexus of manual skill and conceptual analysis.

In the community of scholars interested in human learning, cognitive development and instruction, as well as in a range of neighbouring areas, there is agreement that understanding conceptual change is essential for furthering our knowledge about human thinking. Vosniadou (1994, p. 3), for instance, recently argued that a "theory of conceptual change is a prerequisite for any comprehensive account of learning and can have important implications for instruction". Barsalou (1992) in a similar spirit claims that "concepts constitute the fundamental units of knowledge" (p. 153). My purpose in what follows is to raise some questions and discuss some issues that concern the nature of conceptual knowledge and how people appropriate such knowledge. In particular, I will attempt to outline an alternative to what I refer to as mentalist notions of the nature of conceptual knowledge that dominate current psychological theorizing. This alternative is grounded in a socio-cultural (Vygotsky, 1986; Wertsch, 1985, 1991) and social-cognitive (Rommetveit, 1992) interpretation of human thinking and communicative and practical action. Thus, although I would share the emphasis on the centrality of the role of conceptual change in human learning, I will argue that we need to move away from interpretations of concepts and conceptual change that put concepts solely into the minds of individuals and that disregard the intimate connections between discursive practices and individual learning. We need to consider the situated nature of human conceptual knowledge and that the medium that enabled people to come into contact with concepts is language, or rather communication, and communication is — by definition — first and foremost a collective activity.

A renewed interest in concept formation and conceptual knowledge was one of the important elements of the cognitive revolution in psychology which started in the late 1950s. Concept formation and conceptual thought was studied by Bruner and his colleagues (1956) in a series of classical and well-known experiments that were widely read and that exerted a considerable influence. In this work we find one interpretation of what concepts are and what functions they serve. Thus, Bruner and his colleagues conceived of concepts as categories of thought that enabled people to classify the world and discover differences and similarities. Subjects were exposed to stimulus items that varied in terms of four dimensions: form (circle, cross or square), colour (green, red or black), number of forms that were included in the stimulus (one, two or three circles, squares or crosses) and the border of the stimuli that could contain either one, two or three lines. Concept formation was construed as the ability to identify relevant dimensions in tasks, and use them when deciding what similarities and differences were critical to a particular concept and what were not. Subjects were required to identify the relevant characteristics of a member of a particular class that was chosen by the experimenter by selecting a combination of these four dimensions. The authors also showed that there were two different strategies that subjects seemed to use, wholist and partist strategies, respectively. The former, which implies that subjects started their analysis by forming an overall hypothesis with regard to the correct combination of dimensions, was more effective than the latter strategy, which implies focussing on one dimension at a time through the different exposures.

What Bruner and his colleagues studied can thus be conceived as one type of situation in which concepts are formed and used. The specific nature of the conceptual processes that were studied in these ingenious investigations was of course highly constrained by the demands of the experimental situation. The differences between concepts could be clearly defined and there were no fuzzy boundaries or ambiguities of the kind that are characteristic of concepts in natural language. Thus, there was a kind of purity to the concept formation and utilization of the kind that is characteristic of experimental studies. The exercise was merely one of concept identification and classification, and the significance of the personal biographies of individuals was neutralized by means of a task in which previous knowledge could be made use of in only a very limited way.

Domains of Knowledge and the Social Nature of Thinking

The tendency to regard concept formation as one, basic and in some sense homogeneous psychological process that can be attended to as such, which was characteristic of earlier research, is no longer uniformly accepted amongst scholars in the field. In recent years, there has been a rapid growth of interest in research on concept formation and conceptual knowledge based on the assumption that the specific nature of conceptual knowledge varies across different domains of human activity. A significant proportion of contemporary theorizing and research is concerned with the modes in which people acquire — as the metaphor goes — concepts characteristic of the different sciences and/or expert reasoning in various fields. In particular, the study of concept acquisition has become intense in the areas of teaching and learning within the natural sciences, where the problems of how people adapt to knowledge of a conceptual nature are readily visible. Concepts from physics, such as force, motion, energy and so on, seem to have become favourite objects of research for scholars interested in learning and conceptual change (cf., for instance, Vosniadou, 1994, for several examples).

From a theoretical perspective, this development represents an important step in a new direction, and, as Levine and Resnick (1993) have pointed out, the "recognition of the importance of domain-specific knowledge took the cognitive psychologist on a first step toward eventual inclusion of social factors as part of cognition" (p. 586). The current focus on domains of conceptual knowledge brings issues of how people use and understand concepts into more immediate contact with central and highly visible psychological and educational issues. The research at one level no longer relies on the image of human concept formation and thinking as decontextualized phenomena that take place outside the world of human experience and social practices.

The notion of how social factors are to be included is a tricky one for much of psychology, cognitive science, artificial intelligence and related fields. The success of the cognitive movement was largely a product of the construction of cognitive processes as something that, as it were, lay under or was more fundamental than anything that could possibly be influenced by "social factors". The object of inquiry studied was conceived as a Cartesian machinery manipulating and processing information in a manner that would be independent of social factors that have to do with culture, context and similar "nuisance variables" (Rogoff, 1984, p. 3). Today, however, such nuisance factors are very clearly at the centre of attention.

Interestingly enough, Bruner (1986,1990), in his later writings, appears as one of the most ardent proponents of this attempt to reorient psychological inquiry into human cognition towards a perspective in which social and cultural factors are considered to be relevant for understanding how human mentality is formed. Indeed, he goes so far as to claim that culture is "constitutive of mind" (1990, p. 33), and he is quite critical of the manner in which cognitive psychology developed and became a study of how physical systems manipulate symbolic expressions (cf. Bakurst, 1995).

Even though the recent emphasis on domain-specific knowledge makes the issue of what concepts are and how they are used much more tangible by locating them in scientific theories and other kinds of expertise, there are still clear residues of the basic mentalist ideology that lay behind the more traditional approach in which content was considered less interesting than the general processes of reasoning assumed to be identical across contents and contexts. One of these residues is to associate concepts with something that is exclusively or almost exclusively mental and cognitive. As Lemke (1990) points out, there is a legacy in the history of research on conceptual knowledge, which has taught us "to associate the term 'concept' with the term 'thinking' and to speak of the use of concepts as a 'mental' process" (p. 122). In cognitive psychology there is also a rich repertoire of such psychological terms that are used more or less synonymously with concept, or, alternatively, they are assumed to point to entities that entail conceptual elements. Thus, quite often, terms such as *mental models* [which happened to be the title of two volumes published in the same year by Gentner and Stevens (1983) and Johnson-Laird, (1983), respectively], *representations* and *schemas* are used to refer to entities that appear to have the same ontological status as concept and conceptual structure (or, alternatively, these entities are seen as the aggregation of concepts at more general levels). Following the metaphorics of these perspectives, concepts are mind-stuff and thus the proper target for a psychological — as opposed to a neurological — analysis of the mechanisms of mind. Thinking is essentially a matter of manipulating concepts in algorithmic fashions and something that can be studied outside social practices.

Naive and Less Naive Conceptual Worlds

Thus, in much of the literature there is a tendency to maintain central elements of a dualist perspective and to put concepts and conceptual knowledge within individuals, and to locate problems of learning in the alleged conflict between scientific concepts, on the one hand, and *naive beliefs* (McCloskey, 1983), *children's alternative frameworks* (Driver et al., 1985; Gilbert & Watts, 1983), *common-sense (or lay) theories* (cf. Bliss, 1989; Bliss & Ogborn, 1993) or whatever terms are used, on the other hand (for a bibliography of this literature, see Pfundt & Duit, 1991; for a recent critique, see Caravita & Halldén, 1994). The mentalist orientation of earlier research quite often seems to remain fairly intact, and even in the literature that emphasizes the domain-specific nature of learning and thinking, there is a tendency to decontextualize concepts and to reify them as something that exists *per se*.

To add some substance to my argumentation, let me take a few recent examples that illustrate this conflict between a scientific and commonsensical conceptual understanding of phenomena. In Sweden, there has recently been a national evaluation of the comprehensive school. A substantial proportion of this evaluation has been devoted to studying students' understanding of fundamental scientific concepts in the social and natural sciences. This investigation is also interesting, because it was carried out on statistically representative samples of thousands of students, a procedure that is most unusual in the study of concept formation. I will limit myself to some examples of the results in the studies of concept formation in the natural sciences amongst ninth graders (15- to 16-years old), where we can see what first appears to be a complete clash between everyday and scientific forms of reasoning. Thus, with respect to the concept of atom, the following question was given.

> Think of a wild animal in the forest. It consists of many atoms. The animal dies and it starts to decompose. What happens to the atoms when the animal decomposes and eventually cannot be seen at all? Explain your thinking? (Andersson et al., 1993a, p. 48, my translation).

The accounts given by students indicate that about a quarter of them argue that the atoms disappear or that they are transformed in some fashion; they dissolve, evaporate or vanish. About 4% of these students claimed that the atoms die. In the vocabulary of a student, this is formulated as: "Everything living has atoms in order to survive, and when we die, the atoms die as well", Andersson et al., p. 48, my translation). About 37% of the students gave answers that indicated that they were aware of the fact that atoms cannot dissolve or disappear. These replies include a broad variety of explanations in which some simply state that "Atoms cannot sort of disappear just because the animals die" (p. 49), and those that gave an indication of eco-cycles but without any account of what this implies in functional terms. A mere 5% of students were able to indicate that decomposing is a chemical process through which new molecules are generated by means of reactions and regroupings of atoms. About one-third of the students could not give any explanation of what happens at all or gave replies that were mere restatements of the question.

In terms of conceptual change and the adoption of a scientific model of atoms and how substances are transformed, these results would, at first, appear to be anything but satisfactory. At the end of several years of formal teaching of natural science concepts, there are just as many students who think that atoms die when organisms die as there are students who can indicate that there is a chemical restructuring through which the atoms form new molecules.

According to a standard interpretation within this tradition of research on naive theories, these results reveal "deficiencies in the formation of fundamental concepts held by students" (Andersson et al., 1993a, p. 81, my translation). However, what precisely does this mean? How do we infer that there is something that is problematic beyond the ability of students to coordinate with the language used in the question? Do students really have a concept of how atoms behave that is different, yet on a par with physicists' interpretations, when they claim that atoms die? Before discussing this issue further, let me take another example from the same source.

In one of the other examples used in this evaluation, students' understanding of the qualities and characteristics of air was tested by means of the following task (see Figure 1). The results show that with a liberal interpretation, which accepts alternatives three and four above as correct, 19% of the students manage to give a correct answer. A total of 42% claim that it is impossible to push the plunger into the syringe and this is seen as evidence of the students' lack of understanding of the characteristics of air as a gas that has substance. In the words of the authors, the results "show that pupils have difficulties with very elementary aspects of the concept of gas" (1993b, p. 78), and that they lack knowledge of the fact that "air can be compressed" (p. 75).

Can the plunger be pushed in?

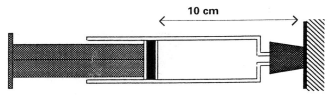

Johan pulls air into a plastic syringe and closes it off with a rubber plug as shown in the figure. No air can now get into or out of the syringe. The distance from the bottom of the syringe to the plunger is 10 cm (see picture). Johan then holds the rubber plug against a wall (see picture) and tries to push the plunger into the syringe. What happens? Mark with a cross!

0   The plunger cannot be pushed into the syringe

0   The plunger can be pushed another millimetre or so

0   The plunger can be pushed in another centimetre or so

0   The plunger can be pushed in several centimetres

These examples illustrate what seems to be the core message of much of this research. Scientific concepts are generally construed as being at odds with everyday reasoning and they are generally seen as abstract, symbolic and formal in contrast to the supposedly more concrete (and sloppier) versions that exist in natural language and that are "naive" or constitute "misconceptions". In the interesting work by Chi and her colleagues on concepts of elementary physics (Chi et al., 1994), to take another example, there is an assumption that there are sharp categorical differences between scientific concepts and those characteristic of everyday language. Thus, Chi et al. argue that the difficulties students have when encountering scientific concepts stem "from the existence of a mismatch or incompatibility between the categorical representation that students bring to an instructional context, and the ontological category to which the science concept truly belongs". Thus "students' naive conceptions represent a concept such as 'forces' as a kind of substance that an object possesses and consumes". And in students' minds, forces are entities that belong to the MATTER category, when in fact forces are a kind of Constraint-Based Interaction between two objects (a PROCESS)". The plunger can be pushed in until it hits the bottom of the syringe.

Cognition and Discourse

The mentalist origin of these accounts of differences between different discursive practices can be noticed on several levels. First, there is a continued use of the mentalist metaphors of concepts as entities that exist in the minds of individuals and that can be expected to appear whenever called for. The main difference seems to be that the concepts are now assumed to be located in domains rather than in general cognitive and logical processes, but this is a difference in degree rather than in principle. These domains in most studies appear as ready-made worlds of a cognitive nature rather than as arenas of shared human practices in which conceptual knowledge is part not only of thought processes but also of discourse, physical equipment and coordinated work (Pea, 1993). Students are exposed to concepts that science supposedly "has" rather than to concepts that scientists "use" in a discursive practice and in relation to concrete observations. These concepts are described as stable and ready to be applied rather than as tools that can be exploited for particular purposes and whose meaning has to be re-established and argued for every time they are used, and by means of which scientific objects are constituted as targets for research. In addition, there is the assumption that different discursive practices — such as science and common-sense — have concepts that represent identical phenomena, yet construe them differently. Thus, and to follow the examples above, "force" is construed as substance in everyday thinking and as an interactive phenomenon in science; atoms are dead objects in one discursive tradition that may not be transformed (except in nuclear fissions), and in another they are alive and can die. This is an interesting claim, which is rooted in a correspondence theory of language and that grossly underestimates the differences between institutionalized languages, such as those of various sciences and everyday thinking. The difference between these languages is not that one is naive and the other less so; the important difference is that human beings have the ability to develop mediational means that serve different purposes. Establishing a vertical dimension in terms of which differences in degree of naivety is the criterion is more a reflection of power structures that construe expertise in science and other institutional languages as something that is beyond the grasp of people who do not master those discursive patterns.

However, the interesting point from a technical and methodological perspective in most of these empirical studies is that student understanding is studied on the basis of how they respond either to specific terms or to problems that have already been formulated to fit scientific forms of reasoning. Thus, there is a tendency by scholars to ascribe certain forms of reasoning to people on the basis of what they say in response to linguistic items rather than to consider these answers as attempts to maintain a discussion by means of terms suggested by the stronger communicative partner, the experimenter or interviewer. Why focus on the answer, and why not assume that the questions posed in these kinds of studies mean very different things to respondents who vary in expertise? Why not assume that conceptual knowledge is constitutive of how we interpret questions and are able to locate them in a particular form of discourse as well?

To conclude, conceptual knowledge is discursive in nature. The mastery of concepts of science is the mastery not of some mystical and obscure thought processes, but of certain discursive practices or, in Vygotskian language, certain mediational means that account for the world in specific manners. There is nothing in our minds or brains that is more funda-mental than that. Since the empirical work in these studies is carried out by means of language, we ask questions, we analyse the replies given by students, and we should be very cautious in assuming what sort of conceptual processes we tap. And why not follow the suggestion made by Lemke (1990) and do away with the middle-man, the concept as a purely cognitive entity? Instead, we could study how people use language in situated practices, such as interviews and experiments, and how they account for phenomena. After all, discourse is all that we have access to when analysing problem-solving, alternative frameworks or whatever (Säljö, 1994). In my opinion, such a research strategy would demystify concepts and conceptual knowledge. Concepts would appear as semiotic tools that people use when talking and thinking.

From my point of view, it is important to note that one of the implications of this is the recognition that the conceptual register that people master when learning what is referred to as subject matter is discursive and very clearly of human origin; the concepts represent modes of understanding reality, communicative traditions and social practices that have evolved over long periods of time; in some of the sciences this history spans over two thousand years. Concept formation and conceptual knowledge, thus, are no longer abstract processes in which the individual can choose how to categorize the world at his or her own discretion. When learning conceptual knowledge, individuals are socialized into patterns of thinking, and into the concrete practices that go along with these patterns, which provide them with perspectives and resources that have been cultivated by others and that are made for action in specialized settings. In this sense, socialization in modern society is largely a matter of learning how to mean within the discursive practices offered by society through schools and other social institutions. In this sense, and to follow Bruner, culture is constitutive of mind and mediated action.

Utilizing such a perspective, I think we would discover that the real problems of the differences between scientific concepts and those characteristic of everyday life have less to do with conceptual difficulties or misconceptions on the part of so-called naive subjects and more to do with the problem that people do not have access to contexts in which science talk is functional and necessary. The laboratories and seminar rooms of scholars in which concepts are created and used, and where it is necessary and functional to make use of science talk, are in a very concrete sense not accessible to everyone. In fact, most people do not have access to any environments in which science talk is functional, and the results of the rich work on alternative frameworks illustrates this very clearly. Analysing classroom discourse against this background, I think we would find that it is very rare, even in science teaching, that students are in situations where they can make use of scientific forms of reasoning as authentic discursive practices.

7

Knowledge, Belief, and Opinion: A Sociologist's View of Conceptual Change

Devorah Kalekin-Fishman

Socrates:	Is not the first rule of good speaking that the mind of the speaker should know the truth of what he is going to say?
Phaedrus:	And yet, Socrates, I have heard that he who would be an orator has ... to do ... only with public opinion about them, and that from this source and not from the truth come the elements of persuasion.

Plato, Dialogues, Vol. 3, Phaedrus, p. 421.

Socrates:	Being is the sphere or subject matter of knowledge, and knowledge is to know the nature of being?
Glaucon:	Yes.
Socrates:	And opinion is to have an opinion?
Glaucon:	Yes.
Socrates:	Reflect: when a man has an opinion, has he not an opinion about something? Can he have an opinion which is an opinion about nothing?
Glaucon:	Impossible.
Socrates:	And not-being is not one thing but, properly speaking, nothing?
Glaucon:	True.
Socrates:	Then opinion is not concerned either with being or with not-being?
Glaucon:	Not with either.
Socrates:	And can therefore neither be ignorance nor knowledge?

Plato, The republic, pp. 219–220.

"A Second Look" at the Peace Process in the Middle East — Israeli Television, Monday, September 12, 1994:

Ehud Ya'ari: ... the problem is to know how to report the details as we know them ...

Amos Keinan (same programme): If in one square centimetre we can perform a revision of the relationship between the third world and the industrialized world by conceiving of how we can share a homeland, we will have created a model for the Arab countries, for the Near East and therefore from Karachi to Algier. And I believe that we can do it! ....

Danny Rabinowitz: The important thing is to have the right to tell their story in their own terms ...

Introduction

Distinguishing knowledge from belief and opinion raises knotty problems for thinkers, and resonates in important ways with the world of action. Each of the Socratic dialogues is at once a substantive claim that true concepts are timeless and a procedural bid to convince people to change the opinions and beliefs they hold. Politically drenched TV debates still devolve on similar problems as the quotes from a recent programme in Israel demonstrate. On the face of it, the three terms refer to different ways of categorizing concepts and predict different levels of difficulty in effecting conceptual change. The contexts for examining the issues are diverse.

Changing naive (and presumably mistaken) belief and opinion into knowledge is currently reconstructed as inquiry into how concepts come to be accepted and how change can be effected. This is a salient issue in all of the human sciences. Sharing an interest in human beings and how they function, the demarcated disciplines of philosophy, economics, political science, sociology and psychology, all focus on achieving descriptions of what people do and attempt to explain why they do them. The disciplines differ, however, in their underlying world views and theoretical assumptions, and thus in the concepts that concern them, the methods they deploy, and in their understanding of what is involved in conceptual change.

In this paper, I will derive a framework for relating to the topic of conceptual change from studies in cognitive psychology. I will then focus on the varied ways in which socio-logical theories contribute to an understanding of the issues involved. Finally I will suggest that some of the ideas can be integrated into theories of instruction. I will begin with some preliminary remarks about the point of departure.

In dealing with the question of conceptual change, psychologists usually premise that knowledge, the truth of which is established with the aid of scientific inquiry, is distinct from opinion or belief. Learners have beliefs and opinions that they think are true knowl-edge. Verifying the degree to which their notions are acceptable, and changing mistaken ideas for correct ones are the essential goals of instruction. Since notions are formulated in concepts, several different kinds of questions present themselves. There is the question of what it is all about — what are these hubs of interest called concepts? There are, further, the issues of how people acquire concepts and how they agree or manage to change them. A key concern is the mechanism of concept acquisition, and the embeddedness of concepts in individual experience. So psychologists look for the roots of mistaken opinions and beliefs, and investigate strategies for effecting changes in concepts at the level of opinion or belief into concepts that represent knowledge. Applying the findings of cognitive science is, hope-fully, the road to effective pedagogy.

In the view of sociology, the initial problematic is that of extra-individual reality. Both the formation of concepts and the possibility of conceptual change are part of the social process that individuals produce. According to this perception, the sources of all kinds of concepts, whether termed knowledge, opinion or belief, are to be found in the social order. Such a view enlarges the boundaries of the puzzle. The global question is how we should define the nature of society and describe its impact on the formation of the individual. Then there are the issues of what is available for conceptualization and how concepts are made accessible or imposed. An additional question is that of the ends to which concepts can, or should be changed. Furthermore, the conceptualization of education, the social institution invested with responsibility for imparting knowledge, is problematic. For sociologists, the structure of the framework, as well as what is presented in educational organizations as knowledge are topics to be analysed.

The foci of psychology and sociology are, then, quite different. There are, however, mutual implications. For one thing, the instructional context is generated by the social order and crafted within the limits of psychological processes. Concretely, instruction is conducted in a setting that produces a community *sui generis* with a decisive effect on individuals. For another, educators and pupils who enter instructional settings shape them by acting on their own surmised knowledge, opinions and beliefs about the nature of the social context and how people function. A responsible theoretical application to schooling of what is known about conceptual change must therefore refer to elements that are at the heart of the disciplinary concerns of both psychology and sociology.

Fundamentally, both disciplines agree in assigning responsibility for defining concepts to the realm of philosophy. We will start there.

What are Concepts and When do They Change?

The Socratic preoccupation with concepts as opposed to beliefs and opinions still engages philosophical discourse. In this century, Wittgenstein (1958) revolutionized thinking about concepts by drafting unconventional angles of vision on language and usage. His work has had far-reaching influence on philosophical explorations of conceptualization (see, for example, Keil, 1989; Peacocke, 1992). In current arguments about epistemic validity, the central philosophical issue is that of the justification for espousing a concept, the grounds for believing in concepts and for accepting that the process of attaining concepts is warranted (Kornblith, 1994; McDowell, 1994; Quine, 1973). Conditions for conceptual change are examined most prominently in writings on the philosophy of science (see, for example, Feyerabend, 1978; Kuhn, 1970; Prigogine & Stengers, 1984).

A nice summary of many of the issues is found in discussions of conceptual "revolutions" by Thagard (1992). I will cite some of his definitions. Finding traditional disputes over whether concepts are "entities" or "non-entities", innate or largely learned, fictions or emergent states, irrelevant, Thagard initiates an investigation of conceptual change by defining concepts as "complex structures ... [which] (1) [give] special priority to kind and part-whole relations that establish hierarchies and (2) [express] factual information in rules that can be more complex than simple slots" (p. 29). He suggests that when conceptualizing, a person holds to a specifiable totalizing scheme in which a concept can be identified as:

A kind of:

(with) Subkinds:

A part of

(with) Parts:

(in terms of) Synonyms:

(in terms of) Antonyms:

In addition a concept encompasses:

Rules: for deduction, explanation, problem solving

(and) Instances:

This definition is the cornerstone for hypothesizing that conceptual change is affected by the addition or deletion of parts, and by reorganization through coalition or decomposition as a result of differentiation. The change may signal a redefinition of the entire hierarchy (cf. Thagard, 1992, pp. 34–37).

Looking at historically verified shifts in scientific thinking, Thagard examines competing theories for coherence, analyses the nature of the concepts involved, their functions, their logical potential for change, and the differences between the rival systems. By combining deductive, statistical, schematic, analogical, causal and pragmatic (linguistic) strands of explanation in a computational model, Thagard concludes that conceptual changes (and most emphatically conceptual revolutions in science) come about when an innovative conceptual system proves to be more rational than the system in use. The helpfulness of this description in explaining the likelihood of conceptual change among children is accepted by many psychologists, as the next section will show.

Conceptual Change in the Eyes of Psychologists

In order to survey psychologists' views, I will look at notions of concepts, processes of configuring concepts, postulated conditions for conceptual change, and plausible mechanisms that make change possible.

Definitions

Echoing philosophical analyses, psychologists assume that concepts reflect recognized regularities such as those of set-subset and whole-part. According to Pines (1985, p. 108), concepts take shape when perceived regularities "are labeled with words" which interpret the world. These categories of description (Johansson et al., 1985) are taken for signs, symbols or isomorphs of perception "and used in thought and communication". Concepts turn into pre-conditions of perception because they organize sense-data (Strike & Posner, 1985, p. 215).

Configurational Processes

Concepts, then, are the "furniture of the conscious mind ..", the resources of consciousness. Configurations of concepts are disclosed when experience is transformed into representations (Burns, 1992; Perner, 1991; Strike & Posner, 1985). As elements that combine into propositions and algorithms, concepts are embedded in skills and episodes (White, 1985), which in turn are encoded in schemata (Norman & Rumelhart, 1975). Usually, new information is encoded with existing schemata, but where concepts are exposed to varied situations, a schema may undergo evolution, or a fresh schema will be created. It will include the organizational patterns, the kinds of information represented, the units of representation (format) and the nature of the relationships among the units of information (Kroll & Deutsch, 1992).

Conditions

Conceptual change is induced when there is some discrepancy between current conceptions and the capacity to explain experience with their help. A condition for accepting new concepts, therefore, is an awareness of their capacity to explain or predict phenomena. A further condition for conceptual change is the consistency of the new conceptualizations with other knowledge (Fiske & Taylor, 1984; Vosniadou, 1994). This description of conditions for change matches conceptual change in lay persons and in learners to paradigmatic shifts in the realm of science (Kuhn, 1970). As a matter of fact, substantial evidence has been assembled in psychological research to the effect that in the areas of cognition and learning, children, and perforce adults, are likely to cognize in ways that differ little from those of scientists (Deloache & Brown, 1987).

Perner (1991) focusses on a broader explanation of the conditions of cognitive development. In his view, conceptual change is intimately connected with developmental changes in behaviour. These changes indicate that representations of desires, goals and reasons for acting in certain ways in situations have been remodelled. Relying on research into children's orientations to others, Perner concludes that such changes are based on evolving theories; for normally-developing children achieve a conceptually configured theory of situations during the first 2 years of life, and a full-blown theory of mind at about the age of 4 years.

Mechanisms

Exploring the relationship between conceptualized reality and the content of concepts, Baron-Cohen (1995) attributes conceptualization to brain mechanisms, which enable the kind of theorizing assumed by Perner. He designates mechanisms such as the interactional

Intentionality Detector (ID), Eye Direction Detector (EDD), and Shared Attention Mechanism (SAM), as well as the Theory of Mind Module (ToMM). These mechanisms of mind
actively obtain cues from others, which are configured into concepts and, when appropriate,
spur conceptual change. Constructs of one or more of these mechanisms have proved
important in diagnosing malfunctions and specifying deficiencies in autism (Cosmides et
al., 1992).

Salomon (1993) specifies some of the relational mechanisms that optimize normal
thinking. His theoretical approach is confirmed in classroom research into the effects of
"social and cultural elements on the acquisition of intellectual skills" (cf. Voss et al., 1995).
Deliberately cultivating the "division of cognition" through collaborative learning is
considered advantageous because, in the views of the psychologists, interaction is a moti-
vator; and mutual criticism spurs clear thinking.

Another aspect of this turn in research is the assertion that because of increasing technological sophistication, children acquire "true knowledge" outside of school as well at a very
early age. Thus, school achievements are linked to learning that goes on outside the classroom and "situated learning", an adaptation of the "apprenticeship model " to activities in
the classroom, is a logical inference (Levine et al., 1993; Voss et al., 1991).

The Need for a Sociological View of Conceptual Change

To show that it is useful to explore conceptual change from a sociological point of view, I
will first point out how both the philosophical and the psychological approaches cited
above converge to issues at the core of the sociological project. Then I will examine how
sociological theorizing can enhance an understanding of conceptual change.

While declaring that he is omitting the "social context of scientific change" (Thagard,
1992, p. 10), and justifying the omission by pointing to algorithms from the area of artificial
intelligence, Thagard (1992, p. 112) actually introduces considerations that require sociological explanation. For one thing, he recognizes that "society" is an entity, although he
defines it as a region completely separate from the world of real science, a region to which
the foibles of individual scientists are relegated. He admits that "even a scientist [is] ...
driven by personal motivations of success and fame ..." but insists that the *prescriptive
norms of the scientific community* [my emphasis] support his view that scientific conceptualization is utterly neutral and independent of "social factors". Waving the magic wand of
rationality, Thagard maintains that science as a whole is able to transcend the personal goals
of its fully human practitioners because of the institutional commitment to experimental
evidence and explanatory argument (Thagard, 1992, p. 113). Paradoxically, the very
defence of "institutional commitment" demonstrates the centrality of the social context, for
it is a commitment based on opinions of a community (a group) of scientists. And the
descriptors represent beliefs that privilege the community of scientists.

The psychological literature at once leads up to the social context and regresses from it. In
the large, psychologists acknowledge that selves are "transactional", for "most of our
approaches to the world are mediated through negotiation with others" (Bruner, 1987, p. 93).
In recent work there are attempts at more precise typologies (see Perkins & Salomon, 1989).
In addition, there is literature in which evidence is marshalled to show that concepts have to

be understood in context (among others, see Fischer et al., 1991; Halldén, 1994; Nunes, 1993; Nunes et al., 1993).

Whether the mechanisms of conceptualization and conceptual change are envisaged as dependent on the perception of regularities achieved through attention to the human environment (Baron-Cohen, 1995; Perner, 1991), on a confrontation with problems that cannot be solved with known concepts (Strike & Posner, 1985), or on the formation of schemata that are adequate to wider and wider ranges of situated actions (Norman & Rumelhart, 1975), psychologists do recognize that concepts are connected with social relations. At this juncture, the province of sociology begins. Our purpose, therefore, is to examine how notions about conceptual change can be enhanced by reference to sociological analyses of the social context.

Sociological Views of Conceptual Change

Since sociology focuses first and foremost on context-social relations embedded in social structure, sociological views of the formation of concepts and of concept change rely in the main on the clarification of the mechanisms that govern social processes. In relating to concept change, therefore, the central sociological questions hinge on the nature of the person presupposed by a theorized social structure, the functions of concepts in constituent relations, and on how meanings are likely to alter across space and over time. These issues are treated quite differently in different schools of sociology. To illustrate, I will summarize some orientations articulated in sociological classics and discuss how each depicts the context, identifies individuals, situates concepts and signals bases for concept change. Following the outline, I will point out some of the connections between the sociological interpretations of concept change and the realizations of processes, conditions and mechanisms elaborated by cognitive psychologists. Finally, I will go on to derive implications for theories of learning and instruction.

Conceptual Change and Approaches to Social Evolution

One persistent notion in sociology is the idea that there is a parallel, or at least an analogy, between phylogeny and ontology. In the view of evolutionists, prevailing concepts are linked to the level of development to which a society has evolved, and changes are traceable to inevitable progression. Despite the fact that theories of this kind all agree on the efficient cause of conceptual change, different views of evolutionary mechanisms lead to different approaches to the sources of concepts and their configurations as well as to conditions of change. I will cite briefly approaches to social evolution that are proposed by Auguste Comte (1798–1857), Herbert Spencer (1820–1903) and the 20th century school of structural-functionalism headed by Talcott Parsons (1902–1979).

The man who named the science of sociology, Auguste Comte, formulated a "law of human progress" for society as a whole much like a theory of development with alternate points of stability and progression (1907)[1]. The scientific investigation of society was therefore to be divided into studies of "social statics" and "social dynamics". In Comte's view, just as creatures conserve an identity as they mature and improve in their functioning, societies, too, pass through successively higher stages. He pinpointed three key phases in the unfolding of societies' potential, characterizing each phase by a type of thinking with its emblematic conceptual configurations. Each phase was notable for the tensions created by the confrontation of conservative mechanisms with mechanisms that herald continued evolutionary change. The dynamic social changes he delineated were the gradual and graduated passage from the "theological" to the "metaphysical", and ultimately, to the "scientific", or the "positive" stage, the stage of highest achievement. Concept change is thus a function of society's transitions from one plane of development to the next, an inevitable unfolding of the core potential of the human race.

In the Comtean framework, the family, as the agency of reproduction, is responsible for relaying to every one of its members, the conceptual configurations appropriate to the society. From birth, individuals acquire concepts that coordinate with the level of evolution attained by the society as a whole to date, and meaningful conceptual change occurs in tandem with evolutionary changes of phase. Only in the stage of positivism, can human beings conceive phenomena rationally and scientifically. To support his inference, Comte could explain the founding of the science of society in 19th century France by the developmental stage of French society.

The British sociologist, Herbert Spencer (1820–1903), addressed the issue of evolution from a different vantage point. By contrast with Comte, he abstracted his description of social development directly from biological growth, fixing on structural complexity as a signal of development and change. The raw material for social structure was, in his view, the shapeless "horde". Because of the need to adapt to the environment, the amorphous band gradually learns how to divide socially necessary tasks among its members, and thus structures a community. Over the course of time, societies evolve from the simplest division of labour (hunting, gathering, reproducing) to sets of increasingly compound structures. Growth and intricacy are the product of constantly expanding needs; they follow from the preceding structures, and, in turn, give promise of further evolution. The traits of human beings and the content of human thinking derive from the relation of a society to its physical and social surround. These evolve because relations to other groups, the social environment, require more highly differentiated internal structures. In Spencer's system, the process of social differentiation is inevitably linked to the differentiation of concepts. Conceptual configurations, ever more complex, mirror social changes (Spencer, 1937).

In the 20th century, the notion of evolution as the basis for concept change has taken on additional gear among sociologists of the functionalist school (e.g. Davis, 1949; Levy, 1966; Merton, 1968; Moore, 1963; Parsons, 1937, 1966, 1977). Concerned with the interrelations of action in different areas of social living, this school has extended the Spencerian view to focus on distinguishing among social functions. The theories of this school are based on the assumption that society is at once an integrated system and a set of analytically isolatable systems in a cybernetic relationship. These include those of the economy (adaptation to the physical environment), the polity (collective decisions about goals and about the means for their attainment), systems of kinship and education (the maintenance of patterns from generation to generation), all driven by a propensity to integration, the creation of a

---

[1]Following the logic of an evolutionary framework, Comte (1907) was certain that investigations of the social should be conducted, like studies of biological organisms, by means of "observation, experimentation, and comparison". Overall, however, the departmentalization of the discipline had, in his view, to be adopted from physics.

common culture, the backbone of which are concepts and modes of conceptualization. The common language, the shared symbols, the collective awareness of transcendental truths are conceptualized as elements in overarching socio-cultural formations.

The cultural system directs the implementation of social relations, fulfilling the operational imperatives of the economy and the polity, regulating the formation of personality and organizing the physical environment. Adequate coordination of these related systems ensures survival. The content of concepts is derived from the cultural system, but their application is effected on the level of collective and personal agency. Agents use concepts in the performance of action. They set goals, select normative means to insure goal attainment, and mobilize energy to achieve their target. In this framework, concept consistency, or non-change, sustains a society's moral right to survive. Concepts change, however, when, over time, actor-agents modify goals, means or motivations in order to maximize functional effectiveness.

Conceptual Change and Approaches to Social Action

The qualities of agency are explored in detail by several different sociological theorists. I will allude to discussions by Max Weber (1864–1920) and then to arguments of the exchange theorists, George Homans (1910–1993) and Peter Blau (b1918).

For his inquiry into social action, action (by "ego") oriented to another, Max Weber delineated "ideal types", sets of abstract conceptual configurations, "subjectively adequate on the level of meaning" (Weber, 1947), which help explain social action and social forms. Two "ideal" orientations to social action have a basis in rationality. When underpinned by instrumentality, social action is configured by a rationality of means and ends (*Zweckrationalität*). When underpinned by a devotion to principle, social action is configured by a desire to preserve cherished values (*Wertrationalität*). Alternatively, there are types of concept configurations that impel social actions according to tradition, or according to a discernment of charisma, the recognition of godly gifts in persons or in their roles. It was clear to Weber that actual relationships originate in a melange of intentionalities, which infuse social action and permeate society. But with the aid of ideal types, he could isolate the mechanisms that determine social action.

In his analysis of macro-social structures Weber investigated the balance of formal and substantive rationality in the conduct of civil society. "Formal rationality" refers to considerations of expediency, the efficiency with which numerical calculations of technical means correlate with demarcated ends. "Substantive rationality", on the other hand, relates to "ultimate ends" which may be "ethical, political, utilitarian, hedonistic, ...[refer to] ... social distinction, ...[or to] ... social equality ..." (Weber, 1947, p. 185). The key to conceptual change in the large then is to be found in the compounding of prevailing technologies and the kinds of significance attributed to the experience of being human. The modern world, with its rapidly growing emphasis on technical rationality, was, to his mind, propelling industry and industrial organization toward an ever more rigid bureaucracy. This constitutes a conflation of substantive with formal rationality. Thus, the accelerating effects of rationalization were turning society into an "iron cage" of means-ends rationality, throttling affective and humane forces.

In society, as Weber described it, conceptualization is invested with the capacity to initiate context. Surface continuity and conceptual stability may be promulgated by a dominant worldview. Individuals' concepts are likely to change as goals are configured for specific domains: religious, political and economic. In the dynamic of the working structures, moreover, the interpenetration of the orientational ideal types ("subjectively adequate on the level of meaning") in specific circumstances is precarious. This understanding contrasts with the approach of the evolutionists in that it endows the stream of situated historical events with prodigious significance.

Exchange Theory and Conceptual Change

In the theoretical framework developed by George Homans and extended by Peter Blau, society is depicted as a marketplace, and social action is regulated by market considerations. Principles of reinforcement and mechanisms of exchange explain the behavioural and affective outcomes of interaction. Under market conditions, the individual's recognition of surfeit is a function of excessive positive reinforcement (Homans, 1961). Blau (1964) argued that these postulates can explain not only the relations between individuals, but also the development of elites as well as the relationships between superordinate and subordinate groups. In his view, the all-encompassing goal of groups and of individuals is to maximize profits by exchanging goods and rewards. Since mutuality is profitable only as long as its rewards are felt to be valuable, conceptions will vary according to supply and demand, i.e. according to the management of programs of reinforcement. Changes in conceptualizations occur as conditions of exchange are transformed. In sum, to conduct the kinds of relationships that exchange theorists postulate, people conceptualize the arena of the "marketplace" in which they negotiate; weigh the likelihood of rewards or sanctions resulting from alternative patterns of action; and plan for maximum profit.

Conceptual Change and Symbolic Interaction

Symbolic interactionists such as George Herbert Mead (1863–1931), and his intellectual descendants (e.g. Becker, 1968; Becker & McCall, 1990; Harré, 1972; Stryker, 1980) define role-taking as the basis of human development. They describe concept formation as the direct outcome of situated encounters in which symbols are exchanged (Mead, 1934). People associate by swapping verbal and non-verbal gestures that embody concepts. At birth, infants act because of physiological pressures. Caretakers' responsive gestures based on interpretations of these actions as symbolic, convey an appreciation of the role of infant, which turns into the heart of the infant's understanding of the world. In the course of early development, children's interaction consists of isolated gestures. Further on in their development, very young children imitate chains of behaviours that are typical behaviours of "significant others". Gradually they crystallize their conceptualization of appropriate conduct to define the configurations of behaviours as an interactional tool, a fully-fledged role. The most significant breakthrough occurs when the concept of any given role is generalized. On the basis of the contextualized generalization, the individual is aware of how she or he, together with others, is interacting in roles so as to conform to the "rules of the game", the norms of her or his society. Thus, the tot may imitate movements made by one of the significant others. Later, she or he may combine movements into a coherent task: Mom puts on a coat and picks up a briefcase. At a later stage, she or he will be capable of locating these operations in a frame of social relations with available others: Mom goes out to meet her colleagues at work.

The model of successively imitating gestures, learning roles and acting according to the rules of some game recurs throughout the life-course. As people take on diverse roles in varieties of affiliations, concepts are extended and changed. There is an accretion of roles as new games are encountered, and, with the "thickening" of experience, a modification of the concepts acquired heretofore.

Mead's description of maturation, as occasioned by chains of situations and their representations, is the foundation of a constructivist view of the individual. The symbols exchanged with significant others and ultimately attributed to "generalized" others are stored on the basis of the interpretations that are necessarily unique to every situation and to every individual. Stores of concepts steer action. In new sites, individuals interpret events and relationships by enlisting the principles that buttress their personal cumulative stock of gestures in order to decide on the roles involved and on seemly actions (Berger & Luckmann, 1972). In every context, the composite systems of construals that prop role partners' constructions of their selves mesh to determine the construction of situations, the nature of the context. In this school of sociological theory, constructivism is a *description* of the human condition rather than a *prescription* that may or may not be heeded[2].

The modes of construction and the generalized motivations are explored in the work of Erving Goffman (1922–1982), who focuses on concrete action in situations. Since *all* action is oriented to others, he described the myriads of concepts that inhere in actual events by compiling "ethologies" of people and their types of reasoning as attuned to different milieux. Goffman adapts mechanisms that Mead stipulates, and details the substance of the mutual interpretations that are presented and re-presented on the basis of concepts, and abstracted (meta-represented) over time as principles. The grounds for conceptualization are notions of self, of others, of the environment, and of the social structures that infuse persons' self-presentations. Information is filtered through a repertoire of dramatically viable scenes. The ability to adopt character changes, and to deploy different sets of concepts according to backdrop is the measure of a person's control over the information that is available "frontstage" or "backstage", and of the reactions of others (Goffman, 1959, 1967). Conditions that facilitate concept change derive from a framework of scenic arrangements, which shift with actors' struggle to guarantee themselves with the regard, the respect and the deference that make life worth living.

Harold Garfinkel and the ethnomethodologists also relate interaction to stores of concepts. Reversing the delineation of concept-into-action (conceptualization as the basis for action), which is the premise of Weber's explication of social action as well those of Mead, Berger and Luckmann, and Goffman; this school of sociology views conceptualization as a retrospective process (Garfinkel, 1967). The macro-social context is an aggregate

[2]Personal construct psychology, as developed by Kelly (1955) and his many followers, is based on similar assumptions. These assumptions are, however, rarely applied in cognitive psychology. In their exploration of students' views of science, Gilbert et al. (1985) use Kelly's technique of the repgrid. They do not, however, draw conclusions beyond the cognitive functioning that is elicited through an "interview-about-instances".

of doing, performing "the marvellous mystery" called society, which is a conglomerate of routine situations. These practices supply an unquestionable, and for the most part unquestioned, background to on-going interchanges. All together, the social mystery is sustained by everybody's reliance on "taken for granted" sited wholes. Conceptualizations can be ignored until actors are pressured by discrepancies to examine performances retrospectively. Having participated in an interchange, people can look back and see, so to speak, what concepts "underlay" their actions. When actions do not take the expected course, searches for meaning are carried out overtly and interactionally.

Garfinkel emphasizes the hazards of the enterprise. Concept change is at once uncontrollable because it takes form only in retrospect, and inevitable by the sheer contingency of experience. In dealing with breaches of the taken-for-granted, we have to compromise with incoherent expectations, choosing among projected alternatives according to roughly predictable probable consequences. We allow room for error, go along with gut feelings about predictability, decide whether it is important to apply the rules at all costs ("Cartesian rules") or whether to put interpersonal solidarities ("tribal rules") to the fore (Garfinkel, 1958). These considerations invade every type of action, including the actual *performance* of scientific research by contrast with the so-called norms of science. Research is, in this view, a common-sense way of applying concepts to a set of routines, like all common-sense accomplishments, and at the mercy of common-sense (see also Schuetz, 1967).

The perception of conceptualization and concept change as inescapably connected with practical routine actions has proven useful in analysing conceptual transformations in the social sciences (Button, 1991). It is echoed in recent bids to construct "a historical sociology of concept formation" by examining "how concepts work as they do" (Somers, 1995, p. 115). If we accept the assumption that all concepts are reflexive and relational, they can only be known "by reconstructing the public histories of their construction", i.e. by examining their usage retrospectively (Somers, 1995, p. 140; see also Hacking, 1990)[3].

Concept Change and Society as Constraint

As we have seen, there are major theoretical differences as to the nature of society, the aspect of the social structure that has the greatest impact on concept formation, the conditions and the mechanisms involved in transmitting concepts. In this section, I will discuss theoreticians who stress the capacity of society to oblige people to accept prevailing concepts.

According to Durkheim (1858–1917), concepts are inevitable products of the physical structure of a society, the division of labour and its religious orientation(s). Together with Mauss, Durkheim (1965 [1915]) demonstrated that the physical disposition of the community,

---

[3]In political science, scrutiny is fixed on how concepts work in relation to historical processes (Skocpol, 1979; Tilly, 1975). A collection of papers by political scientists (Ball et al., 1989) demonstrates an important shift in emphasis by focusing on language change while locating the political context as background. Supporting the axiomatic notion that "a ... political language is a medium of shared understanding and an arena of action because the concepts embedded in it inform the beliefs and practices of political agents" (Ball et al., 1989, p. 1), participating authors examine historical variations in the significance of concepts of government: concepts such as "constitution" "democracy", "the state", "party", "citizenship" "corruption" as well as "property" and "revolution". Overall, the papers examine the hypothesis that conceptual change can be shown to be associated with political innovation.

the topography of the environment as well as the distribution of the population in architectonic structures have had a decisive impact on modes of conceptualizing number and space.

Durkheim theorized that the type of solidarity characteristic of a community is the ground for physical arrangements. Solidarity is, thus, the mainstay of human life and the foundation of viable concept configurations. In older societies labour was divided so that workers were for the most part interchangeable. Such a distribution of labour made for what he called "mechanical" solidarity and imposed fitting types of concepts. By contrast, the division of labour under capitalism is such that the contributions of all the workers combine into a competent whole, like the organs of living creatures. Durkheim recognized these as societies integrated in "organic solidarity". The specific form of social solidarity is realized in the *conscience collective* — an expression that refers to both the *consciousness* of the collective and its *conscience*. Individuals born into a community are constrained to accept the resources that constitute this consciousness through their exposure to physical constructions and their placement in the social structure.

The mechanisms of constraint are embodied in religious practices, with further conceptual complexity deriving from the cardinal distinction between the sacred and the profane. In Durkheim's view, the experience of the collective is identical to the experience of the godhead. For this reason, collective practices of sacred rituals are invigorating, supplying participants with the strength they need to carry out daily life in their diffuse private worlds. In performing the necessary tasks of the profane, energy is dissipated, and, once spent, must be replenished by further participation in the sacred, by renewed contact with the community as a collective. Since the sanctity of the community is realized in regular actions at predetermined moments in pre-defined places, this experience of moral imperatives is an inescapable classification of times as well as spaces. The concrete realization of social solidarity in conditions of the space–time–activity of the sacred generates the strength of personhood.

In sum, then, concepts of self-identity, like concepts of number and causality, and space and time, are inexorably implanted by society. This does not ensure that everyone has reliable knowledge at his or her disposal. There are social conditions that lead to misconceptions, errors of opinion and belief. These are a danger to the collective in that they undermine solidarity and threaten morality. Moreover, they mark a danger to the individual because they may lead to anomie. Such confusion as to acceptable notions and prevailing norms is a social handicap that Durkheim spotted as a situated cause, among others, of suicide (1951 [1897]).

In a sense, it is possible to classify Karl Marx (1818–1883) with the evolutionists. By contrast with the Durkheimian approach, Marxian theories view conceptual change as an indicator of progressive liberation. Marx (1974 [1857–1858]) postulated a historical dialectic that assured linear progress, with the accomplishment of true communism, the "withering away of the state", and the institution of a classless society as the ultimate achievement of social development. In the process, he specified that concepts are thus consequent upon economic and political relations. A "superstructure" of conceptual configurations reinforces existing relations by governing all forms of high culture and knowledge. This super-structure buttresses the advantageous positions of the dominant class. Only when, within the dialectic of relations, the oppressed find ways to overcome subjugation, do changes in the ("base") structures of relations emerge, warranting new conceptual configurations (in the "super-structure"). Meaningful conceptual change achieved in political contest is a redivision of reality, which supports the revised division of labour and newly recognized relations. The inference is that concept change is intricately connected with purposive political action (Marx, 1974 [1857–1858]).

Bourdieu (1991) points out that liberation requires a detailed understanding of the challenges presumably localized in the superstructure. The owners of the means of production control economic capital and have access to political resources. Although the transformation of the base structure is necessary for conceptual change, it is not a sufficient condition. Diverse groups exercise control over symbolic capital — language, mythologies, cultural capital (the arts and distinctions among fine arts and crafts) and over social capital — stratification and the allocation of prestige. To effect modifications, it is necessary to contest the controlling interests in each field. Therefore, concept change may occur at different rates and in different ways depending on the types of capital available to groups and the types of intra-field relations that prevail.

Implications for Learning and Instruction

The practical problems of conceptual change are faced by educators who attempt to bring learners to a desirable level of school achievement. In this section I will point out what is implied for teaching and learning by different types of theories.

A survey of sociological theories was undertaken in order to demonstrate diverse ways in which it is possible to unwrap relevant elements in blanket terms such as "context", "collaboration" and "pedagogy". Limitations of space prevent a complete explication of the topic, but I will summarize some of the lessons that can be learnt by illustrating what different theoretical persuasions imply in regard to the organization of education and its social functions. This will indicate the ramifications of a given sociological point of view for actions related to schooling and pedagogy. First I will discuss theories that shed light on goals regarding education. These include the evolutionary approaches, theories of social action, and some of the interactional paradigms. Then I will point out some approaches, theories of social action, and some of the interactional paradigms. Then I will point out some lessons for understanding processes.

Goals

Evolutionary Models

Sociological models that derive from an evolutionary approach view organized education as the agent that helps individuals and hence the collective as a whole to achieve adaptation. Given that the availability of concepts depends on the developmental stage of the social structure and, that the human being is a "naturally" maturing biological organism, the meeting of the individual with available concepts is mediated by institutionalized education, the socially sanctioned intervention in individuals' lives. Therefore, teaching has to be, and naturally is, coordinated with the felt needs of society. Individuals' success is measured by the extent to which they acquire the skills that the environment demands. The short-range challenge for educators is to match the content and process of learning to the level of adapt-ability that can be expected of children at different ages with the learning of new concepts. The goal is to ease adaptation as an ongoing part of living. Collective success is measured by the capacity of the group to adapt to long-range environmental changes by accepting para-digmatic change. They are "natural" when societies progress to a higher level of ideological functioning (Comte, 1907) or become more complex (Spencer, 1937). In the long term, society can be counted on to convey the kinds of changes that are required to educational institutions (Spencer, 1945).

In current forms of these theories, social evolution is a highly articulated process, and adaptation is conceived to be multidimensional. Society as a whole has to adapt to the phys-ical environment for self-maintenance and survival. But the social system is analysed as one of several systems and, in the overall picture, every system is an environment for every other (Parsons, 1966). Schools have a highly articulated mandate. Instruction has to enable the acquisition of planning skills — the capacity to take decisions and find the means to carry them out. People are constrained to become attuned to the kinship group, and the school, so as not to undermine the patterns that maintain healthy social functioning. And the tool for adaptation is the successive acquisition of adequate representations. These include a grasp of the universalistic values, beliefs, norms and language, which make it possible for actors to get along with others in the environment. Instructors have to work toward adapta-tion by reference to all the social institutions. Language and the verbalized or unverbalized symbols connected with belief systems are the means for attaining appropriate representa-tions. The circularity is intended. Relevant representations make it possible to learn how to define goals and make plans to attain them, and ultimately to adapt to an appropriate status-role in the given social world.

Social Action

From Weber's theoretical approach, we learn that schools are conducted to serve the macro-social order by furthering belief systems that support the intertwining of prevailing formal (technical) rationality and substantive rationality. These orientations infuse the organization and administration of schooling (bureaucracy), as well as the content (Weber, 1947).

In classrooms, the aim is for individual learners to be able to operate with an appropriate repertoire of "subjectively adequate" motives for social action. Because of the ambiguity of most social structures, the dynamic of the interaction of the two types of rationalities presents problems for conceptualization and for conceptual change. To monitor conceptual-izations and their changes, instructors supervise how the learner mixes instrumental rationality and expressive (value-based) rationality; the learner's concern for tradition, and the regard for submission to charisma.

An incapacity to attain conceptual change is signalled by the incongruence of representa-tions. When learners grow up in diverse subcultures, the types of orientation shared by some groups of learners may be incompatible with the forms of schooling and the structures of learning materials. This metacognitive equipment will influence responses to content and the capacity for acquiring new skills. Neither instructor nor learner is likely to be aware of the extent to which there is a readiness to adopt a given weighted mixture of "ideal types" of thought in orienting oneself to social action.

Critical Models

In the critical models of sociological theory, it is axiomatic that schools are organized and curricula formulated to perpetuate existing power relations. Yet if the means of manipulation are understood, the organization and the curriculum content can serve to overturn the loci of power. Researchers of this school of thought to study the practical mechanisms of restricting, controlling, or regulating action and knowledge with a view to providing tools for activism. The presupposition is that the dominated are seduced into an acceptance of the concepts and the representations as well as the skills that serve the given "hegemonic" order (Gramsci, 1985). These all-encompassing representations are presented as *the* modes of perception and conception, brooking no alternatives (Bourdieu, 1994).

Among critical sociologists, organizing education so as to separate out elites and to fix "weak" populations is interpreted as part of a deliberate project to perpetuate the status quo. The extreme formulation of criticism points out that conceptual change is actually a goal only under two distinct sets of conditions. Dissident groups who attain conceptual change can better their situation by taking political action. The dominating groups will then do everything they can to thwart the concept change that portrays a different distribution of power. Dominant groups are also, however, constantly seeking new concepts to further the entrenchment of domination. For the advancement of the existing order, conceptual change that benefits production is the prerogative of the chosen who are deputed to control knowledge (Bernstein, 1971–1990; Giroux, 1989; Popkewitz, 1991).

Symbolic Interaction

In the writings of symbolic interactionists goals in education are implied. Goals underlie myriad agendas for performing a (school) class. Here, however, the goals are viewed from the point of view of the partners to the instructional situation, and of the atmosphere of formal learning. Goffman's dramaturgical approach reminds us that, in every situation, each participant aspires to preserve or to increase self-esteem. Among ethnomethodologists, situated goals are those associated with "keeping things going as they should" (however this is perceived), which is the basis for moral certainty in the performance of everyday living.

Process

The sociological approaches that describe process relate to organization and curriculum as well as to classroom relations. According to Durkheim, schools are necessarily the institutional expression of collective morality and of shared concepts. The modes and content of instruction stem from sources that are inescapable because the imposition of concepts is not a conscious decision, but a natural outgrowth of the life of a collective. Ongoing classroom processes signal the monitoring of congruence (Durkheim, 1956).

Approaches in critical sociology describe educational process as the countenance of control of all capital. The mechanisms of classroom learning rely on the resources the members of the group — instructor(s) and learner(s) — command, the shares they have in the various types of capital available, and in the dispositions toward dominance that they have developed in their lives up to the particular learning situation (Bourdieu & Passeron, 1977). Pedagogical work is imparting a *habitus*, a set of spiritual and intellectual, as well as bodily dispositions (Bourdieu, 1994). In a very tangible sense, then, classroom processes insert social structures into the consciousness, incorporating and perpetuating them in the bodies of those educated. The capital that is "in the hands" of the learner in different areas of (extra-school) living will either facilitate or impede perceptions of meaning, the ability to apply those perceptions to specific events and to conceptual configurations. The incorporated structures ensure the self-censorship that controls representations, modes of planning, anticipated sociation and the structure of the immediate context (Bourdieu, 1991, 1994). No wonder that, eventually, learners develop massive opposition to unregulated initiatives of conceptual change (Kalekin-Fishman, 1987; Willis, 1977).

Awareness in the instructor of limitations on pupils' control of types of capital that are valued at the school, will sensitize her or him to the difficulties learners confront when faced with the subject matter canon. Pedagogy may then actually facilitate the learners' acquisition of symbolic capital.

The self and its needs are at the heart of implications of exchange theory for instructional practice in the classroom. By situating teaching and learning strategies in market rationality, this framework provides a kind of calculus for assessing the rate of conceptual change according to measures of (i) the losses that are likely to be incurred by sticking to existing concepts, and (ii) the relative value of rewards for conservative or revised, progressive conceptualization.

The centrality to instruction and learning of the mechanisms of symbolization and the formation of representations is the global conclusion from an exploration of approaches included under the heading of symbolic interaction. The exchange of gestures that Mead describes is a model for the process of learning and instruction that can be presumed to be going on in every school situation, events with both overt and covert content. The overt content is multileveled, providing a basis of naming (objects, persons, relationships, situations), a proposed set of recipes-for-action, as well as generalizations, or overarching principles that cue the learner into further applications of the set of learned concepts (Berger & Luckmann, 1972). The covert content is the realization of personal agendas.

In instructional situations, characters labour for self-maintenance and for esteem "on stage". The instructor is part of these dramas, and the constant interplay of roles, identities and characters has a deep influence on the process of learning new concepts. Conceptualization of the scenes is based on the work that is done backstage to the classroom-theatre: the home, the neighbourhood, as well as the schoolyard at recess. Thus, even when we talk about a particular school subject, conceptual change is a function of the depth of the grasp of the character presented in instructional incidents. The representation of the content depends on the inescapable involvement of conceptualization with the presentation of self (Goffman, 1958). In these views, conceptualization and the adoption of concept change is not a process of looking at anomalies "out there", and of absorbing an objective view of the world. It is a minute-by-minute process of assessing the importance of one's self in that world and of reckoning whether the game as a whole is understood, whether the character that the learner (or the instructor) is presenting is adequate, and so on.

Concentrating on how people construct situations, ethnomethodologists turn our attention to the holistic scenes in schools and in classrooms in which the activating concepts remain latent except when violated. Hence, change is a possibility when, in their encounters with infractions of unstated rules, learners will look for an illumination of the concepts that they have been using uncritically. The process of conceptual change in instruction, therefore, depends on the extent to which instructors can engineer breaches in action sequences, then drill new actions, and in retrospect clarify the interpretations hitherto taken for granted. In this framework, activity learning has the implication, not of reaching a grasp of the indubitably "right" concepts, but rather that of uncovering aspects of conceptualization that are "wrong" because they do not work.

The centrality of gender to the formation of women's cognitive performance has risen and fallen as a topic of debate. In contemporary sociology, there is no longer any question but that gender is perhaps the most significant marker of social structure. Whether we deal with race, caste and class, ethnicity, or age as the boundaries of human groups, we have to attach a tag for gender to each. And although we may envision a Utopia in which gender differences are overcome by a harmonious cognitive androgynism (Woolf, 1963 [1928]), this is not the condition of women or of girls here and now. The essential sociological consideration of the differences between boys and girls, and men and women, has to be attached to every theoretical standpoint in order to understand the multiplexity of conceptualization and concept change (Smith, 1990). An integral part of instruction, therefore, is the grasp of the kinds of knowledge and the beliefs that are imposed, negotiated, relevant; the opinions into which each gender is socialized, the degree to which we can point to similarities and dissimilarities. This is more than an academic exercise or even a type of classroom research. It is a basic recognition that there are practical consequences for what we think of as cognition and these consequences are with us from the very moment the learner and the instructor enter the classroom.

Knowledge, Belief and Opinion Revisited

When investigating how to make sure that knowledge is indeed acquired, psychologists are interested in what pupils think, say, enjoy or suffer from (Gardner, 1991). This is information that can facilitate the control of conceptualization and of concept change related to the topics schools deal with. Sociology provides a sobering basis for understanding knowledge, the formation of concepts, and conceptual change. Although different schools of sociology assume different forms of the social order, all imply that society determines the limits of what is defined as knowledge, what as belief and what as mere opinion. The curriculum definition of knowledge is seen as a social product rather than as a register of eternal truth. School administration and organization are not evidence of a "natural" order, but confirm prevailing social forms.

In the sociological view, furthermore, society penetrates every aspect of human relations in the schools and in the classrooms. One of the most important aspects of instruction, then, is the world of the teacher. Teachers' biographies are consequential for their approaches to instruction. The view of the world that they bring into the classroom is crucial for an understanding of how they know, believe and opine; how they relate to concepts and how they hope to influence conceptual change. In my own research (Kalekin-Fishman, 1995), I have found, as did Lortie (1975), that in many ways, teachers and educators relate to the knowledge of concepts and to concept change "as if " they accept some of the positions proposed by sociologists. Here, for example, are a few of the widespread presuppositions.

1. Presentism: School subjects that are provided for in the curriculum are granted the exclusive status of "knowledge". Their comprehensive endorsement implies a theory of social evolution in which the current state of affairs reflects the pinnacle of human development and, therefore, current conceptualizations are the only ones possible.
2. Concomitantly, the modes of thought sanctioned in intellectual currents of the day are taught (and, it is hoped, learned) as inexorable laws rather than as negotiated opinions and beliefs.
3. The hierarchization of subjects, ages, roles in instruction and learning as well as in school administration assumes a predetermined and inescapable ranking of social locations and positions, each assigned to a specific level of status-rewards (Parsons, 1966; Weber, 1947).
4. Classroom arrangements assume the prevalence and the legitimacy of only certain types of interaction. School rules and regulations are endowed with a moral and ethical status that brooks no investigation (by pupils *or* teachers). All of these have lasting meaning in terms of political socialization (Kalekin-Fishman, 1995). The basis for every lesson, as well as for the kinds of interchanges that govern the lessons, is the self of the teacher and the selves of the pupils. The gear of beliefs and opinions brought into the classroom, which is tightly joined with the capacities for acquiring concepts and the possibilities of an inclination toward conceptual change, is overlooked.

Given that the view of reality as socially generated is useful, it is worthwhile to look at ways in which naive views of instruction can be expanded by weighing the importance of some quite general conclusions.

a. Conceptualization and conceptual change are always rooted in belief and opinion as well as in what was previously accepted as knowledge.
b. Except when associated with technologies, different bodies of "things to be learned" may not be recognized as knowledge by people whose cultural origins are "different", or by members of different social classes.
c. The more or less naive theorizing about society that both teachers and learners bring into the classroom may inhibit a realization of the potential for conceptualization in institutionalized learning situations.
d. In sum, mechanisms of cognition cannot account for all that goes on in schools and in classrooms. Educational organizations reflect society in manifold ways, and the people who participate in them are each an "entire world" in the full sense of the term.

Even a rudimentary awareness of alternative views of the social foundations of knowledge may affect approaches to the circumstances and the outcomes of schooling. A consciousness of the prevalence of negotiation and its various guises as they are recognized by sociologists (see above: Mead, Goffman, Garfinkel) can alert educators to the actualities of "non-learning" in the classroom. A readiness to ask about interests in the distribution of knowledge and, even more importantly, about the distribution of ignorance, can guide teachers in their choices of sections from the curriculum. In sociological terms, the challenge of conceptual change is an awesome effort. It may turn out to be well worthwhile for educationists and educators to examine in depth when and whether such an effort is indeed necessary.

PART 3

Domain-Specific Aspects

8

Knowledge Restructuring in an Economic Subdomain: Banking

Anna Emilia Berti[1]

Introduction

There is now a very large number of investigations on students' conceptions of physics, mathematics and natural sciences and on the ways such conceptions change (see Confrey, 1990; Eylon & Linn, 1988; Pfundt & Duit, 1994). In comparison, the studies on politics and economics (see Furnham, 1994) are rather scanty, and have been carried out, with few exceptions, outside the conceptual change paradigm. This gap is unjustifiable both on practical and theoretical grounds. On the one hand, useful suggestions for improvement in the teaching social studies could arise from a deeper knowledge of student's societal notions, as in the case of physical conceptions. On the other hand, the understanding of conceptual change should be based on a comparison between various knowledge domains aimed at identifying similarities and differences between them, and at distinguishing general structures and processes from domain specific ones. This requires the extension of research into the domains that have been studied less up to now, namely the societal domain. To contribute to this task, the present paper proposes an examination of similarities and differences in the origins of misconceptions about physical phenomena and economic institutions. It then compares some factors that underlie resistance to change in both fields, and suggests a working hypothesis that conceptual change can be more easily fostered in the economic field. Finally, it presents a series of intervention studies on the concept of banking, aimed at checking this hypothesis.

Factors Underlying Misconceptions About Physical Phenomena and Economic Institutions

The presence of similar mistaken physical conceptions in students from different countries and different school experiences has suggested the existence of common underlying factors.

1. Observation of natural phenomena from which untrue images of the characteristics of physical entities and processes can result. For instance, the Earth appears flat, and the stars much smaller than the sun (Vosniadou & Brewer, 1992). An object falling from a moving carrier appears to follow a straight-down trajectory (McCloskey et al., 1983). Acceleration is hardly perceived by human eye (Champagne et al., 1980).

[1]The investigations presented in this paper were carried out with the help of some students: Cinzia Aquino collected the data for Study 1, and Giovanna Consolati for Study 2. Rosanna Ciccarelli helped plan and implement the curriculum of Study 3. The whole project was funded by the MPI (funds 40% and 60%).

2. Meanings suggested by ways of talking. For instance, expressions such as "turn to heat" or "heat pump" suggest that heat is something that flows (Eylon & Linn, 1988).
3. The wrong use of analogies (Spiro et al., 1989).
4. Inadequate presentation of the topics by textbooks and teachers (Vosniadou, 1991).
5. The constraints of framework theories on interpretation of information from sense experience or verbally taught (Vosniadou, 1994; Vosniadou & Brewer, 1994). Framework theories consist of fundamental ontological and epistemological presuppositions, which develop very early and, according to some authors, are constrained in their turn by innate structures (Gardner, 1991; Spelke, 1991).
6. Lack of background knowledge, that is knowledge that contributes to the construction and evaluation of a certain theory, but is not specifically part of it (Chinn & Brewer, 1993).

Similar to the physical domain, erroneous conceptions concerning economic activities, roles and exchanges have also been found in children from different cultures and social backgrounds (Berti & Bombi, 1988; Furth, 1980; Jahoda, 1979, 1981; Leiser et al., 1990; Strauss, 1952). In order to identify similarities and differences in the origin of these misconceptions, each of the above listed factors will now be examined with reference to the economic domain.

Inappropriate Analogies and Generalizations

Some economic misconceptions appear to arise from inappropriate analogies and generalizations that children use to fill the gaps in their information. For instance, at 8- to 10-years, when the idea of employee develops, many children believe that the owners of factories, banks and buses get the money to pay employees from their own job (Berti & Bombi, 1988). This misconception originates with an inference from the correct belief, developing at about the age of 6–7 years, that people work to earn money. A different, and less widespread, misconception is that people have to pay a fee in order to get a job, thus allowing the owners to pay their employees with the money collected in this way. This conception, found in children from such different nations as Italy (Berti & Bombi, 1988), Mexico, Spain and the United States (Delval, 1994), appears to spring from the idea that you must pay in order to get something you want.

Ways of Talking and Presentation of Topics at School

In Italian the same word *guadagno* [earning] is commonly used both for money paid for a job and for profit, that is for the difference between revenue and expenses. This confirms children's spontaneous idea that shopkeepers make a living by selling at cost, for in this way they also receive some money.

In Italian elementary schools, the notions of profit, expenses and revenue are usually presented in the context of arithmetic in the third or fourth grade. Textbooks limit themselves to stating that shopkeepers sell goods at higher prices than they have paid, without explaining why. Many third grade children do not know that by selling at cost one gets back the same money one has spent. Not understanding the reason for price increase, these children conclude that shopkeepers change prices at will, decreasing or increasing them according to their generosity or greed for money (Berti, 1992). In junior high schools, in the history and geography curricula, more complex economic notions such as market or planned economy are touched upon or treated in depth, but in both cases in barely understandable ways (Berti, 1991).

Lack of Background Knowledge

Some economic misconceptions stem from the lack of prerequisite arithmetic, and fade as it is acquired. For instance, up to 7–8 years of age many children believe that shopkeepers give change so that customers do not find themselves without money. This conception is abandoned when children understand that the change compensates for a difference between the amount paid and the price of the goods bought (Berti & Bombi, 1981). The idea that shopkeepers make a living also by selling at cost survives only until children understand that in this way accounts do not balance (Berti et al., 1986; Berti & De Beni, 1988).

Constraining Framework Theories

As economics concerns specific classes of human actions, economic misconceptions should also reflect presuppositions concerning human nature and the motives underlying human behaviour. The hypothesis that societal understanding in children was hindered by a framework theory was put forward by Hans Furth and Gustav Jahoda, even if not in these words. According to Furth (1980), up to adolescence children are not able to differentiate personal and societal domains. As a consequence of both their immature thinking and their poor engagement in societal relations, they interpret economic and political institutions in terms of rules and motivations governing the personal relations that have involved them since infancy. Jahoda (1981) appealed to this hypothesis to explain why the notions of interest and bank profit are barely understood even at 16 years, whereas shopkeepers' profit is understood by 10- to 11-year-olds. According to Jahoda, the operation of a bank tends to be conceived in terms of the same principles of equality and strict reciprocity governing the transactions between siblings and friends: "if you borrow something you return the same, no more and no less — anything else would not be 'fair'" (Jahoda, 1981, p. 84).

Observation

Up to now, I have shown that the same factors underlie misconceptions about both physical and economic phenomena. Now I argue that observation plays a different role in the two domains. The physical domain comprises processes and material objects whose properties can be observed. However, as seen before, observation can sometimes result in misleading information because of the limitations of human visual system. On the other hand, the societal domain comprises roles, relations and rules that are not perceivable, although underlying perceivable behaviour. For instance, property is a relation between human beings (or institutions) and objects, consisting of a set of rights of the former over the latter, which allow a variety of overt behaviours, sometimes resulting in spatial proximity, some-times not. Owners of cars very often drive them personally, but owners of bus companies very seldom do so, having the buses driven by employees.

Therefore, in the economic domain, mistakes do not arise from observation, but from interpretation of what is observed. The perception of a person driving the bus is truthful, while the perception of the straight-down fall of an object dropped by a moving carrier is not. The mistake is in the inference, drawn by most children from the ages of 4–5 to 8–9 years, that the bus driver is also the owner of the bus (Berti et al., 1982).

Cognitive Factors Underlying Resistance to Change of Prior Conceptions

It has been frequently observed that students, independently of age, are very reluctant to abandon their physical misconceptions: most never acquire or misinterpret scientific notions taught in class, or revert to pre-instructional conceptions after leaving school (see Gardner, 1991). When a change occurs, it takes a long time (see Carey, 1985; Vosniadou & Brewer, 1992). Three main kinds of cognitive explanations for resistance to change have been put forward (for a discussion of motivational factors see Pintrich et al., 1993).

Nature of the Change Involved

According to some scholars, the acquisition of scientific knowledge often does not require the simple accretion or enrichment of pre-existing conceptions, i.e. the addition of knowl-edge to pre-existing structures, but their restructuring (Carey 1985, 1991; Vosniadou & Brewer, 1987). Two kinds of restructuring have been identified. In weak restructuring, the relations between concepts change (as in the substitution of "no motion without a force" with "no acceleration without a force"), and higher level concepts that subsume lower level ones are added (Chi et al., 1982). According to Susan Carey (1985), in radical or strong restruc-turing, which can be compared to scientific revolutions (Kuhn, 1970), changes also occur in the individual concepts, the domain of phenomena explained and the criteria of explanations.

Restructuring, both of the weak and radical types, are considered as inherently complex and time consuming processes (Carey, 1985, p. 192). Resistance to change, in this view, appears to derive from the operation of the processes transforming a theory-like cognitive structure into another one. However, no justification of why restructuring should be so time consuming is offered beyond the analogy with scientific revolution. This analogy has been challenged by other authors, according to whom children's and non-scientist adults' concepts undergo a simple accretion through the addition and deletion of concepts and beliefs, rather than revolutionary changes (Spelke, 1991; Thagard, 1992).

Entrenchment of Prior Conceptions

For other scholars, the resistance to change or the long time needed depends on the entrenchment of prior conceptions. A conception is entrenched when it contains a belief that is either deeply embedded in a network of other beliefs — which has much support from evidence, or participates in a broad range of explanations in various domains — or satisfies strong personal or social goals (Chinn & Brewer, 1993, p. 15). In this view, the long time needed for children to transform their conceptions on specific phenomena is a consequence of the long time needed to reinterpret the framework theories embedding them (Vosniadou & Brewer, 1994).

The Complexity and Abstractness of the Concepts to be Acquired

This point has been underlined in the neo-behaviouristic literature on learning and in the neo-Piagetian theories of cognitive development rather than in literature on conceptual change. Some concepts are formed by other concepts, which involve more elementary skills. This hierarchy of components must be mirrored by a learning hierarchy (Gagné, 1985). The acquisition of concepts involving abstract relations between abstract concepts requires a sequence of steps that moves from the development of concrete concepts, through the construction of single abstract concepts, to the connection of these concepts by single and, lastly, multiple abstract relations (Fisher, 1980). Before arriving at the end of the sequence, children show concrete, simplified and sometimes erroneous versions of the target concepts. The sequence requires a long time to be covered because of the number of component concepts and relations involved, each of which must be separately constructed, and also the limited capacity of the working memory, in which concrete instances are compared and abstract concepts an relations are constructed (Case, 1985).

How Resistant to Change are Economic Misconceptions?

Whether or not we should expect children's misconceptions about economic institutions to be resistant to change depends on the factors we assume to underlie such resistance. My assumption is that only two of the above factors are effective, that is (i) the entrenchment of prior beliefs and (ii) the abstractness and complexity of the target conception, compared with the previous one. Restructuring — that is, the construction of new relations between concepts, the formation of higher order concepts and, in the case of radical restructuring, changes in pre-existing concepts — in my view, can be easily achieved when the other two factors are not operating. This is the case when children already possess the prerequisite background knowledge, their wrong beliefs are not entrenched, and they are confronted with the operation of individual subsystems (as for instance bank, factory or shop), rather than with abstract notions (as for instance *enterprise* or *profit* meant in general terms, as opposed to shop profit, bank profit or factory profit), or systems including other systems (as would be the case if children were taught about the relations between banks and industry).

One source of entrenchment identified for physical concepts, the fact that they arise from observation and therefore are deeply rooted in daily life, does not apply to economic misconceptions, as seen above. Another source of entrenchment for these concepts could reside in their being embedded in a framework theory, as suggested by Furth (1980) and Jahoda (1981). However, this has been put forward by both authors as an interpretative hypothesis without being explicitly tested, and might prove to be wrong. Children's construction of societal phenomena in terms of rules relevant to the personal domain could reflect the occasional use of analogical reasoning in order to fill gaps in their knowledge, rather than the systematic constraint of a framework theory.

If, as I expect, children's concepts about economic institutions are not entrenched, they should be easily changed through explicit instruction. Furthermore, the correct notions, once acquired, should persist. Far from being disconfirmed by daily encounters with the world, they should offer new perspectives on things children hear about from parents, teachers and media, or that they observe personally. The success of the few training studies on economic concepts, when children already possess the necessary background knowledge, supports the view that economic misconceptions are easily abandoned (Ajello et al., 1986, 1987; Berti, 1992, 1993; Berti et al., 1986). Studies on economic instruction in elementary grades and at secondary levels show its effectiveness (Schug & Walstad, 1991).

To test if knowledge restructuring can actually be easily achieved in economic subdomains, I have carried out a series of studies aimed at teaching children the operation of one economic subsystem: banking.

Children's Conceptions of Banking

Understanding banking has been examined in different parts of the world, showing a stage-like sequence of conceptions in children from kindergarten to 10th grade (Berti & Bombi, 1988; Jahoda, 1981; Jahoda & Woerdenbagch, 1982; Ng, 1982; Takahashi & Hatano, 1994). At level 0 there is a *total absence of ideas on banking*. At level 1 (*the bank is a source of money*) children think that anybody can go to the bank and get money. At level 2 (*the bank looks after money*) children believe that only people who have previously deposited money to protect it from thieves can go and get it. At level 3 (*the bank also lends money*) children are aware of the existence of loans, but they do not relate deposits to loans: the deposit money is locked in a safe in separate envelopes or boxes and never touched again until it is returned to its owner, whereas loan money is obtained from external sources, such as the state or local council. At level 4 (*the bank lends money deposited*) children make the connection between deposits and loans.

At these levels, knowledge about interest is fragmentary. Some children do not know about it, some know one type of interest only, and others know both types but cannot correctly explain how the bank gets the money to pay the interest on deposits. Lastly, at level 5 (*connection between loan and deposit interest*), children are aware of interest on both deposits and loans and connect them, stating that the bank can pay deposit interest thanks to the interest that it receives, in turn, from loans. This level was found in a minority of youngsters at 14 (Berti & Bombi, 1988) and 16 (Jahoda, 1981). Some stated that the amount of the two kinds of interest was the same, others maintained that loan interest was lower than deposit. Only a small minority of 16 year-olds recognized that loan interest was higher than deposit interest, thus allowing banks to pay their employees and earn a profit.

Some characteristics of the above sequence suggest that knowledge restructuring rather than mere enrichment is involved.

1. The transition from the most incorrect conception to the correct one is slow and gradual.
2. In the transition from one level to the next, new relations between concepts are introduced: between the money taken from the bank and that previously deposited; between deposits and loans; between loan interest and deposit interest; between bank earnings and the difference between loan interest and deposit interest.
3. In the most advanced conception, the superordinate concept of interest, intended as "money paid to keep somebody else's money for a certain time", appears. These three characteristics suggest that the transition between levels involves at least a weak restructuring. The two subsequent characteristics suggest that even radical restructuring occurs.
4. There are changes in individual concepts. For instance, the bank, initially conceived as a place where money is kept safe, becomes an institution providing for the circulation of money.
5. The domain of phenomena explained by the conceptions also changes. Thanks to the difference between deposit and loan interest the source of money for bank employees can be identified.

Aims of the Intervention Studies

In order to test whether economic conceptions can be easily and permanently changed, three intervention studies have been carried out by teaching children of different grades how the bank works. A second purpose of these studies was to check whether children really applied the rule of strict reciprocity to the economic domain, by explicitly asking them if deposit and loan interest are fair or unfair.

The conditions identified by several scholars (see Chinn & Brewer, 1994; Strike & Posner, 1985; Vosniadou, 1991) as facilitating deep changes in knowledge structures are the following.

1. Dissatisfaction with existing conceptions.
2. Possibility of understanding the new one, at least minimally.
3. Compatibility between the new conception, background knowledge and framework theories already possessed.
4. Fruitfulness of the new conception.
5. The learner's memory capacity should be taken into account (Case, 1985).

In the studies described in this chapter, I have strived to meet conditions 1, 2, 4 and 5 and to check where condition 3 was satisfied. Children's erroneous ideas were explicitly disconfirmed, and the correct notions were presented in terms suitable to them. With children already possessing the notion of shopkeeper's profit, the analogy between shops and banks was introduced to explain how banks pay their employees and make a profit through the difference between deposit and loan interest. In order not to overload children's memory capacity, the information on banking was distributed over two lessons in the first two studies, repeating the explanations several times and sketching the main points on the blackboard. As this turned out to be insufficient for children whose starting level was far from the target one, in Study 3 a curriculum of several units was implemented.

Besides arithmetic, background knowledge with respect to the notion of banking comprises conceptions about other economic systems, such as shops and factories. The idea of shopkeepers' profit is mastered by the age of 9–10; from the age of 10–11 children state that factory owners pay their workers with the money obtained by selling their products, abandoning the idea, typical of 7- to 9-year-olds, that the owners obtain the money from external sources such as banks, the state, the local council, or from their savings or work (Berti & Bombi, 1988). As these notions should also help in understanding how the bank works, 10- to 11-year-old children are expected to understand explanations on this topic. This view was also supported by an exploratory study carried out with fifth graders. After only one lesson on banking, the majority had succeeded in relating deposits, loans and interest (Berti, 1993).

The first of the studies presented in this paper was carried out with 10- to 11-year-olds with two purposes: (i) To examine the effects of two class lessons depending on the learners' background knowledge of shops and factories, and (ii) to check whether 10- to 11-year-olds do judge interest as unfair, thus applying the framework theory of equality and reciprocity in interpersonal transactions to the bank. In Study 2, the same lessons were addressed to 8- to 9-year-olds, to check the effects on children more backward in both banking and background knowledge. Study 3 was carried out with 9- to 10-year-olds, to evaluate the results of a longer intervention and to check the persistence of change through a delayed post-test presented 8 months after the completion of the curriculum.

In all three studies, a pre-experimental design was chosen. All the children were administered a pre- and post-test and attended class lessons. In Jahoda's (1981) study, the impact of the interview on children's conceptions was also evaluated, and it turned out to be very low on all subjects, especially in the youngest ones (11- to 12-year-olds). Therefore, I preferred to make a comparison between subgroups of children showing different conceptions at pre-test, rather than dividing the children into experimental and control groups.

Study 1: Fifth-Graders' Ideas on Bank Functions and Interest Before and After Two Lessons on Banking

Procedure

Four fifth grade classes, from three State run elementary schools in a lower-middle class area near Milan (Northern Italy) collaborated in this study. A total of 71 children (mean age 10.7 years; boys = 36, girls = 35) participated in all phases (pre- and post-test, and class lesson). The intervention was comprised of three parts:

1. A pre-test, intended to ascertain children's conceptions of shop profit, payment of factory employees, and banking, which consisted of a semi-structured interview (see the schema in the Appendix).
2. Explanation of bank operation, through two class lessons involving discussions, explanations and diagrams on the blackboard. The first, which was devoted to the notions of deposits, loans and interest, took place 1 week after the pre-test. The second, which took

place the day after the first test, was devoted to a recapitulation and comparison between banks and shops. The structure is presented in Table 1.

3. A post-test, conducted 2 weeks after the lesson, asked the same questions on banking again.

Table 1: Summary of the lessons on banking. Aim and content of each step

---

1. Aim: Focus children's attention on the fact that some of theirs ideas are wrong.

The interviews showed that some concepts were known by all children, while other questions could not be answered correctly. As banking is very important, although difficult to understand, this lesson will explain what banking is for and how it works.

2. Aim: Clarify that deposit money is not kept separate.

Many children thought that the money each person brings to the bank is kept in a separate container such as an envelope, sack or box, so that when they go to take it back, they receive their own money, as if it were kept in a personal money-box. Things do not work in this way. Everybody's money is kept together in a big safe. In order to remember how much money each person has brought the bank employees write the amount in a computer.

3. Aim: Explain the main functions of banks.

How is the money kept (*discussion*)? Everyone's deposit money is kept together. As many children rightly said, banks have two main aims: to look after people's money, and give loans. Banks have other functions, but these are the most important. Why do people put their money in the bank? Many children said that people do so to protect it from thieves. This is correct but incomplete. People put money in the bank not only because they are afraid of thieves, but also for another reason, mentioned by some children (*stimulate a short class discussion*). People put money in the bank because, when they get it back, the bank gives them more than they put in.

4. Aim: Give information about the existence of interest on deposits, explicitly disclaiming wrong ideas.

For example, if people put a million lire in the bank and leave it there for one year, when they go to get the money back they receive their million plus another 70.000 lire (*write on the blackboard*). This extra money is called interest. This is important and children must try to remember it. Banks do not get paid to look after people's money. On the contrary, they give them extra money. Why? (*brief discussion*).

5. Aim: Justifying interest on deposits. Illustrate the connection between deposits and loans.

Banks pay interest on deposits to encourage people to put money in the bank. Banks do not in fact keep all the money in safes, but use it. How do they use it? (*short discussion*). By lending it.

Almost all children talked about loans, but many of them did not know how banks manage to have money to lend. Here is how they do it: they use the deposit money to give loans. Of course, the people taking money to the bank are aware that their money is used to give loans. They know this and agree to it, because they have no doubt that their money will be returned to them later.

6. Aim: To introduce the concept of interest on loans.

When people receive a loan from the bank, after a period of time they must give the money back. In addition, they pay some more money called interest. For example, if someone asks for one million lire as a loan and gives it back after one year, she/he will have to give back one million plus another 150,000 lire: the money loaned plus the interest (*write on the blackboard*).

7. Aim: To define interest in general terms.

The bank keeps the deposit money for a period of time and pays interest on it; the people receiving loans keep the money for a period of time and then pay interest on it. Interest represents money paid to keep other people's money for a period of time. In short, the function of the bank is to collect money, obtaining it from people who have it, and then loaning it out.

8. Aim: To introduce an analogy between banks and shops.

Banks can be compared to shops. Shopkeepers buy from factories and sell to people. Banks get money from savers and then give it out to people who ask for loans. The owner of the bank, like the shopkeeper, wants to make a profit.

9. Aim: To recapitulate the preceding points

Children are invited to discuss the point of the previous lessons, that is, deposits, loans, interest.

10. Aim: To justify the difference between the amounts of active and passive interest.

How do shopkeepers make profits? (*ask for answers and then summarize*). Shopkeepers buy goods at a certain price and then sell them at a higher price. Banks give depositors a certain amount of interest and then ask for higher interest when they loan money out. For example, they give savers 70,000 lire per million but ask for 150,000 lire per million lent (*write on the blackboard*). In this way the owner of the bank manages to pay the interest on deposits, pay her/his employees' salaries, electricity bills, heating, cleaning the bank, etc., and also make a profit. (*Stimulate children to express doubts or ask questions.*)

The children were examined individually in a quiet room made available by the school. All interviews were recorded and transcribed to allow accurate analysis of their content. Answer classification was carried out by two independent judges who agreed in 98% of cases. The significance of the differences between pre- and post-test was checked by McNemar or Sign tests, depending on the measures involved (dichotomic classification versus level sequences).

Children's Conception Before the Intervention

At pre-test, all the children knew that shopkeepers sell their goods at a higher price than they pay, and they judged this increase necessary and fair. However, only 35 children (49%) stated that factory employees' wages were paid by money received from selling products. The remaining children either answered "don't know" ($n = 12$; 17%) or mentioned other sources such as local council, state or other banks ($n = 24$; 34%). The children's conceptions of banking and interest are presented in Table 2, which shows that most children either did not know about bank loans or did not connect them to deposits. Furthermore, most children (65%) either did not know about interest or knew of only one type. Most children ($n = 42$; 59%) also believed that an individual's money is kept in separate drawers, envelopes or bags. The reason people bring their money to the bank most often mentioned was protection from thieves ($n = 60$; 85%). Only 16 children (22%) said the money deposited increased.

Table 2: 10- to 11-year-old children's ideas on bank functions and interest at pre-test

Ideas on banking	Knowledge of interest						
	0	**D**	**L**	**D > L**	**D = L**	**L > D**	**Total**
Banks look after money	4	3	0	0	0	0	7
Banks lend money	14	4	11	3	5	7	44
Banks lend deposit money	6	1	3	1	1	4	19
Deposit interest paid with loan interest	0	0	0	0	0	1	1
Total	24	8	14	4	9	12	71

0 No kind of interest is known.
D, Only interest on deposits is known.
L, Only interest on loans is known.
D > L, Interest on both deposits and loans is known, and the former is considered higher.
D = L, Interest on both deposits and loans is known, and is believed to be the same amount.
L > D, Interest on loans is believed to be higher than interest on deposits.

A total of 27 (82%) children out of 33 who mentioned deposit interest (either using this word, or saying that banks give back more money than has been deposited), and 21 (54%) out of 39 who mentioned loan interest, were not able to explain why interest is paid. Their answers were "don't know" or tautologies ("you have to pay interest"). Only three of the 33 children (9%) and eight of the 39 children (20%) gave economic explanations for deposit and loan interest, respectively; stating in the first case that the bank uses deposit money, and in the second that the bank needs money for expenses and earnings.

Some children interpreted interest as a "thank you", from the bank for being preferred ($n = 3$), or from the people who borrowed money ($n = 10$, 26%). These answers show that some children do apply interpersonal rules to the economic domain, but this — contrary to Furth's and Jahoda's hypotheses — helps rather than hinders their understanding. On the other hand, a high number of children regarded deposit interest (n = 12; 36%) and loan interest ($n = 12$; 31%) as unfair, which is coherent with Furth's and Jahoda's hypothesis. However, this judgement could also be because of children's lack of knowledge of the banking system and the role of interest. Finally, only 11 children (15%) stated that bank employees are paid through interest money. All the others mentioned different sources, such as tax, other bank, money earned by the owners from their jobs, or answered "don't know".

Children's Conceptions After the Intervention

At post-test, all answers turned out to be significantly different on all points examined. All children stated that everyone's deposit money was put in the safe together. The difference in respect to pre-test was significant ($\chi^2 = 40$, d.f. $= 1$, $P < 0.0001$). Loans were mentioned by all the children who, with only one exception, also connected them with deposits. Furthermore, 48 children (68%) also connected the two types of interest, reaching the higher level of the sequence. The sign test showed the difference between pre- and post-test to be significant ($P < 0.001$). All children mentioned both deposit and loan interest ($\chi^2 = 44$, d.f. $= 1$, $P < 0.001$) and used the word *interest*, which only 16 children knew at pre-test.

Table 3: 10- to 11-year-old children's ideas on bank functions and interest at post-test

Ideas on banking	Knowledge of interest		
	D = L	**L > D**	**Total**
Banks lend money	0	1	1
Banks lend deposit money	3	19	22
Deposit interest paid with loan interest	2	46	48
Total	5	66	71

See Table 2 footnote.

According to the majority ($n = 66$; 93%), loan interest was higher than deposit interest, whereas, according to the remaining five children, the amount was the same. Economic explanations were given for deposit interest by 62 (87%) children ($\chi^2 = 57$, d.f. $= 1$, $P < 0.001$) and for loan interest by 48 (68%) ($\chi^2 = 33$, d.f. $= 1$, $P < 0.001$). Lastly, all children stated that both deposit and loan interest were fair, thus showing that interest evaluation depends on the understanding of how the bank works rather than on the generalization of interpersonal rules to the economic domain.

Also, ideas about the payment of bank employees turned out to be very different from pre-test. Most children ($n = 59$; 83%) stated that banks obtained their money through the difference between deposit and loan interest ($\chi^2 = 44$, d.f. $= 1$, $P < 0.001$). This answer was given by all the 48 children who had stated that deposit interest is paid through the money received from loan interest.

In conclusion, 68% of children attained a full understanding of what they had been taught, reaching a target in a couple of hours that, according to cross-sectional studies, they would have reached at least 5 years later, if they had not been taught. The other children had also changed their ideas, although not mastering all the notions furnished.

A comparison between the pre-test answers of the children who at post-test reached a full understanding (FU) of the banking and those who did not (NFU) showed some significant differences. The percentage of FU children who at pre-test knew none, one or both kinds of interest was 21, 35 and 44%, respectively, compared with 59, 23 and 18% in NFU children ($\chi^2 = 9.3$, d.f. $= 2$, $P < 0.01$). Awareness that deposit money is kept together was shown by 65% of FU children versus 17% of NFU ($\chi^2 = 13.8$, d.f. $= 1$, $P < 0.001$). Knowledge that factory workers are paid with the money earned by selling goods was expressed by 52% of FU children, versus 17% NFU ($\chi^2 = 13.8$, d.f. $= 1$, $P < 0.001$).

Children's prior knowledge of banking could have helped their progress by reducing the distance between starting and target levels, whereas knowledge of factories could have allowed children to transfer an already known notion rather than constructing it *ex novo*. The fast progress realized, thanks to the two lessons, could also have been helped by (i) background knowledge of shopkeepers' profit, which allowed the analogy between shops and banks to be introduced during the lessons, and (ii) the absence of a framework theory of strict reciprocity in transactions, which would have conflicted with the notion of interest. As the first requirement was met by all the children and the second by the majority, it was not possible to check their weight. Therefore, a second study was carried out with younger children.

Study 2: Third Graders' Understanding of Bank Functions and Interest Before and After Two Lessons on Banking

Procedure

A total of 53 third grade lower-middle class children (mean age 8.8; 19 girls, 34 boys), from a village near Brescia (Northern Italy) participated in all phases of the intervention. The same procedure as the previous study was followed, with one modification. The analogy between banks and shops was not introduced, because most children turned out not to possess the notion of shopkeeper's profit, as expected. The first lesson was devoted to the notions of deposit, loan and their relationship; the second to interest. The study was carried out towards the end of the school year, when the children had already studied the arithmetic operations.

Children's Conceptions Before the Intervention

At pre-test, only 16 children (30%) answered the questions about shops by stating and justifying that retail prices are higher than wholesale prices. The remainder stated that shopkeepers sell either at cost or at a lower price ($n = 15$; 27%), or mentioned price increase without being able to justify it ($n = 22$; 42%). Only 14 children (26%) mentioned the sale of products as the source of factory employees' wages, while the remainder mentioned other sources ($n = 25$; 48%) or answered "don't know" ($n = 14$, 26%). The children's conceptions of banking and interest are shown in Table 4. Nearly half the children were not aware of bank loans and the majority of those who knew about them did not connect them to deposits. Four children even believed the bank gave money to anyone who needed it. Few knew about interest. Of the 49 children who mentioned deposit, 38 (77%) thought the money was kept in separate containers. Only two (4%) mentioned money increasing as a motivation for putting money in the bank, while the others spoke about protection from thieves ($n = 49$; 73%) or the possibility of having it back when needed ($n = 9$, 18%).

Table 4: 8- to 9-year-old children's ideas on bank functions and interest at pre-test

Ideas on banking	Knowledge of interest					
	0	**D**	**L**	**D = L**	**L > D**	**Total**
Banks are sources of money	4	0	0	0	0	4
Banks look after money	19	1	0	0	0	20
Banks lend money	15	3	2	1	0	21
Banks lend deposit money	7	0	1	0	0	8
Total	45	4	3	1	0	53

See Table 2 footnote.

Children's Conceptions After the Intervention

At post-test, nearly all children ($n = 50$; 93%) stated that deposit money was kept together, showing significant progress compared with pre-test ($\chi^2 = 37$, d.f. = 1, $P < 0.001$). Conceptions on bank functions and interest changed significantly, as can be seen in Table 5 (sign test, $z = 6.4$, $P < 0.001$). Although the number of children that spoke of at least one type of interest increased significantly from eight to 40 ($\chi^2 = 30$, d.f. = 1, $P < 0.001$), only 12 out 34 children who mentioned deposit interest, and 16 of 28 of those mentioning loan interest gave economic justifications, whereas the others answered in the same ways as found in Study 1 at pre-test.

Deposit interest was considered unfair by 13 children (38%), according to whom the bank ought to give back the same money as it received. Loan interest was considered unfair by 14 children (46%). As none of the seven children reaching the higher level viewed loan interest as unfair, such an evaluation appears to reflect poor understanding of bank operations rather than a generalization of the principle of strict reciprocity. Lastly, at post-test, 13 children (24%) stated that bank employees were paid through loan interest ($\chi^2 = 11$, d.f. = 1, $P < 0.001$).

Table 5: 8- to 9-year-old children's ideas on bank functions and interest at post-test

Ideas on banking	Knowledge of interest						
	0	**D**	**L**	**D > L**	**D = L**	**L > D**	**Total**
Banks look after money	1	3	0	0	0	0	4
Banks lend money	0	1	0	0	1	0	2
Banks lend deposit money	12	8	6	2	8	4	40
Deposit interest paid with loan interest	0	0	0	0	0	7	7
Total	13	12	6	2	9	11	53

See Table 2 footnote.

In conclusion, 8- to 9-year-olds remained at an intermediate level, different from Study 1, where the 10- to 11-year-olds retained most of the information given during the lessons and reached the highest level of the sequence. Although the majority learned that banks are not limited to keeping people's money in safes but use it to give loans, only a minority acquired the notion of interest on both deposits and loans. The difference between 10- to 11-year-olds and 8- to 9-year-olds can be easily connected to their different starting levels, both in their conceptions of banking and in their background knowledge of factories and shops. Whether the younger children were also hindered by a framework theory of strict reciprocity is controversial. On the one hand, the high number of children that regarded interest as unfair suggests that 8- to 9-year-olds, as opposed to 10- to 11-year-olds, apply the rules of strict reciprocity to the bank. On the other hand, the lack of understanding of the role of interest in banking by most children suggests that the judgement of unfairness can derive from a lack of specific knowledge.

If children have no framework theory that contrasts with the understanding of bank interest, they should be able to learn how the bank works through a prolonged and gradual intervention that disconfirms their misconceptions and gives them all the information required, regardless of pre-existing knowledge gaps and erroneous ideas. Such an intervention was carried out in Study 3. In addition, this study had two other objectives: (i) to test the permanence of the notions acquired, through a delayed post-test, and (ii) to ascertain whether the previous teaching of shopkeeper's profit facilitated understanding of banking.

If the delay in the age at which children understand banking compared with shop profit is because of the greater familiarity of shops, and to the fact that, at least in Italy, shop profit is usually taught whereas banking is not, the order in which these notions are taught should not affect learning. If, on the other hand, bank profit is more difficult to understand because of conflict with the rule of strict reciprocity, previously learning the notion of profit in the easier context of shops should make this task simpler.

Study 3 : Understanding of Bank and Shop Functions in Fourth Graders After a Three-Month Curriculum

Procedure

A total of 38 lower-middle class children (17 boys, 21 girls), from a village near Varese (Northern Italy), attending two fourth grade classes, participated in the study. Their mean age at the pre-test was 9.4 years. The first part of the study (pre- and post-test and the instructional intervention) was carried out from November 1993 until March 1994. A delayed post-test was given 8 months after the first, in November 1994. At that time, a child was absent because his family had moved.

The pre-test and first post-test were the same as in the two previous studies, and were carried out through individual interviews, 1 week before and 2 weeks after the intervention. The delayed post-test consisted of a written questionnaire, with open questions. Children were first invited to explain the functions of the bank to an imaginary child who had not participated in the lessons the year before. Then, more specific questions, similar to those already asked in the first post-tests, on deposits, loans, interest, payment of employees and shopkeepers, followed. The class teacher taught about shops and banking during normal school hours, at one unit a week for about 3 months, with some interruptions because of elections and Christmas.

The curriculum on banking was implemented along the same lines as the structure used in the two previous studies. It was spread over a greater number of lessons and was integrated with arithmetic problems. A bank employee was also invited to the classes, to be interviewed by the children. The curriculum on buying and selling was set up along the same principles. Its structure is presented in Table 6. In one class, shops were presented first, followed by banking; in the other, the order was reversed. In both classes, the last lesson was devoted to a comparison between banks and shops. One column on the blackboard was given to each. The teacher wrote a sentence in the shop column, inviting the children to suggest a similar one for the bank. The first couple of sentences were "The shop obtains goods from producers — The bank obtains money from savers". The last couple were "The money which the owner of the shop/bank has after paying all expenses is called profit".

Table 6: Structure of the curriculum about shop profit

Unit 1. Length: 2 hours. Method: discussion, role play (children play shop game, selling goods at cost according to their idea of pricing).

Aims

1. Call children's attention to shopkeepers' expenses.

2. Show that by selling at cost shopkeepers get the same as they spent to replenish their shops.

3. Show that by selling at cost shopkeepers cannot deal with expenses.
   Suggest that shopkeepers sell goods at higher prices than they paid for them.

Unit 2. Length: 1.30 hours. Method: discussion, individual exercises (completing the shopkeeper's thought bubble with her reflections when deciding about prices).

Aims

1. To sum up the previous unit.

2. To focus on the expenses needed to run a shop.

Unit 3. Length: 1 hour. Method: discussion, class lesson, individual arithmetic exercises (e.g.: calculate unitary profit, given cost and revenue of goods).

Aims

1. To sum up the previous units.

2. To introduce the terms *profit, expenses, revenue*.

3. To train children in the arithmetic operations involved in buying and selling, with reference to unitary price.

Unit 4. Length: 2 hours. Method: discussion, class lesson, individual arithmetic exercises

Aim

1. To sum up the previous units.

Children's Conception Before the Intervention

At pre-test, only five children (13%) mentioned retail price increase, and also explained the reasons. The others stated that shopkeepers sell at cost ($n = 24$; 63%) or mentioned price increase without justifying it ($n = 9$; 24%). The source of money to pay factory employees was identified by 15 children (39%) as product sales. Conceptions on the bank and its functions are presented in Table 7, which shows that hardly any children knew about interest and only a minority (26%) were able to connect deposits and loans. The majority of children ($n = 31$; 81%) thought money was kept in separate containers. Only one child stated that bank employees are paid with the money earned through loan interest. Other sources mentioned were owner's personal money ($n = 14$; 37%) and tax ($n = 7$; 18%).

Table 7: 9- to 10-year- old children's ideas on bank functions and interest at pre-test

Ideas on banking	Knowledge of interest						
	0	**D**	**L**	**D > L**	**D = L**	**L > D**	**Total**
Banks look after money	17	1	0	0	0	0	18
Banks lend money	9	0	1	0	0	0	10
Banks lend deposit money	8	0	1	0	1	0	10
Total	34	1	2	0	1	0	38

See Table 2 footnote.

Children's Conception Two Weeks After the Intervention

At the first post-test, all children stated that shopkeepers increased their prices and explained why. The difference with pre-test was highly significant ($\chi^2 = 25$, $P < 0.001$). All children but one said that everyone's deposit money is kept together ($\chi^2 = 28$, $P < 0.001$). A total of 35 children (92%) stated that deposit interest is paid through loan interest, reaching the highest level of the sequence, whereas three children stopped one level lower ($\chi^2 = 33$, $P < 0.001$) (see Table 8).

Table 8: 9- to 10-year-old children ideas on bank functions and interest at post-test

Ideas on banking	Knowledge of interest			
	D	D = L	L > D	Total
Banks lend money	3	0	0	3
Banks lend deposit money	0	12	23	35
Total	3	12	23	38

See Table 2 footnote.

Deposit interest was mentioned by all children, and the majority ($n = 33$; 87%) said it was fair, even if only a minority ($n = 9$; 22%) justified it with economic reasons. Loan interest was known by 35 children (92%), justified with economic reasons by 20 (57%), and judged as fair by 30 (86%). As in Study 1, some children interpreted loan interest as a "thank you" ($n = 9$, 26%). Of the 35 children who were aware of both types of interest, five (14%) believed the amounts to be the same, while the remaining 27 (76%) stated that loan interest is higher than deposit interest.

According to 23 children (60%) bank employees are paid through loan interest ($\chi^2 = 20$, $P < 0.001$). These answers were given by 80% of the children who had correctly identified the source of money for factory workers compared with 48% of those who did not. As in Study 1, ideas about payment in the factories and banks turned out to be significantly associated ($\chi^2 = 3.9$, $P < 0.05$). Lastly, at no point was there any significant difference between the two classes (shops first versus banking first).

Children's Conception Eight Months After the Intervention

At the delayed post-test, all children but two expressed a correct conception of shopkeeper profit. More regressions were found in the answers about banking, even if, on the whole, most children expressed the same conceptions as 8 months before. A total of nine children who had previously connected deposits and loans gave different answers, in two cases they reverted to the type already expressed at pre-test (loans are given with the owner's money). In the other seven cases the children overgeneralized information offered during the lessons, stating that the money for loans comes from loans interest.

Deposit interest was mentioned by all children but two, and loan interest by all but one. Loan interest was said to be higher than deposit interest by 28 children, while all the others regarded them as equal. In comparison with the previous post-test, three children regressed and four progressed. Bank employees were said to be paid through loan interest by 17 children, with nine regressions ($\chi^2 = 4$, d.f. = 1, $P < 0.05$), all involving children who, during the pre-test, had not described the sale of goods as a source of money for factory workers wages. The association between factory and bank answers thus became higher than in the previous post-test ($\chi^2 = 9.9$, d.f. = 1, $P < 0.01$). Bank owners were said to earn money through loan interest, by the same 17 children who mentioned this source of money for bank employees, plus two other children.

On the whole, Study 3 showed that gradual and comprehensive teaching, together with arithmetic exercises, permits most 9-year-old children, who are unaware of bank interest and think that shopkeepers sell at cost, to acquire the notion of shopkeeper profit and understand banking operations. Most children had conserved these conceptions 8 months after the completion of the curriculum. Ideas on payment for work turned out to be rather resistant, which suggests that a curriculum specifically devoted to this topic should be designed.

General Discussion

In this series of studies, children of different ages successfully acquired knowledge on the essential characteristics of banking by interventions whose length was inversely proportional to their pre-existing economic knowledge, which in turn depended on age. All 10- to 11-year-olds already knew about shopkeeper's profit, half had the right idea about the source of money that employers use to pay their employees, and nearly all knew about bank loans. Further, the majority knew about at least one type of interest. These children needed only a couple of hours of lessons to disconfirm erroneous conceptions, establish new connections between concepts, acquire superordinate concepts such as interest, and to add further components to their pre-existing concepts of deposit and banking. As has been argued in the introduction, such changes in children's conceptions represent at least a weak type of restructuring.

Things were different with 8- to 9-year-olds, whose knowledge of banking and other systems was very backward. Of all the information supplied during the lessons, these children focussed on loans and their links to deposits, while assimilating the information on interest to a much smaller extent. In this way, they went up one level in the sequence of knowledge of banking, thus reaching approximately the same level as 10- to 11-year-olds before the intervention.

These changes apparently represent accretion rather than restructuring, as the view of the bank looking after money is enriched by the idea of the bank lending money, while the individual concepts remain substantially unchanged: bank deposit is still seen as a way to protect one's own money from thieves; the bank is not yet understood as a going concern earning money from the difference between costs and income for services supplied. However, a slight change in concepts also occurred and a new relation was introduced: bank deposits are not seen as individual packets of money kept in separate containers waiting to be returned to their owners, but as money circulating as bank loans. Thanks to these changes, the gap between children's conceptions and how the bank actually works decreased. The distinction between restructuring and accretion appears therefore less clear-cut than Carey (1985) suggested. What looks like accretion may be a step in a sequence of changes, at the end of which a conception differs from the initial one in a way that charac-terizes weak or strong restructuring.

A prolonged intervention produced stable restructuring even in 9- to 10-year-olds, whose ideas on the target notions and background knowledge of other economic systems were extremely backward. Half these children did not know about bank loans and only a minority connected them to deposits. Interest, whether active or passive, was almost totally unknown. Moreover, the greater majority of these children had no idea of profit, believing that shopkeepers sell at cost, nor did they know where the money to pay factory workers came from.

With these children, analogies or transfer of pre-existing notions could not be applied to the bank. New concepts and connections had to be introduced one at a time without the support of background economic knowledge. Study 3 has shown that this could be done over a short period of time. Although the curricula on the bank and shop were implemented over 3 months, the number of hours involved was only 18. Over this period of time, the same ground was covered that would have required several years without instruction.

The short time over which these changes occurred, disconfirms the theory that concep-tual restructuring needs months, if not years. This estimate of the time required for restructuring mirrors the results of the cross-sectional studies, showing a distance of years from the most mistaken conceptions to the more correct ones. The view that this is the time actually required for conceptual restructuring to occur assumes implicitly that people are thinking about a certain domain of phenomena continuously during that period of time, which is of course false. More plausibly, even over a period of years, the time actually devoted to a particular topic, reflecting or receiving and elaborating information about it, would not add up to more than a few hours. If this is true, then teaching the same few hours could be concentrated or spread over a few weeks or months instead of years, on the condi-tion of choosing the age levels when children already possess the necessary background knowledge and establishing that prior conceptions are not entrenched.

Instead, discarding a framework theory, or differentiating the contexts in which it can or cannot be applied (see Caravita & Halldén, 1994) may in fact take years. This process, however, is quite different from restructuring conceptions about specific phenomena, and requires separate investigation. In any case, hindering framework theories seem to constrain conceptions about physical objects but not about economic institutions. The studies presented in this paper have highlighted that children, starting at least from the age of 8–9 years, do not possess framework theories on human behaviour that may impede comprehen-sion of bank operations. I expect that this is also true for other economic systems and that it is possible to successfully teach third, fourth and fifth graders a wide variety of notions on economic activities, roles and institutions.

The results of the few studies already carried out (Ajello et al., 1986, 1987; Berti, 1992; Berti et al., 1986) point in this direction. Instead, a contrasting framework theory may well exist in younger children. However, it would not be of primary importance compared with the main obstacle to the understanding of concepts such as profit and interest, represented by poor arithmetical knowledge. Therefore, younger children should only be introduced to economic notions that require little or no arithmetical knowledge, such as production of goods, work as a paid activity, function and value of money, employed and self-employed (Ajello & Bombi, 1988).

I would like to conclude by presenting some anecdotal data referred by the teacher who implemented the curriculum in Study 3. The children were enthusiastic about the curricula. At the end of the intervention, they asked for further similar initiatives. Moreover, low achievers in traditional school activities turned out to be equally or even more competent than their classmates at pre-test, participated in the lessons with interest and performed quite well at post-tests. This suggests that children are highly motivated to understand the society in which they live, even those who are not particularly successful at school. Besides its more direct effects, teaching economic notions may also improve the relationship between child and school.

Appendix

Structure of Interview

This is a list of points to be asked. Question order and wording will depend on children's answers (in italics) and on the words they use themselves. Follow-up questions must be asked when children's answers need clarification.

Shopkeeper's Profit

A stationer buys pens at 300 lire each. What price can she sell them at? Why? Do you think this is right?

Factory Employee's Wages

How do factory owners get the money to pay their employees?

Banks

Do you know what a bank is? What is a bank for?

1. *To put money in.*

How is the money kept, everybody's all together or in separate containers?

Why do people take money to the bank?

What does the bank do with that money?

One day a person takes a million lire to the bank. After one year she decides to get all her money back and goes to the bank to ask for it. How much money will she get? Why?

If children mention interest, ask: How does the bank get the funds to give this extra money?

Do you think it is fair that you receive back more than you have deposited?

2. *To obtain money.* (Ascertain whether it is a present, salary or a loan, asking if anybody can get money from the bank and if they can keep it for ever.)

How does the bank get the money for loans?

A person asks the bank for a loan of one million lire. After one year she pays the money back. How much money will she have to pay back? Why?

If children mention interest, ask: Do you think it is fair that you have to give back more than you borrowed?

If children mention point 2 first and do not mention deposits, ask: We have seen that banks pay salaries and lend money. Are these their only functions or do they have others?

If children mentioned both deposit and loan interest, invite them to compare the two amounts. Let's see again how much more money the bank can give you if you deposit one million lire for one year (suggest 50.000 lire if the child does not suggest a precise amount). If you borrow one million lire for one year, how much more do you have to give back? Why?

Who pays the people working in the bank?

How does she or he get the money to pay them?

9

Conflicting Data and Conceptual Change in History Experts

Margarita Limón and Mario Carretero[1]

Introduction

It can be said that knowledge acquisition in history has not been a very attractive topic for researchers in the last decades (see Voss et al., 1995 for a review). Two reasons, among others, can be mentioned as responsible for this lack of attention. On the one hand, society in general considers scientific literacy much more important than social and historical literacy and, on the other hand, history in itself is a rather ill-defined and fuzzy domain where it is always difficult to design cognitive tasks to be explored.

The study of reasoning in history has not been considered until now from the point of view of its relationship with domain-specific knowledge and conceptual change, but, rather, takes into account a subject's causal representation of historical situations. Even the relationship between evidence and reasoning strategies has not been studied. Only a few studies about social contents (e.g. Kuhn et al., 1994) and historical document evaluation e.g. Rouet et al.. (1996); Wineburg, (1991) can be mentioned. For example, Wineburg (1991) presented his subjects (eight historians and eight students) with a problem-solving task about the battle of Lexington. Eight documents about the battle were presented. His results showed that the more expert subjects — the historians — used three heuristics to solve the task: (i) the corroboration heuristic: historians corroborated in different documents the information and details they considered important; (ii) the sourcing heuristic: historians paid attention to the source of the documents presented, in order to assess their importance and reliability, and (iii) the contextualization heuristic: historians confronted the document information with their general knowledge to contextualize the historical event in its particular time and space.

Rouet et al. (1996) presented seven documents and a chronology of the main events of the Panamá Channel. They were asked to write an essay about four controversial issues about the Channel construction. For example, they asked if the US military intervention during the 1903 Panamanian revolution was justified. In their first study, the participants were 24 undergraduate students, and in the second study there were 19 subjects: eight history graduates and 11 psychology graduates. Results from the second study showed that both experts and novices used the corroboration and the sourcing heuristics. Nevertheless, contextualizations were more frequent and qualitatively different in experts' essays compared with novices'. Experts' contextual statements were more elaborated and intermediate between specific knowledge and general world knowledge.

We have pointed out (Carretero et al., 1994) that history is a discipline where, it seems to us, extremely important to characterize historical cognition and, particularly, knowledge acquisition. For example, social and individual values and ideology often have a strong

[1]We are grateful for the grants PB93-0245 and PB5-541A-2-640 received from DGICYT supervised by the second author. We are also grateful to the participants in the studies described.

influence in how historical events are understood and taught in schools. In comparison to the domain of science, historical content seems to be much more influenced by these ideological factors and, therefore, it is quite frequent to find different interpretations of the same historical event. To give an example, the reader can think about the "Discovery" of America by Columbus. In Spanish textbooks, the term "Discovery" appears, and for a long period most of them related this event as epic and glorious conquering by the Spanish Monarchy. However, the same event was reported in quite a different way in South America. In 1992, when the fifth centenary of the "Discovery" was celebrated, the term "meeting" of two cultures was proposed instead of "discovery". Leaving aside the anecdote, the change proposed seems to us very meaningful in emphasizing how society values and ideology affect the representation people build of historical events. The national identity and the collective historical consciousness is tightly related to these historical representations.

The acquisition of historical knowledge involves understanding that different interpretations and explanations of historical events are possible. On the other hand, historians have sustained different historiographical positions, such as the Annales school, the Marxist theory of history, or the History of Mentalities (Carretero et al., 1994). These positions differ in their conception of history and, therefore, on their selection and search for evidence to explain historical events.

In contrast to the situation in the domain of history, enormous progress has been made in the study of cognitive processes in relation to the science domain (Chi et al., 1988). Much of these efforts have come from studies that consider the enormous importance of a subject-specific knowledge base for conceptual change (Carey, 1985; Vosniadou, 1991; Vosniadou & Brewer, 1987). Some studies have focused on children and adults' logical reasoning skills, to try and find similarities and differences between experts, children and lay subjects (Kuhn et al., 1988; Kuhn, 1989). Kuhn (1993) proposed that the characterization of science as argument allows the establishment of links between the scientific thinking of the child, adolescent or adult and, the professional scientist. For her, both scientific and informal theories must be regarded as possible states of affairs that are subject to confirmation and disconfirmation by evidence. This recognition entails awareness of the theory and, therefore, the possibility of reflecting on it. At that rate, by bringing evidence to bear on it, the theory can be evaluated. But this evidence needs to be considered as an object of cognition that is different from the theory. It is only in this way that the evidence becomes capable of disconfirming the theory. According to Kuhn (1993), both the ability of recognizing the possible falsehood of a theory and the identification of evidence capable of disconfirming, would be abilities that belong to both the informal and the scientific reasoning.

From our point of view, these abilities are also involved in the process of conceptual change. If someone is going to change his/her theory it seems important to (i) distinguish theory and evidence, (ii) be aware of both theory and evidence in order to reflect about them, (iii) recognize the possible falsehood of a theory, and (iv) identify the evidence capable of disconfirming the theory. The presentation of conflicting or anomalous data may facilitate recognition of the possible falsehood of a theory and identify evidence capable of disconfirming the evidence.

Nevertheless, it is important to point out that in the domain of history, which is an open, ill-defined and fuzzy domain, falsification in the Popperian sense, i.e. understood as the testing of a hypothesis against counter-evidence using deductive logic and by mean of a crucial experiment, is not always possible. Disconfirming evidence can change to some extent the theory or the hypothesis, but often it is not enough to definitely discard the theory. For example, in the case of the microhistorical problem we pose in the empirical study presented below, evidence to support that the nobility did not benefit from the expulsion of the Morisco population in Spain can be found, but this disconfirming evidence is not enough to discard this hypothesis. In fact, it is possible to find evidence that supports it. Depending on subjects' selection and evaluation of evidence, it is possible to find confirming and disconfirming evidence. History is the study of the past, and one of its features is that this study may change with time: a new methodology to study historical evidence can be used, new evidence can be discovered, the historiographical positions may change leading to a different analysis of the evidence. In sum, this "reconstruction" of the past could be considered never-ending, and almost always remains open. Therefore, falsification in the Popperian sense is rather rare — if not impossible — in the domain of history. In other words, in general, no instant rejection of a theory is possible.

Thagard (1992) analysed some conceptual revolutions in science and he proposed a theory of conceptual change [see Limón & Carretero, 1997 for a review]. He stated that, in most science revolutions, there is a large explanation-driven component, in which concepts and hypotheses are generated to explain puzzling facts or anomalous data. Although he refers to the relationships between old and new theories, he distinguishes four kind of relationships between successive theories. These are ordered by decreasing amounts of cumulativeness and can be related to responses to anomalous data, as proposed by Chinn and Brewer (1993), and the alpha, beta and gamma behaviours described by Piaget (1975) (see Table 1). These four kinds of relations are incorporation, sublation, supplantation and disregard. If a new theory T2 completely absorbs the previous theory T1, then T2 incorporates T1. Therefore, T2 is just an extension of T1. If T2 partially incorporates T1 while rejecting aspects of T1, then T2 sublates T1. If T2 involves the near-total rejection of T1, then T2 supplants T1. Finally, if the adoption of T2 comes about simply by ignoring T1, then T2 disregards T1.

Chinn and Brewer (1993) proposed seven types of response to anomalous data: ignoring, rejecting, excluding, hold them in abeyance, reinterpreting, peripheral changes and theory change. Anomalous data are not accepted when the individual ignores or rejects them. In contrast, they are accepted in the other types of responses. Anomalous data are explained by the individual when some changes in the individual's theory are produced (peripheral or theory change). When conflicting data are ignored, rejected or held in abeyance, the individual is not able to explain them. No theory change is achieved in any of these responses, except when a peripheral change or a theory change is made. They considered that the fundamental ways in which scientists react to anomalous data appear to be identical to the ways in which non-scientist adults and science students react to such data. Therefore, these responses to conflicting or anomalous data could also be applied to the domain of history.

On describing the processes of equilibration, Piaget (1975) distinguishes adapted and unadapted reactions to anomalous data. Unadapted ones are produced when subjects do not realize the conflict between the new information and the old. Adapted responses are classified into three types. Subjects ignore or do not take into account the conflicting data in "alpha" behaviours. "Beta" behaviours are characterized by producing partial modifications in the subject's theory. New data are considered a variation and are integrated into the subjects' theory. This includes data in an explicative schema that before was not used to explain them (generalization), or excluding those data from a schema that was previously employed, and which explained them by a different schema or even by building an "*ad hoc*" principle (differentiation). These partial modifications never affect the central core of the subject's theory. Generalization and differentiation are used to solve data-theory conflicts. Nevertheless, "gamma" behaviours involve the modification of the central core of the theory. Conceptual modifications need to be made in this type of behaviour to suppress the conflict. Thus, "gamma" behaviours would imply a strong restructuring (Carey, 1985) of the subject's theory.

Our research is related to recent efforts to establish a fruitful relationship between cognitive conflict and conceptual change. Both traditional cognitive developmental theories, Piagetian and more recent approaches in science education (see Duit, this volume for a review), consider cognitive conflict as a necessary but not sufficient requisite to produce conceptual change, at least in the field of science (Dagher, 1994; Dreyfus et al.; 1990).

In general, it can be predicted that historical content tends to raise more resistance to conceptual change than scientific content. This could be because of a strong relationship between historical content and the subjects affective and ideological attitudes (Carretero et al, 1994; Chinn and Brewer, 1993). For example, apparently it should be easier for novices studying history to change their ideas about a physics problem, such as a falling body problem, than to change their representations about the independence of their country.

We were interested in the study of the interaction between reasoning strategies, such as evidence selection and evaluation to develop an explanation — an argumentation — and domain-specific knowledge. Therefore, we decided to include in our research a sample made up of high domain-specific knowledge individuals, in order to study the strategies experts employ, and because it was supposed that they should be able to more easily avoid ideological and affective influences.

An Empirical Study on the Expulsion of the Moriscos from Spain in the 17th Century

We posed a microhistorical problem about a very specific topic: the expulsion of the Moriscos from Spain in 1609. The Moriscos were people who were forced by the Spanish monarchy to convert to Catholicism between 1499 and 1526. However, these people continued living according to the Arab customs until they were definitively expelled from Spain in 1609. The general objectives of the studies were:

a. To study the interaction between reasoning strategies and domain-specific knowledge.
b. To study how historical evidence is selected, interpreted and employed to build an explanation — a hypothesis — to solve a historical problem by subjects with a high domain-specific knowledge about the content of the problem.
c. To study the effect of presenting conflicting data in subjects with a high level of domain-specific knowledge in the subject of history.

In this paper, we will focus on the results obtained for the third of these objectives.[2]

---

[2]Results concerning the "a" and "b" objectives can be found in Limón and Carretero (1998) and Limón (1995).

Table 1: Reactions to anomalous data and degree of conceptual change

Responses to anomalous data		Chinn & Brewer (1993)	Degree of conceptual change	Relation between the old and the new theory
Piaget (1975)		**Chinn & Brewer (1993)**		**Thagard (1992)**
Unadapted responses	Unawareness of contradiction	Ignore[a]	No conceptual change at all	T1
Adapted responses (awareness of contradiction)	Alpha	Ignore, Reject, Exclude, Abeyance	No conceptual change but awareness of contradiction	T1
	Beta	Reinterpret data maintaining T1	Weak restructuring	Incorporating (T2 is just an extension of T1) Sublating (T1 & T2)
		Peripheral changes to T1		Sublating (T1 & T2), Supplanting (T1 & T2)
	Gamma	Accept the data and change of theory	Strong restructuring	Disregarding (T2)

[a]Subjects can ignore the anomalous data being unaware of the contradiction they involve, or being aware of it, but putting the data aside.

Study 1

Subjects

Two groups participated in this study. Fifteen final-year history undergraduates made up Group 1 (G1) and 15 specialists in modern history (15th to 17th centuries) made up Group 2 (G2).

Procedure

Part One

The aim of Part One was to examine subjects' ideas about the expulsion of the Moriscos from Spain in 1609. A closed-item questionnaire was presented to the subjects, who had to select from three possible answers the one they considered closest to their beliefs and ideas about the expulsion of the Moriscos. However, if they considered that none of the possibilities coincided with their view, they could introduce a new option or make any changes they wished to the ones presented, always explaining their changes to the experimenter. Our aim was to allow people to express their own ideas about the topics explored.

The questionnaire presented to Group 1 had 38 items. The first 18 items (Part A) were basic questions about the customs and way of life of the Moriscos, the relationships between them and the Christian population, the areas where the Moriscos lived and the general context prior to the expulsion. The aim of these questions was to measure the previous knowledge students had about the Moriscos and their expulsion. The remaining 20 items were designed to explore the subjects' evaluation of the Moriscos, their ideological point of view, and their ideas concerning their expulsion from Spain and to whose advantage and disadvantage it was.

Group 2 had to complete only the last 20 items of the questionnaire (Part B). It was considered that the experience of these subjects as teachers and researchers guaranteed that their basic knowledge about the topic was extensive enough to deal with the task; a time factor also played a part in this decision.

Once they had finished the questionnaire, subjects underwent a short interview where they had to outline their global evaluation of the expulsion, its causes and its consequences, and to decide to whose advantage and disadvantage it was.

Part Two

This part was divided into three phases.

Phase 1

Subjects were given a short text — about 20 lines, or 200 words — where they were introduced to the historical problem they had to solve. They were told about the situation of the

Duchy of Gandía in 1609 (the expulsion date). The expulsion occurred and it had several consequences for the Duchy and its inhabitants. Five documents with data about the situation of the Duchy of Gandía before and after 1609 were presented. They provided information and evidence for participants to support their answer to the following question: to whose advantage was the expulsion of the Moriscos in the Duchy of Gandía? Four possibilities were presented:

a. The Duke of Gandía.
b. A local oligarchy, most of whose members had important positions in the government of the town of Gandía.
c. Neither of these (neither the Duke nor the oligarchy).
d. Both of them (both the Duke and the oligarchy).

Subjects were asked to read carefully and to examine the data presented in the five documents. Once they had studied the data, they answered the question. They were asked to justify their answer and to indicate the documents they used to elaborate their explanation.

Phase 2

Subjects were given five more documents containing more data about the situation of the Duchy of Gandia before and after 1609, and were asked to examine these new data. Then, they were asked to answer the same question again, taking into account the documents presented in both Phases 1 and 2: to whose advantage was the expulsion of the Moriscos in the Duchy of Gandía? The same four possibilities were presented as in Phase 1. Again, they were asked to explain and justify their answers, indicating on which documents these were based.

Phase 3

Each subject was presented with a table containing data, extracted from documents 1 to 10 (see Appendix, Tables A, B, C and D). The information included in these tables conflicted with the choice subjects made in Phase 2. For instance, if the answer given in Phase 2 was "B" (it was to the advantage of a local oligarchy), the table presented in this phase was Table "B", where arguments and data conflicting with this choice appeared. If the answer given in Phase 2 was "A" (it was to the advantage of the Duke), the table presented in Phase 3 was Table "A" (conflicting data about the hypothesis of the Duke's profits). The same procedure was carried out when the answers given in Phase 2 were "C" or "D".

Description of the Documents

The documents included data about the situation in Gandía before and after the Morisco expulsion in 1609. Data supporting the four possibilities were included in the documents, which referred to five key factors involved in the problem presented.

1. The repopulation of the area from which the Moriscos were expelled. On the one hand, this repopulation gave rise to new economic conditions that were favourable to the land-owners (Document 1); but on the other hand, the departure of the Moriscos led to a redistribution of the lands they had occupied (Document 6).
2. Incomes in the Duchy before and after 1609, centred around the cultivation of sugar cane. Moriscos were specialists in this crop, the main source of income in Gandía until 1609. When the Moriscos were expelled, sugar cane production decreased spectacularly (Documents 2 and 7).
3. Social, political and cultural factors involved in the expulsion (Documents 3 and 8).
4. Demographical evolution of the Duchy during the 17th century. As shown in the Document 4, a considerable proportion of the Duchy's population was Morisco. Thus, their expulsion had relevant consequences for its demography (Document 9), repopulation and economy.
5. Economic data of the Duchy. Evolution of incomes and expenses throughout the 17th century (Documents 5 and 10).
   One document representing each key factor was presented in each of Phase 1 and 2.

Results

In order to study the process followed by the subjects we analysed the answer given by each subject throughout the task. Table 2 shows the subjects' prior hypothesis (H0) and their choice in Phases 1, 2 and 3 (P1, P2 and P3, respectively).

Two or more options appear in H_0 when more than one option could be chosen by the subject, taking into account his/her answers in the prior knowledge questionnaire and the interview. Two or three letters appear in rows P1, P2 and P3 when subjects gave a mixed answer. For instance, Subject 6 from Group 2 said that in the short term, and from an economic point of view, no-one benefited from the expulsion of the Moriscos (Answer "C"), that in the medium term the oligarchy (Answer "B") gained economic, political and social advantages, and that in the long term, and from a political and social perspective, both groups obtained advantages (Answer "D"). To study the effect of presenting conflicting data, we have evaluated which and how many subjects changed their Phase 2 choice after Phase 3 (where conflicting data were presented). Five of 15 subjects from Group 1 (33.4%) did not change the answer they gave in Phase 2 after Phase 3. Ten of 15 subjects from Group 1 (66.7%) changed their answer after being presented with the conflicting data in Phase 3. In Group 2, six of 15 subjects (40%) did not change their answer and nine of 15 (60%) did change it. A chi-square test was performed and showed no significant differences between the number of subjects who changed their answer in Phase 3 in Groups 1 and 2.

Subjects' answers were classified according to the categories described below in order to have a more qualitative analysis of the answers provided and the degree of change achieved after presenting conflicting data. The complete process followed by each subject (Table 2) was taken into account to categorize subjects' answers.

Table 2: Answers given in the three phases in Study 1

Subjects

	Group 1 (Students) (n=15)															Group 2 (Professors) (n=15)														
	S1	S2	S3	S4	S5	S6	S7	S8	S9	S10	S11	S12	S13	S14	S15	S1	S2	S3	S4	S5	S6	S7	S8	S9	S10	S11	S12	S13	S14	S15
H0	C	C	C	C	C	C	C	C	C	C	C	C	C	C	C	C	C	C	A	C	C	C	D	D	C	A	C	C	C	C
		A					B			A				B				D	D	D		A		D	C		A			
																		B												
P1	D	B	C	C	C	C	B	B	B	C	C	C	C	C	C	C	C	C	A	C	C	A	D	D	C	A	C	C	C	C
	C								B															B						
P2	D	B	B	D	B	B	B	B	B	D	B	D	B	D	B	B	B	B	A	B	B	B	D	D	B	B	A	D	B	B
	C								D															B				B		
P3	D	B	B	C	C	B	B	B	D	B	B	C	C	C	C	C	B	B	D	C	C	B	B	D	D	C	B	C	C	B
	C		C						D	D						B				D	B		C		B		D	B	B	B
																					D									

Category 1

Subjects who maintained their hypothesis. These subjects appeared to be "insensible" to the conflicting data presented. All Group 1 subjects and subjects 9 and 10 of Group 2 were "insensible" to the information presented throughout the task, they maintained their prior hypothesis without changing it.

Example: Subject 2 from Group 1 (history undergraduate) said the following in Phase 2:

> The oligarchy benefited because they obtained lands and titles of nobility (Documents 6 and 8). The Duke lost out because his expenses were the same before and after the expulsion, while incomes decreased, in spite of the changes in the main resource of the Duchy — sugar cane (Document 7). On the other hand, Document 6 shows that the land redistribution was chaotic, and this led to a lack of profitability.

Therefore, his answer was "B". In Phase 3, after Table "B" was presented (see Appendix) he accepted Point 3 in Table "B" (demographic crisis) and the probable economic losses of the oligarchy, though he indicated that there were insufficient data to state something like this. Even taking these points into account, he considered the social improvement of the oligarchy as the most important aspect, since this was the main goal in the historical period where the expulsion occurred. Nevertheless, he continued thinking that the most correct hypothesis was "B" (The oligarchy benefited from the expulsion of the Moriscos in Gandía).

Category 2

Subjects who maintained their hypothesis, but who modified it slightly after reading the conflicting data. In this case, conflicting data seemed to have an effect — albeit slight — on subjects' hypotheses.

Example: Subject 3 from Group 1 (undergraduate in history) said in Phase 2:

> The oligarchy benefited because:
>
> — The Duke's income is lower than his expenses (Document 10).
> — The comparison between Documents 2 and 7 shows the dramatic decrease in sugar cane production.
> — The comparison between Documents 4 and 9 shows that there is depopulation in the area.
> — Morisco lands are going to become the property of the principal officers of the city (Documents 6 and 8).

After seeing Table B, she accepted that there was a demographic crisis, but she thought there were insufficient direct economic data about the oligarchy to claim that they also suffered an economic crisis, or that their economy was influenced by the Duke's. She indicated the Duke's expenses continued to be higher than his incomes (Document 10), and that the members of the oligarchy would become the owners of the lands abandoned by the Moriscos. She concluded that the oligarchy benefited, but only slightly.

Category 3

Subjects who changed the answer given in Phase 2 in Phase 3. After presenting conflicting data, these subjects moved back to their initial hypothesis, but added some of the data presented in Phase 3; in fact, they added only data that coincided with their hypothesis.

Example: According to the prior knowledge questionnaire and the initial interview, Subject 6, from Group 1 (undergraduate in history) would have chosen Option "C" (no-one benefited from the expulsion of the Moriscos in Gandía). His answer in Phase 1 was "C":

> The new conditions the Duke can now introduce [after the expulsion] are a possible advantage for him (Document 1). Document 5 shows the Duke's economic losses. In spite of some signs of recovery, incomes decrease gradually. Although there is no [direct] data about the oligarchy, the population decrease (Document 4) would be a disadvantage for them since, as a result of the decreasing population, the Duke would probably eliminate some of the municipal offices.

In Phase 2, his answer was "D" (both of them benefited):

> The Duke's benefits are considerable: the economic balance is positive after 1636 (Document 10), and there is a demographic recovery: the birth rate in Gandía is higher than in Valencia (Document 9). The comparison between Documents 2 and 7 shows an increase in incomes, despite the disappearance of the sugar cane income. The members of the oligarchy benefit because they obtain tax-free lands and nobility titles (Documents 6 and 8).

In Phase 3, after carefully reading Table D (see Appendix) he again chose Option "C" (no-one benefited), and based his answer on Points 1, 2 and 3 of Table D:

> The expulsion causes a demographic crisis. Therefore, the lands abandoned by the Moriscos would not be occupied very quickly. Moreover, there were some problems with the taxes and charges inherited from the Moriscos, which the new owners of the lands had to pay.
>
> — The Duke suffers an economic crisis, exacerbated by currency depreciation.
> — The oligarchy would also suffer an economic crisis, as they would be unable to recover the loans they made to the Duke.

This subject added to his initial hypothesis (nobody benefited, the expulsion had only negative consequences, and was strongly damaging from an economic point of view) some of the data presented in Table D that confirmed and reinforced his hypothesis.

Category 4

As in the case of Category 3, these subjects changed the answer they made in Phase 2 during Phase 3. They did not merely add data, but rather adapted their hypothesis and modified it (distinguishing short-, medium- and long-term effects and the type of advantage — social, political and/or economic) to assimilate the new and conflicting data. In sum, they extended their hypothesis to include the new data.

Example: Subject 6 from Group 2 (modern history specialist) said in Phase 2:

> Apparently, the oligarchy benefited, because they obtained lands and nobility titles, but the economic data does not show that the Duke benefited. However, this seems to me a contradiction, because it does not coincide with typical situations where power networks exist. In these networks, if one benefits, everybody benefits. There is a demographic increase, according to Documents 4 and 9, and a comparison between Document 2 and Document 7 shows that the sugar cane crop was lost. Thus, the answer I consider to be the most correct is "B" (the oligarchy benefited).

In Phase 3, after seeing Table B, she said:

> In the short term the Duke does not benefit on an economic level, although perhaps he does so on a political level (he may obtain greater political control in Gandía, since the main offices were held by people belonging to his network — though it would be necessary to know more details, for instance, the family relationships between the Duke and members of the oligarchy). In the long term, there are political benefits for the Duke. With regard to the oligarchy, in the short term, particularly during the years immediately after the expulsion, they could lose out from an economic point of view, but in the medium term, they benefited because they obtained lands and political power. In the long term, they also benefited, because their social position improved, and they constituted a group with political–social power to face the Royal Court. Lands became an instrument for acquiring socio-political power, as was usual in that historical period.

In short, her final answer was in the short term, at an economic level, "C" (neither of them); in the medium term, "B" (the oligarchy), from an economic, social and political point of view; and in the long term, "D" (both of them), from a social and political perspective.

According to the prior knowledge questionnaire and the initial interview, her answer would be "C" (neither of them"), and this was the answer she chose in Phase 1. Thus, this subject extended her hypothesis and integrated the new data into it, differentiating the effects of the expulsion according to a temporal dimension (effects in the short-, medium- and long-term), and to a type-of-benefit dimension (economic, political and social). This "extended" hypothesis did not contradict her hypothesis after Phase 2. She integrated some of her prior ideas: first, the expulsion was damaging at an economic level in the short term, but beneficial at a political and social level in the long term; second, in that period it was usual to find the establishment of networks of power motivated by a desire for social improvement (in the case of the oligarchy) and for the power of the privileged groups to be maintained.

Category 5

In this case, subjects' changed their initial hypothesis partially, after they were presented with the conflicting data. Obviously, these subjects chose a different option in Phase 3 from that chosen in Phase 2.

Example: Subject 11 from Group 1 (undergraduate in history) chose "C" (neither of them) in Phase 1. He argued that the Duke suffered an economic crisis (Document 5) and that, consequently, the oligarchy would have suffered too, although some particular individuals may obtain some benefits. In Phase 2, he said:

> The oligarchy benefits because its members obtain lands and social improvement (Documents 6 and 8). The Duke tries to recover his economic equilibrium. Finally, expenses and incomes are balanced, and he makes neither a profit nor a loss (Document 10).

Therefore, his choice was "B" in Phase 3, he chose Option "D" (both of them). He accepted the economic losses of both (Point 2 in Table B) and the close relationship between their economies (Point 5 in Table B). However, he considered that, to some extent, there was a demographic recovery. This recovery was beneficial for both of them (see Point 3 in Table B). He also thought that both benefited at a social and political level, which made up for the economic losses and led to a recovery of the economic balance.

In this case, a change was produced: at the beginning, he thought neither of them benefited. Nevertheless, after reviewing the documents, he considered the oligarchy benefited. Finally, after presenting the conflicting data, his opinion was that both of them benefited from the expulsion. The "recovery of the economic balance" point was already present in his answer in Phase 2, but it was in Phase 3 where he introduced (because of the information presented in Table B) the political and social benefits and the interrelationship between the two groups that made economic recovery possible. Although he did not completely change his initial hypothesis (both were damaged at an economic level), there was a new element included from Table B: the political and social benefits as a consequence of the interrelationship between the Duke and the oligarchy. These five categories were ordered from one to five, according to the effect produced by the conflicting data presented: from effect zero (Category 1) to a partial change of the subject's hypothesis (Category 5). The results are shown in Table 3.

An ANOVA on the answers given to the conflicting data (scored from one to five, according to the category where their answers was classified, i.e. Category 1 = one point ; Category 2 = two points, etc.) with one between subjects factor (domain-specific knowledge level: students and historians) was performed. The results showed no significant differences between undergraduates and professors.

Table 3: Categorization of the answers after presenting conflicting information

	Group 1 (Students) (n = 15)		Group 2 (Professors) (n =15)	
Category 1: Subjects who maintained their hypothesis	S1, S2, S8, S9, S10	5 (33.3%)	S2, S3, S7, S9, S10, S15	6 (40%)
Category 2: Subjects who maintained their hypothesis, but slightly changed	S3	1 (6.67%)	S1, S8	2 (13.3%)
Category 3: Subjects who moved back to H0, but added some confirming data	S5, S6, S14, S15	4 (26.7%)		0 (0%)
Category 4: Subjects who extended their hypothesis to include the new data	S4, S13	2 (13.3%)	S4, S5, S6, S11, S12, S13, S14	
Category 5: Subjects who changed their initial hypothesis partially	S7, S12, S11	3 (20%)		

Study 2

Subjects[3]

Two groups participated in this study. Fifteen final-year history undergraduates made up Group 1 (G1) and 15 specialists in modern history (15th to 17th centuries) made up Group 2 (G2).

Procedure

The procedure followed in Study 2 was exactly the same as that in Study 1 except for Phase 3 of the second part of the task. In this case, instead of presenting conflicting data, subjects were asked to review all the documents presented in Phase 1 and Phase 2, one by one. They had to explain who took advantage and who took disadvantage of the expulsion of the Moriscos in the Gandía Duchy taking into account just the information included in each document. The answers were recorded by the experimenter.

After they reviewed all the documents, they were asked to again answer the question posed at the end of Phase 1 and Phase 2.

Results

To study the process followed by the subjects we analysed the answer given by each subject throughout the task. Table 4 shows the subjects' prior hypothesis (H_0) and their choice in Phases 1, 2 and 3 (P1, P2 and P3), respectively. Two or more options appear in H_0 when more than one option could be chosen by the subject, taking into account her/his answers in the prior knowledge questionnaire and the interview. Two or three letters appear in rows P1, P2 and P3 when subjects gave a mixed answer.

As in Study 1, we have evaluated which and how many subjects changed their Phase 2 choice after Phase 3 (where they reviewed the documents presented). Ten of 15 subjects from Group 1 (66.7%) did not change the answer they gave in Phase 2 after Phase 3. Five of 15 subjects from Group 1 (33.4%) changed their answer after being presented with the conflicting data in Phase 3. In Group 2, eight of 15 subjects (53.4%) did not change their answer and seven of 15 subjects (46.7%) did change. A chi-square test was performed, and showed no significant differences between the number of subjects who changed their answer in Phase 3 in Groups 1 or 2.

Subjects' answers were classified according to the same categories described in the Results section of Study 1, in order to analyse, from a qualitative point of view, the answers provided and the degree of change achieved after reviewing the documents presented. The complete process followed by each subject (Table 4) was taken into account to categorize the subjects' answers. Table 5 shows the results obtained.

---

[3]Participants in Studies 1 and 2 were different people, although they were extracted from the same population.

Table 4:   Answers given in the three phases in Study 2

Subjects

	Group 1 (Students) (n = 15)															Group 2 (Professors) (n = 15)														
	S1	S2	S3	S4	S5	S6	S7	S8	S9	S10	S11	S12	S13	S14	S15	S1	S2	S3	S4	S5	S6	S7	S8	S9	S10	S11	S12	S13	S14	S15
H_0	C	A	C	C	C	C	A	C	C	C	C	D	C	D	D	C	C	C	C	C	C	A	A	C	C	C	D	B	B	C
P_1	C	C	C	C	C	C	C	C	C	C	C	D	D	B	C	C	C	B	A	A	C	C	C	A	C	C	D	B	B	A
P_2	B	B	B	C	B	B	B	B	C	B	B	B	D	B	B	B	B	B	B	D	B	B	B	B	B	D	D	B	D	C
P_3	B	B	C	C	B	D	B	B	C	B	B	B	B	D	B	D	C	D	B	D	B	B	D	B	C	D	B	B	D	C

Table 5:   Categorization of the answers after reviewing the information presented

	Group 1 (Students) (n = 15)		Group 2 (Professors) (n = 15)	
Category 1: Subjects who maintained their hypothesis	S1, S2, S4,S5,S7,S8, S9,S11,S12, S15	10 (66.7%)	S4,S5,S6,S7, S10,S13, S14,S15	8 (53.3%)
Category 2: Subjects who maintained their hypothesis, but slightly changed	S13	1 (6.7%)		0 (0%)
Category 3: Subjects who moved back to H_0, but added some confirming data	S3	1 (6.7%)	S1	1 (6.7%)
Category 4: Subjects who extended their hypothesis to include the new data	S6,S10, S14	3 (20%)	S2, S8, S9, S11, S12	5 (33.3%)
Category 5: Subjects who changed their initial hypothesis partially	0 (0%)		S3	1 (6.7%)

An ANOVA on the answers given to the conflicting data (scored from one to five, according to the category where their answers were classified, i.e. Category 1 = one point ; Category 2 = two points, etc.) with one-between-subjects factor (domain-specific knowledge level: students and historians) was performed. The results showed no significant differences between undergraduates and professors.

Discussion

As can be seen from the results section, about a half of the participants in both studies did not change their initial hypothesis at all during the three phases of the task (see Tables 2 and 4). Totals were 18 of 30 subjects (60%) from Study 2 and 11 of 30 subjects (36.7%) from Study 1 (see Tables 3 and 5). These results could be linked up to the well-known tendency of humans to "protect" their hypothesis and the great difficulties in changing or modifying it (e.g. Klayman & Ha, 1987; Koslowsky & Maqueda, 1993; Mynatt et al., 1977; Wason, 1960). The answers provided by these subjects belonged to the "unadapted responses" or "alpha responses" according to Piaget (1975). These participants showed an awareness of contradiction, but ignored, rejected, excluded or held in abeyance the conflicting data or all those that did not fit their explanation of the problem (see Table 1).

From a qualitative point of view, the presentation of conflicting data made the subjects change their hypothesis more, and a higher degree of conceptual change seemed to occur. The answers given by the subjects who changed their answer after presenting conflicting data or reviewing the information presented were mostly "beta answers" (except the Category 2 explanations that were "alpha answers"). Following Chinn and Brewer's (1993) terminology, they reinterpreted the data, although maintaining their hypothesis. This type of change involved a weak restructuring of their ideas, because some of them incorporated the conflicting data as an extension of their hypothesis (Category 3 explanations).

Just a few of subjects (Category 4), mainly some of the professors, reinterpreted the data and extended their hypothesis, employing generalization and differentiation (Piaget, 1975) according to three dimensions that seem to be linked to expertise in history (Carretero & Limón, 1995; Limón, 1995): (i) temporal dimension, (ii) a type-of-benefit dimension, and (iii) historical contextualization of the problem. Many of the explanations categorized in Category 4 point out that a different choice should be made if the historical event — the expulsion of the Moriscos in this case — was assessed in the short, medium or long term. Many of them referred to the level of analysis of the problem. In our problem, for example, specialists seemed to weigh more the social and the political aspects (particularly the typical situation that resulted from the power networks and the desires of a rising bourgeoisie) than the economical aspects, supported by their general knowledge of the period. Nevertheless, students used to interpreting the problem mainly from an economical point of view, employed their contemporary criteria to evaluate and interpret the information presented. Historians clearly contextualize their answer to the problem, confirming the results obtained by Wineburg (1991) and Rouet et al. (1996). Only 6% of the participants made a peripheral change of their hypothesis (Category 5 answers).

In conclusion, no radical conceptual change was achieved, but it is also true that our task posed a microhistorical problem; that is, it was similar to other situations that occurred in that period. To achieve a strong restructuring and, consequently, to develop a new hypothesis about the expulsion of the Moriscos, the analysis of more evidence would probably have been required. On the other hand, as has been emphasized in the domain of science (i.e. Vosniadou, 1994), the conceptual change process, understood as a strong restructuring, is an effortful, difficult and time-consuming process; therefore, such deep change was not expected in a task such as the one presented here.

From a instructional point of view, it is interesting to emphasize that both experimental conditions (presentation of conflicting data and documents review) were useful in promoting a certain degree of conceptual change: about 50% of the subjects made a weak restructuring of their prior hypothesis. Nevertheless, the presentation of conflicting data was more useful for students than for professors in promoting change. In Study 1, 10 of 15 subjects changed their hypothesis after looking at the conflicting data, whereas in Study 2, five of 15 subjects changed their hypothesis in Phase 3. The conflicting data presentation seemed to make them change their answer, although their arguments were not as clear as those of the professors, who, in general, were able to distinguish the dimensions that we have referred to.

Further research is needed to study further the role of the domain-specific knowledge level. Our subjects had a high-level of knowledge of the topic (even the students group), but it would be interesting to study if these strategies (presentation of conflicting data and reviewing the information presented) could work to promote some degree of conceptual change in people with a lower level of domain knowledge.

Appendix

General Information Presented at the Beginning of the Task

In 1609, the Duchy of Gandía belonged to the Borja family. The map we are giving you shows the Duke's possessions in Gandía after 1609.

The Duchy of Gandía was the nerve centre of Borja's possessions in the Kingdom of Valencia and, together with Oliva, the most profitable. They are both located on a fertile fluvial plain washed by the Vernissa and Alcoy rivers (now called Serpis) set between the sea and the mountain chain that encloses the plain on its west side. This location permits the development of a microclimate that favours the growing of tropical crops such as sugar cane. The village of Gandía was located close to the coast. Moriscos, who represented the majority of the inhabitants of the Duchy, were irreplaceable experts in the cultivation of cane sugar.

On the 22nd of September 1609, the Marquis of Caracena published an edict in which he announced a Royal Decree (of the 4th of August) by which Philip the III decreed the expulsion of the Moriscos from the Kingdom of Valencia, arguing religious reasons (failure of previous conversion attempts) and political reasons (Moriscos disturbed Christian kingdoms).

The Edict was published in Gandía on the 27th of September, giving the Moriscos three days to leave for Genova.

We are now going to present to you some documents that provide you with more information about the Moriscos and about the Duchy of Gandía before and after the expulsion. You must evaluate each of these documents carefully and, based on the information they provide, answer the question:

To Whose Advantage Was The Expulsion Of The Moriscos?

Select the option you consider the most suitable from the following:

a. The nobility (in this particular case the Duke of Gandía)
b. The local oligarchy, many of whom occupied important positions in the government of Gandía.
c. Neither of these.
d. Both the Duke and the local oligarchy.

After your selection, you must explain your choice and the documents on which you based it.

Tables Presented in Phase 3 (Study 1)

Table A: Given to subjects who chose Option A in Phase 2)

Duke's Falling Profits

As Table 5 (Document 5) shows, the Duke of Gandía's profit (net income) in 1605 was 5727 pounds, whilst in 1612 (three years after the expulsion) he made a net loss of 8327 pounds. His profits in 1699 fell by 78% compared to those of 1605.

Worsening of Duke's Economic Situation. Depreciation of the Currency

As can be seen on Document 10, the Duke's income fell by 42% between 1605 and 1612. Between 1605 and 1699 the fall was 33%. It should be borne in mind that, due to the depreciation of the currency, the pounds in 1699 were worth less than those of 1605, so that the Duke's real losses were even greater.

Fall in Population

According to Document 4, 60% of the Duchy's inhabitants were Moriscos, so that the expulsion led to a considerable fall in population. In 1712–1713 the total number of houses in the Duchy was 1643 (Document 9), whilst the 1609 (Document 4) figure had been 2015. Even a century later this loss of population had not been made up.

Loss of the Sugar Crop, Principal Source of Income for the Duchy

According to Document 2, by far the main source of income for the Duke before 1609 was the sugar crop (50.0% of his income). The Moriscos — as mentioned in information presented at the beginning of Phase 1 — were experts in this crop. According to Document 7, after 1609 only 4.12% of the Duke's income came from sugar. This crop was, moreover, specific to the area, due to its peculiar climatic conditions (as explained in the initial information).

Re-Distribution of the Moriscos' Lands After the Expulsion. Social Improvement of Those Who Received Them

According to Document 6, 58% of the lands formerly occupied by the Moriscos fell — tax free — into the hands of a select few. Some of these occupied offices in the government of Gandía (Document 8), and even managed to obtain titles of nobility (Table 8.2, Document 8).

Table B: Given to those who chose Option B in Phase 2

Distribution of the Moriscos' Lands: Duke's Greater Control

As Document 6 shows, a high proportion of those who received the Moriscos' lands were people connected with the Duke (relatives, officers of his court, etc.). According to Document 8, some of them occupied posts in the government of Gandía. In this way, the expulsion allowed the Duke to gain greater control over the lands formerly occupied by the Moriscos, and at the same time over the government of the city. Moreover, by giving lands tax-free, he succeeded in gaining the favour of the city's governors (for example, obtaining loans, as indicated on Document 10).

Money-Lenders in the Oligarchy Affected by the Duke's Economic Crisis

According to Document 10, the Duke's money-lenders seized his profits in 1604 and 1611 as a result of his serious economic crisis (as shown on Documents 5 and 10). If the Duke did not pay the money-lenders — the governors of Gandía frequently lent him money — they could not recover their money, and would themselves be the victims of an economic crisis.

Demographic Crisis: Lack of People to Work the Land

According to Document 4, 60% of the Duchy's inhabitants were Moriscos, so that the expulsion led to a considerable fall in population. In 1712–1713 the total number of houses in the Duchy was 1643 (Document 9), whilst the 1609 (Document 4) figure had been 2015. Even a century later this loss of population had not been made up. In a situation of demographic crisis, even though the members of the oligarchy received lands (Document 6) and were paid in kind (Document 1), there would be no people to work the lands.

Increase in the Duke's Income From Taxes on Houses and Lands. New "Cartas Puebla" Conditions

As shown by a comparison of the data on Documents 2 and 7, the taxes received by the Duke from houses and lands increased considerably after 1609 (his income from taxes on lands rose by 5.87%, and that from house taxes doubled). Thus, although the expulsion resulted in a 60% fall in population (Document 4) and, therefore, of an important part of the income from taxes on houses and lands, the Duke's income increased considerably as a result of the new system of charges outlined on Document 1. The expulsion allowed the Duke to establish new conditions on his properties (new cartas puebla) and in the exploitation of monopolies and commerce (Document 1). There is a type of "refeudalization" of the area.

Endogenous Repopulation; Economic Interdependence of the Two Groups

A considerable proportion of the lands (56.3%, Document 6) were given to citizens of Gandía (endogenous repopulation), many of whom had connections with the Duke (Document 6), and some of whom occupied important posts in the government (Document 8) and were money-lenders to the Duke.

Thus, their economy appears to be closely connected to the Duke's, so that if the Duke suffers a serious economic crisis (Documents 5 and 10) and the repopulation is endogenous — i.e. there is no influx of settlers from outside who could revitalize the economy — then it is unlikely that the situation of the oligarchy would be much better.

Table C: Given to subjects who chose Option "C" in Phase 2

More Peaceful Situation in the Duchy at a Social, Political and Religious Level

According to Document 3, clashes between Moriscos and Christians were frequent in the years leading up to 1609. The expulsion resulted in a more peaceful social, political and religious situation. Moreover, the fact that the expulsion was in line with the wishes of the Royal Court would result in political and even economic benefits for the Duchy.

New "Cartas Puebla" Conditions

According to Document 1, the expulsion allowed for the imposition of new conditions on the new vassals, and for the reintroduction of payment in kind in order to avoid losses due to inflation. The new conditions of "distribution of fruits" were always favourable to the landowner (i.e. to the Duke and the oligarchy).

The Duke Succeeds in Palliating His Crisis and the Oligarchy, in Improving Their Social Position

The Duke of Gandía was, even before 1609, immersed in a serious economic crisis (according to Table 5, his profits went from 20,896 pounds in 1582 to 5727 pounds in 1605; Document 10 tells us that his profits were seized in 1604). He needed money, which he obtained thanks to the new conditions imposed in the new cartas puebla (Document 1), and also from the money-lenders (many of whom were those who received tax-free ex-Morisco lands — according to Documents 6 and 8), as shown by his debt in 1605 and 1612 (although he didn't pay, he still received loans) — Document 10. He probably obtained loans in exchange for the concession of tax-free lands. Members of the oligarchy received lands and, in the longer term, improved their social position (they received titles: Table 8.2, Document 8).

A Degree of Economic Recovery

Document 10 shows that there was a degree of economic recovery in the Duchy after 1636: administration costs increased and the debt fell considerably. The "distribution of fruits" became the principal source of income after 1609: there had been a change (sugar replaced by other crops, such as citrus fruits, grapes, olives), which appears to have been beneficial.

Positive Demographic Evolution

The birthrate (Table 9.2, Document 9) is higher in Gandía than in the País Valenciano as a whole. The increase is particularly notable from 1650, which appears to confirm the economic recovery of the area. The population level, considering that it suffers from the expulsion and from a plague epidemic between 1649 and 1652 (Document 9), undergoes a clear recovery after 1682 (between 1650 and 1682 it nearly doubles). In the city of Gandía in 1712, there are 20% more houses than before the expulsion (Document 4675 houses, as against 816 in 1712), which appears to suggest an economic recovery.

Table D: Given to those who chose Option D in Phase 2

Demographic Crisis: Lack of People to Work the Land

According to Document 4, 60% of the Duchy's population were Moriscos, so that the expulsion led to a considerable fall in population. In 1712–1713 the total number of houses in the Duchy was 1643 (Document 9), whilst the 1609 (Document 4) figure had been 2015. Even a century later this loss of population had not been made up. This demographic crisis meant that there was a lack of people to work the lands.

Duke's Economic Crisis

As Table 5 (Document 5) shows, the Duke of Gandía's profits (net income) in 1605 were 5727 pounds, whilst in 1612 (three years after the expulsion) he made a net loss of 8327 pounds. His profits in 1699 fell by 78% compared to those of 1605. As can be seen on Document 10, the Duke's income fell by 42% between 1605 and 1612. Between 1605 and 1699 the fall was 33%. It should be borne in mind that, due to the depreciation of the currency, the pounds of 1699 were worth less than those of 1605, so that the Duke's real losses were even greater.

Economic Crisis of the Duke's Money-Lenders

As Document 10 shows, the Duke's money-lenders, among whom were officials of the city of Gandía (many of whom received tax-free former Morisco lands — Documents 6 and 8) succeeded in seizing his profits in 1604 and 1611, given his grave economic crisis (see Documents 5 and 10). The non-repayment of these loans would lead to a serious economic crisis for the money-lenders.

Loss of the Sugar Crop

According to Document 2, by far the main source of income for the Duke before 1609 was the sugar crop (50.02% of his income). The Moriscos — as mentioned in the initial information — were experts in this crop. According to Document 7. after 1609 only 4.12% of the Duke's income came from sugar. According to Document 1, the "distribution of fruits" was introduced after the departure of the Moriscos (experts in sugar cultivation), and, given that sugar was the most heavily taxed crop under the new system of payments, other produce, such as tree-fruits, grapes and olives, began to be cultivated more. This type of produce was also grown in areas adjacent to the Duchy, whilst sugar — as explained in the initial information — was a crop specific to Gandía, due to its peculiar climatic conditions. Thus, the loss of the sugar crop led to a drop in the commercial profitability of the Duchy.

Slow and Endogenous Repopulation

According to Document 6, the repopulation was endogenous (58.83% of the former Morisco lands passed to a few members of the Duke's entourage) and slow, due to the problem of rent charges (taxes imposed on the Morisco lands). Thus, the lands left vacant as a result of the expulsion could not be reoccupied by people with a sound economic base, and this was an obstacle to the rapid economic reactivation of the area.

10

When Change Does Not Mean Replacement: Different Representations for Different Contexts

Juan Ignacio Pozo, Miguel Angel Gómez and Angeles Sanz[1]

The Nature of Conceptual Change About the Nature of Matter

In the last decade, studies about science learning and instruction, and their application to education, have been mostly devoted to the identification and understanding of students' alternative frameworks or ideas about scientific phenomena. Many studies in various domains of science (physics, chemistry, biology, etc.) have shown that students hold informal or intuitive ideas for interpreting physical or chemical situations, which are alternative to those defended by scientists, and that students maintain these alternative ideas even after receiving specific science teaching in those domains. Indeed, in the last 15 years we have gathered more studies on these alternative ideas than we can possibly read, as shown by the comprehensive bibliography compiled by Pfundt and Duit (1994).

Most of these studies are descriptive in nature (Hashweh, 1988), as they are aimed only at identifying and describing the most common interpretations held by students with different ages and levels of instruction. These studies, the majority carried out by science teachers, usually refer to these intuitive ideas as misconceptions, emphasizing that they are erroneous from a scientific point of view. Other studies are more theoretical, trying to discover the cognitive and educational processes that are at the origin of these alternative frameworks. These studies tend to conceive these ideas as part of broader alternative or implicit theories held by students in different domains (e.g. Chi et al., 1994; Claxton, 1991; Pozo & Carretero, 1992; Vosniadou, 1994). According to these interpretations, the ideas held by students could be explained in terms of the cognitive processes used for interpreting everyday situations, which produce ontological and structural categories (or implicit theories) different from those maintained by scientific theories.

Many of the pervasive data supporting this research approach are indeed concerned with the persistence, or non-replacement, of these alternative or implicit theories after specific science teaching. Thus, after studying mechanics many students still maintain pre-Newtonian beliefs about force or movement (e.g. Pozo & Carretero, 1992), also, after studying biology many students still explain natural selection in terms of inherited changes in individuals instead of using Darwinian explanations. A similar pattern of results has been found in the specific domain of chemistry, in which we are going to centre our study. In order to learn secondary school chemistry, students must understand that, beyond its observable appearance, matter is discontinuous, as it is composed of particles (molecules, atoms, etc.) in constant movement and separated by a vacuum space. These particles interact in complex ways to produce the different states in which matter can appear (gaseous, liquid and solid),

[1]This work has been possible thanks to the financial support of the Spanish Ministry of Education through a subvention from the CIDE and the DGICYT grant PB94-0188 for research supervised by the first author.

which, beyond their observable differences, share the same chemical composition and mechanisms.

However, after studying chemistry in secondary school and even at university, many students still maintain their intuitive representations of matter. Instead of interpreting matter in terms of microscopic representations based on the intrinsic motion of particles, students keep their macroscopic representations, based on the direct appearance of reality, that conceive matter as continuous, usually static and without vacuum space between parts (e.g. Andersson, 1990; Nussbaum, 1985). Although all the empirical studies agree in the persistence of these "misconceptions" about the nature of matter, there is no agreement about the extent of this persistence. Thus, while some studies show that around 50% of adolescent students use the particle theory of matter to interpret the tasks they are confronted with (Dickinson, 1987; Nussbaum, 1985), other studies reduce this percentage to a bare 20% (Rollnick & Rutherford, 1990; Stavy, 1988). Similarly, the influence of specific chemistry teaching on the assimilation of microscopic representations is different from one study to another. In general, it increases the assimilation of the idea of particles as the building blocks of matter, but students usually attribute to particles properties of the observable macroscopic world, such as the colour, shape and size that can be observed in the real objects they compose (Andersson, 1990; Gómez et al., 1995). For instance, they think that when a balloon is inflated the particles of air inside the balloon also increase their size. Thus, students do not replace one kind of representation with another, but rather merge them in a new non-scientific assimilation of the particle theory of matter.

Results of chemistry learning would suggest that, as occurs in other science domains, personal theories (in this case based on macroscopic representations) are not replaced in the majority of students by the scientific theory taught (based on microscopic representations). However, whilst students do not give up their implicit theories about the nature of matter, they can still undergo some kind of conceptual change. According to the first models of conceptual change, based on the promotion and solution of cognitive conflicts (e.g. Posner et al., 1982), in order to learn scientific theories students should become dissatisfied with their conceptions as they acquire a new scientific conception that appears more explanatory, plausible and intelligible. In fact, in their efforts to assimilate scientific theories that they have been taught, such as the particle theory of matter, students produce "synthetic models" (Vosniadou & Brewer, 1992), in which certain scientific notions, such as the concept of particle, are synthesized with some previous presuppositions (or implicit theories), such as the idea present in their framework theory that things are as they appear to be (Vosniadou, 1994). This gives rise to an erroneous assimilation of the scientific model, so that students conceive of particles not as a new level of analysis of matter, but as a part of observable reality (atoms and molecules are pieces of matter). This synthesis leads, as we have indicated, to their attributing to particles properties observable in the macroscopic world.

This confusion between different levels of analysis of material is caused by an absence of conceptual differentiation between these theoretical levels, given that students would lack the metacognitive awareness that could be expected in more expert subjects (Vosniadou, 1994). As has been observed in numerous domains of knowledge (Chi et al., 1988; Ericsson & Smith, 1991; Glaser, 1992), including that of chemistry (Pozo et al., 1993), expert subjects are more aware of the theories they are using for interpreting problems, so that they discriminate better between different levels of theoretical analysis of the nature of the material. In fact, although there are no empirical studies in the chemistry domain, it is likely that even experts do not abandon common-sense theories of matter, but rather learn to differentiate them metacognitively from scientific theories.

Perhaps conceptual change does not necessarily involve the replacement of one kind of representation by another, but the coexistence and integration of different representations for different tasks. Perhaps, as Spada (1994, p. 115) has suggested:

> Many so-called naive concepts and problem solution strategies are very helpful in almost all situations of daily life. Scientific reasoning is not in the position to replace commonness thinking. Both types do complement each other. The student has to learn to discriminate in which situations which concepts and problem solution strategies are adequate.

This interpretation is consistent with recent theories of cognitive representation, such as mental models, that stress the existence of multiple mental representation competing for their activation in each task or for each content. Moreover, this perspective on conceptual change considers commonness interpretations of scientific phenomena as a fruitful outcome of the functioning of the cognitive system (di Sessa, 1993), instead of seeing them only as conceptual mistakes, in comparison with scientific theories. In this sense, Spada (1994) comments that science teaching should not be aimed at replacing commonness theories but at making students more efficient in the contextual activation of their multiple alternative representations.

Thus we should accept that after science learning the two kinds of representations could coexist and be used in a different way by subjects according to the context. However, we are still lacking empirical data about the contextual variables that influence the activation pattern of both alternative and scientific theories (Chi, 1992). This shortage of relevant empirical data is caused by, in part, the scant importance given, in most studies about science learning, to the contextual variables in the activation of knowledge. With some outstanding exceptions (e.g. Engel Clough & Driver, 1986) most research has confronted subjects with only one task, inferring from it that subjects would use the same interpretation for other problems involving the same scientific concepts.

In the domain of chemistry, studies have attempted to discriminate between subjects using scientific (i.e. microscopic) representations and subjects using personal (i.e. macroscopic) representations. The lack of agreement in results, which we mentioned before, could be related to the scant attention paid to contextual variables in these studies. Perhaps subjects use different representations according to the task context or format. In order to find the answer, we need studies that consider the influence of task and subject variables in the representations used by different subjects when faced with different tasks involving similar scientific contents.

Objectives and Hypotheses

Within a wider study on chemistry learning (Pozo et al., 1993), this research aimed at analysing the influence of different variables on the activation of subjects' representations of the nature of matter. Our interest was not to know what kind of representation the subjects hold, but when they use them. We assumed that subjects have different alternative representations for interpreting similar problems involving the chemical structure of matter, and that they use them discriminately according to the task's demands. This use would depend on the instruction received by subjects, in terms of both their specific training in chemistry and their general educational level.

Specifically, our main objectives were (i) to study the effects of task demands on the activation of macroscopic or microscopic representation, and compare tasks that require spontaneous answers with tasks that suggest more academic interpretations; and (ii) to study the effect of both specific and general instruction on the representations activation pattern in the different tasks, and compare subjects with different expertise in chemistry but the same educational level.

With regard to the first objective, we expected that, in spontaneous answer tasks, subjects would use mostly macroscopic representations, based on the observable properties of matter, whereas the use of microscopic interpretations, based on the relationships between particles that compose the matter, would be more frequent the closer the task was to academic contexts. However, we also expected that this activation pattern would vary according to subjects' instructional level. Thus, we hypothesized that subjects with more knowledge in chemistry would not give up their personal or macroscopic representations, as some models of conceptual change suppose, but that they would use them more discriminately than subjects with lower expertise in chemistry. In fact, we expected that subjects with less chemistry knowledge would use both kinds of representations, but in a confused way, frequently attributing macroscopic properties to the microscopic particles. On the other hand, we thought that experts in chemistry would differentiate between the two kinds of representations, using them as really alternative frameworks, rather than as a synthetic model. Moreover, we expected that chemistry learning would increase the use of microscopic representations for experts in every task.

Finally, as we found in other related research (Gómez et al., 1995), university students without training in chemistry performed surprisingly well in chemistry tasks. We were interested in comparing the results of this subject group with those obtained by university chemistry students, in order to consider the effects of education from a broader point of view than the teaching received in specific domains.

Method

Tasks and Procedure

We designed three paper-and-pencil tests involving several qualitative chemical situations. The problems were the same in the three tasks, and they concerned everyday situations (e.g. what happens when a piece of sugar is dissolved in a coffee cup?). The only difference between tests was the kind of answer requested, manipulated through task format or context. The three tests were applied in a 20- to 25-minute session in a constant order, corresponding to that of the following presentation. The purpose of this presentation sequence was to avoid interference of tasks on subsequent tasks.

Task 1 (Free Task) required spontaneous answers to explain five different situations. Any reference to particles or chemical jargon was carefully avoided in the problem statements. Subjects were asked to answer them freely, without any restriction (see Appendix 1 for an example). Task 2 (Descriptive Task) offered four answer alternatives for each one of the eight items. All the alternatives presented were descriptive in nature, since they do not involve the causal mechanisms of the phenomena. Two alternatives were based on microscopic representations, as they made reference to particles, and two were based on macroscopic interpretations (see Appendix 2 for examples of the answer alternatives). One of each kind of representation was scientifically correct, whilst the other contained a conceptual mistake (or "misconception"), usually implying no discrimination between macroscopic and microscopic models of matter. Finally, Task 3 (Explanatory Task) was identical in structure to the Descriptive Task, presenting eight problems with the four answer alternatives as described above. However, in this test, microscopic answers made explicit reference to kinetic theory, not only to describe but also to explain the relationships between particle interactions and the observable appearance of matter (see Appendix 3 for an example).

Subjects

The sample was composed of 120 Spanish subjects, divided into six groups of 20, differing in age and instruction in chemistry. There were four groups of adolescent students and two groups of university students with different expertise in chemistry.[1] The adolescent groups corresponded to seventh grade (12–13 years old), ninth grade (14–15 years old), eleventh grade with science studies (16–17 years old and a science group) and eleventh grade without science studies (16–17 years old, non-science group.) The university groups were final year students of chemistry (chemistry group) and psychology (psychology group), and had similar ages.

Data Analysis

We began by computing the total number of answers in each category for each subject. In the Free Task, subjects' answers were classified according to the same four answer categories provided in the Descriptive and Explanatory Tests (see Appendix 1 for examples), namely (i) macroscopic correct, (ii) macroscopic wrong, (iii) microscopic correct and (iv) microscopic wrong. We considered that an answer involved a microscopic representation only when it included a explicit reference to some kind of particles composing matter. We classified it as wrong macroscopic or microscopic when there was an obvious conceptual mistake.

We also computed the proportion in which each answer category was used for each one of the two independent variables studied: group and test. In this way, taking the mean proportion of category use, we made two analyses of variance (ANOVA). The first one was based on a factorial design $6 \times 3 \times 2$, between-groups for the first factor (six groups) and within-group for the test (Free, Descriptive and Explanatory) and answer category (macroscopic and microscopic only). The second one was a factorial design $6 \times 3 \times 4$, between-groups for the first factor (six groups) and within-group for test (the three tests) and answer category (the four answer alternatives). Post-hoc analyses were carried out using Tukey's test.

---

[1] Because we were more interested in the novice end of the expert–novice continuum, the tasks designed were too easy for professional chemists. Thus, we were convinced that the best sample of "experts" for these tasks was final year students. Whilst they could hardly be considered experts in chemistry, they had enough experience to correctly solve the elementary chemistry tasks presented.

Results

First of all, we shall present the overall results about the use of each kind of representation. We shall then present the effect of independent variables, group and test, and finally the interaction between them. For purposes of clarity, for each variable effect, we shall present first the results of the first ANOVA (considering only the kind of representation) and then the second (concerned with the correctness of these representations)..

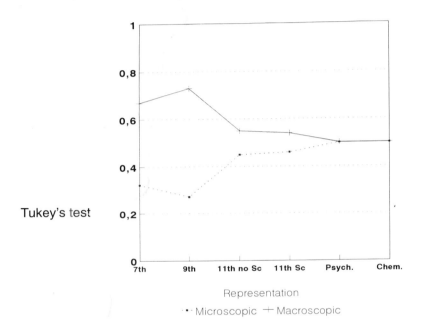

Subjects refers to grade of students.
11th no Sc = 11th graders with no science studies;
11th Sc = 11th graders with science studies;
Psych. = University psychology group;
Chem. = University chemistry group.

Figure 1: Mean proportion of each kind of representation by group.

In general, the ANOVA showed a significant effect for the kind of representation ($F(1,114) = 39.22$; $P < 0.0001$). According to Tukey's test, subjects resorted more to personal or macroscopic representations ($M = 0.58$) than to microscopic or chemical models ($M = 0.42$). Moreover, they made significantly more conceptual mistakes ($P = 0.05$) when they used chemical models based on particles than when they approached situations from the macroscopic dimensions of the observable world.

These results are far from surprising. More interesting is the interaction between kind of representation and group. The ANOVA also showed significant differences by group

($F(5,114) = 9.11$; $P < 0.0001$). In fact, two different representation patterns were found for the groups (see Figure 1). Younger adolescents (groups aged 12–13 and 14–15) more often used macroscopic than microscopic representations ($P < 0.05$ according to Tukey's test). On the other hand, the remaining groups, who were older and more educated, employed the two kinds of representations in a similar proportion, and there was no significant difference between these groups. The pattern of results by groups is different when we consider the correctness of the representations, and the effect is significant ($F(15,342) = 10.56$; $P < 0.05$). As Figure 2 shows, the use of macroscopic correct representations, which make up our intuitive or common-sense chemistry, does not change at all from one group to another. With independence of age and instruction, all the groups gave over 40% of answers based on correct macroscopic representations. However, younger subjects (groups aged 12–13 and 14–15) made more mistakes when using these macroscopic representations than did the remaining groups ($P < 0.05$). Moreover, subjects with expertise in chemistry differed from the remaining groups, except the psychology group, in using correct representations more frequently based on microscopic particles ($M = 0.42$; $P < 0.05$), and the psychology group used them more often ($M = 0.33$) than 12- to 13-year-old and 14- to 15-year-old adolescents.

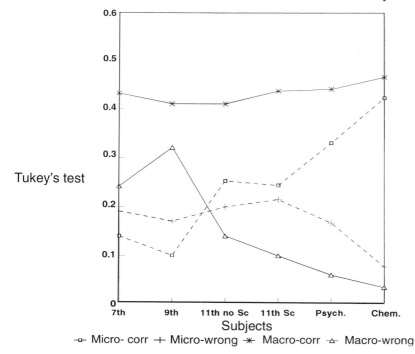

Subjects refers to grade of students.
11th no Sc = 11th graders with no science studies;
11th Sc = 11th graders with science studies;
Psych. = University psychology group;
Chem. = University chemistry group

Figure 2: Mean proportion of each representation (including mistakes) by group.

If we compare Figures 1 and 2, we can see that the similarity of the results observed for the four older groups in Figure 1 has clearly disappeared in Figure 2. Whereas the chemistry group scarcely made any erroneous interpretations based on the particulate nature of matter, the science and non-science 16- to 17-year-old groups made mistakes in about half of their microscopic representations. Psychology group results were at an intermediate level. As noted before, these mistakes are mostly caused by an insufficient differentiation between the macroscopic world and microscopic particles, which causes students to attribute properties of the observable world to the particles.

With regard to the effects of the test variable on the kind of representation, the ANOVA also showed a main effect ($F(2,228) = 115.72$; $P < 0.0001$). Whilst the Free Test produced nearly 80% of macroscopic answers, in both Descriptive and Explanatory Tests the two kinds of representation were equally probable (see Figure 3). Thus, the Free Test elicited more macroscopic representations than the other tests ($P < 0.05$). Also, when we considered possible mistakes, the most interesting result is the increase in erroneous interpretations based on particles in the Explanatory Test, as compared with the Descriptive one ($P < 0.05$).

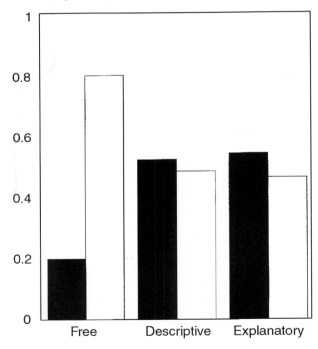

Figure 3: Mean proportion of each kind of representation by task.

Finally, we shall describe the results of the interaction between the two independent variables of group and test, which was also significant for the kind of representation used ($F(10,228) = 5.85$; $P < 0.0001$). Figure 4 represents the results obtained. In the Free Test, there were the following significant differences ($P < 0.05$): the chemistry group made microscopic interpretations ($M = 0.43$) more often than any of the remaining groups; the psychology group used particle concepts significantly more than 12- to 13-year-old, 14- to

15-year-old and non-science 16- to 17-year-old groups; the 16- to 17-year-old science group used particles more than 12- to 13-year-old and 14- to 15-year-old groups ($P < 0.05$). The Descriptive Test results showed that the two groups of 16- to 17-year-olds, with and without specific science training (with means of 0.59 and 0.66), along with the psychology group, resorted more to microscopic representations than, not only the two younger adolescent groups, but also the chemistry group ($P < 0.05$). Finally, in the Explanatory Test, the most outstanding result was that only the two university groups, both psychologists ($M = 0.58$) and chemists ($M = 0.59$), chose significantly more microscopic representations than macroscopic ones.

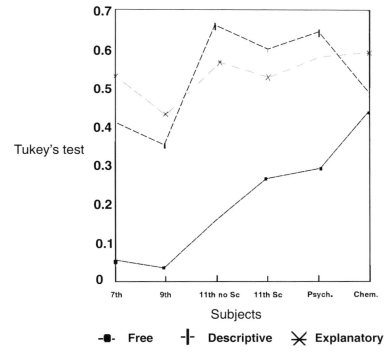

Subjects refers to grade of students.
11th no Sc = 11th graders with no science studies;
11th Sc = 11th graders with science studies;
Psych. = University psychology group;
Chem. =University chemistry group.

Figure 4: Mean proportion of microscopic representation by task and group.

When we compared the results of the Descriptive and Explanatory Tests we found an interesting result: both the younger adolescent groups (12- to 13-year-olds and 14- to 15-year-olds) and the chemists employed the concept of particle composition of matter more when the task required an explanation than when it was merely descriptive ($P < 0.05$). In the three intermediate groups, the results were exactly the opposite, as they used the concept of particles more to describe than to explain ($P < 0.05$).

However, when we also consider the mistakes committed ($F(30,684) = 6.76$; $P < 0.0001$), this apparently confused pattern of results becomes clearer. Summarizing only the more relevant results, the increase of microscopic answers in the Explanatory Test for the younger adolescent groups was accompanied by a parallel increase in conceptual mistakes, whereas the chemistry group scarcely made erroneous interpretations, and used more correct microscopic representations than the remaining groups ($P < 0.05$). In other words, when younger students attempted to resort to particle models they did not differentiate them correctly from their macroscopic observations, and they attributed properties to the particles that they observe in reality. On the other hand, chemists were able to differentiate both kinds of matter representation.

Summary and Conclusions

We shall summarize the main results obtained in relation to our objectives before returning to more theoretical considerations as a conclusion. With respect to our first objective, we found a main effect of test format and context on the kind of representation activated by the subjects. As predicted, spontaneous representations are mostly based in the macroscopic properties of matter. In the Free Test, only 20% of answers were based on the particle model. On the other hand, when the task format prompted it, in Descriptive and Explanatory Tests, microscopic representations increased, though achieving barely 50%, and thus not surpassing macroscopic answers. These two percentages are quite similar to those obtained by previous studies on chemistry learning and are in apparent contradiction; they showed a mastery of the particulate theory of matter that varied from 20 to 50%. These differences may have been produced by the different contextual demands of the tasks used in each study, which favoured the activation of different representations of matter.

As for our second objective, we also found important group differences. There were two major trends in results. First, younger adolescent subjects, aged from 12 to 15, when they usually begin learning chemistry, gave mainly macroscopic answers, whereas the remaining groups, older and with more education, used the two kinds of representations in a similar proportion.

From these results we can draw several conclusions. Above all, as expected, we found that all the groups used at least two different representations of matter, one based on its observable properties and the other conceived in terms of the particle composition of matter. In other words, instruction has not removed the macroscopic representation of matter, nor replaced it by particle theory. On the contrary, the two models coexist and are used as representational alternatives, even in subjects who are relatively expert in chemistry.

The persistence of intuitive representations after instruction has usually been interpreted by researchers as a proof of a poor understanding of scientific models. Even though this may sometimes be the case, it is possible that conceptual change does not usually require the replacement of one representation by another, because both could be useful in different contexts (Spada, 1994). Indeed, in other related studies we have found that university chemistry students show an expert understanding of most chemical concepts, such as conservation of matter and substance, intrinsic motion of particles, etc (Gómez et al., 1995;

Pozo et al., 1993). They do not lack chemical understanding, but merely have different models for different problems.

However, if all of the groups, including chemists, use both macroscopic and microscopic models, does instruction make any difference to students' representation of chemistry tasks? According to the results we have obtained, the answer must be affirmative. Although different groups do not differ in what kind of representation they have, they do differ in when they use them and, consequently, in the function and meaning that they attribute to each representation. Taking into account especially when each group referred to microscopic representations and the conceptual mistakes made in doing so, we can identify three different uses or conceptions of the particulate theory of matter.

First of all, 12- to 13-year-old and 14- to 15-year-old students, who are beginning to learn chemistry in secondary school, scarcely make interpretations in terms of particles, but they are more inclined to use them in the Explanatory Test. This tendency does not reflect a better understanding of the particle theory of matter, because very often it is accompanied by erroneous interpretations, attributing many properties to particles that in fact belong to the macroscopic world. In sum, because of the overlapping of macroscopic and microscopic representations, subjects do not conceive particles and their relationships as a different way to explain changes in matter, but as an unobservable part of the observable matter or, as it were, the submerged part of the iceberg of reality.

At an intermediate level, we have the two 16- to 17-year-old adolescent groups, with and without science teaching, and the psychology group. There were no differences between science and non-science students, showing that, in this case, specific science instruction was not efficient. This result is surprising, because in other aspects of chemistry understanding this instruction does make some difference, though not as great a difference as might be desired (Pozo et al., 1993). As far as the psychology group is concerned, their performance is better than expected, bearing in mind that they have no specific instruction in chemistry. As we have suggested elsewhere (Gómez et al., 1995), this result may reflect the influence of some general conceptual models (such as, for instance, the concept of interaction or the function of models in scientific explanation), which might be partially transferred from one domain to another. These cross-domain conceptual models could be conceptually related to the ontological categories postulated by Chi (1992) in her theory of conceptual change.

In any case, these three groups share, with some slight differences, a similar trend, consisting in using particles more in the Descriptive Test than in the Explanatory Test. For these groups, particles appear to serve more for describing than for explaining the macroscopic world. In fact, in the Explanatory Test they return, to a significant extent, to macroscopic representations. This trend is different from the pattern shown by chemists, who use microscopic representations more in the Explanatory Test, and without making erroneous interpretations about the functional mechanisms of particles. However, chemistry students use the particle theory less than expected. In fact, the effect of expertise was smaller than in other domains of chemistry learning (Pozo et al., 1993). Perhaps the tasks we used in this experiment were too elemental for chemistry students, who were not inclined to use their academic knowledge to solve them.

We consider this change in the cognitive function of microscopic representations — from descriptive to explanatory — to be a core objective of conceptual change in chemistry. Learning chemistry may not so much require the replacement of previous representations, but rather a change in their cognitive function, integrating them into new theories or conceptual models, which would provide the old representations with a different, more theoretical, meaning. As di Sessa (1993) has pointed out, intuitive science is mostly descriptive in nature, whereas formal science is more concerned with the search for explanatory principles. Thus, macroscopic representations, as useful for describing the world we live in, would not necessarily be removed, but merely changed in the sense of interpreting them from a new theoretical point of view. In this sense, science teaching should not aim to replace "misconceptions" by scientific concepts, but to make students reflect upon the conceptual and functional differences between these two apparently overlapping systems of knowledge through the process of metacognitive awareness (Vosniadou, 1994). Learning chemistry would not involve replacing representations but, rather, differentiating and integrating them into a common theoretical framework.

Appendix 1

Example of Questions and Answers in the Free Test

When we hang out a wet shirt in the sun, we can observe that, some time later, the shirt becomes dry.

Why do you think this occurs?

Macroscopic Correct

"... heat evaporates water" (all the groups)

"... the sun's radiation emits heat that makes the shirt dry" (chemistry group)

Macroscopic Wrong

"... the air acts as a hair-drier" (psychology group)

"... heat eliminates humidity" (16- to 17-year-old non-science group)

Microscopic Correct

"... as temperature increases water molecules increase their mobility" (chemistry group)

Microscopic Wrong

"… the molecules of water are transformed, because of the heat, into gas" (16- to 17-year-old science group)

Appendix 2

Example of Item from the Descriptive Test

If we put a lump sugar into a glass of water and we stir it with a spoon, a few moments later we can observe that the water has acquired a sweet taste.

Why do you think this occurs?

Macroscopic Correct

"… the sugar is merged with the water and thus the sweet taste appears"

Macroscopic Wrong

"… the sugar releases a substance that interacts with the water giving it a sweet taste"

Microscopic Correct

"… the particles of sugar are merged with the particles of water, giving it the sweet taste"

Microscopic Wrong

"… as the particles of sugar are broken, they release a sweet substance that gives the taste to the water"

Appendix 3

Example of Item in the Explanatory Test

When we heat cold soup, as the soup heats, its smell increases in the room.

Why do you think this occurs?

Macroscopic Correct

"… by the heat action, there is a change from liquid to vapour and this leads to the diffusion of the soup smell in the room"

Macroscopic Wrong

"… when the soup is heated, part of the water that composes the soup is evaporated, and thus the smell is more concentrated, as occurs also with its taste"

Microscopic Correct

"… when the soup is heated, the particles of the soup begin to move faster; they become liberated from the attraction of other particles, and move through the air"

Microscopic Wrong

"… the heat causes the particles of soup to break and they release in the form of vapour the smell that they have inside them"

11

Children's Conceptions about the Role of Real-World Knowledge in Mathematical Modelling: Analysis and Improvement

Lieven Verschaffel, Erik De Corte and Sabien Lasure

Introduction

As for many other subject-matter domains, the development of mathematical competence consists of many steps, some of which involve only small and simple additions of new information to the learner's existing knowledge base, while others require drastic changes in the available knowledge base. In the latter case, conceptual change can be very difficult to achieve (Vosniadou, 1994). For example, research has convincingly documented the severe problems children have in revising their conceptualizations of the operations of multiplication and division with natural numbers, beyond the integer domain. Moreover, this research has revealed that many of the inadequate conceptions about multiplicative concepts in children and even in adults (such as the belief that multiplication always makes larger and division always makes smaller) result from deficiencies in the curricular experiences provided by the school (such as the narrow range of problem situations used as models of these operations during instruction) (Behr et al., 1992). In this chapter, we address another, more fundamental kind of conceptual change in the domain of mathematics education, which relates to children's concepts and beliefs about the process of modelling arithmetic word problems itself (see also: De Corte & Verschaffel, 1985; Freudenthal, 1991; Greer, 1993; Kilpatrick, 1987; Nesher, 1980; Reusser, 1986; Säljö, 1991; Schoenfeld, 1991; Treffers, 1987; Verschaffel & De Corte, 1997a). In Studies 1 and 2 it will be argued and documented that as a result of years of experience with traditional mathematics instruction in general, and with an artificial and stereotyped diet of standard word problems in particular, children gradually develop a narrow and limited but deep-rooted conceptualization of mathematical modelling, whereby this process is reduced to selecting the correct formal-arithmetic operation with the numbers given in the problem, without seriously taking into account their common-sense knowledge and realistic considerations about the problem context. Study 3 will demonstrate that it is nevertheless possible to change children's (mis)conceptions about the role of real-world knowledge in mathematical modelling and problem solving. A major feature of this new approach is that word problems are not conceived as artificial, puzzle-like tasks that can always be unambiguously solved by performing one (or a combination) of the four basic arithmetic operations with the given numbers, but as genuine exercises in realistic mathematical modelling.

Study 1

Method

Subjects were 75 pupils (10- to 11-year-old boys and girls) from three fifth-grade classes of three schools in which word problem solving was taught in the traditional way. This implies that the pupils had been frequently confronted with traditional school word problems rather than with authentic problem situations, and that realistic modelling had not been systematically addressed in teaching (see also De Corte & Verschaffel, 1989).

A paper-and-pencil test was constructed consisting of 10 matched pairs of items. Each pair consisted of:

1. a standard item (S-item) that can be solved unambiguously by applying the most obvious arithmetic operation(s) with the given numbers (e.g. "Steve has bought 5 planks of 2 metres each. How many planks of 1 metre can he saw out of these planks?"); and
2. a parallel problematic item (P-item) for which the appropriate mathematical model is less obvious and indisputable, at least if one seriously takes into account the realities of the context evoked by the problem statement (e.g. "Steve has bought 4 planks of 2.5 metres each. How many planks of 1 metre can he saw out of these planks?").

The 10 P-items are listed in Table 1.

Table 1: Ten P-items involved in Study 1

P1	Carl has 5 friends and Georges has 6 friends. Carl and Georges decide to give a party together. They invite all their friends. All friends are present. How many friends are there at the party? (= the "birthday" item)
P2	Steve has bought 4 planks of 2.5 metre each. How many planks of 1 metre can he get out of these planks? (= the "planks" item)
P3	What will be the temperature of water in a container if you pour 1 litre of water at 80°C and 1 litre of water of 40°C into it? (= the "water" item)
P4	450 soldiers must be bussed to the their training site. Each army bus can hold 36 soldiers. How many buses are needed? (= the "buses" item)
P5	John's best time to run 100 metres is 17 seconds. How long will it take to travel 1 kilometre? (= the "runner" item)
P6	Bruce and Alice go to the same school. Bruce lives at a distance of 17 kilometres from the school and Alice at 8 kilometres. How far do Bruce and Alice live from each other? (= the "school distance" item)
P7	Grandfather gives his 4 grandchildren a box containing 18 balloons, which they share equally. How many balloons does each grandchild get? (= the "balloons" item)
P8	Rob was born in 1978. Now it's 1993. How old is he? (= the "age" item)
P9	A man wants to have a rope long enough to stretch between two poles 12 metres apart, but he has only pieces of rope 1.5 metres long. How many of these pieces would he need to tie together to stretch between the poles? (= the "rope" item)

P10   This flask is being filled from a tap at a constant rate. If the depth of the water is 4 cm after 10 seconds, how deep will it be after 30 seconds? (This problem was accompanied by a drawing of a cone-shaped flask) (= the "flask" item)

The 10 pairs of problems were administered on the same day in two series, each containing the P-variant of five problem pairs and the S-variant of the five other pairs.

The problems in each series were presented in two different orders, and in each class one half of the children started with one series while the other half was given the other series first. The administration of the problems was done by the class teacher as part of a normal mathematics lesson.

The problems were presented on A4-sheets. With respect to each problem, pupils were asked to write down not only their answer, but also how they arrived at this answer (e.g. by mentioning the calculations), and possible other comments they might have (e.g. explaining their stumbling block when they were not able to solve the problem, supplementing their numerical answer with some comments, criticizing the problem statement, etc.).

Analysis

Children's reactions to the problems were analysed in two ways for evidence of the activation and use of real-world knowledge and realistic considerations about the problem context:

1. by distinguishing in their answers between realistic answers and non-realistic ones; and
2. by distinguishing in their computations and additional comments between realistic comments and non-realistic comments.

When a child gave an answer to the problem that was scored as realistic or produced a non-realistic answer that was accompanied by a realistic comment, his/her overall reaction to that particular problem was scored as a "realistic reaction" (RR). Take, for example, the "planks" item mentioned above. A RR score was not only given to a child who produced the realistic answer "$4 \times 2 = 8$; he can saw 8 planks of 1 metre", but also to a child who responded with "10 planks" but who added the comment that "Steve would have a hard time putting together the remaining pieces of 0.5 metre". The code NR ("non-realistic reaction") was given for children who answered a problem in a non-realistic manner and did not give any further realistic comments (e.g. answering the "planks" problem as follows: "$4 \times 2.5 = 10$; he can saw 10 planks of 1 metre"). For examples of non-realistic reactions (NRs) and realistic reactions (RRs) for the 10 P-items we refer the reader to Verschaffel et al. (1994).

Hypotheses

The overall hypothesis of the first study was that, because of (i) their extensive experience with an impoverished diet of standard word problems, and (ii) the lack of systematic attention at the mathematical modelling perspective in their mathematics lessons, pupils would demonstrate a strong tendency to exclude real-world knowledge and context-bound consid-erations from their problem-solving endeavours of the P-items, and — consequently — would solve them as if they were not at all problematic.

Results and Discussion

Table 2 gives the number of pupils who reacted in a realistic (RR) and in a non-realistic (NR) way for each of the 10 P-items from Table 1.

Table 2: Number and percentage of non-realistic (NRs) and realistic (RRs) pupil reactions to the 10 P-items in Study 1*

P-item	NRs		RRs	
	n	*%*	*n*	*%*
1. Birthday	60	80	15	20
2. Planks	65	87	10	13
3. Water	62	83	13	17
4. Buses	38	51	37	49
5. Runner	73	97	2	3
6. School	73	97	2	3
7. Balloons	31	41	44	59
8. Age	73	97	2	3
9. Rope	75	100	0	0
10. Flask	72	96	3	4
Total	622	83	128	17

*RRs stands for "realistic reactions", i.e. all reactions reflecting activation of context-dependent real-world knowledge in the solution of the problem or in the additional comments.

The data in Table 2 strongly support the hypothesis. As predicted, the pupils demon-strated a very strong overall tendency to exclude real-world knowledge and realistic considerations when confronted with the problematic versions of the problems. In total, only 128 out of the 750 reactions to the P-items (= 17%) could be considered as realistic (RR), either because the pupil wrote a realistic answer or made an additional realistic comment.

Table 2 also shows that, for two of the 10 P-items, a considerable number of realistic answers or comments were observed for the "buses" item (P4) and the "balloons" item (P7). The question arises why these two problems elicited considerably more RRs than the other P-items. A common characteristic that differentiates P4 and P7 from the other P-items is that, in P4 and P7, the modelling difficulty is restricted to the last phase of the solution process, wherein the pupil has to make sense of the result of this arithmetic operation, namely a quotient with a remainder (Silver et al., 1993). In all other P-items, the underlying realistic modelling difficulty requires context-based adaptations at the beginning of the solution process, namely the construction of the mathematical model, rather than at the end of it (Verschaffel et al., 1994).

Finally, to have an indication of the interindividual differences in the disposition towards (non-)realistic modelling, we counted the total number of RRs on the 10 P-items for each pupil separately. Fifty-nine of the 75 pupils (78%) reacted in a realistic way to fewer than three of the 10 P-items. Almost all RRs of these pupils were found on the "buses" and the "balloons" problem. Only 16 pupils (22%) provided RRs on at least three P-items, and only two of them did so on more than half of the 10 P-items (see Verschaffel et al., 1994, for more details).

Although Study 1 provides empirical evidence for pupils' strong tendency to exclude real-world knowledge and realistic considerations from their understanding and solving of word problems, its findings need to be put into perspective because of an important methodological limitation of the data-gathering technique used, namely a collective paper-and-pencil test. Indeed, one could argue that, during their (private) solutions of the P-items, some pupils may have activated real-world knowledge that was not reflected in their written answers, simply because they finally decided to react in a "conformist" rather than a "realist" way in line with their beliefs and conceptions about the prevailing rules and conventions of the game of school arithmetic word problems (De Corte & Verschaffel, 1985). This may have led to a significant underestimation of the number of realistic considerations in this first investigation. Therefore, we set up a second study in which we assessed whether two rather simple forms of scaffolding during an individual interview were sufficient to transform children's non-realistic solutions into realistic ones.

Study 2

Method

Study 2 consisted of two stages. In the first stage, seven matched pairs of word problems used in Study 1 were collectively administered to a group of 64 fifth-graders from three different schools. The seven problematic items (P-items) selected were: P1 (the "birthday-party" item), P2 (the "planks" item), P4 (the "buses" item), P5 (the "running" item), P6 (the "school-distance" item), P9 (the "rope" item), and P10 (the "flask" item) (see Table 1). The administration of the test and the scoring of the answers were done in the same way as in Study 1. Based on the results on this paper-and-pencil test, the five most "realistic" and the five most "non-realistic" problem solvers from each of the three fifth-grade classes were selected to participate in the second stage of the investigation. During this second stage, which took place 1–2 days later, these 15 realistic and 15 non-realistic problem solvers were individually administered the same seven problem pairs once again.

To assess the strength of children's tendency towards non-realistic mathematical modelling, the following interviewing procedure was followed with respect to each P-item solved with a non-realistic answer (NR) on the paper-and-pencil test.

First, the pupil was asked to read aloud the problem followed by his own NR written down on the answer sheet (e.g. "4 × 2.5 = 10 planks" for the "planks" item).

Then a cognitive conflict was produced by confronting the pupil with the written notes of a fictitious classmate who had responded the same problem in a realistic manner. For instance, with respect to the "planks" item the interviewer said: "As you can see on this sheet, one of your classmates responded: 4 × 2 = 8 planks. What is the best answer? Why?" If the pupil stuck to the initial NR (i.e."10 planks") after this first and weak form of scaffolding, a second and stronger scaffold in the direction of realistic modelling was provided. The interviewer said: "Can you draw the planks? Can you also draw what happened with these planks according to the problem statement? Can you see on your drawing how many planks of 1 metre Steve can saw out of these 4 planks?" In Table 3 we present the weak and the strong scaffold for each of the seven P-items separately.

Table 3: Weak (S1) and strong (S2) scaffolds used for the seven P-items of Study 2

P1-item (the "birthday" item)

S1:   One of your classmates said that it is impossible to solve this problem. Who is right? You or your classmate?

S2:   Can you give me the name of a good friend in the class? Imagine you and ... are giving a party together and that you both invite your best friends. Imagine that your five best friends are present, and that the six best friends of ... are present. Are you sure that there are 11 guests at the party?

P2-item (the "planks" item)

S1:   One of your classmates responded in this way: 4 × 2 = 8; Steve can saw 8 planks. Who is right?

S2:   Can you draw the planks? Can you also draw what happened with these planks according to the story. Can you see on this drawing how many planks of 1 metre Steve can saw out of these 4 planks?

P4-item (the "buses" item)

S1:   One of your classmates responded in this way: 450/36 = 12.5; they will need 13 buses. Who is right?

S2:   You have answered that they will need 12.5 buses. What does that answer mean to you? 12.5 buses?

P5-item (the "school distance" item)

S1:   One of your classmates said that it is impossible to solve this problem. Who is right? You or your classmate?

S2:   Can you make a drawing of the situation described in the problem? Is this the only drawing you can make out of this problem statement?

P6-item (the "runner" item)

S1:   One of your classmates responded that it is impossible to know precisely how long it would take John to run 1 kilometre. Who is right?

S2:   Do you know your best time on the 100 metre? Imagine that it is 17 sec. If you had to run 1 kilometre, do you think that you would succeed in running every remaining 100 metre in that same best time?

P9-item (the "rope" item)

S1:   One of your classmates responded in the following way: I don't know exactly, but the answer will certainly be more than 8 pieces. Who is right?

S2:   Here is a picture of the man who is tying together the pieces of rope to stretch between the two poles. Do you still think that 8 pieces will be enough to stretch between the two poles?

P10-item (the "flask" item)

S1:   One of your classmates said that it is impossible to give a precise answer to that question. Who is right?

S2:   If this is the part of the flask that was filled after 10 sec (interviewer points at the coloured part of the cone-shaped flask on the pupil's response sheet), can you indicate on this figure what the level of the water will be after 20 sec? And after 30 sec?

In order to control for possible disturbing effects of the interviewing technique, the same procedure (involving similar kinds of provocation and scaffolding) was applied with respect to the P-items that were solved with a RR (e.g. answering the "planks" problem with "4 × 2 = 8 planks") during the paper-and-pencil test. In these cases, the pupil was confronted with the fictitious written reaction of a non-realistic responder (e.g. "4 × 2.5 = 10 planks"). The same interviewing procedure was also applied with respect to the seven "unproblematic" S-items: pupils who had given a correct answer to a S-item from the paper-and-pencil test were confronted with an incorrect response resulting from the application of a wrong operation with the given numbers (e.g. a multiplication instead of a division), while those who had given an incorrect answer were confronted with the correct one.

Analysis

For all 30 pupils and for all seven P-items the following kinds of data were used for analysis.

1. The initial reaction to the problem during the paper-and-pencil test; this reaction was scored either as RR or NR;
2. The reaction to the confrontation with the RR of a fictitious classmate (= weak scaffold) in case of an initial NR during the paper-and-pencil test; this reaction was also scored either as RR or NR;

3. Eventually, the reaction to the second and strongest form of scaffolding; this reaction was again scored either as RR or NR.

Whereas the pupils' total number of RRs to the seven P-items of the paper-and-pencil test provide a measure of their actual level of realistic modelling, i.e. the level at which they can perform independently, their sensitivity to scaffolds towards realistic modelling of the P-items that were initially answered with a NR reflects their zone of proximal development (Vygotky, 1962) or their learning potential (Hamers et al., 1993), i.e. those behaviours that they cannot yet perform independently but could with help from others. To measure this zone of proximal development or learning potential, a score of 2, 1 or 0 was given for each P-item not yet solved in a realistic manner during the paper-and-pencil test.

- 2 = The pupil produced a NR during the paper-and-pencil test, but replaced it by a RR after being confronted with the realistic alternative during the first, weak form of scaffolding.
- 1 = The pupil produced a NR during the paper-and-pencil test, did not replace it by a RR after being confronted with the realistic alternative, but produced a RR after receiving the second, strong scaffold.
- 0 = The pupil produced a NR during the paper-and-pencil test, and this reaction remained unchanged even after the second and strongest scaffold.

The mean of these scores (their sum divided by the number of P-items not yet answered with a RR during the paper-and-pencil test) was considered as a measure of a pupil's learning potential, i.e. a score that indicated how much a pupil gained from increasingly stronger forms of scaffolds towards realistic modelling on those P-items he could not answer in a realistic manner himself.

Hypotheses

First, it was hypothesized that — as in Study 1 — the overall number of RRs generated on the seven P-items of the paper-and-pencil test would be alarmingly low. Therefore, we predicted that the overall percentage of RRs on that test would not differ significantly from the percentage of RRs found in Study 1, which was 17%.

Second, a positive effect of the scaffolds on the number of RRs was anticipated. Therefore, we predicted that the percentage of RRs of the 30 pupils at the end of the individual interview would be significantly higher than on the paper-and-pencil test. However, we also expected that this overall percentage of RRs at the end of the individual interviews would still be dramatically low. This latter prediction was based on the assumption that pupils' tendency towards routine-based and non-realistic modelling would be so strong, that the confrontation with the RR (= scaffold 1) and even the subsequent hint towards the realistic reasoning underlying this RR (= scaffold 2) would frequently be insufficient to make them change their initial NR into a RR.

Third, we hypothesized that the so-called realistic problem solvers of the P-items from the paper-and-pencil test would benefit more from the two forms of scaffolding than the pupils with little or no RRs on that test (the so-called non-realistic problem solvers). Their greater tendency towards realistic modelling — as expressed in their better performance on the P-items during the paper-and-pencil test — would make them also more sensitive to the two scaffolds provided during the individual interview. Therefore, we predicted a significantly greater mean learning potential score for the 15 realistic than for the 15 non-realistic problem solvers on the P-items not yet solved with a RR during the paper-and-pencil test.

Results and Discussion

In line with our first hypothesis and with the findings of Study 1, the results on the collective test revealed a very strong tendency among the pupils to exclude real-world knowledge and context-based considerations from their solutions of school arithmetic word problems: only 16% of all the reactions of the 64 pupils to the seven P-items of the paper-and-pencil test were classified as realistic. This percentage is almost exactly the same as in Study 1, where the overall percentage of RRs was 17%. As in Study 1, the "buses" problem elicited again the largest number of RRs, namely 64%. The percentages of RRs for the six other P-items used in Study 2 varied between 17 and 1%.

As was said before, from each of the three classes, wherein the paper-and-pencil test was administered, the five pupils with the highest number of RRs and the five pupils with the lowest number of RRs were selected to participate in the second part of the study. This resulted in a group of 15 realistic and a group of 15 non-realistic problem solvers. The percentage of RRs in these groups of realistic and non-realistic problem solvers was 39% (i.e. 41 RRs out of a total of 105 responses) and 8% (i.e. 8 RRs out of 105 responses), respectively. A one-tailed Student's t-test showed that the difference between the two groups was significant, $t(28) = 8.58$, $P < 0.01$. All 15 non-realistic problem solvers produced either one or no RR on the paper-and-pencil test, and all RRs from this group occurred on the "buses" item. The 15 realistic problem solvers, on the other hand, produced either two RRs (seven pupils), three RRs (six pupils), four RRs (one pupil) or five RRs (one pupil) on the paper-and-pencil test. These findings show that the 15 so-called realistic problem solvers could certainly not be considered as genuine "experts" in realistic mathematical modelling. Characterizing them as pupils with a weaker tendency towards non-realistic modelling, seemed more correct.

In line with the second hypothesis, a significant effect of the two forms of scaffolding was found. Altogether, the two scaffolds resulted in an increase in the cumulative number of RRs from 23% (i.e. 49 RRs out of a total 210 responses) during the paper-and-pencil test to 57% (i.e. 120 RRs out of a total of 210 responses) at the end of the individual interviews (see Table 5). A one-tailed t-test revealed that this increase was significant, $t(29) = 12.97$, $P < 0.001$. Additional one-tailed t-tests revealed that both forms of scaffolding contributed equally to this increase: the first, weak scaffold resulted in an increase of the cumulative percentage of RRs from 23% (i.e. 49 RRs out of 210 responses) to 40% (i.e. 83 RRs out of 210 responses), $t(29) = 5.61$, $P < 0.001$, and the second and stronger scaffold produced an additional significant increase from 40% (i.e. 83 RRs out of 210 responses) to 57% RRs (i.e. 120 RRs out of 210 responses), $t(29) = 6.95$, $P < 0.001$.

Although the scaffolds led to a significant increase in the number of RRs, the cumulative percentage of RRs at the end of the individual interviews was still alarmingly low. Indeed, in 43% of all cases (i.e. 90 out of a total of 210) the pupils still reacted in an unrealistic way even after the second and strongest scaffold towards realistic modelling. This percentage is higher than that of the cases where either form of scaffolding resulted in a shift from a NR to a RR (see Table 4).

Table 4: Number and cumulative number, and percentage and cumulative percentage of realistic reactions of the 30 pupils to the seven problematic items at the different stages of Study 2

		IRR*	RRF	RRS	NRR
Absolute	N	49	34	37	90
	%	23%	165	18%	43%
Cumulative	N	49	83	120	210
	%	23%	39%	57%	100%

IRR = immediate realistic reaction during the collective test
RRF = realistic reaction after the first, weak scaffold
RRS = realistic reaction after the second, strong scaffold
NRR = still a non-realistic reaction at the end of the individual interview

Third, the results also confirmed the hypothesis that the realistic problem solvers would benefit more from the two scaffolds than the non-realistic ones. This was evidenced by comparing the mean learning potential scores (maximum = 2; minimum = 0) of the 15 realistic and the 15 non-realistic problem solvers. The mean learning potential score was 0.88 and 0.52 for the realistic group and the non-realistic group, respectively. A one-tailed t-test revealed that this difference was significant, $t(28) = 2.55$, $P < 0.01$.

So, while the results of the second study strongly confirm elementary school pupils' disposition towards non-realistic modelling of school arithmetic word problems, they provide, at the same time, evidence for the existence of interindividual differences in this disposition, by showing that pupils of different levels of actual performance with respect to realistic modelling, differ also in terms of their zone of proximal development, in the sense that they are differently sensitive to scaffolds towards realistic modelling on problems they could not initially properly solve themselves.

The results of Study 1 and 2 support the general hypothesis that, as a consequence of traditional teaching, elementary school pupils have developed a strong tendency to exclude real-world knowledge and realistic considerations from their understanding and solutions of school arithmetic word problems. Indeed, the results on the P-items from the paper-and-pencil tests used in Studies 1 and 2 show that pupils' answers only rarely reflect adjustments for realistic constraints based on realistic considerations. Moreover, the results of the individual interviews in Study 2 suggest that this tendency is very strong and resistant to change; although confronting the pupil with the correct answer (= scaffold 1) and with the underlying reasoning (=scaffold 2) led to a significant increase in the number of RRs, almost half of the P-items were still answered in an non-realistic way at the end of the interview. Apparently, the simple forms of scaffolding used in Study 2 did not lead to the desired changes in children's conceptions and beliefs about the role of real-world knowledge in mathematical modelling of arithmetic world problems.

Starting from these findings, we set up a third study in which we tried to change pupils' conceptions of the role of real-world knowledge in mathematical modelling and problem solving, and to develop in them a disposition towards realistic mathematical modelling and problem solving (Verschaffel & De Corte, 1997b). This was attempted by immersing them into a new classroom culture in which word problems are explicitly conceived and used as exercises in realistic mathematical modelling.

Study 3

Method

Three classes from the same school participated in the experiment: one experimental (E) class of 19 fifth-grade children, and two control classes (C1 and C2) of 18 and 17 sixth-grade children, respectively.

The pupils from the E-class participated in an experimental programme on realistic modelling that consisted of five teaching/learning units (TLU) of about 2.5 hours each, spread over a period of about 15 days. The major characteristics of the programme were as follows.

First, the impoverished and stereotyped diet of standard word problems offered in traditional mathematics classrooms was replaced by a set of more realistic non-routine problem situations that were especially designed to stimulate pupils to pay attention at the complexities involved in realistic mathematical modelling, and at distinguishing between realistic and stereotyped solutions of mathematical applications. Each TLU focused on one prototypical problematic topic of realistic modelling. The topic of the first TLU was: making appropriate use of real-world knowledge and realistic considerations when interpreting the outcome of a division problem involving a remainder. The opening problem involved a story about a regiment of 300 soldiers doing several military activities. Each part of the story was accompanied with a question, which always asked for the same arithmetic operation (namely 300/8 = ?) but required each time a different answer (respectively, "38", "37", "37.5" and "37 remainder 4"). The theme of the second TLU was the union or separation of two sets with joint elements. The opening problem was an (unsolvable) problem about a boy who already possessed a given number of comic strips from the popular series *Suske and Wiske* and got a package of second-hand albums of *Suske and Wiske* from his older cousins (who had lost their interest in these comics). The pupils had to determine how many albums of *Suske and Wiske* there were still missing in the boy's collection after getting this present, given the total number of available albums in this series (i.e. 236), the number of albums in the boy's collection before the gift (i.e. 96), and the number of albums in the package he got from his cousins (i.e. 45). The third TLU focused on problem situations wherein it is not immediately clear whether the result of adding or subtracting two given numbers yields the appropriate answer, or an answer that is 1 more or 1 less than the correct one. In the opening problem, pupils were given the number of the first and the last ticket sold at the cash desk of a swimming pool on a particular day (i.e. ticket no. 524 and no. 616, respectively), and they had to decide how many tickets were sold that day. The fourth TLU started with a problem about a boy who wanted to make a swing and had to decide about the amount of rope needed for fastening the swing at a horizontal branch of a big old tree at a height of 5 metres. In that session, pupils had to experience that in many application problems one has to take into account several relevant elements that are not explicitly nor immediately "given" in the problem statement but that belong to one's common-sense knowledge base. The fifth and last TLU dealt with the principle of proportionality and, more particularly, with how to discriminate between cases where solutions based on direct proportional reasoning are, or are not, appropriate. The starting problem was about a young athlete whose best time to run 100 metres was given, and pupils were asked to predict his best time at 400 metres.

Second, not only the problems but also the teaching methods differed considerably from traditional mathematics classroom practice. The opening problem of each TLU was solved in mixed-ability groups of three to four pupils. This group assignment was followed by a whole-class discussion, in which the answers, the solution processes and possible additional comments of the different groups were compared. Then, each mixed-ability group was given a set of four or five new problems, some with and some without the same underlying modelling difficulty as the opening problem. This group assignment was again followed by a whole-class discussion. Finally, each pupil was individually administered one problem that involved once again the topical modelling difficulty. Pupils' reactions to this individual assignment were also discussed afterwards during a whole-class discussion.

Third, a new classroom culture was established by explicitly negotiating new socio-mathematical norms about the role of the teacher and the students in a (mathematics) classroom, and about what counts as a good mathematical problem, a good solution procedure, or a good response (see Cobb et al., 1992; Gravemeijer, 1995). During the experiment, the pupils from the two control classes followed the regular mathematics curriculum.

Before the experimental programme was applied in the E-class, the three groups were given the same pre-test, which contained 10 P-items (= 2 items per TLU) and five standard problems which functioned as buffer items. One problem in each pair of P-items was similar to an item from the corresponding session of the experimental programme (= learning item), while in the other problem the same underlying mathematical modelling difficulty had to be handled in a different problem context (= near-transfer item).

At the end of the experimental course a parallel version of the pre-test was administered in all three classes as a post-test. However, in one of the control classes — namely C1 — the post-test was preceded by a 15-minutes introduction in which they were explicitly warned that the test would contain several problems for which routine solutions based on adding, subtracting, multiplying or devising the given numbers, were inappropriate.

One month after the post-test, the pupils from the E-class were administered a retention test consisting again of 10 P-items, half of which were parallel versions of the near-transfer items from the pre-test and post-test (= near-transfer items), whereas the other half were even more remote from those encountered during the experimental programme, such as the "water" item (P3) and the "school distance" item (P6) from Table 1 (= far-transfer items).

To evaluate the effects of the experimental programme, an analysis of variance was performed with group (E versus C1 versus C2), time (pre-test versus post-test) and problem

type (learning items versus near-transfer items) as the independent variables and the proportion of "realistic reactions" (RRs) on the P-items as the dependent variable.

Hypotheses

First, in line with the results of Studies 1 and 2, we hypothesized that on the pre-test the
pupils would demonstrate a strong tendency to exclude real-world knowledge when
confronted with the problematic versions of the problems. Therefore, we predicted that, on
the P-items of the pre-test, the pupils of the three classes (E, C1 and C2) would produce a
percentage of RRs that would not differ significantly from the 17% RRs and 16% RRs
obtained in the first and the second studies, respectively.

Second, we hypothesized that the experimental programme would induce conceptual
change in students, and result in a disposition toward realistic modelling and interpreting of
arithmetic word problems. Therefore, we predicted a significant increase in the number of
RRs on the P-items from pre-test to post-test for the E-group. For the two other groups, no
significant increase from pre-test to post-test was expected.

Third, a positive transfer effect of the experimental programme was hypothesized.
Therefore, we predicted that the increase in the percentage of RRs in the E-group from pre-
test to post-test, would not only be significant for the five items that were similar to those
from the experimental programme (= learning items), but also for the five near-transfer
items.

A final hypothesis was that the positive effect of the experimental programme would be
lasting. Consequently, we predicted that there would be no significant difference between
the percentage of RRs of the E-group on the P-items of the retention test and their parallel
problems of the post-test.

Results and Discussion

As predicted in the first hypothesis, the pupils from all three classes demonstrated a strong
overall tendency to exclude real-world knowledge and realistic considerations from their
problem solutions during the pre-test. Overall, the percentage of RRs on the 10 P-items of
the pre-test was only 15%. The fifth-graders from the E-class produced fewer RRs than the
sixth-graders from the C1- and the C2-classes: the percentages were 7, 20 and 18%, respectively. But according to Tukey's *a posteriori* tests the differences were not significant.

To test the second hypothesis, we analysed whether there was an interaction effect
between the independent variables "Group" (E, C1 and C2) and "Time" (pre-test versus
post-test). The analysis of variance revealed that this "Group × Time" interaction was
indeed significant ($P < 0.0001$). Tukey's *a posteriori* tests showed that there was a significant increase in the number of RRs from pre-test to post-test for the E-group: from 7% RRs
on the pre-test to 51% RRs on the post-test. To the contrary, in the two control classes, the
progress in the number of RRs from pre-test to post-test was not significant, namely from
20 to 34% for C1, and from 18 to 23% for C2.

The third hypothesis about the transfer effect was tested by analysing separately the
results of the E-class on the five learning items and the five near-transfer items. The lack of

a significant "Group × Time × Problem Type" interaction indicates that the increase in the percentage of RRs in the E-class from pre-test to post-test, cannot be considered as a task-specific training effect. Indeed, while the increase in the percentage of RRs in the E-class was larger for the five learning items (from 9 to 60%) than for the five near-transfer items (from 6 to 41%), Tukey's *a posteriori* tests revealed that the increase was significant for both kinds of problems.

Finally, the positive results of the E-class on the retention test confirmed the fourth hypothesis. The percentage of RRs for the five near-transfer items of the retention test was 40%, which is almost the same as the result for the five parallel near-transfer items from the immediate post-test (i.e. 41%, see Table 6). Remarkably, the five far-transfer items from the retention test elicited almost the same mean percentage of RRs, namely 39%. This is considerably higher than the percentages observed in equivalent groups of pupils who solved the same P-items without special training in realistic mathematical modelling (see Studies 1 and 2; see also Greer, 1993). This finding provides additional evidence that the effect of the programme was not task-specific.

The results reported above warrant a positive conclusion about the feasibility of changing the conception about the role of real-world knowledge in mathematical modelling and problem solving in children of upper elementary school age, and of developing in them a disposition toward realistic mathematical modelling of school word problems. Nevertheless, some caution is in order. First, the reported positive results are jeopardized by some methodological weaknesses of the present exploratory teaching experiment, such as the small size of the experimental and control groups, and the absence of a retention test in the two control classes. Second, we remind the reader that, on the post-test and the retention test, the overall percentage of RRs of the pupils of the E-class was still relatively low. Moreover, exploratory analyses of the individual test scores revealed substantial interindividual differences in the pupils' learning potential as reflected in the increase in RRs from pre-test to post-test and to retention test: the high-ability pupils from the E-class were more susceptible to the instruction than their average-ability and low-ability peers. Similarly, the increase in the number of RRs was considerably greater for some types of P-items than for others; the programme's success was most visible for the items about the interpretation of the outcome of a division with a remainder (TLU 1) (for more details see Verschaffel & De Corte, 1997b).

General Discussion

In this chapter, three related studies on upper elementary school children's conceptions about the role of real-world knowledge in mathematical modelling of school word problems, have been reported.

The findings from the first study show that, as a consequence of current classroom practice in teaching arithmetic word problem solving, pupils have gradually built up a very strong tendency to solve arithmetic word problems in a stereotyped way: they apply one (or a combination) of the basic arithmetic operations with the two given numbers in the problem, without any consideration of the possible problematic modelling assumptions underlying their proposed solution. The results of the second study confirm this tendency among upper elementary school children, and indicate that it is rooted in very strong conceptions and beliefs about the role of real-world knowledge in mathematical modelling of school word problems, which are resistant to conceptual change. However, both studies also revealed considerable interindividual differences in pupils' actual level of performance with respect to the use of everyday knowledge in mathematical modelling (see Study 1), as well as in their learning potential (or their zone of proximal development) as reflected in their reactions to simple forms of scaffolding aimed at triggering the activation of that knowledge (see Study 2).

The third study assessed whether it was possible to change children's inappropriate conceptions and beliefs about mathematical modelling and about the role of real-world knowledge in it. In view of inducing conceptual change, they were immersed into a new classroom culture in which word problems were effectively treated as exercises in realistic mathematical modelling. In this new classroom culture, a set of challenging, non-standard problem situations and a number of instructional techniques, such as small-group work and whole-class discussions, were systematically used to produce a cognitive conflict (or disequilibrium) in the pupils, which was considered necessary to produce the desired revision of their beliefs about the role of everyday knowledge in mathematical applications. The results of this study again revealed substantial interindividual differences between pupils' zone of proximal development as manifested in their susceptibility to the instructional efforts aimed at conceptual change. But these findings also provide good and promising support for the hypothesis that it is possible to change pupils' conceptions about, and their disposition toward, the activation of real-world knowledge in mathematical modelling of school word problems.

PART 4

Instructional Aspects

12

Task-Dependent Construction of Mental Models as a Basis for Conceptual Change

Wolfgang Schnotz and Achim Preuß

Introduction

There is a broad consensus today among cognitive and educational psychologists that learners are active constructors of their own knowledge rather than passive recipients of information. When children enter school at about 6 years, they have already had numerous experiences and have attained a common-sense understanding of many everyday phenomena. This common-sense view, often referred to as "naive prior knowledge", interacts with the new knowledge to be acquired in school. On the one hand, prior knowledge is a prerequisite for the acquisition of new knowledge, on the other, prior knowledge can also impede comprehension and learning because it is frequently incompatible with the new knowledge to be acquired. Therefore, learning requires not only the acquisition of new knowledge, but frequently the reorganization of existing knowledge, a process that is usually referred to as conceptual change (cf. Caravita & Halldén, 1994; Carey, 1985, 1991; Chi, 1992; di Sessa 1988, 1993; Duit, 1994; Vosniadou, 1994a; Vosniadou & Brewer, 1987, 1992, 1994).

The process of conceptual change that results from the interaction between prior knowledge and new knowledge is not only a central issue for a theory on cognitive learning, it is also relevant under practical aspects for the design of instruction. Many studies have shown that students have acquired, on the basis of their everyday experiences, so-called alternative frames of reference that can be considered as misconceptions from a scientific point of view. In school, these students acquire the scientific vocabulary, learn to reproduce the knowledge and to answer the teacher's questions in examinations. Outside school, however, they continue to use their old everyday knowledge, and even after many years of formal instruction, concepts from this old knowledge co-exist beside the scientific concepts (cf. Clement, 1983; Driver & Easley, 1978; Gilbert & Watts, 1983; McCloskey, 1983; Pfundt & Duit, 1991).

The following paper describes a theoretical framework for the analysis of conceptual change within learning and instruction that is based on existing work on the reorganization of knowledge. According to this framework, conceptual knowledge is a generative cognitive tool for the task-oriented construction of different mental representations, and conceptual change is assumed to result from an interaction between these representations. The paper also reports on an empirical study that investigated the possibilities to foster conceptual change by presenting students with well-defined tasks that stimulate the construction of elaborated mental representations as well as an intensive interaction between these representations.

Theoretical Framework

Previous Views on Conceptual Change

Various scholars of psychology and education have been concerned with the interaction between prior knowledge and new knowledge, although they frequently use different terminologies. Some of the most important early research in this area has been done by Vygotsky (1962). He argued that the difficulty of integrating everyday knowledge and scientific knowledge results from the fact that the so-called naive concepts acquired on the basis of everyday experiences and the scientific concepts taught in school belong to qualitatively different conceptual systems. On the one hand, concepts acquired on the basis of everyday experiences are closely related to the world of real phenomena in the learners' everyday life, but are not part of a coherent system, on the other, the scientific concepts taught in school form coherent systems, but are not sufficiently related to the phenomena in the learners' everyday experience. Accordingly, the function of school should be to help the different systems grow together. Learners should integrate their spontaneously acquired everyday concepts into coherent systems, and should apply the concepts presented in school to their everyday experiences. However, such an integration of different conceptual systems is frequently impossible because the respective knowledge systems are not compatible. Accordingly, a reorganization of knowledge seems to be necessary before an integration can take place.

Reorganization of knowledge or cognitive structures, respectively, played an important role in Piaget's (1950, 1985) theory of intellectual development. Piaget assumed that the human mind possesses an inherent tendency towards equilibration. Accordingly, the cognitive system strives for a balanced mental state that is free of cognitive conflicts. Cognitive development is triggered by active attempts to avoid such conflicts and proceeds by qualitative jumps from one level of intellectual functioning to the next, or from one kind of cognitive equilibrium to another, respectively. Although this theory stimulated much research on cognitive development, it described conceptual change only as global restructuring and could not explain why learners have specific difficulties in reorganizing their knowledge in specific domains.

Another theoretical approach on cognitive restructuring that can be considered as more domain-specific was developed by the Gestalt psychologists (Duncker, 1935; Köhler, 1921; Wertheimer, 1925). These researchers were not very interested in the acquisition of knowledge *per se*. Rather, they analysed processes of cognitive restructuring in thinking or problem solving and gave very detailed descriptions of such reorganization processes. What really causes the respective cognitive restructuring, however, remained undiscovered. An attempt to reanalyse the Gestalt psychology of cognitive restructuring in terms of modern cognitive psychology was made by Ohlson (1984a, b) and by Montgomery (1984). Ohlson argued that cognitive reorganization requires specific information that can either be found internally by the individual in long-term memory or externally in the respective problem situation. This information allows the learner to describe the problem in a new way and, therefore, to detect new interrelations that had remained unnoticed before. Montgomery has pointed out that the reorganization of a Gestalt can also be viewed as transforming a mental model into a structural balance that avoids generating cognitive conflicts. We will discuss this in more detail later.

Reorganization of knowledge was also analysed within the framework of cognitive schema theory, which, for its part, was also strongly influenced by the Gestalt concept. Rumelhart and Norman (1978), for example, have described knowledge reorganization as one of three different kinds of learning. Whereas *accretion* implies the elaboration of existing conceptual structures and *tuning* means the adjustment of existing concepts to new experiences by refinement of default expectancies or adjusting the range of possible data, *restructuring* refers to a reorganization of existing conceptual structures by adding new relations and omitting old relations between concepts. However, this categorization had only a descriptive rather than an explanatory function, and the distinctions are frequently difficult to apply in detail.

Strike and Posner (1982) have described the reorganization of knowledge as a replacement of old ideas by new ones. Accordingly, an individual's old knowledge is challenged by new experiences that create cognitive conflicts, which finally result in a replacement of old misconceptions by new, more adequate concepts. Such replacements are assumed to require that the learner is dissatisfied with her/his old concepts, that there are alternative concepts available that he/she is able to understand, and that the alternative concepts are plausible and promise to be fruitful (cf. Posner et al., 1982). However, cognitive conflicts do not generally result in conceptual change. Learners frequently consider conflicting evidence simply as exceptions that can be explained by *ad-hoc* assumptions (Beveridge, 1985; Rowell & Dawson, 1983). Furthermore, misconceptions are frequently not replaced, but, rather, co-exist beside the new conceptions (Caravita & Halldén, 1994; Pfundt & Duit, 1991).

More recently, various researchers have tried to analyse more precisely the interaction between prior knowledge and new knowledge, as well as the reorganization of existing knowledge, on the basis of concepts from cognitive and developmental psychology. di Sessa (1988, 1993) argues that the intuitive common-sense knowledge acquired from everyday experiences consists of isolated and fragmented knowledge pieces created on the basis of primitive phenomenological principles. According to this view, conceptual change is primarily an increase of coherence and consistency of knowledge caused by a progressive integration of phenomenological principles. Carey (1985, 1991), in comparison, considers an individual's intuitive everyday knowledge not as consisting of fragmented knowledge pieces, but rather as a coherent and systematic theory-like structure. According to this view, conceptual change is a radical restructuring of an individual's intuitive theory, that is, a sudden shift to a new perspective based on alternative core concepts and the new relations between them.

Vosniadou and Brewer (1992, 1994) have introduced a distinction between specific theories and framework theories within learners' intuitive knowledge. Specific theories consist of the domain-specific assumptions that an individual has about reality. Framework theories consist of general ontological and epistemological assumptions as, for example, that flat-looking things really are flat, and that gravity always operates in a top-down fashion from the observer's point of view. These assumptions are referred to as entrenched beliefs, because they are deeply rooted in everyday experience. Kuhn (1989) has pointed out that children do not spontaneously differentiate between hypotheses and evidence. Similarly, they are usually not aware of the theoretical status of their ontological and epistemological assumptions, that is, they do not consider them as hypotheses that can be verified or falsified.

Chi (1992) has argued that concepts are assigned to specific ontological categories that affect the content of these concepts (Chi et al., 1994). According to this approach, misconceptions are the result of inadequate ontological categorizations as, for example, the view that electricity is matter instead of a process. This is only a syntactical view of knowledge reorganization, however. Additional assumptions have to be made in order to explain why some reorganization processes can be performed rather easily whereas others are very difficult for the learner, and why conceptual changes across ontological categories are more difficult than changes within a category.

Another line of research has been presented by Caravita and Halldén (1994) who argue that the difficulties encountered by students in trying to understand scientific concepts should not be considered a problem of replacing old incorrect ideas by correct ones, but rather as a problem of embedding concepts within a specific situational and linguistic context (Halldén, this volume). What is usually referred to as conceptual change is seen here as a process of differentiating and integrating various contexts. Similarly, Säljö (this volume) has pointed out that research on knowledge reorganization should take into account the situated nature of human conceptual knowledge. He suggests that we should analyse, in particular, the connections between an individual's learning and the social and discursive practices within his or her culture. Most work on conceptual change has dealt with cognitive or socio-cognitive aspects of human knowledge. The role of motivational factors in conceptual change has only recently been emphasized (Pintrich et al., 1993).

Concepts as Tools for Knowledge Construction

A theory of cognitive learning that deals with the reorganization of knowledge has, of course, to make specific assumptions about the nature of this knowledge. Most researchers on human cognition agree that knowledge is not something that exists as an isolated entity in an individual's mind. Knowledge is, rather, an instrument that has to be useful for human practice. It is a tool that provides orientation about the world, that allows the creation of new information from old information, and enables an individual to anticipate events or to communicate with others about the present, the past and the future. As a tool, it is embedded — as all other tools — in specific social and communicative practices; it originates from these practices and is also sustained by them (Brown et al., 1989; Resnick et al., 1991; Säljö, this volume).

The fact that knowledge is not an isolated mental entity, but rather a tool embedded in human cooperative activities mediated by language, and that knowledge has to be useful in the respective social contexts, does not imply that the structure of knowledge is irrelevant. The usefulness of a tool serving a specific function is always dependent upon its specific structure and the specific procedures that operate on it. Similarly, the usefulness of knowledge as a tool for orientation and communication is also related to its structure or, more generally, to the structure and functioning of the human cognitive system, which is a product of an evolutionary process. A theory of cognitive learning that includes the reorganization of knowledge should therefore analyse the situatedness of knowledge, its embeddedness in contexts where it is used as a tool for orientation, without neglecting the fact that this usefulness of knowledge results from a specific structure and functioning of the human cognitive system. It is the interplay of both perspectives that promises progress in this field rather than disregarding the one or the other side.

We will argue in this paper that conceptual knowledge is a general and generic cognitive tool that serves to create other more specific tools. We assume that conceptual knowledge is represented in the human mind in the form of cognitive schemata. These schemata are considered as hierarchically-organized active and generative cognitive units that represent typical instances and interrelations within a domain (cf. Anderson & Pearson, 1984; Brewer & Nakamura, 1984; Rumelhart, 1980). If an individual comprehends a specific situation, a scenario, or a corresponding verbal description, then he/she activates a set of cognitive schemata and tries, by interacting bottom-up and top-down processes, to find a schema configuration that best fits the available data. This schema configuration then serves as a basis to create different kinds of mental representations.

A main distinction can be made between propositional representations, on the one hand, and mental models, on the other (Johnson-Laird, 1989; Morrow et al., 1987; Perrig & Kintsch, 1985). Propositional representations consist of complex symbols (propositions) that are similar to the sentences and phrases of natural language, composed of more simple symbols according to specific syntactic rules and, therefore, possess a specific constituent structure. Under a semantic aspect, a proposition denotes that a specific relation exists between specific entities. Therefore, a propositional representation is an internal description of the represented object or scenario by a hypothetical mental language and, thus, is assumed to have a close relation to natural language. Mental models, in comparison, are hypothetical internal quasi-objects that hold a structural or functional analogy to another object or scenario, which they represent on the basis of this analogy. Similar to other analogous models — for example, analogue computers — the represented attributes and the representing attributes may be quite different. In other words, there is, in the sense of Palmer (1978), no physical, but only a natural isomorphy required. For the same reason, mental models do not have to be images of the represented object. They can also represent a subject matter that is not perceivable at all as, for example, international trade relationships. As mental models are characterized by an analogy between their inherent structure or function and the inherent structure or function of the represented object or scenario, they have a closer relation to the respective subject matter than to its verbal description. It is important to note that mental models are not stored in long-term memory. Rather, they should be considered as temporary analogue mental representations that are constructed in working memory to solve specific tasks at hand.

We have argued that concepts (or cognitive schemata, respectively) are general cognitive tools that serve to create propositional representations and mental models as more specific cognitive tools for orientation about a specific subject matter. As cognitive tools, these different mental representations have to be useful. Using a representation is always related to specific procedures operating on it, because a representation never contains more information than can be extracted from it with the help of available procedures (Palmer, 1978). Mental representations can also be considered as internal sign systems. A specific sign system always enables and constrains cognitive processing, because such a system always supports specific operations and simultaneously constrains the kinds of operations that can be performed (Nunes, 1993, this volume). Accordingly, propositional representations and mental models can be considered as different internal sign systems that enable and constrain cognitive processing in different ways.

Symbol processing inference

rule:

isTime(A, ATime): -
  isDiff(A, Greenwich, ADiff),
  isTime(B, BTime),
  isDiff(B, Greenwich, BDiff),
  ATime = BTime + ADiff - BDiff

given propositions:
  isTime(Mexico, 14 h)
  isDiff(Mexico, Greenwich, -6 h)
  isDiff(Rio, Greenwich, -3 h)

goal:
  isTime(Rio, RioTime)

rule application:
  RioTime = 14 h + (-3 h) - (-6 h) = 17 h

inferred proposition:
  isTime(Rio, 17 h)

Model-based inference

model construction:

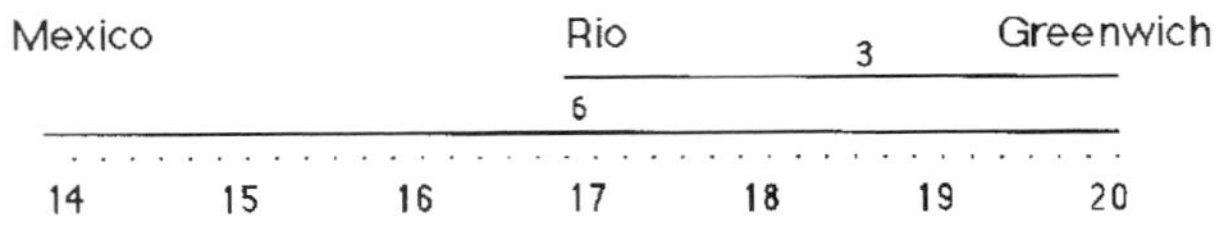

model inspection:

  rightOf(Rio, Mexico, 3 units)
  ->   eastOf(Rio, Mexico, 3 time zones)
  ->   laterThan(RioTime, MexicoTime, 3 h)

  MexicoTime = 14 h

  RioTime = 17 h

Figure 1: Symbol processing and model-based inferences. Example: What is the time in Rio, when it is 14 h in Mexico?

If a propositional representation is used to infer new information, symbol processing rules can be applied that create new propositions on the basis of existing propositions. An example of such a symbol processing inference is shown in the upper part of Figure 1. If an individual wants to infer what time it is in Rio de Janeiro when it is 14:00 h in Mexico, he or she can apply a symbol processing rule that can be described in the following way: *If the time at location A is given and the time at location B is to be determined, then add the difference between location B and Greenwich to the time at location A, subtract the time difference between location A and Greenwich, and set the result equal to the time at location B*. If this rule is applied on the respective propositions concerning the time in Mexico, the time differences between Mexico and Greenwich, and the difference between Rio and Greenwich, a new proposition is created, which indicates that the time in Rio is 17:00 h. Such a rule can be applied in a purely syntactical way without any reference to the respective object, without knowing where the respective cities are, and what the term "time difference" means. The process of inferring new information with a mental model is very different from the application of symbol processing rules. An example of such a model-based inference is shown in the lower part of Figure 1. If the task is to infer what time it is in Rio when it is 14:00 h in Mexico, an individual would first construct a mental quasi-spatial array that corresponds to the graphical configuration shown in Figure 1. Then, he or she could read off from this array that the sign *Rio* is depicted 3 units to the right of the sign *Mexico*, that Rio therefore lies 3 time zones further eastward, and so that it must be 3 hours later there than in Mexico. Furthermore, the individual could read off (by counting) that if the time in Mexico is 14:00 h, it is 17:00 h in Rio. Instead of applying symbol processing rules, inferring new information with a mental model requires procedures for model construction and model inspection. Model construction procedures serve to generate an initial mental model, and, if necessary, to elaborate or reorganize it. Model inspection procedures serve to search for specific entities and to determine the relations that exist between these entities. In other words, these procedures serve to read off information from the model.

Construction of propositional representations and of mental models is not performed in a linear order. Propositional representations can give rise to the construction of a mental model, which is generally assumed to be the case in text comprehension (cf. van Dijk & Kintsch, 1983). However, it is also possible that a mental model gives rise to the formation of a propositional representation. This is the case, for example, in picture comprehension, as iconic information provides a more direct way to construct a mental model than verbal information (cf. Mayer, 1994; Schnotz et al., 1993). We assume a continuous interaction between propositional representations and mental models because of the interplay of model construction and model inspection: On the one hand, mental models are constructed or elaborated on the basis of propositional representations, on the other, propositional representations are constructed or elaborated on the basis of mental models because these models can be used to read off new information that is made explicit in the form of new propositions.

Mental model construction, as well as mental model inspection, are assumed to be performed with the help of cognitive schemata. Mental model construction is the result of a comprehension process. During comprehension, an individual activates a configuration of cognitive schemata that best fits the available information. Such a schema-configuration, which also includes specific information about the particular object or situation at hand, is equivalent to the respective propositional representation that acts as a description of the represented object or scenario and of the mental model to be constructed. Because a description of a specific object does not only fit this object, but also numerous other objects, it would, in principle, be possible to construct an infinite number of mental models on the basis of a propositional representation. However, an individual usually constructs only one mental model during comprehension, and the constructed model represents a typical instance of the described object or scenario. This tendency to construct mental models of high typicality can be explained by the functioning of cognitive schemata during model construction, because schemata and schema-configurations describe typical instances and, thus, lead to corresponding models (cf. Denis, 1982; Greenspan, 1986; Walker & Yekovich, 1984). Cognitive schemata are also a tool for mental model inspection. During such an inspection process the individual has to search for specific entities within the model and has to identify the relations that hold between these entities. The search for entities and the identification of relations between them also requires finding a schema-configuration that best fits the structure of the mental model to be analysed.

To summarize the above thoughts: Conceptual knowledge can be seen as a general instrument that is used to create propositional representations and mental models as more specific cognitive tools for orientation. This conceptual knowledge is implemented as an inventory of cognitive schemata that creates propositional representations as well as mental models. The propositional representations are internal descriptions of the mental models and, thus, serve as a data base for the model construction. On the other hand, these models are the subject of model inspection, which creates or elaborates the respective propositional representations. Thus, propositional structures and mental models are complementary kinds of mental representations that continuously interact by schema-driven processes of model construction and model inspection. The respective cognitive schemata can be seen as active units of conceptual knowledge that enable and constrain model construction and model inspection.

Of course, this view provides only a theoretical framework that needs further specification as well as empirical evidence for its various assumptions. As we will try to demonstrate in the following, it might be helpful to clarify some fundamental concepts in the study of conceptual change and to explain some phenomena that would be difficult to understand otherwise.

Incoherence and Inconsistency of Knowledge

Various researchers have argued that the common-sense knowledge acquired from everyday experience does not possess a coherent structure, but, rather, consists of isolated and fragmented knowledge pieces. Accordingly, common-sense knowledge is seen as incoherent and inconsistent (di Sessa, 1988, 1993). Furthermore, it has been assumed that learners frequently fail to notice this incoherence and inconsistency because of inadequate standards of comprehension, that they do not notice when they do not sufficiently understand a topic, and that they do not systematically check the consistency of their knowledge. According to this view, problems of knowledge reorganization result from metacognitive deficits in noticing incoherence and inconsistency of knowledge (cf. Baker, 1985; Glenberg et al., 1982).

If we assume that knowledge reorganization results from an interaction between propositional representations and mental models, such a view of knowledge incoherence and inconsistency proves itself as problematic. This can be illustrated, for example, by the work of Vosniadou and Brewer (1992) on children's concepts about the shape of the Earth. The authors found that knowledge reorganization is usually neither a sudden replacement of incorrect concepts by correct concepts, nor do individuals simply replace incorrect mental models by correct ones. Instead, knowledge reorganization appears to be a gradual transformation of mental models. For example, if children have assumed for some time that the

Earth is flat and that people live on this flat Earth, and are then confronted with the new information that the Earth is a sphere, then they frequently give answers that seem to be incoherent and inconsistent. Upon being asked about the shape of the Earth, a child may answer, for example: "It is a sphere". Answering the question whether a man who walks straight ahead all the time would ever reach the end of the Earth, the child could say: "No, he would never reach the end". The child could also answer to a corresponding question: "People cannot fall from the Earth". Afterwards, however, the same child could nevertheless state that the Earth has an end, and that someone who lives on the spherical surface of the Earth would fall from the Earth. Old and new knowledge seem to co-exist here in a totally unrelated way, and the child's knowledge appears to be clearly inconsistent.

Figure 2: Example of a child's synthetic model of the Earth (from Vosniadou, 1994b, modified)

However, there is no inconsistency at all if the child has constructed a specific kind of mental model. Vosniadou and Brewer found that children sometimes imagine the Earth as a hollow sphere, similar to a goldfish bowl with a flat bottom where people are assumed to live, as is illustrated in Figure 2. With this image of the Earth, the child's answers make perfect sense: The Earth is a sphere; a man walking straight ahead does not reach the end of the Earth because there are mountains and oceans in between; nevertheless, the Earth has an end, which is on the top and can be reached only by a rocket; people cannot fall from the Earth, because they are living inside on the flat bottom, but an individual living outside on the spherical surface would, of course, fall down.

These findings show that misconceptions sometimes do not result from difficulties in understanding new information, rather, they result from children's creative attempts to reconcile new information with old assumptions about the respective subject matter, and to construct "synthetic models" (Vosniadou & Brewer, 1992) that correspond to both kinds of information as far as possible. Vosniadou and Brewer assume that children possess implicit framework theories consisting of general ontological and epistemological assumptions, so-called "entrenched beliefs", which are deeply rooted in everyday experience. Such beliefs are, for example, that flat-looking things are really flat, or that gravity always operates in a top-down fashion from the observer's point of view. If a child holds these assumptions and then learns that the Earth is a sphere, the child will try to interpret this new information within his or her old framework theory and, thus, construct an updated model taking into account the available information as far as possible. The problem is, in these cases, not to understand the new information correctly, but to release the model construction from inadequate constraints. Children need support to reconcile their experiences of a flat-looking Earth with the new idea of a round Earth. They have to understand that round things can look flat under specific conditions and that gravity does indeed always operate from top-to-bottom, but that "top-down" denotes different directions at different places on the Earth (Vosniadou, 1994b).

Of course, the term "framework theory" should be used with caution, because the fact that children behave *as if* their thinking follows some epistemological and ontological beliefs does not imply that they really *possess* the respective theoretical assumptions and *operate* with them as part of their implicit or explicit knowledge. A child's (mis)interpretation of new information could also result simply from a lack of necessary conceptual differentiations as, for example, between the appearance of an object (e.g. flat) and the nature of this object (e.g. round), or between different kinds of spatial reference (e.g. top-down here and top-down there), because such a differentiation was not yet required, instead of epistemological and ontological assumptions in the child's mind. Nevertheless, this work is very important because it clearly demonstrates that problems of conceptual change or reorganization of knowledge, respectively, sometimes do not result from incoherence of knowledge or from metacognitive deficits in detecting knowledge inconsistencies. Instead, a learner's misconceptions can also result from active (and successful!) attempts of coherence formation, that is, attempts to construct a mental model that satisfies constraints both from old and from new knowledge. As the example presented above has shown, learners sometimes find rather creative solutions to this problem.

The example presented above also demonstrates that inconsistency of knowledge has nothing to do with the co-existence of correct and incorrect pieces of knowledge. The fact that some of the child's answers mentioned before were correct and others were incorrect does not have implications for the consistency or inconsistency of the respective knowledge. The essential point is whether these answers are compatible or incompatible, that is, whether all the respective propositions can be true for some possible world. In the present example, such a world does exist, namely the Earth as a hollow sphere, and as long as the propositions that describe (and constrain) this world do not contradict each other, there is no reason to consider the child's knowledge as inconsistent.

According to our view, knowledge can be seen as *consistent* as long as its *propositions are compatible*. Compatibility of propositions means that it is *possible* to construct at least one mental model that fits *all* the respective propositions. Accordingly, *knowledge is inconsistent if (and only if) it is impossible to construct a model that fits all the respective propositions.* In other words, knowledge is inconsistent if every model that can be constructed from parts of the propositional data base is necessarily incompatible with other parts of this data base.

We have already mentioned that mental models are not stored permanently in long-term memory, but should be considered as temporary mental representations in working memory. This implies that mental models only have limited stability. For example, it is possible that a learner uses a mental model and takes into account its entities at one moment, and then ignores some of these entities a few moments later. Accordingly, contradicting propositions can also be the result of fluctuations in the structure of a mental model, because the respective model does not yet possess sufficiently high stability. However, the possibility of unstable mental models leading to contradicting propositions does not affect our definition of knowledge inconsistency. If we say that knowledge is inconsistent if (and only if) it is impossible to construct a mental model that fits all available propositions, we do not assume that learners do not construct mental models when their propositional knowledge is inconsistent, instead, learners can also construct mental models on the basis of inconsistent propositional knowledge, taking only parts of this knowledge into account. In addition, these models can lack stability, which may lead to further contradicting propositions. However, none of the mental models constructed under such conditions would fit all these propositions. Thus, our definition of knowledge inconsistency can be maintained: Knowledge is inconsistent if every model that can be constructed from parts of the propositional data base is necessarily incompatible with other parts of this data base. It has to be added, however, that consistency of knowledge requires sufficient stability of the respective mental models.

The theoretical view presented here has another important implication that refers to the question of where exactly the contradictions exist in the human mind, when we talk about inconsistency of knowledge. Our answer is that these contradictions exist only between propositions, not between mental models, and that contradictions can therefore be detected only on the level of propositional representations. Of course, this claim can be challenged because, at first glance, it appears that contradictions can exist between mental models also. One could argue, for example, that a hollow sphere model of the Earth contradicts the scientifically correct model, because the real Earth is not a hollow sphere. Although this sounds plausible, such an argument is too simplistic and ultimately incorrect, as we will try to show with the following example.

If learners try to understand why different times and dates simultaneously exist on Earth, they can construct very different models: They can project the Earth's surface on a cylinder, unwrap the cylinder on a rectangle, and then imagine that this rectangle is moving like a flying carpet along the time axis as shown in Figure 3a. An alternative would be to imagine the Earth as a sphere (or circle) that rotates within a shell of different time states as shown in Figure 3b. A further possibility would be to depict the Earth surface repeatedly as a rectangle, forming an endless Earth tape as shown in Figure 3c, and to imagine a "time window" that moves along this tape and defines the actual space–time relations.

All these models look very different, and none of them has much similarity to the real Earth. But despite their different appearances, they are equivalent in reference to informational content because all the information about time and date differences between specific cities that can be read from one model can also be read from the other models (Larkin & Simon, 1987). Thus, there is no contradiction between these models. Similarly, it would be incorrect to argue that a hollow sphere model of the Earth contradicts the scientifically

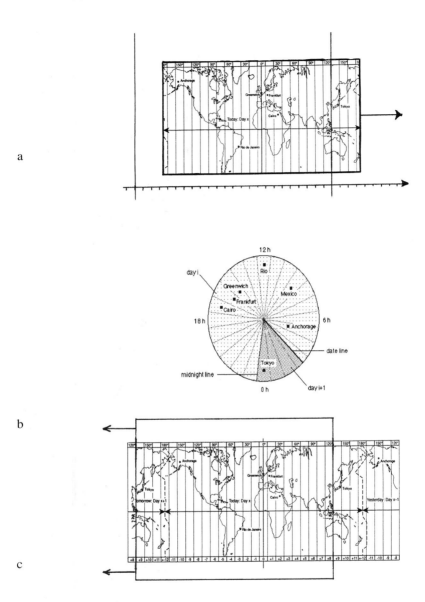

Figure 3: Examples of different models of time differences on the Earth: The Earth's surface as a rectangle moving along the time axis (top); the Earth's surface as a sphere/circle rotating in a shell of time states (middle); the Earth's surface as an endless tape constrained by a gliding time-window (bottom)

correct model, because the Earth is not a hollow sphere. The Earth is indeed not a hollow sphere, but neither is the Earth a rectangle moving along a time axis nor an endless tape with a "time window". Nevertheless, these models are scientifically correct and equivalent representations — as far as the informational content is concerned — of time and date differences on the Earth. Obviously, the shape or structure of a model *per se* does not matter. The relevant point is what information can be read from the model. On the one hand, it is possible to read the same information from very different models, if these models are equivalent in information as in the example above, on the other, it is possible to read off contradicting information from very similar models (as, for example, an Earth model with and without a dateline).

Thus, cognitive conflicts or inconsistencies do not exist between mental models themselves, rather, they exist on the level of propositional representations. Accordingly, mental models can give rise to inconsistencies only via inspection procedures applied on a model. These procedures read off information from the model and encode this information as propositions, which may then contradict other propositions. In other words, cognitive conflicts or inconsistencies arise from the interaction between mental models and propositions, and they manifest themselves on the *propositional* level.

Knowledge Application and Conceptual Change

The studies mentioned above have made obvious that knowledge sometimes seems to be inconsistent without really being inconsistent. This does not imply, however, that the common-sense view of children or adults is coherent in general, that no inconsistencies exist in their knowledge, and that learners do not show metacognitive deficits in the detection of such inconsistencies. In fact, the notion of incoherent, fragmented knowledge does not really contradict the notion of spontaneous coherence formation by learners who construct synthetic mental models if one assumes that the former corresponds to a more global view, whereas the latter represents a more local view on the organization of human knowledge (cf. di Sessa, 1988, 1993; Vosniadou, 1994b; Vosniadou & Brewer, 1992).

In the following we will describe some examples, in which deficits in conceptual knowledge remained unnoticed and obviously led to the construction of inadequate mental models and to inconsistent propositional representations. We will then discuss under what conditions these conceptual deficits can be detected and removed. The examples are taken from a study, in which we tried to analyse the conceptions of adults about times and dates on the Earth. Of course, these subjects knew that the Earth is a sphere, that it rotates around its north–south-axis in an eastern direction, that the sun rises in the east and sets in the west, that a day begins at midnight 0:00 h and ends at midnight 24:00 h. Nevertheless, they had considerable difficulties in forming a sufficiently elaborated mental model and a consistent propositional representation. Frequent conceptual deficits were the lack of relevant concepts, the failure to discriminate between relevant concepts, and inadequate conceptual embeddings. To illustrate these deficits, we give some examples:

1. If a city is located in the west, a sunrise occurs later there. Accordingly, clocks have to be put forward 1 hour if one enters a new time zone to the west ...
2. After having crossed all time zones during a day, we enter a new date zone ...

3. The date line is the meridian on the Earth where it is always midnight ...
4. Because of the rotation of the Earth, the date line is continuously moving to the west ...
5. A date zone is an area that consists of all the time zones on the Earth ...

In example (1), the subject does not discriminate between the relations "occurs later" and "is later". In (2), entities of space and entities of time are mixed up, as time zones and date zones are seen as time intervals instead of spatial entities. In (3) and (4), the date line is categorized as a spatial entity, but considered a variable entity on the Earth. Finally, in (5), the subject considers a date zone as the sum of all existing time zones. Because this would correspond to the whole Earth, the subject fails to discriminate between areas on the Earth where different days exist.

Frequently, subjects also do not recognize the function of the date line and its relation to time zones. The following statements are typical examples:

6. If someone travels eastward and enters a new time zone, he has to add 1 hour to the time. If he crosses the date line in the Pacific, he has to add 1 day.
7. As the sun rises earlier in the east, the time in a time zone lying to the east is later than the time in a zone lying to the west. ... East of the date line we have a day later than west of the date line.

In both (6) and (7) the subject fails to recognize that the date line and the time zones have totally different influences on time, because the 24 steps of increasing the daytime by 1 hour during one circumnavigation eastward are compensated by 1 decrease of 24 hours at the date line. Examples of inadequate conceptual embeddings are:

8. The different daytimes that exist simultaneously on Earth are caused by the Earth orbiting around the sun and the inclination of the Earth's rotation axis.
9. Countries in the northern hemisphere and countries in the southern hemisphere belong to different time zones and have different daytimes.
10. If it is 0:00 at the North Pole then it is 12:00 at the South Pole. If one would orbit around the South Pole and return to the North Pole, the time there would be 24:00 of the same day.

In (8), (9) and (10), the concept of daytime is not adequately embedded, because it is connected with other concepts that are irrelevant in this context (orbiting of the Earth around the sun, inclination of the Earth's rotation axis, northern and southern hemisphere). because of failures to discriminate between relevant concepts and the inadequate conceptual embeddings, subjects frequently show explicit contradictions, which indicate inconsistent propositional knowledge. The following are some examples:

11. The date line is located on the 180th meridian in the Pacific. If it is 12:00 in Greenwich, it is the same day all over the world. Then the date line moves westward with a speed of 1 time zone per hour.
12. Time changes continuously everywhere in the world. Because of the rotation of the Earth around its own axis, the change from an old day to a new day at any place on

the Earth occurs at midnight, 24:00. This change takes place at the date line, which is located on the 180th meridian and crosses the Pacific.

13. At any place on the Earth, the date changes after 24 hours ... The date line is an arbitrary line that divides the Earth into two halves where different days exist. ... If someone circumnavigates the Earth westward once within 24 hours, he has to put back his watch 24 times, 1 hour at each new time zone. If he started on a Tuesday afternoon, for example, he would return to the place where he started on Tuesday afternoon.

In example (11), the date line is at first seen by the subject as a stationary entity and then, two sentences later, as an entity with a variable location. So, the date line is stationary and variable (i.e. not stationary) at the same time. In (12) the subject assumes that a new day begins at midnight and that this event occurs at the date line which is located in the Pacific. Accordingly, it would always be midnight at that place in the Pacific, which contradicts the previous proposition that time changes continuously everywhere in the world. In (13) the subject mentions the date line as a borderline between two areas where different days exist. Nevertheless, the subject then ignores the date line mentioned directly before and assumes that after a circumnavigation westward the date is put back one day. So, the subject comes up with two different days existing simultaneously at one place on Earth.

The question arises under which conditions such conceptual deficits can be detected by the learner. A central point in this respect is that knowledge can be seen as a tool. If a tool is not adequately constructed, its deficits are manifested when the tool is used. Similarly, when knowledge is considered a tool, knowledge deficits should become apparent during the use of this knowledge. As we have characterized conceptual knowledge as a general cognitive tool for the construction of specific interacting mental representations, namely propositional structures and mental models, deficits in an individual's conceptual knowledge should become evident in the construction and interaction of these propositional representations and mental models.

We assume that conceptual knowledge is used in a task-oriented way according to the principle of cognitive economy. In other words, we assume that an individual tries to construct with as little cognitive effort as necessary a mental representation that is useful for the respective task at hand, and that this usefulness requires that the mental representation has a specific structure. If a model needs to have a specific task-adequate structure, the model has to include specific entities that form a specific configuration (cf. White & Frederiksen, 1990). We can illustrate this again with time-difference phenomena on the Earth, where it is possible to present rather different tasks or to ask rather different questions as, for example, in (Q1) and (Q2):

(Q1)   What is the time in Rio de Janeiro, when it is 14:00 h in Mexico?
(Q2)   A space shuttle starts from Moscow at 14:00 h, orbits two times around the Earth within 3 hours and then returns to its starting point. The crew always adjusts the shuttle calendar to the date of the respective part of the Earth. How often do they switch the date during their journey?

Questions like (Q1) will be referred to in the following as *time-difference tasks*. Such questions can be answered in a purely syntactical (algorithmic) way without constructing a mental model. If the learner tries to answer questions like (Q1) with the help of a mental model, then this model needs to have only a minimal structure, because it has to contain only meridians and time zones with the respective cities. Questions like (Q2) will be referred to in the following as *circumnavigation tasks*. In order to solve such tasks, the model needs to have a more complex structure: It has to include, not only meridians and time zones, but also the date line and date zones. Otherwise, it would be either impossible to read off the required information from the model, or this information would be contradictory. If the model contained no date zones, it would not be possible to read off where each day exists on the Earth. If the model did not encompass a date line, it would be possible to simultaneously read off different days at one and the same place: If it is Tuesday 14:00 in Mexico, for example, the learner could infer that it is Tuesday 17:00 in Rio, because the time in Rio is 3 hours later than in Mexico. However, the learner could also infer that it is Monday 17:00 in Rio, because according to the model, the time in Rio is also 21 hours earlier than in Mexico. In general, mental models have to be elaborated according to the task at hand to attain a "structural balance", that is, a model structure that allows operation of the model without running into contradictions (Montgomery, 1984).

If we assume that mental models are constructed as temporary mental representations in working memory according to specific tasks at hand, and if we further assume that this construction process follows the principle of cognitive economy, then we can conclude that the structure of these models will *not* go beyond the requirements of the tasks at hand. For example, mental model construction would be assumed to progress less far when learners have to solve time-difference tasks than when they have to solve circumnavigation tasks.

We have assumed that conceptual deficits become obvious in the construction of mental models with an inappropriate structure and in the task-induced interplay of these models with propositional representations. Accordingly, the likelihood that existing conceptual deficits will be detected by the learners affected by the kind of task he/she is trying to solve. If a learner tries to solve a task and the respective model has an inappropriate structure, it is either impossible to read off the required information, or different propositions can be read of the model that contradict each other. However, such deficits can only be detected if the learner is dealing with appropriate tasks that require the construction of a sufficiently elaborated model and the use of this model in sufficiently different ways. If a mental model is used in a too restricted way for the task at hand, insofar as there is no need to read off specific information, and as contradicting information never enters working memory simultaneously, conceptual deficits can remain unnoticed.

Failure to detect conceptual deficits can also result from the specific context in which the respective knowledge is applied. Because of the previously mentioned situatedness of knowledge, learners frequently use one part of their knowledge in a specific context and another part of their knowledge in another (cf. Halldén, 1990). According to this context-specific use of knowledge, learners can construct different mental models in different contexts, and read off information from these models that contradict each other. But these inconsistencies can remain unnoticed if the respective contexts are rather distinct because the respective contradicting propositions never enter working memory simultaneously and because of the large distance between these contexts (cf. Caravita & Halldén, 1994).

What Changes in Conceptual Change?

We have described conceptual knowledge as a cognitive tool for the construction of mental models and propositional representations. Accordingly, processes of conceptual change manifest themselves as a reorganization or transformation of mental models and propositional representations. The term "transformation" should be used with caution in this context, however. As mental models are temporary representations constructed in working memory according to the specific tasks at hand, they do not exist permanently in long-term memory. Even if the same mental model is used again and again, it must always be reconstructed to be used. From this point of view, no old models exist in the mind that can be transformed into new models. Instead, mental models are always constructed according to specific configurations of activated cognitive schemata. If a schema configuration is activated that has already been used for constructing a previous mental model of a specific learning content, the new model will have the same structure as the previous one, and the previous model is said to be reconstructed. If a new schema configuration is activated, the construction process will lead to a new model structure that differs from the previous structure, and the previous mental model seems to have undergone a "transformation".

One can assume that the activation of schema configurations that have frequently been used successfully in the past requires less cognitive effort than the activation of new configurations. Thus, it can be expected that, according to the principle of cognitive economy, the frequently used schema configurations have a higher likelihood of being activated and of guiding the mental model construction than new configurations. This assumption can help to explain different phenomena. First, although mental models are not stored in long-term memory, learners show a strong tendency to preserve the structure of the mental models they have used so far, because the respective schema configurations have a higher likelihood than other configurations to be reactivated and, thus, to construct a mental model with the same structure as before. Second, the construction of a mental model with a new, alternative structure requires more cognitive effort, because the respective schema configuration is not as well established as the previous configuration. Accordingly, it is also more difficult to maintain the respective model structure in working memory, which might explain why, at the beginning of learning about a complex subject matter, the individual's mental models have a lower stability than when learning is more advanced.

Finally, it is a well-known fact that scientifically incorrect common-sense conceptions frequently remain alive and can be reactivated even after many years of schooling under specific circumstances. According to our theoretical view, one can assume that cognitive schemata from a previously used schema configuration generally continue to exist and that they can also be used in other configurations. Accordingly, there exists a general possibility that even if an old schema configuration has not been used for a long time, it can be reactivated in a specific context, if other competitive configurations are not sufficiently activated. This implies that there is never a real replacement of old concepts by new concepts, but rather a competition between alternative concepts with a different likelihood of being activated according to their former usefulness and the respective context conditions. Such an impossibility to really replace old, scientifically incorrect concepts might appear as an impediment in education. However, it also provides an important advantage, because the coexistence of various (scientifically correct or incorrect) conceptions can be a basis for higher cognitive flexibility. If an individual does not act as a learner, but as a teacher, such a flexibility to temporarily adopt scientifically incorrect views even plays a central role, because it gives the teacher a chance to understand the thinking of his/her students and to reconstruct their incorrect mental models too.

Many studies of conceptual change on the basis of mental model theory have been conducted primarily under a developmental perspective. In the following, we will describe an empirical study on conceptual change that has been conducted with the previously described theoretical framework under the perspective of learning and instruction.

A Study of Task-Induced Conceptual Change

Research Questions and Hypotheses

Knowledge has been described above as a tool that has to be useful. This implies that, on the one hand, there is no need to modify knowledge as long as it is sufficiently useful and, on the other, that knowledge has to be used in order to be reorganized. Knowledge application implies that conceptual knowledge is used to construct specific propositional representations and mental models that interact through schema-driven processes. According to this view, it should be possible to foster conceptual change by presenting students with well-defined tasks that stimulate the construction of elaborated mental models as well as an intensive interaction between these models and the corresponding propositional representations. In order to test this general assumption we tried to analyse both the influence of knowledge application on knowledge acquisition and the influence of knowledge application on the reorganization of knowledge.

Research Questions

With regard to the influence of knowledge application on knowledge acquisition, the study aimed at answering the following questions:

(1a)   What influence do learning tasks that trigger a specific kind of knowledge application have on the construction of mental models and propositional representations?

(1b)   What influence do individual learning prerequisites have on the construction process?

With regard to the influence of knowledge application on knowledge modification the following questions were asked:

(2a)   What influence do learning tasks that trigger a specific kind of knowledge application have on the repair of conceptual deficits?

(2b)   What influence do individual learning prerequisites have on this task-dependent repair of conceptual deficits?

Hypotheses

If the construction of mental models and propositional representations is a task-oriented process, we can assume that learners will place different emphasis on these representations depending on the tasks to be solved. The above mentioned time-difference tasks, for example, require a relatively rich propositional representation, because many details about the time-coordinates of various cities have to be encoded on the propositional level, whereas the mental model (if one is constructed at all) does not have to be very elaborated. On the contrary, circumnavigation tasks require a more elaborated model, which must also include the date line and date zones, whereas the propositional representation needs to contain less detail information. These considerations lead to the following hypothesis:

(H1.1)   The construction of a propositional representation is emphasized more if learners are solving time-difference tasks than if they are solving circumnavigation tasks. On the other hand, the mental model construction becomes more differentiated if learners solve circumnavigation tasks, because the date line and date zones are added more frequently than if learners solve time-difference tasks.

We assume that the construction of these different mental representations needs different cognitive prerequisites and that individuals differ with regard to these prerequisites. Because of the close relationship between propositional representations and verbal information, a learner's performance in verbal reasoning tasks can be considered an index of her/his ability to process verbal information and to encode its semantic content in a propositional format. We will refer to the corresponding ability to process verbal information and to solve verbal reasoning tasks (which is, of course, based on verbal semantic knowledge, cognitive schemata and the respective functioning of working memory) as an individual's verbal-reasoning skills. Because of the close relationship between mental models and the spatial or quasi-spatial structure of the represented subject matter, a learner's performance in spatial reasoning tasks can be considered an index of his/her ability to construct and manipulate mental models. We will refer to the corresponding ability to process spatial information and to solve spatial reasoning tasks (which is, of course, based on spatial semantic knowledge, cognitive schemata and the respective functioning of working memory) as an individual's spatial-reasoning skills. Therefore, one can formulate the following hypotheses.

(H1.2a)   Verbal-reasoning skills have a higher influence on the construction of a propositional representation than on mental model construction.

(H1.2b)   Spatial-reasoning skills have a higher influence on mental model construction than on the construction of a propositional representation.

According to the considerations presented above, conceptual deficits result in the construction of mental models with an inadequate structure. If these models are used in a sufficiently variable way, contradicting information will be read from the model and enter working memory. Accordingly, learners who work on tasks that require them to operate their mental models in a more varied way are more likely to detect such conceptual deficits than learners who work on tasks that require a less variable use of their mental models. We have assumed above that model construction develops further, and that mental models are used in a more varied way, if learners solve circumnavigation tasks than if they solve time-difference tasks. Accordingly, we arrive at the following hypothesis:

(H2.1)   Learners who solve circumnavigation tasks will detect more conceptual deficits and will repair these deficits more frequently than learners who solve time-difference tasks.

The process of detection and repair of conceptual deficits can be assumed to progress differently depending on individual cognitive learning prerequisites. We have assumed above that high spatial-reasoning skills provide a better basis for mental model construction than low spatial-reasoning skills, and that learners scoring high in verbal reasoning can construct more elaborated propositional structures than learners scoring low in verbal reasoning. As the repair of conceptual deficits is based on an interaction of propositional representations and mental models, both learners with high spatial-reasoning skills and learners with high verbal-reasoning skills should benefit more from an intensive interaction between mental models and propositional structures than learners with low spatial- or verbal-reasoning scores. Accordingly, we can formulate the following hypotheses:

(H2.2a)   The increased repair of conceptual deficits by learners who solve circum-navigation tasks as compared with those who solve time-difference tasks is more pronounced if learners have high spatial-reasoning scores.

(H2.2b)   The increased repair of conceptual deficits by learners who solve circum-navigation tasks as compared with those who solve time-difference tasks is more pronounced if these learners have high verbal-reasoning scores.

Method

Subjects and Learning Material

Forty university students from different faculties, whose ages ranged from 22 to 30 years, participated in the study. The subjects were randomly assigned into two groups of 20 students. As learning material, all subjects received an instructional text printed on paper that explained why different times and dates exist on the Earth. This text covered the following themes: Time zones on the Earth, time differences on the Earth, date differences on the Earth, and date zones on the Earth. The text length was 2750 words. In addition, the two groups of subjects were presented with two different sets of learning questions on a sheet of paper. One set consisted of six questions about time differences between various cities on the Earth (*time-difference tasks*), and the other set consisted of six questions about changes in time and date during circumnavigations around the Earth (*circumnavigation tasks*).

Procedure

The study was run in two separate sessions of 2–3 hours each with a 1-week interval. During the first session, the subjects were presented with a verbal reasoning and a spatial reasoning test. The verbal reasoning test (VMG1) required the students to precisely understand verbal statements and their implications. The spatial reasoning test (cube test of Amthauer IST-70) required them to recognize three-dimensional objects after rotation. The subjects were then asked to explain, in a short essay, why different times and dates exist on Earth.

In the second session the subjects received the instructional text and one of the two sets of learning questions as learning material. One group of subjects received the text combined with time-difference questions. The other group of subjects got the text combined with circumnavigation questions. The subjects were asked to read the text carefully in order to answer the respective questions. There was no time limit during this learning phase. After learning, the subjects were again asked to explain, in a short essay, why different times and dates exist on Earth. Finally, the subjects had to apply their knowledge on time and differences in a test that consisted of 35 items concerning time and date on Earth. Eighteen items were time-difference questions, and 17 items were orbiting questions. The two sets of questions were presented in a randomized sequence.

Scoring

The subjects' verbal-reasoning scores were determined as an index of their ability to mentally encode the semantic content of verbal material in a propositional format. The spatial-reasoning scores of the subjects were determined as an index of their ability to construct and manipulate three-dimensional mental models. The subjects' essays on time and date differences on the Earth were considered as descriptions of their temporary mental models, or as verbalizations of the underlying conceptual structures, respectively. Verbal reference to relevant spatial entities (such as *meridians, time zones, date line* and *date zones*) was assumed to indicate the existence of the respective entities in the subject's mental model. The frequency of conceptual deficits (lack of relevant concepts, failure to discriminate between relevant concepts and inadequate conceptual embeddings) was determined for each essay. Furthermore, the number of cities mentioned with correctly remembered time-coordinates was determined for each subject. This score was considered an indicator of the elaborateness of the underlying propositional representation. Regarding the final test, both the number of correctly answered time-difference questions and the number of correctly answered circumnavigation questions were determined.

Results

Knowledge Application and Knowledge Acquisition

The essays written by the students before and after learning were analysed with respect to the frequencies of reference to *meridians*, *time zones*, the *date line* and *date zones*, because these entities were considered as the critical milestones in the progressive model construction. Before learning, the concept "meridians" was mentioned 0.13 times on average (SD = 0.22) by the time-difference group and 0.25 times (SD = 0.38) by the circumnavigation group. This difference was not significant. After learning, the mean frequency of mentioning meridians had neither increased nor decreased in the time-difference group (SD = 0.28), and it had slightly decreased by 0.10 (SD = 0.31) in the circumnavigation group. This difference between both groups was not statistically significant. Before learning, the concept "time zones" was mentioned on average 0.52 times (SD = 0.32) by the time-difference group and 0.53 times (SD = 0.35) by the circumnavigation group. This difference was not significant. After the learning phase, the mean frequency of mentioning time zones had increased by 0.33 (SD = 0.31) in the time-difference group and by 0.28 (SD = 0.35) in the circumnavigation group. This difference between the two groups was not significant.

Prior to learning, the concept "date line" was mentioned on average 0.23 times (SD = 0.26) by the time-difference group and 0.20 times (SD = 0.30) by the circumnavigation group. This difference was not significant. After the learning phase, the mean frequency of mentioning the date line had increased by 0.28 (SD = 0.38) in the time-difference group and by 0.33 (SD = 0.34) in the circumnavigation group. This difference between both groups, again, was not significant. The concept "date zones" was mentioned before learning on average 0.05 times (SD = 0.22) by the time-difference group and 0.10 times (SD = 0.31) by the circumnavigation group. This difference was not significant. Following the learning phase, the mean frequency of mentioning date zones increased by 0.10 (SD = 0.31) in the time-difference group, whereas it increased by 0.35 (SD = 0.59) in the circumnavigation group. The increase of mentioning date zones within the circumnavigation group was significantly higher than the increase within the time-difference group (t(38) = 1,69; P < 0.05). The change in frequency of mentioning the different entities is shown in Figure 4.

The essays written by the students were also analysed with respect to the number of correctly remembered time-coordinates of different cities as an indicator of a well-encoded propositional representation, which also includes detail information. Before learning, the members of the time-difference group mentioned the time-coordinates of 1.25 cities (SD = 1.59) on average, whereas the subjects in the circumnavigation group mentioned the time-coordinates of 1.00 cities (SD = 1.72); this difference was not significant. After the learning phase, these values had increased by 0.75 (SD = 1.59) in the time-difference group and by 0.50 (SD = 2.12) in the circumnavigation group. This difference was also not significant. These results support hypothesis (H1.1) to some extent. On the one hand, the process of mental model construction was progressing more when learners had solved circumnavigation tasks: The subjects of this group inferred date zones as mental entities significantly more frequently than the subjects who had solved time-difference tasks. However, there was only a slight, but not significant, difference with regard to the date line between the two groups, which indicates that the subjects of the

Task-Oriented Propositional Encoding and Mental Model Construction

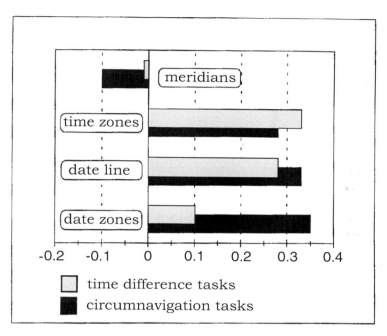

Figure 4: Increasing reference to critical entities in mental model construction by learners who solved time-difference tasks and learners who solved circumnavigation tasks

time-difference groups also had inferred this entity in their models, although this was not required by their tasks. The fact that no significant differences between the two groups were found with regard to the time zones and meridians did correspond to our assumption that there is no difference with respect to these entities. The *decreasing* frequency of reference to meridians by the circumnavigation group could be explained by the fact that the focus of the subjects' attention gradually shifted during the progressive mental model construction from older entities to new entities that had only been included previously into the model. As the model construction was more advanced in the circumnavigation group, the older entities (meridians) were more likely to become out of focus than in the time-difference group. On the one hand, there was a tendency for learners who solved time-difference tasks to focus more on the formation of a propositional representation than learners who solved circumnavigation tasks, although this was not statistically significant.

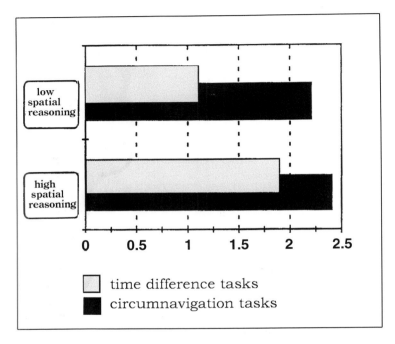

Figure 5: Decrease of conceptual deficits of learners scoring low and those scoring high in spatial reasoning after solving time-difference or circumnavigation tasks

Individual Differences

We had assumed that the formation of a propositional representation and a mental model required different cognitive skills. More specifically, we had hypothesized that verbal-reasoning skills had a higher influence on the formation of a propositional representation than on mental model construction, whereas spatial-reasoning skills had a higher influence on mental model construction than on the formation of a propositional representation. A highly elaborated propositional representation should be especially helpful to solve time-difference tasks, because detailed information about the time-coordinates of various cities are required here. A highly elaborated mental model should be especially helpful to solve circumnavigation tasks, because these tasks require model-based inferences. We indeed found, on the one hand, a highly significant correlation between the time-difference scores of all subjects in the final comprehension test and their verbal-reasoning scores ($r = 0.37$; $P < 0.01$), whereas no significant correlation was found between circumnavigation scores and verbal reasoning ($r = 0.22$). On the other hand, a highly significant correlation was found between circumnavigation scores in the final comprehension test and spatial-reasoning scores ($r = 0.40$; $P < 0.01$), whereas the correlation between time-difference scores and spatial reasoning was not significant ($r = 0.18$). Although the correlation differences themselves were not statistically significant, the results lean in the direction of our assumptions (H1.2a) and (H1.2b), namely that the construction and use of the different mental representations make different demands on cognitive requirements.

When we analysed the correlational patterns of the subject groups separately, we found an interesting difference between both groups. On the one hand, there were no significant correlations within the time-difference group. (Verbal reasoning had a correlation of $r = 0.23$ with the time-difference score, and the correlation with the circumnavigation score was $r = 0.06$. Spatial reasoning had a correlation of $r = 0.28$ with the time-difference score, and the correlation with the circumnavigation score was $r = 0.27$.) On the other hand, we found high correlations between cognitive prerequisites and test scores within the circumnavigation group: Verbal-reasoning scores had a highly significant correlation with time-difference scores ($r = 0.68$; $P < 0.001$), and spatial-reasoning scores showed a significant correlation with the circumnavigation scores ($r = 0.47$; $P < 0.05$). Verbal reasoning had only a correlation of $r = 0.09$ with the circumnavigation scores, and spatial reasoning correlated only with $r = 0.28$ with the time-difference scores.

These results indicate that learners with high verbal-reasoning skills were obviously ready to encode as propositions, not only the information that is necessary for mental model construction, but also detailed information regarding time-coordinates of various cities, even when they had to concentrate primarily on the construction of a mental model. Afterwards, these subjects could therefore show good performance in solving time-difference tasks, although these tasks had not been expected. In other words, the high correlation between verbal reasoning and time-difference scores can be explained by the willingness of learners to process and encode information that is not required by the task. Learners who were solving time-difference tasks, on the contrary, concentrated their processing primarily on the propositional encoding of detail information. This propositional encoding was obviously neither difficult for subjects with high or low verbal-reasoning scores. Accordingly, there was only a low correlation between verbal-reasoning scores and time-difference scores within the time-difference group. Learners with high spatial-reasoning scores were probably better able to construct a mental model than learners with low spatial-reasoning scores. Accordingly, a high correlation was found in the circumnavigation group, because only these subjects received tasks that required the construction of an elaborated mental model.

Of course, the question arises as to why there was only a low correlation within the time-difference group between the subjects' spatial-reasoning scores and their performance in solving circumnavigation tasks during the final comprehension test. It has to be kept in mind that the subjects from the time-difference group were not required to construct a mental model and were not prepared to solve circumnavigation tasks. Thus, even when they had constructed a mental model, they were not in a position to anticipate the specific use of their model. High spatial-reasoning abilities were not very helpful in this case. The reason might be that it is difficult to postpone the initial construction of a mental model and to start with this construction only after the learning phase. Accordingly, high spatial-reasoning skills do not help a learner very much in the case of such unexpected tasks, when no appropriate mental model has been constructed before. It might also be possible that subjects with high spatial-reasoning scores really did construct a mental model even when they had to solve only time-difference tasks, but as they could not anticipate the circumnavigation tasks that they had to solve afterwards, the learners' mental models were not appropriate for this purpose.

Knowledge Application and Knowledge Modification

Task-Oriented Repair of Conceptual Deficits

We had assumed that conceptual deficits become visible when learners work on tasks that require elaborated mental models and when they operate on these models in a sufficiently variable way. Accordingly, we had assumed that learners who solve circumnavigation tasks will detect and repair more conceptual deficits than learners who solve time-difference tasks. Before learning, the subjects showed an average number of 4.15 conceptual deficits (SD = 1.04) in the time-difference group and a mean number of 4.50 conceptual deficits (SD = 1.64) in the circumnavigation group. This difference was not significant. During the learning phase, the average number of conceptual deficits decreased by 1.45 (SD = 1.15) in the time-difference group, and by 2.30 (SD = 1.78) in the circumnavigation group. That is, the number of conceptual deficits was reduced significantly more when learners solved circumnavigation tasks than when they solved time-difference tasks ($t = 1.80$; $P < 0.05$). This result supports hypothesis (H2.1). Accordingly, tasks that require elaborated mental models and force learners to operate on these models in multiple ways, help students to detect and repair conceptual deficits.

Individual Differences

We had also assumed that the repair of conceptual deficits was based on an interaction of propositional representations and mental models. Therefore, it had been hypothesized that both learners with high spatial-reasoning skills and learners with high verbal-reasoning skills should benefit more from tasks that required an intensive interaction between mental models and propositional structures than learners with poorer skills. Accordingly, we had expected that the difference regarding the repair of conceptual deficits between learners with time-difference tasks and learners with circumnavigation tasks would be more pronounced if the subjects had higher spatial-reasoning skills. Similarly, we had expected that the difference between the two groups concerning the repair of conceptual deficits would be more pronounced if learners had higher verbal-reasoning scores. The whole sample of 40 subjects was, therefore, divided by a median split into a subsample of 19 subjects scoring high and a subsample of 21 subjects scoring low in spatial reasoning. Likewise, the subjects were divided into a subsample of 19 subjects scoring high and a subsample of 21 subjects scoring low in verbal reasoning.

Contrary to our expectations there was no significant difference regarding the repair of conceptual deficits between time-difference subjects and circumnavigation subjects with high spatial-reasoning scores. Before learning, the average number of conceptual deficits among these subjects was 4.22 (SD = 0.83) in the time-difference group (nine subjects) and 3.90 (SD = 1.91) in the circumnavigation group (10 subjects), which was not a significant difference. After learning, the average number of conceptual deficits had decreased by 1.89 (SD = 1.45) in the time-difference group and by 2.40 (SD = 2.12) in the circumnavigation group. This difference in the decrease of conceptual deficits was not significant. However, there was a strong difference in the reduction of conceptual deficits among learners with low spatial-reasoning scores: Before learning, the average number of conceptual deficits among these subjects was 4.09 (SD = 1.22) in the time-difference group (10 subjects) and 5.10 (SD = 1.10) in the circumnavigation group (11 subjects), which was not significantly different. The average decrease of conceptual deficits after learning was only 1.09 (SD = 0.07) in the time-difference group (10 subjects), whereas it was 2.20 (SD = 1.48) in the circumnavigation group (11 subjects). This difference between both groups was significant [$t(19) = 2.23$; $P < 0.05$]. The different rates in the reduction of conceptual deficits are shown in Figure 5.

These results did not correspond to hypothesis (H2.2a). Our interpretation of this finding is that learners with high spatial-reasoning scores were willing to construct an elaborated mental model even when they only had to solve time-difference tasks. Therefore, they were able to detect nearly as many conceptual deficits as when they had to solve circumnavigation tasks. However, learners with low spatial-reasoning scores did not spontaneously construct an elaborated mental model when they were solving time-difference tasks. Accordingly, they detected fewer conceptual deficits than when they solved circumnavigation tasks. The strong reduction of conceptual deficits among low spatial-reasoning subjects who solved circumnavigation tasks suggests that these learners were definitely able to construct a mental model of the learning content. However, they obviously needed appropriate learning tasks as a stimulation to construct such a model.

We found exactly the opposite pattern of results when we differentiated between low and high verbal-reasoning scores. Among the learners with low verbal-reasoning scores, the average number of conceptual deficits before learning was 4.39 (SD = 0.96) in the time-difference group (13 subjects) and 4.75 (SD = 1.04) in the circumnavigation group (8 subjects), which was not significantly different. After learning, the average number of conceptual deficits had decreased by 1.69 (SD = 1.26) in the time-difference group and by 2.38 (SD = 1.60) in the circumnavigation group. This difference also was not statistically significant. Among the learners with high verbal-reasoning scores, the number of conceptual deficits before learning was 3.72 (SD = 1.11) in the time-difference group (7 subjects) and 4.33 (SD = 1.97) in the circumnavigation group (12 subjects), which was not significantly different. After learning, the average number of conceptual deficits had decreased by 1.00 (SD = 0.82) in the time-difference group, whereas it decreased by 2.25 (SD = 1.96) in the circumnavigation group. This difference in the reduction of conceptual deficits was significant [$t(16) = 1.96$; $P < 0.05$]. The different rates in the reduction of conceptual deficits are shown in Figure 6.

These results seem to support hypothesis (H2.2b), because there were significantly fewer conceptual deficits among learners who worked on circumnavigation tasks than among learners who solved time-difference tasks, when verbal-reasoning skills were high. It should be noted, however, that this difference did not result from a *marked* decrease of conceptual deficits in the circumnavigation group but from a *slight* decrease in the time-difference group. Insofar, this finding was also unexpected. The results can be explained in the following way: Time-difference tasks required the learner to encode much detailed information about the time-coordinates of various cities in a propositional format. As learners with high verbal-reasoning scores had high skills in this kind of processing, they were willing to invest a great deal of their cognitive capacity in this propositional encoding. Accordingly, they had fewer cognitive resources available for the construction of a mental model and, thus, could not detect as many conceptual deficits. In other words, these subjects were disadvantaged in their learning, because they received a task with limited demands and because they had *good abilities* to solve this task, which prevented them from constructing an elaborated mental model and detecting conceptual deficits.

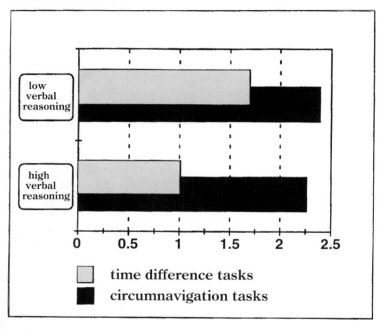

Figure 6: Decrease of conceptual deficits of learners scoring low and learners scoring high in verbal reasoning after solving time-difference or circumnavigation tasks

Discussion

The data of the study described above give some indication that the theoretical view presented could be a useful framework for the study of conceptual change within short-term processes of learning and instruction. According to this view, conceptual change is the result of a specific kind of knowledge application. Conceptual knowledge is considered as a general tool for the task-oriented construction of specific propositional structures and mental models. Accordingly, conceptual change takes place in the framework of a task-oriented interaction between propositional structures and mental models. Depending on the kind of anticipated use of knowledge, the mental model construction proceeds differently. Conceptual deficits lead to inadequately structured mental models. If these models are used in a sufficiently varied way, model inspection processes either cannot be applied or lead to contradictory results on the propositional level, which makes the existence of conceptual deficits obvious. If models are only used in a limited way, however, such deficits can remain unnoticed. Increasing coherence and consistency of conceptual knowledge is therefore the result of a sufficiently broad use of mental models of increasing stability.

The construction of the different mental representations is influenced by different cognitive prerequisites. On the one hand, learners with high spatial-reasoning skills are not only better able to construct a spatial mental model, they are also willing to exceed the model structure that is required for the task at hand. These learners construct and use relatively elaborate mental models, even with less demanding tasks, and, thus, are able to detect conceptual deficits nearly to the same extent as for the more demanding tasks. Learners with lower spatial-reasoning skills, on the contrary, need appropriate tasks as an external stimulation in order to construct such mental models and use them in a sufficiently variable way. On the other hand, learners with high verbal-reasoning skills are willing, even in cases when the main focus lies on the construction of an elaborated mental model, to encode on the propositional level detailed information that is not required for mental model construction. Therefore, these learners show high performance when they receive unexpected tasks that require the respective detail information. However, if learners with high verbal-reasoning skills receive tasks that require a propositional encoding of detail information rather than the construction of an elaborated mental model, they can, paradoxically, be hindered in their acquisition and modification of knowledge because of their good abilities to fulfil this requirement.

Concerning the question of how it is possible to foster conceptual change, various suggestions have been made. The relatively simple view of Strike and Posner (1982), who assumed that instruction should challenge the students' misconceptions and create cognitive conflicts in order to replace these misconceptions by new, scientifically more adequate conceptions, has been challenged by recent, more refined theoretical views. Researchers such as Caravita and Halldén (1994) and Säljö (this volume) have emphasized the situatedness of human concepts, which implies that concepts are always used and sustained by specific contexts. Accordingly, conceptual change could be supported by helping students to differentiate between contexts that are associated with the use of specific knowledge or to integrate previously distinct contexts. Vosniadou and Brewer (1994) have pointed out that conceptual change is frequently difficult because learners construct mental models that are constrained by framework theories consisting of inappropriate ontological and epistemological assumptions. Accordingly, conceptual change could be fostered by helping students to exempt their mental model construction from inadequate constraints (Vosniadou, 1994b).

The theoretical framework described in this paper supplements these views as it emphasizes the necessity of knowledge application and the construction of mental models as temporary analogue representations for the evaluation of conceptual knowledge. According to this view, it should be possible to foster conceptual change by learning tasks that stimulate individuals to construct mental models and use these models in a sufficiently variable way that enables the detection of existing conceptual deficits. Such learning tasks should be designed and sequenced in a way that requires a progressive mental model construction towards a certain model structure. These tasks should initiate a use of these models that makes conceptual deficits obvious. The view of a progressive mental model construction on the basis of conceptual knowledge, and the notion of a task-oriented interaction between these models and corresponding propositional representations, which helps to evaluate the coherence and consistency of conceptual knowledge, might, therefore, not only be a useful framework for the study of conceptual change in instructional settings, but also a heuristic for constructing and sequencing appropriate tasks in the design of learning environments that foster conceptual change.

13

Constraints on the Effectiveness of Diagrams as Resources for Conceptual Change

Richard Lowe

Introduction

The conceptual change associated with learning can be seen as a process that involves a progression of mental models (Gentner & Stevens, 1983; Vosniadou, 1994; White & Frederiksen, 1986). Formation of the initial mental model in such a progression has been attributed to an individual's everyday interaction with the physical world. Vosniadou (1994) has obtained evidence from a variety of subject domains that progression from this initial mental model to a culturally-accepted model is by way of a combined mental model that incorporates features of both types of models. Vosniadou characterizes conceptual change as being particularly difficult to achieve if the construction of a new mental model involves apparent contradictions of a naive framework theory in which the target concept is embedded. A naive framework theory is hypothesized to contain presuppositions based upon an individual's everyday experience and to form the foundation for the development of subsequent knowledge structures. Such theories can be in fundamental conflict with the scientifically-accepted foundation for a particular knowledge domain.

As a way of reconciling new information presented during the course of instruction, with the coherent system of explanation provided by a robust naive framework theory, students appear to construct what Vosniadou has termed "synthetic" mental models. These are a product of assimilating contradictory information into existing conceptual structures and typically result in scientifically-inappropriate responses to generative questions (i.e. questions that require consideration of phenomena not directly experienced before by the respondent). From the preceding analysis, it seems unlikely that many established teaching approaches, which tend to emphasize the *enrichment* of an existing conceptual structure, would be capable of dealing with the dominant, obstructive effect exerted by a naive framework theory. Interventions directed toward a fundamental *revision* of that structure appear to hold greater potential as a way to engender change towards a more scientifically-acceptable concept. However, before such a revision can be contemplated, it is necessary to characterize the naive framework theory that is to be addressed by an intervention.

Conceptual Change and University Study

There is a tradition in conceptual change to examine the influence of naive concepts on subsequent conceptual development and to deal with the introduction of fundamental science concepts in school settings (e.g. Bliss et al., 1989; Driver et al., 1985; Osborne et al., 1983). However, there are many domains in which formal, intensive study of the subject matter does not begin until university level. Presumably students who reach this level have had a considerable measure of success in undergoing the conceptual changes necessary to develop basic science concepts that are in accord with what is accepted scientifically. Nevertheless, when they begin their university studies in an essentially unfamiliar domain, it is possible that the process of learning concepts in that domain is subject to constraints on conceptual change that are somewhat analogous to those that operate with much younger students. Although university students would almost certainly not possess the same sorts of naive framework theories that have been suggested by Vosniadou and her colleagues for much younger children, the general notion of a naive framework theory as an impediment to conceptual change appears, at least in principle, transferable to learning at university level.

The study reported here is set in the domain of meteorology and deals with the underlying conceptual structures that exist for Australian weather maps. Although in-depth tuition in meteorology occurs only at university level in Australia, those who enrol in such courses have typically already had extensive exposure to weather maps. This exposure comes both from low-level formal instruction in schools (in classes such as geography and general science) and from weather forecast segments in the media. Previous research indicates that university students' mental representations of weather maps differ in quite fundamental ways from those of professional meteorologists, suggesting that their previous exposure to weather-map information has produced some underlying conceptual structures that are quite inappropriate from a scientific point of view (Lowe, 1989, 1993, 1994a,b). The general nature of these differences appears likely to be a serious hindrance to beginning meteorology students' efforts to learn how to process weather maps effectively. Anecdotal evidence from university teachers of meteorology suggests that such students do indeed have persistent problems in making effective use of weather maps and the nature of these problems appear to be related to the differences found during research. Therefore, it is important to determine the origin of these differences as a basis for designing instructional interventions to help students develop the capacity to construct suitable mental models from this type of depiction. Such models should have features that facilitate rather than hinder the progress of conceptual change towards a meteorologically-acceptable concept of a weather map.

The present research explored the effect of meteorological expertise on the mental models of weather-map diagrams that are generated while processing these depictions. The investigation used a generative task (prediction) to elucidate the features of the constructed mental model on the assumption that the characteristics of the output from prediction processing will reflect the nature of the mental model upon which that processing was based. Mental model features deduced from predictions made by meteorologists and non-meteorologists were used as evidence for larger theoretical structures in which their concepts of weather maps were embedded and by which these concepts were constrained.

Mental Models and Diagrams

Mental models represent situations in an analogue fashion and can be manipulated in various ways to perform processes such as inference and prediction (Johnson-Laird, 1983). They have been found to be a useful theoretical construct for considering the way people deal with novel situations and solve problems, especially where technical systems are involved (e.g. De Kleer & Brown, 1981; Hegarty et al., 1988; Kieras & Bovair, 1984; Payne, 1991). So that they can cope with changing situations, mental models are considered as flexible representations that have the capacity to be updated with additional information as required. Running a mental model of a physical or conceptual system forwards in time from its original state is hypothesized as a mechanism for the generation of predictions. By this account, the quality of a prediction would depend on the characteristics of the mental model that was run to produce the new state of affairs.

There is empirical evidence to support the view that diagrams are effective as a means of facilitating the processing of information because they can support the construction of mental models that are a suitable basis for that processing (e.g. Glenberg & Langston, 1992; Hegarty & Just, 1993). To qualify as "suitable" in this regard, a mental model would need to be complete as well as accurate with respect to both the tokens that stand for the entities that the model represents, and the structuring that the model includes to represent the relations that exist amongst those entities. In order to construct a mental model with these characteristics from a diagram, the individual must first process the diagrammatic depiction appropriately. If the person studying the diagram is both familiar with its general subject matter domain and adept in processing that particular type of diagrammatic display, it is likely that the construction of a suitable mental model will ensue. This is the type of situation that appears to have been the focus in most of the research on diagrams and mental models to date (e.g. Mayer & Gallini, 1990). However, there are instructional situations in which neither of these conditions can really be said to apply. For example, consider an individual who is faced with a highly abstract diagram of a technical system and who lacks a well-developed domain-specific mental representation of the diagrammatic genre to which that depiction belongs. This is the sort of situation that could occur with a beginning student of a specialized scientific domain such as meteorology. It seems unlikely that such a person would have the capacity to process the diagram appropriately in the first instance and so construct a suitable mental model of the depicted system. This is not to say that there would be no attempt to construct a mental model from the diagram; however, the sort of model that could be constructed under these conditions would probably be neither complete nor accurate.

Subsequent cognitive processing carried out on the basis of an incomplete, inaccurate mental model could be expected to be flawed, particularly if higher level operations such as inference or prediction were involved. Conclusions based upon the running of a model with these inadequacies should reflect the nature of the model's weaknesses and the basis upon which it was constructed (that is, the effectiveness of the diagram processing underlying building of the mental model). If conceptual change occurs by way of a progression of mental models, knowledge of these aspects of beginning student models should be considered when devising instructional interventions designed to promote effective conceptual change. This is likely to be particularly important when change to a scientifically-acceptable concept is hampered by the presence of a persistent naive framework theory that continues to produce or reinforce misconceptions as new information is added to the existing knowledge base.

Weather Maps as Instructional Diagrams

How Weather Maps Change over Time

The weather we experience at any given time is a consequence of the state of the atmosphere that surrounds us. Energy from the sun activates the atmosphere so that this global mass of gaseous fluid behaves as a huge dynamic system. The atmosphere is in a continual state of flux and the interaction of local meteorological influences with broader global factors determines the weather experienced within a given region. The weather map for a region uses a highly specialized graphic language to depict some consequences of this interaction. From a visuo-spatial perspective, a weather map mostly consists of sequences of smoothly curving lines spaced across the part of the Earth's surface dealt with by the map. These lines are the isobars that join locations with the same atmospheric pressure and, thus, collectively show the distribution of pressure across the map region. High and low pressure centres marked within the isobar sequences identify local pressure extremes; these pressure centres are often surrounded by a number of concentric closed isobars (i.e. isobars in the form of complete closed loops) that define a high or low pressure cell. Structures such as these provide a basis for chunking the complete set of meteorological markings shown on a weather map into a smaller number of local features. The other main components of a weather map are the fronts, which mark significant temperature discontinuities. Although fronts are also marked by lines, they are distinguished from isobars by having additional symbols attached to them (triangular barbs in the case of cold fronts).

The graphic forms used to define components such as isobars or fronts change over time to reflect the behaviour of the meteorological entities they represent. For a weather map to represent properly the way the meteorological situation changes from one day to the next, the visuo-spatial characteristics of its markings must be altered strictly in accordance with the appropriate meteorological principles and situational features. At a macro level, this can involve broad changes in which graphic forms (that together comprise the overall meteorological pattern) move across the surface of the map. These changes make up a complex choreography in which different components of this pattern perform their own characteristic movements. The precise direction and extent of these movements varies according to the nature and context of the meteorological phenomena concerned. For example, there is typically an easterly progression of features overall in the southern half of the Australian weather map region during summer while features in the northern half are generally much less active. However this general trend is modulated considerably according to the specifics of each particular meteorological situation. The macro level changes in the overall pattern of meteorological markings are accompanied by more localized micro level changes. These involve alterations in the visuo-spatial characteristics of graphic forms that reflect small-scale regional meteorological influences. For example, when the isobars making up a high pressure cell are shifted via the general easterly movement of features so that they change from being over the sea to being over the land, their profile typically "adapts" (bends) to reflect the local change in surface temperature conditions. The central issue in determining the way weather-map markings at any level should be treated is that meteorologically-appropriate meaning and significance are given to this visuo-spatial information.

Weather Maps and Selectivity

The type of weather map normally used for presenting weather forecasts is a mean sea level chart that displays only a small part of the Earth's total meteorological environment. In effect, a person viewing the chart is looking through a small window that provides fragmentary information about isolated, local aspects of a much more comprehensive global meteorological system. In addition to this spatial selectivity, weather maps are usually presented as single diagrams, which means they also give a temporally selective view of broader meteorological processes.

It was stated earlier that beginning students of university-level meteorology typically acquired their background knowledge of weather maps from a very limited amount of school instruction and a far more extended period of exposure to the media. Consider the sorts of treatment that weather maps would be given in these situations. Even when presentation of a weather map is accompanied by generalized comments about changes expected for the next day, this elaboration is typically superficial and covers only a limited period. In the interests of simplicity and accessibility, the focus tends to be on a limited number of specific meteorological features (such as the retreat of a high pressure cell or the approach of a cold front) that can be referred to in a concrete fashion when "explaining" the forthcoming weather. It is usual to discuss these features in isolation from the broader, meteorological situation such that they are treated as discrete objects rather than as transitory phenomenon within a global mass of gaseous fluid. This highly selective experience of meteorological phenomena gives non-meteorologists (such as beginning students of meteorology) a very limited range of opportunities to develop appropriately contextualized mental models of meteorological systems. In many ways, it resembles the situation that small children experience when they learn about the Earth and its relation to the day–night cycle as a result of their everyday observations (Vosniadou, 1994). In both situations, the nature of the mental model that can be constructed is constrained by the limited scope of the available information.

However, there are important differences. Because a weather map is an artificial and highly abstract device constructed by humans (rather than a natural object or phenomenon), there is no simple, readily discernable relation between events we have experienced in our everyday surroundings and the graphic pattern of meteorological information displayed on the map. This is caused by both the way the map depicts information about the atmosphere and by the nature of the atmosphere itself. Vosniadou (1994) suggests that misconceptions developed during the process of conceptual change arise from attempts to reconcile a culturally-accepted scientific explanation with initial explanations that individuals develop as a result of their everyday experiences. This explanation assumes that there is sufficient perceived commonality between the situation as experienced and the situation as dealt with in the scientific explanation to permit the construction of a synthetic mental model that combines aspects of an initial model with aspects of the culturally-accepted model. While this account is well suited to cases such as the explanation of the day- and night-cycle explored by Vosniadou and colleagues, it does not appear sufficient in the case of weather maps. The abstraction in a weather map is so great that it would be unreasonable to expect misconceptions to be generated as a result of *direct* conflict between (i) the individual's experience of the Earth and its weather and (ii) the map's graphic representation. However, this does not preclude the generation of misconceptions caused by attempts to "reconcile"

some *other* aspects of our experience with scientific information presented in this specialized graphic.

Framework Theories and Concepts of Weather Maps

When processing a weather map, non-meteorologists do have *general* experience that they
can draw upon about the way objects in our world behave and how these are represented
pictorially. Our direct experience of the way the world works is dominated by the behaviour
of the solid objects in our immediate locality at any given time. The tendency for elementary explanations of weather maps to refer to meteorological features, such as high cells and
cold fronts, as if they were discrete objects may encourage meteorological novices to make
analogies between solid objects and these much less tangible and qualitatively different
gaseous phenomena. This would be understandable, given the nature of our surroundings.
Despite the fact that fluid states of matter (liquids and gases) play a very significant role in
our lives, we are often unaware of either their presence, or the energy that drives their
behaviour. Our experience of these fluid states is particularly limited with respect to their
dynamic behaviour, especially as far as large-scale dynamics are concerned. For example,
although we live in an "ocean" of air, its distinctive properties (invisibility, permeability,
etc.) mean that its presence and behaviour are generally imperceptible. We usually become
aware of this gaseous fluid only when there is substantial local movement involved (such as
when we feel the wind blow and see the curtains move or when we hear and see a champagne cork pop from a bottle).

The broader-scale and often more subtle fluid behaviours of the atmosphere that are
reflected in a weather map are not an immediate part of our everyday experience. A probable consequence is that this deficit in our everyday experience of the gaseous systems
represented in weather maps forces non-meteorologists to rely on their experience of the
properties and behaviour of the (more perceptible) solid objects in our environment when
given weather-map processing tasks. When such tasks require the drawing of weather-map
markings, it may follow that these markings are generated in accord with the individual's
experience of pictorial representations of everyday subject matter (which almost exclusively deal with arrangements of solid objects). On this analysis, it could be expected that
the mental models that non-meteorologists construct from a given weather map as a basis
for drawing weather-map patterns, would be dominated by entities whose properties are
largely those of solids and whose representation in graphic form accords with generalized
pictorial conventions for depicting solid systems. This would suggest the non-meteorologists possessed an underlying naive framework theory constraining the generation of such
models based upon the following presuppositions.

a. A weather map represents a system that behaves as if it is comprised of an essentially
    finite set of discrete ("solid") objects.
b. The changes in the weather-map pattern that result from this behaviour can be generated
    from a simple visuo-spatial approach that manipulates graphic forms as if they were
    comprised of solid objects.

In contrast, the corresponding aspects of meteorologists' framework theory would be as follows.

a. A weather map represents part of a much more extensive and continuous gaseous fluid system.
b. The changes in the weather-map pattern that result from the way this system behaves must be generated by an approach that subjugates visuo-spatial manipulation of graphic forms to the meteorological complexities involved.

Non-Meteorologists' Approach to Weather Maps

Previous research indicates major qualitative differences between meteorologists and non-meteorologists in the way that they deal with weather-map diagrams. These findings have been interpreted as evidence that these two groups possess conceptual structures for weather maps that are founded upon fundamentally different bases. The nature of these differences appears to be consistent with the different framework theories suggested above for meteorologists and non-meteorologists. It would be expected that when given a specific weather map to process, the mental model that members of these different groups construct from that map would reflect the differences in their particular framework theories. The consequences of these differences in their mental models should be manifested in the type of predictions made as a result of running such models to generate future weather-map patterns.

Findings from research on the performance of weather-map processing tasks provide some clues about how non-meteorologists' predictions might differ from those of meteorologists if they were operating on the basis of the naive framework theory as suggested. In one study (Lowe, 1994b), meteorologists and non-meteorologists were given a standard weather map of the Australian region and asked to draw the meteorological markings they would expect to find in the region beyond that shown in the given map. This expansion task was an investigation of both the types of entities that populated subjects' mental representations of weather-map diagrams and the extent to which these representations included a regional map's wider meteorological context. The findings indicated that the non-meteorologists' repertoire of entities tended to be more limited than it was for meteorologists with a small number of highly stereotypical and regular graphic forms being generated. In their attempts to draw additional markings to fill the region beyond the given map, it appeared that the non-meteorologists were far more reliant than the meteorologists on the meteorological markings that were already provided. It was concluded that the non-meteorologists' mental representations were contextually impoverished whereas those of the meteorologists subsumed regional weather maps into much larger meteorological systems that operated well beyond the regional scale. The non-meteorologists' production of highly localized patterning of well-defined, regular graphic elements in their attempts to deal with the map expansion task is consistent with their apparent lack of contextual knowledge.

An earlier study (Lowe, 1989) in which subjects engaged in a progressive search task to uncover parts of a hidden weather map and then attempted to complete the remaining missing sections also suggested that non-meteorologists have a tendency to characterize meteorological markings as regular graphic forms. Their completion of information within a regional map area (as opposed to beyond it, as was the case in the study mentioned above) favoured the production of concentric closed loop structures. They appeared to be trying to turn poorly-defined curved isobar fragments into coherent graphic structures that had the form of well-defined visual "objects". Compared with meteorologist subjects, there was a noticeable absence of attempts to organize these local graphic structures into broader composite assemblies. This tendency was consistent with their predominantly visuo-spatial strategies for addressing other aspects of the experimental task. A similar focus amongst non-meteorologists on the formation of graphic objects was found in a study of the way meteorological markings were copied from a weather map and later recalled (Lowe, 1993). In that study, the predominantly visuo-spatial approach taken by the non-meteorologists to the processing involved in the copy-recall task contrasted sharply with the overriding meteorological approach of the meteorologists. Of particular interest to the current research is that non-meteorologists exhibited comparatively poor performance in copying and recalling more subtle graphic characteristics of weather-map markings, such as local variations within isobars that could be regarded as perturbations in what was otherwise a regular shape or structure overall. It was as if the coarse characteristics of a pattern such as a concentric group of closed isobars had a privileged status over its finer details.

By making a number of assumptions from these previous findings and considering the basis for the proposed naive framework theory, it is possible to suggest some aspects of the type of mental model that non-meteorologists would produce when faced with a weather-map prediction task. Given their previous exposure to simple ideas about weather maps, it appears likely that the mental model generated will be a synthetic model that reconciles non-meteorologists' rudimentary meteorological knowledge with their everyday experience. Thus the meteorologically-legitimate general action of moving graphic forms across the map over time (as emphasized in elementary instruction about meteorology and the treatment of this subject in the media) will be combined with quite inappropriate approaches for dealing with specific changes that should simultaneously occur in the details of the meteorological pattern. An overarching assumption is that superficial visuo-spatial rather than deeper meteorological considerations will determine the characteristics of the mental model generated. As far as the individual entities are concerned, the mental model would be expected to characterize these entities as objects that retain their integrity rather than being subject to changes in their intrinsic properties. As a result, when an entity moved, its location would change but characteristics such as its size, shape and structure would tend to be unaffected, especially if its form appeared to be particularly cohesive from a visuo-spatial perspective. There would be no provision in the model for any but the most obvious forms of interaction between entities, thus excluding interactions in situations such as those in which entities are distant from each other. It is also what would be expected from individuals who tend to focus upon the coarse characteristics of graphic structures and who lack the domain-specific knowledge to alter the finer details accordingly. These aspects of the proposed mental model can be related to the way different types of substances behave. Where the behaviour of solids is the main focus, the coherence of discrete objects is a major determinant of the type of change that occurs. However, for gaseous fluids, physical continuity throughout the fluid system and the change of properties with distance are fundamental.

A further assumption is that the motion of entities is relatively uniform in both direction and magnitude. In other words, rather than there being a complex set of meteorological constraints on where different types of entities can legitimately move to and how far they can shift in a given time, movement would tend to be concerted. An approximate analogy here might be to consider the meteorological markings as if they were all painted onto a strip of paper that was drawn past the window made by the weather-map boundary. However, this suggestion raises the question of what lies beyond the boundary ready to enter the window as other elements leave the window area. Because non-meteorologists' mental representations do not seem to encompass what lies beyond the weather-map boundary, it seems reasonable to assume that another simplification would be that the mental model built from a given map should be of very limited geographic scope. Essentially, the construction of a mental model would rely for its raw material on the array of markings explicitly presented on a given map.

Hypotheses

In this study, evidence was gathered about the mental models of a given weather map constructed by meteorologists and non-meteorologists. The research task involved subjects drawing their predictions of the markings they would expect to appear on the weather map one full day later than the given map. The general expectation was that weather-map predictions drawn by non-meteorologists would differ from those generated by meteorologists in ways that indicated the presence of fundamentally different framework theories underpinning the construction of mental models by each group. This would in turn result in two quite different sets of characteristics in the predictions drawn as a consequence of running these dissimilar mental models. The meteorologists would subjugate the visuo-spatial characteristics of the predictions to the demands of a framework theory that incorporated presuppositions consistent with the nature of the atmosphere as a global mass of gaseous fluid. In contrast, the non-meteorologists' predictions would reflect the construction from the original weather map of mental models based upon a framework theory derived from their everyday experience of local sets of solid objects and pictorial conventions for treating these objects in diagrammatic form. This difference in framework theories led to two specific hypotheses.

a. The meteorologists' predictions will treat a regional weather-map display contained within the bounds of its frame as an integral part of a larger fluid system whereas the non-meteorologists' predictions will tend not to reflect this wider context. As a result, the non-meteorologists' predictions will be more limited than those of the meteorologists by the markings that were present within the original weather map's frame.
b. In the meteorologists' predictions, treatment of graphic forms and their arrangement will reflect the fluid nature of the gaseous atmospheric system represented in a weather map whereas the non-meteorologists' predictions will be more consistent with the representation of discrete objects in an everyday solid system. At a macro level, this will be indicated by the individual features in the meteorologists' predictions having undergone more independent patterns of displacement from their original positions than those drawn by the non-meteorologists. At a micro level, it will be indicated by the graphic elements comprising individual features in the meteorologists' predictions having undergone more substantial changes in size, shape and structure from their characteristics in the original map than those drawn by the non-meteorologists.

Method

Subjects

Sixteen meteorologists were forecasters in the Western Australian Regional Bureau of Meteorology who had from 3 to 30 years of professional experience in their field. Sixteen non-meteorologists were university graduates from a variety of disciplines who were engaged in postgraduate diploma studies. These subjects were without specialist training in meteorology and reported that their main experience with weather maps came from viewing television weather presentations or from the weather section of newspapers.

Materials

Subjects were provided with an A4-sized sheet showing a typical summer weather-map diagram for the Australian region (Figure 1). This will be referred to the as the "original" map. In addition to this map showing the meteorological markings, subjects were given an A4-sheet of tracing paper that was identical to the original except that it showed no meteorological markings (this will be referred to as the "prediction" map).

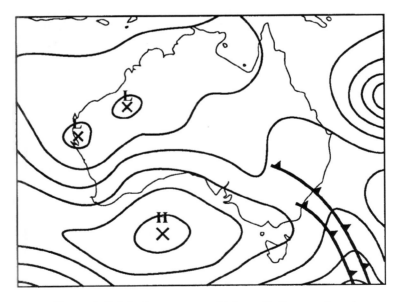

Figure 1: Original map upon which prediction was based

Procedure

Subjects were given the task of drawing the meteorological markings they thought would be present at one full day after those that were depicted on the original map. Each subject performed this task individually with the experimenter, and to facilitate their drawing of the prediction markings, subjects superimposed the prediction map on the original.

Data Analysis

Some preliminary treatment was applied to prediction maps to prepare them for analysis. After being digitized to produce computer files, the outline of the Australian continent was removed from each map using an image processing package so that only meteorological markings remained. Next, various characteristics of the meteorological markings (which will be referred to as "elements") were measured using an image analysis program. These measurements ranged from those concerned with the intrinsic graphic properties of individual elements themselves (such as their size and shape) to those that identified the position of the elements within the frame of the map (such as the coordinates of their centres of mass and the location of their extremities). A set of corresponding measurements was also made for the original map so that differences between the original and prediction measurements could be calculated for each subject. This process required the identification of corresponding graphic elements on the original and prediction maps, a task carried out in collaboration with two consultant professional meteorologists. Where the function of markings such as the barbs on cold fronts and alphabetic letters indicating the meteorological identity of a pressure system was simply to label features (rather than forming an essential part of the total meteorological pattern), these were omitted from the main analysis. These omissions meant that 24 of the total 34 elements present on the original map were considered in the analysis process. However, as described in the Results section, an indexing system further reduced this to a more manageable subset chosen from these remaining 24 elements. When considering the maps of individual subjects, a threshold was set to decide whether or not there had been an intentional change in element position. If the position of a prediction map element changed from its original position by a distance of greater than 5% of the overall height or width of the map frame, it was classed as having been moved deliberately by the subject.

Results

As mentioned above, 10 of the 34 individual graphic elements from the original map were not considered of sufficient meteorological importance to be included in the analysis. For the sake of simplicity and economy in reporting, the measurements presented here deal with only an illustrative subset of the remaining 24 elements Figure 2 shows (a) this subset of elements and (b) the identity of the major features that will be referred to in presenting the results.

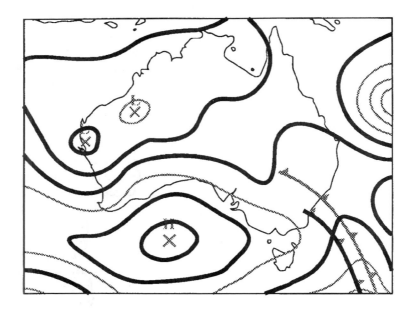

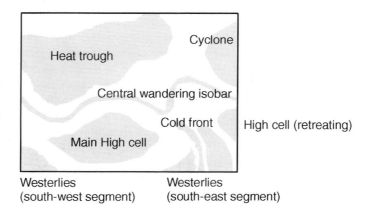

Figure 2: (a) Bold lines show index elements used to compare characteristics of features on original and prediction maps. (b) Identity of major features in original map

The primary consideration for selecting the particular subset of index elements (shown in Figure 2a) was that they gave clear indications about subjects' treatment of meteorologically-significant features of which these elements formed a part. A further consideration was that, whenever possible, the elements selected were produced in substantial numbers by both subject groups. In most cases, each meteorologically-significant feature was comprised of several elements. However, only one or two of these elements were usually necessary to fulfil an indexing role for the feature as a whole.

In order to facilitate presentation of the results, discussion will be structured around a comparison of an illustrative example of a specific non-meteorologist prediction map (Figure 3) and a corresponding map generated by a meteorologist (Figure 4).

Although this treatment of two individual examples is a convenient way to make the findings more concrete, it should be noted that the summary results presented refer to the subject groups. In addition, because many patterns of findings were repeated across a number of meteorological features, the findings included here deal only with representative features that illustrate widespread trends. To make salient characteristics of the patterns easier to distinguish, Figure 5 isolates aspects of the sets of prediction markings produced by the non-meteorologist and meteorologist, and these are used as illustrative examples in the presentation of the results. These aspects, which will be referred to periodically during this Results section, are shown in pairs of windows grouped around the original map that forms the centrepiece of Figure 5. For each of the six aspects displayed, the non-meteorologist's rendition is in the top window of the pair.

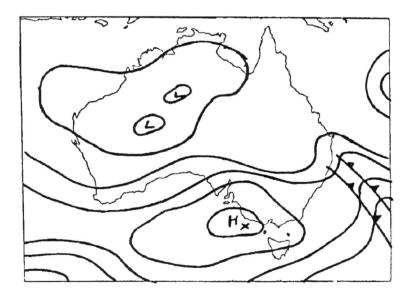

Figure 3: Non-meteorologist prediction map

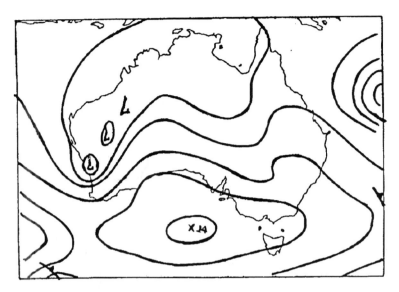

Figure 4: Meteorologist prediction map

Map as Part of a Large Fluid System

Comparison of the example non-meteorologist and meteorologist predictions for the south-west corner (Figure 5d) with the original map illustrates the way that meteorologists were more likely to add to the map new markings that have no obvious visuo-spatial antecedents in the original map. In the meteorologist map, the two lines curving in from the map's western border are two isobars fragments that indicate the arrival of a high pressure cell from the area to the west that is beyond the scope of this map. Another "arrival" from the map's wider context can be seen at the western end of the southern border. This line carrying a triangular barb is a cold front that indicates a temperature discontinuity associated with cold air from the Antarctic to the south entering the map region. In comparison, the corresponding non-meteorologist prediction map example shows that neither of these features is present; that is, nothing has been brought into the map region from its wider context. The difference illustrated in these examples reflects the results of the meteorologist and non-meteorologist groups as a whole. Overall, the meteorologists' prediction maps tended to contain more meteorologically-significant elements than those of the non-meteorologists (M-met = 22.06, SD = 2.29; M-non-met = 18.00, SD = 4.6; $t(30) = 3.16$, $P < 0.005$). Of these totals, the mean number of elements on the prediction map that were not present on the original was significantly greater for the meteorologists ($M = 2.44$, SD = 1.79) than for the non-meteorologists ($M = 0.88$, SD = 1.78; $t(30) = 2.47$, $P < 0.05$). All of the meteorologists added at least one non-original element to their prediction map whereas 75% of the non-meteorologists added no elements at all. These new elements were almost exclusively added to the western side of the map.

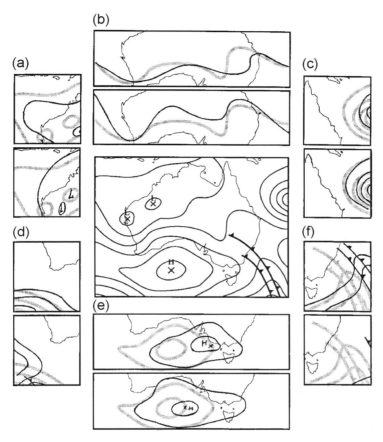

Figure 5: The central original map is surrounded by pairs of windows that compare the non-meteorologist (top) rendition of a particular aspect of the map with that of the meteorologist (bottom). The thick grey markings in the background of each window show the relevant part of the original map

Continuous Fluid Mass Versus Discrete Solid Objects

Evidence was obtained at both the macro and micro levels that the meteorologists and non-meteorologists took fundamentally different approaches to changing the markings on the map from the original to the predicted pattern. The meteorologists' predictions involved altering the marking pattern in a variety of often quite radical ways that were consistent with what would be expected in a fluid system under the influence of complex energy flows. In contrast, the alterations that the non-meteorologists made to the original array of markings were much more conservative. They were consistent with the influence of a much simpler energy flow regime acting upon a system consisting of relatively discrete objects that each maintained a high degree of individual integrity.

Macro-Level Changes (Movement of Features)

There were clear differences in the extent to which meteorologists' and non-meteorologists' patterns of meteorological markings taken across the map as a whole maintained their structural cohesion from original to prediction maps. Comparison of the overall arrangement of features and localized patterning in the example non-meteorologist's map with these characteristics in the meteorologist's map reveals the non-meteorologist's much greater degree of broad coordination between different sets of markings. Figure 6 compares the prediction maps superimposed on grey regions representing the location of main features of the original map.

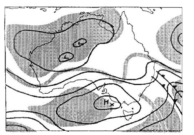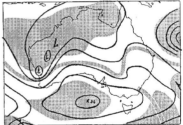

Figure 6: Non-meteorologist (a) and meteorologist (b) prediction maps superimposed over original features. Note that much of the non-meteorologist prediction approximates uniform translation of features

In the non-meteorologist prediction example, there is a pronounced tendency for the majority of features, or graphic patterns formed by visuo-spatially related groups, to have been moved in concert rather than with some degree of independence. With few exceptions, this movement is essentially a simple progression of the whole pattern of meteorological markings from west to east. However, in the meteorologist prediction example, there is considerably more variety in the way the various features have been moved, both in terms of the extent of movement and the direction. Some features, such as the cold fronts, have been moved a considerable distance whereas others, such as the cyclone, have remained in much the same location. In addition, different features have moved (or "grown") in different directions; although the high cell and fronts moved eastwards (but at different rates), part of the large heat low and its included smaller low cells have progressed southwards.

The general trends described for these meteorologist and non-meteorologist examples were reflected across the two subject groups as a whole. Figure 7 is a visual summary that compares one of the major differences between the groups: the degree of coordination with which features were moved in an easterly direction between original and prediction.

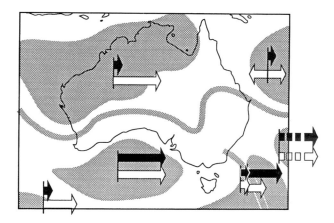

Figure 7: Summary of overall easterly movement of main features by meteorologist (black arrows) and non-meteorologist (white arrows). Not to scale

For the non-meteorologists, the similarity in the lengths of the white arrows attached to different features indicates the concerted movement of markings in general to the east. In contrast, the extent to which the meteorologists moved different features (as indicated by the black arrows) was much more variable. Overall, the meteorologists' movement of features tended to be more varied both in terms of direction and extent than that produced by the non-meteorologists. In other words, the meteorologists treated the features in a manner consistent with their being highly flexible, loosely connected entities whereas the non-meteorologists treated them as if they were far more rigid and closely coupled.

Two exceptions to the generally eastward movement of features found with the non-meteorologists should be noted. The first exception is the comparatively small *extent* of the non-meteorologists' change in the cold fronts' position as illustrated by Figure 5f. As a result, the difference in the original and predicted positions of the west-most front in the south-east corner tended to be significantly greater for the meteorologists (M-met = 1.70 cm, SD = 0.44) than for the non-meteorologists (M-non-met = 1.07 cm, SD = 0.83; $t(26)$ = 2.58, $P < 0.05$). The net effect of this difference was that the non-meteorologists typically kept most of the front's original form still visible within the map region whereas, for the meteorologists, only a trace of the front remained. The second exception is the variability of the cyclone's *direction* of movement. The majority of the non-meteorologists tended either to move the cyclone considerably to the west, bringing it much closer to the Australian coast or else to move it much further to the east, so that it almost left the map. In contrast, one-half of the meteorologist group did not move the cyclone appreciably at all while the other half of this group shifted it only very slightly to the east.

Micro-Level Changes (Alteration of Intrinsic Characteristics)

The previous section considered changes in the structure of the weather-map pattern as a whole that were generated in the course of producing predictions. However, there were also changes at a smaller scale. These changes concerned the internal structure of the subsets of markings that make up individual features. Although it is convenient to describe these changes separately in terms of the size, shape and structure of markings, it should be noted that it was typical for two or more of these changes to occur together.

Size Change

There was a general tendency for meteorologists' predictions to embody significantly greater change in the size of features than occurred in the non-meteorologists' predictions. This trend was present across a wide range of features and involved both increases and decreases in size. Two major features are used here as examples of this widespread pattern. A feature that was a noticeable exception to this trend is also reported.

The first feature that will be considered is the main high pressure cell, which in the original map is located just to the south of the Australian continent. The changes in this cell that can be seen by comparing the original map with the two predictions to illustrate the comparative reluctance of the non-meteorologists to alter the size, shape or structure of map features (Figure 5e). For the meteorologist, there is a noticeable increase in the size of the high cell (as indicated by the larger overall area included within the high cell's outer closed isobar). However, in the non-meteorologist's prediction, there is no obvious change in the size of the high cell. This difference exemplifies the trend across both subject groups with respect to changes in the overall size of the high cell (as indicated by the area of a box required to just enclose its outer isobar). The difference between the areas of the original and prediction enclosing boxes for the high tended to be greater for the meteorologists than for the non-meteorologists (M-met = 14.93 cm^2, SD = 9.53, M-non-met = 7.9 cm^2, SD = 5.04; $t(30) = 2.62$, $P < 0.05$).

A further example of size change can be seen in the case of the cold fronts (Figure 5f). Although a reduction in the size of the cold front symbols can be seen on both the meteorologist and non-meteorologist example prediction maps (compared with the original), there is a far greater change involved in the meteorologist's prediction. Considering both subject groups as a whole, the meteorologists' cold fronts became smaller because of the removal of their southern sections, which is consistent with progressing this part of a front beyond the map frame. However, the non-meteorologists either made no change in the size of the front or else actually increased its size. These differences in size change of the cold fronts between original and prediction map are shown by the change in the area of the enclosing box that would just contain the west-most front, which was significantly greater for the meteorologists (M-met = 7.68 cm^2, SD = 6.37) than for the non-meteorologists (M-non-met = 3.33 cm^2, SD = 3.57; $t(26) = 2.18$, $P < 0.05$).

An important exception to the general tendency in predictions for meteorologists to change the size of features more than the non-meteorologists occurred with the tropical cyclone located in the north-east corner of the map (Figure 5c). In the examples given, the meteorologist's prediction shows little change in the cyclone whereas, in the non-meteorologist's prediction, it is substantially reduced in size. Across the subject groups, the size of the cyclone's outer isobar tended to change less for the meteorologists than for the non-meteorologists. This was shown by differences in the area of a bounding box drawn to enclose the isobar (M-met = 5.00 cm^2, SD = 2.87; M-non-met = 8.82 cm^2, SD = 4.19, $t(26) = 2.86$, $P < 0.01$).

Change in Shape

In drawing their predictions, the meteorologists tended to change the original shape of features far more extensively than did the non-meteorologists. A useful reflection of this general trend is embodied in the wandering isobar that extends from west to east across the middle of the map. Comparison of the shape of this isobar (Figure 5b) illustrates one aspect of these changes in which the undulations in its path become more exaggerated in the meteorologists' prediction, particularly with respect to the dip and bump on the western half of the isobar. As a result, the isobar's overall proportions change and it becomes less symmetrical. The position and size of the various dips and bumps that comprise this isobar's path are coordinated with changes in the range of graphic elements that surround it on either side. Thus its overall change in shape is a useful indicator of the degree to which markings generally change between original and predicted maps. The shape of this isobar tended to change more between the original and prediction map for the meteorologists as a group than it did for the non-meteorologists. This difference is captured by both a change in the length ratio of the sides of this isobar's enclosing box (indicating its proportions) and a change in the symmetry of the isobar along its major axis. The change in the length ratio for the meteorologists ($M = 0.20$, SD = 0.11) tended to be greater than that for the non-meteorologists ($M = 0.08$, SD = 0.12; $t(28) = 2.70$, $P < 0.05$). For the meteorologists, the isobar also tended to become more asymmetrical with respect to its major axis than it did for the non-meteorologists (M-met = 1.18, SD = 0.70; M-non-met = 0.51, SD = 0.50; $t(28) = 2.96$, $P < 0.01$).

This tendency for meteorologists to change the shape of markings more than the non-meteorologists was not confined to the region around this wandering isobar. This difference also occurred for markings that were quite distant from this central isobar as can be seen with the looped isobar in the south-east corner of the map (Figure 5f). There was a difference in the extent to which the isobar changed shape between the original and predicted maps as reflected in the ratio of the lengths of the isobar's major and minor axes (M-met = 0.35, SD = 0.06; M-non-met = 0.21, SD = 0.10, $t(14) = 3.31$, $P < 0.01$). This appeared to be largely because of the non-meteorologists tending to retain the humped shape of the original isobar while shifting it eastwards, whereas many of the meteorologists changed its shape as well as its position.

Change in Structure

The previous results for size and shape report data about individual graphic elements. However, in some cases, a number of these elements can be considered together because they collectively comprise a weather-map feature. For example, the main high cell on the original map contains two concentric closed isobars. Where such groupings of elements exist, it is appropriate to go beyond the characteristics of the individual component elements to consider the structure of the assembly they constitute because of the highly localized changes in properties that can occur over time in a fluid system. For the high cell in the non-meteorologist prediction example shown in Figure 5e, the relative positions of the inner and outer closed isobars are little changed from their arrangement in the original map (the separation of the inner and outer isobars being larger on the western side of the high cell in both cases). However, in the meteorologist example, the separation of these isobars is larger on the eastern side because of changes, such as an extension of the eastern lobe of the outer isobar. This type of alteration in the internal structure of a meteorological feature was much more pronounced among the meteorologist group than for the non-meteorologists. There was no significant difference between the groups in the extent to which the outer isobar's position changed from original to prediction map (M-met = 2.51 cm, SD = 0.90; M-non-met = 2.91 cm, SD = 2.15). However, the non-meteorologists tended to move the inner isobar significantly further than the meteorologists (M-non-met = 1.21 cm, SD = 1.51; M-met = 0.16 cm, SD = 0.14; $t(26)$ = 2.38, $P < 0.05$). These results reflect the fact that the meteorologists changed the outer isobar of this high cell much more independently of the inner isobar than was the case with the non-meteorologists, who showed a substantial degree of coordination in the way they moved these isobars. For the meteorologists, the change was far more asymmetrical, with the central section of the high cell typically holding its original position while the eastern part of the outer high isobar expanded.

Discussion

There were pronounced differences in the way the two groups of subjects changed the pattern of markings on the original map in order to produce their predictions. These differences in approach generally support the two hypotheses advanced above. The hypotheses will now be considered in turn.

The first hypothesis concerned the extent to which subjects' results would reflect the wider context of the original weather map. As predicted, the meteorologists' predictions were consistent with a characterization of the weather-map area as a window depicting meteorological information about just part of the larger global mass of gaseous fluid that makes up the Earth's atmosphere. Because they were able to bring in new features from beyond the map's border, it appears that the mental model meteorologists generated from the original map incorporated its wider context. In contrast, the results indicate that non-meteorologists' mental models were far more limited because their prediction maps tended to be confined to features that already existed in the original. These models do not appear to provide information about what exists beyond the border of the original map. This implies that, when non-meteorologists ran their mental models, although these models specified that the markings *en masse* be moved from west to east, they were not able to provide new markings to fill the notional vacancies produced as a consequence of this movement. It should be noted in passing however, that this did not actually result in gaps in the marking pattern of non-meteorologists' prediction maps because the graphic material near the western border of the map tended to be "stretched" in an apparent attempt to preserve the overall visuo-spatial effect. If the non-meteorologists' mental models were largely devoid of meteorological context as proposed, this would be consistent with a weather map's contents being characterized as an essentially finite system rather than as part of a larger fluid system.

The second hypothesis dealt with whether subjects would tend to treat the original map's markings as if they represented a continuous gaseous fluid or as if they were more discrete objects with quasi-solid characteristics. The relatively undiscriminating treatment of the markings by the non-meteorologists contrasted with the highly differentiated treatment given by the meteorologists. The non-meteorologists' macro level movement of most features from east to west in a coordinated fashion suggests that the type of mental model used to generate this aspect of their predictions was very unsophisticated in terms of its treatment of the dynamic character of meteorological systems. While the east–west movement does capture one major component of the changes that occur in these systems, the way the non-meteorologists implemented this movement tended to be overgeneralized (only the southern half of the map should actually respond in this way) and to not incorporate changes in the intrinsic characteristics of the markings involved (such as their size, shape and structure).

The concerted movement of markings and their lack of responsiveness to new meteorological circumstances is consistent with running a mental model that represents the original map as being comprised of a set of quite firmly connected, discrete quasi-solid objects that retain their integrity and respond as a group as weather patterns change. As well as providing non-meteorologists with a comparatively simple solution to the problem of how to shift elements, it also avoids the need to know the delineation of individual meteorological features (where one meteorological feature is properly considered to end and another to begin). Both of these aspects are a great advantage for individuals who have very limited knowledge of meteorology. The much greater differentiation in the treatment of the various original markings by the meteorologists when responding to the prediction task suggests a type of mental model that is constructed on a very different basis. In a variety of ways, this treatment was consistent with the dynamics that would be expected in part of a large-scale gaseous fluid system.

The results reported an exception to the non-meteorologists' generally greater reluctance to alter intrinsic characteristics in the case of the tropical cyclone, where it was the meteorologists who were the more conservative. Discounting differences caused by the non-meteorologists moving more of the cyclone off the map, these subjects produced a far greater range of cyclone sizes than the meteorologists. However, with this particular feature this result is not really the contradiction it appears to be. Compared with other sorts of meteorological features, cyclones are unusual because they tend to be very stable in the sense of retaining their intrinsic structure despite changes in the surrounding meteorological environment. Therefore, it is quite appropriate from a meteorological perspective for the cyclone to be treated differently from its less stable neighbours. This example suggests that the relative stabilities of different types of meteorological features is another aspect that is not addressed by the non-meteorologists' mental models. Another exception to the general trends noted in the results section was the tendency for the non-meteorologists to partially exempt the pair of cold fronts in the south-east corner from the general shift of markings in an easterly direction. By shifting the cold front symbols a much smaller distance, most of these highly conspicuous components of the pattern were kept within the map frame. This perhaps reflects an unwillingness on the part of the non-meteorologists to dispense with perceptually arresting parts of the pattern and may be a further indication of the dominance of visuo-spatial considerations in these subjects.

Despite the fundamental differences in the characteristics of the mental models proposed for meteorologists and non-meteorologists, there is evidence from the present findings to suggest that the non-meteorologists have a very primitive form of synthetic model, rather than one that is completely naive. This comes from the way that the non-meteorologists included one of the main dynamic characteristics of meteorological systems in this region; the general drift of features toward the east. The origin of this more meteorologically-oriented aspect is probably the simplistic treatments of the behaviour of weather systems given by the media or in school classrooms. However, the overgeneralized application of this characteristic and the inappropriate treatment of the markings involved in this move-ment suggests that the model has deeply-rooted inadequacies. The nature of these inadequacies is consistent with the type of naive framework theory that has been suggested for non-meteorologists.

Conclusion

This study compared meteorologists'and non-meteorologists' predictions to investigate the possibility that the underlying cause of beginning meteorology students' persistent inade-quacies in dealing with weather maps is that they possess naive framework theories that are an impediment to conceptual change. The findings obtained were consistent with the exist-ence of such theories. They indicated that non-meteorologists constructed mental models that represented meteorological patterns in terms of visuo-spatial characteristics and quasi-solid objects. Because beginning students of meteorology are essential non-meteorologists when they commence their courses in this area, the findings are likely to be applicable to such students.

If beginning meteorology students' learning about weather maps is hampered by naive framework theories as suggested, then instructional interventions need to address these deeply rooted origins of their mental models (rather than simply enriching their knowledge base with additional meteorological information or dealing with the symptoms in a piece-meal fashion). This goal of bringing about a fundamental revision of the basis for this area of knowledge could be tackled by helping students to address the implicit presuppositions that underlie the way they process weather-map markings. A suitable type of intervention would involve characterizing the map contents as part of a much larger continuous gaseous fluid system in which the graphic rules for depicting visuo-spatial information are different from those involved in systems made up from solid elements. An important aspect of this revision would be a change in the relative status of knowledge components within the conceptual structure so that visuo-spatial information was subordinated to meteorological imperatives.

The question arises as to how such an intervention might be put into practice. This is a challenging problem because our everyday interaction with our immediate environment does not provide relevant experience of gaseous fluid behaviour and because our senses are not equipped for adequate perception of this type of behaviour as it occurs in nature.

A possible approach is to develop instructional resources that provide artificial opportunities that help students develop both overt and tacit knowledge of appropriate gaseous fluid behaviour. This may be as much a matter of developing an intuitive feeling for the way gaseous fluids behave (as we have profound and semantically powerful intuitions about how solid systems behave) as it is of conscious learning of well-defined facts and principles. One promising approach for providing the sort of artificial experience that might support revision of beginning meteorology students' naive framework theories is the use of interactive weather-map animations delivered by means of computer (Lowe, 1995). This type of intervention aims to give individual students opportunities to construct, test and revise a series of mental models by allowing them to interact with an animated weather-map sequence (which indirectly provides a wider implied spatial context as well as directly providing a wider temporal context). The theoretical basis of the intervention is the posited capacity of mental models to be upgraded as a consequence of new information and the assumption is made that it permits the incremental reinterpretation of visuo-spatial information in terms of gaseous fluid dynamics. Preliminary results show that students who have worked with this resource produce prediction maps that are more consistent with the framework theories indicated for meteorologists.

This research suggests that constraints on the learning of scientifically-accepted concepts caused by the effect of naive framework theories on conceptual change is not limited to children in school settings. It appears that a similar account may be useful in understanding the origin of barriers to conceptual change in learners who are considerably older than those studied by Vosniadou and colleagues, and who have proven success in learning about fundamental concepts. Although this research dealt specifically with weather-map diagrams, this type of depiction was used to illustrate more general issues that arise when using diagrams in instruction. The findings raise questions about just how reasonable it is to expect beginning students in technical domains to use diagrams effectively as resources for learning conceptually demanding content if naive framework theories prevent them from building satisfactory mental models. It seems likely that those who are naive with respect to the domain's subject matter need instruction, not just in the course content itself, but also in what is required to make the best use of the specialist diagrams that are so frequently used to present that content. On the evidence of the present research, this may involve helping students to reinterpret the visuo-spatial characteristics of the diagrams in a way that will support appropriate conceptual change.

14

Computer-Assisted Instructional Strategies for Promoting Conceptual Change

Harm J. A. Biemans and P. Robert-Jan Simons

Introduction

The idea that learning should be active is widespread among teachers and educational researchers already. Based upon an analysis of science education-curriculum and instruction trends for the period 1953–1992, Kelly (1993) identified the assumption that students should be actively involved in learning processes to improve retention and application of scientific knowledge as a major trend in current science education. Recently, however, many instructional approaches take into account that active learning is not an easy thing for learners to do: students can only be active learners if they believe in the benefits of active learning, if they know how to learn in an active way, if they get rewarded for active learning, if they have the necessary thinking and learning skills, if they are learning in a stimulating learning environment, etc.

An essential aspect of active learning is searching for and using prior knowledge in understanding new information. Recent constructivist learning theories (e.g. Hegland & Andre, 1992) consider the active use of prior knowledge to be a key strategy for constructing rich and useful mental representations. Hegland and Andre (1992, p. 233) stated that "at any given point, the learner has a store of knowledge about scientific topics that are his or her constructions of reality based upon his or her experiences or interactions with the real world". At any given moment, this prior knowledge can serve as starting-point for future learning. Therefore, the cumulative nature of learning is considered the most fundamental assumption concerning the learning process (Voss, 1987). If the learner has constructed representations of a certain domain that is based upon learning experiences in the past, he or she can use this prior knowledge when she or he has to study related material. Prior knowledge can enable the learner to relate concepts, to think of examples, to structure the learning material, etc. (Vermunt, 1992). Thus, prior knowledge activation can support knowledge construction processes with deeper understanding as a result. Prior knowledge activation, however, can also promote (major) restructuring of already existing knowledge (conceptual change) to provide students with a more fruitful conceptual framework for particular contexts (see also Duit, this volume). In this chapter, the question is addressed of how prior knowledge activation can be fostered through (computer-assisted) instruction and how conceptual change can be achieved. In this respect, this chapter relates to another major trend in science education: The idea that science teaching should focus on concepts and conceptual change to enhance student understanding (see Kelly, 1993).

Theoretical Background

Prior Knowledge

Many previous studies have shown the determining influence of prior knowledge on learning processes and learning performance (e.g. Ausubel, 1968; Dochy, 1992; Duit, this volume; Weinert, 1989). Prior knowledge can be described as all the knowledge that learners have when entering a learning environment, which is potentially relevant for constructing new knowledge. With respect to the terminology used in this chapter, "prior knowledge", "preconceptions", "informal knowledge", "naive theories", "alternative conceptions", "alternative frameworks", and "original ideas" should be regarded as synonyms. Conceptions reflect the way learners look at certain phenomena. Thus, preconceptions can be defined as domain-specific conceptions constructed by students based upon their concrete everyday experiences with particular natural phenomena before formal instruction. Many learners do not appear to hold correct preconceptions (i.e. preconceptions being in accordance with generally accepted scientific views) before formal instruction: Often, their prior knowledge is not in accordance with generally accepted scientific views, or only partially (see also Eylon & Linn, 1988). At this point, it should be noted that generally accepted scientific views especially exist in well-structured knowledge domains, for example in the domain of basic physical geography, which is treated in our studies. The distinction between incorrect and incomplete conceptions, on the one hand, and correct conceptions, on the other, is far less clear when advanced knowledge construction in complex, ill-structured domains is concerned (see Spiro et al., 1991). The existence of generally accepted scientific views in basic, well-structured knowledge domains does not necessarily imply that the particular concepts can be easily understood by students, simply because they concern basic knowledge: Incorrect and incomplete (pre)conceptions (in basic, well-structured knowledge domains) are well documented in the literature on cognitive psychology, educational technology, science instruction, intelligent tutoring systems and other related fields (see Pfundt & Duit, 1994).

As has been shown in many studies (e.g. Ali, 1990; Brown, 1992; Gunstone, 1988), incorrect or partially incorrect prior knowledge is relatively stable and tends to resist change: Even after years of formal instruction on scientific theories contradicting them, many of these incorrect and/or incomplete preconceptions (re)appear in the answers students give when solving problems (Eylon & Linn, 1988). Incorrect and incomplete conceptions can block knowledge construction processes if they are not diagnosed and corrected during learning (see also Chinn & Brewer, 1993; Prawat, 1989; Vosniadou, 1994). Therefore, the existence of students' incorrect and incomplete preconceptions implies that learning does not only involve acquiring or constructing new concepts, but also restructuring of existing concepts, i.e. conceptual change.

On the other hand, students also have prior knowledge that is in accordance with generally accepted scientific views. Even if the preconceptions of the learner are correct, however, successful learning processes are not guaranteed. In many learning situations, these preconceptions do not enter automatically in the learning process: Often, learners should do this consciously themselves or an instructional system should take over. Although it is common wisdom that it is good to make close connections between new information to be learned and existing prior knowledge (see Ausubel, 1968; Dochy, 1992), few students use their prior knowledge intentionally, spontaneously and actively (see De Jong & Simons, 1990; Dochy, 1992). When students do not use their preconceptions while learning new information, this new information may be learned "in isolation" (see Schmidt, 1982). Consequently, students may experience difficulties applying the new knowledge in novel situations (see Saxena, 1991).

Various phenomena can occur during learning that may explain why students do not always use their prior knowledge in concrete learning situations: (i) they may not know which part of their prior knowledge is in accordance with generally accepted scientific views and which part is not, or only partially; (ii) students may be cautious that interference of new knowledge from the learning task may occur with their preconceptions; (iii) they may not know which prior knowledge is relevant in a particular learning situation and which is not; (iv) learners may not be aware of the importance of using their prior knowledge in an active way; (v) they may not be aware of the various kinds of prior knowledge and the consequences for learning; (vi) students may use some of their preconceptions automatically, without even realizing that they do so; and (vii) they may not be able to use their prior knowledge adequately because they lack the necessary learning skills, etc. With respect to text processing, Roth (1985) found that only students using a conceptual change strategy for processing expository texts were successful in giving up or modifying their incorrect prior knowledge in favour of text explanations.

Based upon the research findings mentioned above, the central question is how instructional systems can help students to use their correct or partially correct prior knowledge without creating interference and, simultaneously, to deal with incorrect or partially incorrect prior knowledge that tends to resist change.

Conceptual Change

How and to what extent instruction should promote integration of new knowledge into students' preconceptions, in our view, depends on the quality of these preconceptions: Assimilation of new information into students' preconceptions can only be recommended if these preconceptions can serve as a reliable basis for integration; if this is not so, instructional strategies should be aimed at conceptual change. Conceptual change refers to a partial or radical change of existing conceptions, as opposed to integration of new information into preconceptions without really changing these ideas.

Conceptual change, in other words, requires (major) restructuring of already existing knowledge to provide students with a more fruitful conceptual framework for particular contexts (see also Duit, this volume). In this respect, more traditionally oriented approaches have claimed that incorrect conceptions have to be totally extinguished and replaced by new conceptions. Based upon an overwhelming set of empirical data from conceptual change studies (see Chinn & Brewer, 1993), most constructivist approaches reject this knowledge replacement and transmission idea (see also Geddis, 1991): The basic assumption underlying most influential cognitive change approaches is "the key constructivist idea that construction of new conceptions (learning) is possible only on the basis of the already existing conceptions" (Duit, 1994, p. 11).

Although certain instructional strategies have been shown to contribute to knowledge restructuring, Tergan and Oestermeier (1993, p. 1–2) conclude: "There is a need for research concerning the cognitive processes of knowledge restructuring as well as the instructional conditions that may foster processes of conceptual change" (...) "There is also a need for the development of powerful learning environments (...) to promote processes of conceptual change." Therefore, in the next paragraph, we will focus on instructional conditions to promote knowledge (re)construction processes.

Instructional Theories of Conceptual Change

Nussbaum and Novick (1982) formulated one of the first instructional theories of conceptual change. In their view, instructional strategies to promote conceptual change should (i) make students aware of their own preconceptions (or the preconceptions of others) through an "exposing event", (ii) create a cognitive conflict through a "discrepant event" and (iii) support students' search for a solution to this conflict and encourage conceptual change. This so-called "cognitive conflict" approach of conceptual change has been implemented in many instructional strategies ever since (e.g. Hesse, 1989; Tirosh & Graeber, 1990). Reviewing research on reading and science education, Guzetti et al. (1993) stated that instructional strategies and approaches that were effective in fostering conceptual change had a common element of producing conceptual conflict. Duit (1994, p. 7), however, stated that "there are many studies available in the domain of students' science conceptions that counter-evidence does not necessarily change students' point of view as is explicitly or implicitly assumed in many teaching and learning approaches that build on the cognitive conflict". In his view, cognitive conflict strategies are often not very effective because students do not "see" the conflict and because they experience difficulties in dealing with anomalous data (see also Chinn & Brewer, 1993).

Strike and Posner (1985) proposed one of the most influential conceptual change approaches (see also Duit, this volume). In their instructional theory, four conditions were discerned to foster conceptual change processes: (i) students should feel dissatisfaction with their current conceptions; (ii) the new conceptions must be intelligible; (iii) the new conceptions must appear initially plausible; and (iv) the new conceptions must be fruitful. According to their theory, students should be activated to make close connections between new information to be learned and existing prior knowledge and to correct their preconceptions if necessary. Although Strike and Posner's conceptual change theory has become "very popular and useful" (Pintrich et al., 1993, p. 169), several points of critique of their theory have been formulated (see also Duit, this volume; Lederman, 1992). Pintrich et al. (1993) claimed that Strike and Posner's theory puts too much emphasis on the rational and neglected affective and social ("non-rational") issues of conceptual change: In their view, several motivational constructs and classroom contextual factors are potential mediators of conceptual change processes (see also Linn & Songer, 1991). Moreover, Linder (1993) argued that instruction should build upon examples drawn from students' everyday lives ("more authentic learning environments") and should enable students to develop more meaningful person–world relationships with the new conceptions, based upon context. Finally, metaconceptual and metacognitive aspects of learning, which were not explicitly included in Strike and Posner's theory, appear to affect conceptual change processes as well (see Duit, this volume; Hennessey, 1991).

Based upon these (and other) points of critique, Strike and Posner (1992) revised their initial conceptual change theory: They proposed to take both rational and affective and social factors of conceptual change into account. Moreover, in their revised theory, they put more emphasis on the interaction between preconceptions and new conceptions. Strike and Posner (1992) stressed that the view of conceptual change must be more dynamic and developmental. In this respect, they agreed with Lott's (1989) conclusion that prior studies have focused on "static" views of students' conceptions and have not examined the "dynamics" of conceptual change over time. Nowadays, most constructivist approaches of learning and instruction put key emphasis on dynamic conceptual change processes and include "supporting conditions" of conceptual change. It should be noted, however, that conceptual change on the content level is still a key concern of constructivist science instruction (see Duit, this volume).

Examples of Instructional Strategies to Foster Conceptual Change

Inspired by current conceptual change approaches (e.g. Nussbaum & Novick, 1982; Prawat, 1989; Strike & Posner, 1985, 1992), Ali (1990) and the authors of this chapter (Biemans & Simons, 1995, 1996) have created several instructional strategies to promote both prior knowledge activation and conceptual change in the context of reading comprehension. The training texts dealt with the domain of basic physical geography, and dealt with concepts such as equator, Earth rotation, rain, wind, atmospheric pressure, etc. The target population concerned fifth- and sixth-graders (primary education).

The CONTACT Strategy

As part of her last study, Ali (1990) designed the CONTACT strategy. The CONTACT strategy is typified by continuous, computer-assisted activation of the conceptions of individual learners in text-processing. Computer-assisted instructional strategies aimed at conceptual change can enable individual students to use their own conceptions as a starting-point for knowledge (re)construction processes, which can hardly be realized in concrete classroom situations. Moreover, computer-assisted instructional strategies can activate the student to perform learning activities aimed at conceptual change and provide support whenever the student needs this.

The CONTACT strategy is based upon a process-oriented, heuristic activation model consisting of five steps aimed at conceptual change.

1. Searching for own preconceptions.
2. Comparing and contrasting these preconceptions with the new information.
3. Formulating new conceptions, based upon the previous step.
4. Applying the new conceptions.
5. Evaluating the new conceptions, based upon the previous step.

The CONTACT steps can also be depicted as a flowchart (Figure 1).

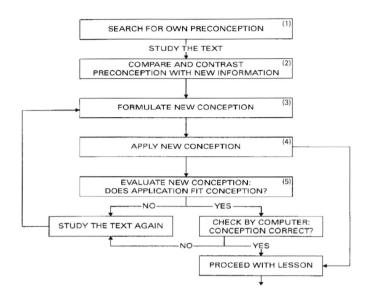

Figure 1: The steps of the CONTACT strategy (Ali, 1990.)

First, students have to search for their preconception by answering the particular idea question (the "exposing event" — see Nussbaum & Novick, 1982). This step is aimed at making students aware of their own ideas with respect to the topic(s) of the particular text (see also Prawat, 1989). An idea question can be described as a concrete problem that has to be solved by relating the central concepts from the corresponding training text. For example, the idea question from the seventh training session ran as follows:

> When Columbus set sail in 1492, the wind did not blow him straight to the equator. Instead, he was blown to America with a curve to the right. Can you explain this?

Students have to choose from six answer alternatives corresponding to different, frequently found conceptions of the relations between the central concepts from the text. One of these answer alternatives corresponds to the generally accepted scientific notion as explained in the text. Students also have to provide written argumentation for the answer they choose. The answer given by the particular student is regarded as his or her initial idea or preconception.

When students have answered the idea question, they have to study the first part of the (new) information from the text. The training texts are all relatively short (7–8 text screens plus 2–3 pictures; 400–550 words).

After studying the first part of the text, students have to compare and contrast their preconception with the essential information from the text. They have to state whether their initial idea is in accordance with the textual information or not. Additionally, students have to write down similarities and/or differences. Relating preconceptions and new information activates students to identify possible differences between both types of notions, as a result of which they may conclude whether their preconceptions are incomplete and/or incorrect or not. Moreover, students are assumed to construct a framework in which the new information can be integrated (see also Strike & Posner, 1985, 1992).

Next, students have to review their preconception and construct a new conception (formulate a new idea), based upon their conclusions from the previous step (see also Prawat, 1989): the idea question is presented again. This implies that it is possible that their conception has not changed. If students are convinced that their original idea is correct, they are instructed to select the same answer alternative; if they think that their initial idea is incorrect or incomplete, however, they are told to pick another, better alternative. In this case, written argumentation is required again. With this step, it is crucial that students really accept the new conception and do not construct isolated new knowledge.

With the fourth instructional step ("applying the new conceptions"), students explore whether their new conception is adequate or not. A main condition for accepting a new conception is that students consider this conception to be plausible (see also Strike & Posner, 1985, 1992). The plausibility of a new conception is supposed to increase if students discover that they can solve problems by applying the new conception (which they could not solve with their original conception). Therefore, students have to apply their new conception by answering a so-called practice question (a concrete problem that is directly related to the particular idea question): Based upon their new idea, they have to choose from four answer alternatives.

Students have to evaluate their new conception by comparing and contrasting their new idea with their answer to the practice question from the previous step (see also Strike & Posner, 1985, 1992): They have to state whether both answers are in accordance with one another or not. Again, students have to write down possible similarities and/or differences. Based upon the results of this evaluation process, they may conclude that their new conception is more fruitful than their preconception and accept the new conception.

If they state that both answers are not in accordance with one another, students have to study the most important part of the text again to discover the mistakes they have made. After rereading the text, they have to construct a new conception (formulate a new idea) and apply this conception again. The same procedure has to be followed if the students' new conception is not correct (yet). Therefore, their idea is checked by the computer.

With all CONTACT steps, strategic information in "How" and "Why" parts is provided (see also Biemans, 1989, 1994; Biemans & Simons, 1992; De Jong & Simons, 1990). The "How" parts contain information about how that particular step can be realized in terms of concrete learning activities and in the "Why" parts, the relevance of the particular step is explained. In some training lessons, the "How" and "Why" parts were presented to all students. In the other lessons, these parts could be consulted by the students whenever they wanted to do so (see Ali, 1990). The CONTACT steps are presented as visual metaphors (cartoons) as well.

The sequence of instructional steps as described above is performed twice during each training session. At the end of the second sequence of steps, students have to state their final conception by answering the particular idea question. Their answer is regarded as their final idea or conception.

A basic principle of the activation model is to stimulate students to discover inconsistencies themselves, e.g. by comparing their conceptions with the information from the text and by checking whether they can solve problems by applying their conceptions. The underlying rationale is that students will have more reasons and arguments to change their conceptions if they discover inconsistencies themselves. Conceptual change, in other words, is supposed to occur through reasoning (see also Strike & Posner, 1985, 1992).

At this point, it should be noted that the CONTACT strategy should be considered as an instructional strategy that is especially useful for knowledge domains in which incorrect conceptions need to be changed, incomplete conceptions need to be enriched, and/or new conceptions need to be constructed (see Vosniadou, 1994). This instructional strategy was not designed to help students to solve metacognitive problems, like becoming aware of the functions of the various kinds of prior knowledge, the critical role of incorrect and/or incomplete conceptions, etc. Moreover, (variants of) the CONTACT strategy can only be useful when considerable knowledge exists about the particular preconceptions that are frequently held by students.

The CONTACT strategy was evaluated by comparing its effects with the effects of a strategy characterized by activation both before and after the presentation of the (new) textual information [the so-called before–after (BeAft) strategy] (see for a more extended report Ali, 1990). As part of the BeAft strategy, students' conceptions were activated by presenting the particular idea question (see step 1 of the CONTACT strategy) both at the beginning and at the end of each of the nine training sessions: One of Ali's (1990) previous studies had shown that before–after-activation was more effective in fostering conceptual change than no activation or activation either before or after studying the text. Subjects in this study were 87 sixth-graders (primary education).

The CONTACT strategy turned out to lead to final conceptions of a higher quality and to higher learning performance than the BeAft strategy (see for more details Ali, 1990). Time costs for continuous activation were high at first but diminished later. According to Ali (1990), all instructional steps included in the CONTACT strategy seemed necessary to foster conceptual change.

Various interpretations of the results of this study, however, remained possible. The study did show that the CONTACT strategy was effective in promoting conceptual change, but not why it was, because the two instructional strategies (the CONTACT strategy and the BeAft strategy) differed in several respects. Therefore, the question arose which aspects of the CONTACT strategy were responsible for the differences in quality of conceptions and learning performance that showed up. Is it the feedback loop? Is it because the relevance of activating and using prior knowledge is made more clear to the students? Is it because students learn how they can activate and use their prior knowledge? Is it because students are stimulated to be active? Or is it a combination of some or all of these (or other) explanations? To conclude, although the CONTACT strategy appeared to lead to conceptions of a higher quality and to higher learning performance, Ali's last study (1990) did raise several questions.

The Project "Prior Knowledge Activation and Self-Regulation"

Therefore, in our own research project "Prior knowledge activation and self-regulation", the effectiveness of the CONTACT strategy was subjected to closer inquiry. The project was aimed at answering the following research questions:

1. To what extent do the various steps of the CONTACT strategy contribute to its effectiveness?
2. Can the effects of the CONTACT strategy be increased by making the strategy more flexible?

The corresponding studies are described and discussed in the next paragraphs of this chapter.

Study 1

Effects of the Various Steps of the CONTACT Strategy

The aim of our first study, being a replication of Ali's (1990) study with respect to materials and tests, was to examine which steps of the CONTACT strategy contributed to the effects found in Ali's study (see for a more extended report Biemans & Simons, 1995). Therefore, the CONTACT strategy was dismantled in a systematic way: The full instructional strategy was compared with two stripped versions and with a no activation control condition. In this study, subjects (46 fifth- and 40 sixth-graders, primary education) had to study seven training texts, supported by the particular instructional strategy.

Subjects assigned to the first instructional condition ($n = 21$) studied the training texts supported by the CONTACT strategy (see Ali, 1990). In the second instructional condition (the NEW IDEA condition; $n = 21$), the fourth and fifth CONTACT step were not included in the instructional strategy. Subjects assigned to the third instructional condition (the OLD IDEA condition; $n = 21$) only had to perform the first CONTACT step ("searching for own preconceptions"). Finally, in the fourth instructional condition, the No Activation condition ($n = 23$), subjects only had to study the texts without their preconceptions and final ideas being activated.

The results from this study showed that the complete CONTACT strategy was more effective in promoting conceptual change than the second and third condition: Students assigned to the complete CONTACT condition constructed conceptions representing the relations between the central physical geography concepts from the training texts more accurately (students from the instructional condition No Activation were not included in this analysis because their final ideas had not been activated). The condition OLD IDEA (in which students only had to perform the first step "searching for own preconceptions"), on the other hand, led to final conceptions of the lowest quality. Apparently, to be able to construct better conceptions, students needed more help (as provided by the complete CONTACT strategy). This conclusion was in accordance with the findings of Ali's (1990) study.

Nevertheless, the CONTACT strategy appeared to have a negative side-effect: Students mainly focused on constructing correct conceptions, while disregarding information that was less directly related to the central concepts from the texts. This led to lower learning performance scores on less directly related performance test questions as compared with the no activation control group. These findings were in accordance with the selective-attention hypothesis (see also Anderson & Pichert, 1978; Goetz et al., 1983). According to Machiels-Bongaerts (1993, p. 113), who tested the selective-attention hypothesis in expository text processing, "... activating prior knowledge results in a selection process during information processing. Only information corresponding to the knowledge activated would be processed in depth, resulting in better recall of that information."

Overall, the various instructional conditions did not differ with respect to the students' learning performance scores. In this respect, it proved impossible to dismantle the training effects that had been found by Ali (1990), because the effects themselves were not replicated. A remarkable outcome of this study was the lack of retention loss for the CONTACT group (the retention test was given 2 weeks after the last training session). All other groups performed much lower at retention time than at post-test time, but the CONTACT group remained on the same level. This finding combined with the results concerning the students' conceptions gave some hope that the underlying activation model might be effective after all.

How can one explain the different findings from this study and Ali's (1990) experiment, in which the CONTACT strategy was superior to the before–after (BeAft) strategy, which had been superior to a no activation control group in a previous study? One explanation might be the involvement of fifth-grade students in this study. Perhaps the strategy is too complicated for the younger students. *Post-hoc* analyses, however, did not reveal any differences between fifth- and sixth-graders. Another explanation might be that shortening the training from nine to seven sessions is responsible for the differences between both studies. In Ali's study, there were indeed more differences between the CONTACT group and the BeAft group at the end of the training than in the beginning. Students need to learn how to work with their prior knowledge and to use the help being offered. An additional explanation might be found in the competence level of the students. There are some indications that the students in Ali's study were of a higher competence level than the present ones. Finally, the different research outcomes may be caused by interference effects: Students had to study conceptual information and had to learn how to learn simultaneously. Informal observations showed that the students in this study had more of these problems and more problems in maintaining their concentration than the students in Ali's study. To conclude, instead of denying the effectiveness of the CONTACT strategy, trying to improve it seems better.

Study 2

The CONTACT-2 Strategy

In our second study, an attempt was made to improve the CONTACT strategy in several respects and to replicate the effects of Ali's (1990) study (see for a more extended report Biemans & Simons, 1996). In our view, the strategy should become more flexible and should offer still more help to the less competent students. Therefore, a revised variant of the CONTACT strategy, the CONTACT-2 strategy, was constructed. The CONTACT-2 strategy was characterized both by adaptations to solve the problem of selective attention mentioned above and by adaptations to increase the efficiency and flexibility of the strategy.

To increase the efficiency and flexibility of the strategy, various adaptations aimed at supporting conceptual change processes were made.

1. With all the steps of the original CONTACT strategy, additional strategic information in "How" and "Why" parts was included (see also Biemans, 1989, 1994; Biemans & Simons, 1992). The "How" parts contain information about how that particular step can be realized and in the "Why" parts, the relevance of the particular step is explained. When the student is executing a particular step of the CONTACT-2 strategy, however, the corresponding "How" and "Why" parts are optional. During the first sequence of steps, the monitoring question "Do you understand what to do with this step?" is always posed before the student can execute the particular step. In case of a negative answer, the student has to study the corresponding "How" parts before executing the step. In case of an affirmative answer, the student can execute the step immediately. During the second sequence of steps, the "How" and "Why" parts are fully optional: monitoring questions are omitted.
2. If the student has a correct conception at the end of the first sequence of steps, the second sequence is not presented: The CONTACT-2 strategy is more sensitive to the student's progress than the original CONTACT strategy.
3. All learning activities corresponding to a particular step of the CONTACT-2 strategy have to be performed on one "execution screen" of which all elements are labelled in different colours: The "execution screens" of the various steps are more surveyable.
4. After each "execution screen", the student is asked whether he or she has written down the requested information on the worksheet to ensure that he or she executes the particular step in a profound way.
5. With the steps "searching for own preconceptions", "formulating new conceptions", and "applying the new conceptions", the student can ask for a corresponding picture: Both textual and visual presentation modes are used to optimize the student's opportunities to activate his or her conception ("multiple bridging"; see also Spiro et al., 1991).
6. With the steps "comparing and contrasting the preconceptions with the new information" and "evaluating the new conceptions", crucial concepts are accentuated in different colours to focus the student's attention on the essential elements from his or her conception and from the text.

To solve the problem of selective attention, the strategy was adapted in several respects. These adaptations were aimed at spreading the student's attention.

7. At the beginning of each training session, the goal of the training (comprehension of the whole text) is stressed.
8. Crucial concepts and relations between concepts are accentuated in red to focus the student's attention on all important information from the text.
9. The student is given the opportunity to search for information on other text screens: scrolling options are optimized.
10. The amount of strategic information the student is obliged to read is reduced so the student can pay more attention to the text itself.

11. If the student has a correct conception at the end of the first sequence of steps, the second sequence is not presented so the student can pay more attention to the text itself.

As part of our second study, the CONTACT-2 strategy was evaluated as well (see for a more extended report Biemans & Simons, 1996). Subjects in this study were 29 fifth-graders and 45 sixth-graders (primary education). They were assigned to three instructional conditions: the original CONTACT condition ($n = 25$), the CONTACT-2 condition ($n = 25$) and the No Activation control condition ($n = 24$). The CONTACT condition and the No Activation condition were identical to the conditions of the same name used in the previous study (see for more details Biemans & Simons, 1995).

The results of our second study were rather clear-cut. The CONTACT-2 strategy was more effective as a process-oriented instructional strategy aimed at supporting the process of conceptual change than the original CONTACT strategy and the control condition No Activation: The adaptations of the original CONTACT strategy did result in an overall superiority over the other two conditions on all dependent variables.

Students who studied the training texts guided by the CONTACT-2 strategy had better conceptions after the training than students from the conditions CONTACT and No Activation and applied these conceptions in a more adequate way. Thus, the CONTACT-2 strategy appears to lead to conceptions of the highest quality, which can be transferred to other problem-solving situations, even after a longer period. In other words, students who are supported by the CONTACT-2 strategy construct more valid conceptions with more adequate retrieval paths (see also Schmidt, 1982; Simons & Verschaffel, 1992). The original CONTACT strategy, on the other hand, does not lead to better conceptions (in the longer term) than the control condition No Activation.

Concerning the students' learning performance, a comparable training effect was found: Students from the CONTACT-2 condition had higher learning performance scores than students from the conditions CONTACT and No Activation (no significant difference was found between the conditions No Activation and CONTACT). Thus, the CONTACT-2 strategy does not only lead to conceptions of the highest quality but also to the best learning performance both at post-test and at retention time.

Moreover, the selective attention problem had been overcome: Students who had been assigned to the CONTACT-2 condition achieved the best learning performance scores, both on test questions that were directly related to the central concepts from the particular training text and on less directly related questions. Thus, it appears to be possible to help students in using their prior knowledge and in restructuring their preconceptions and to prevent the selective attention effect (which was found in the previous study) from showing up. In our view, students who study texts guided by the CONTACT-2 strategy have more information-processing capacity left for studying the other information from the learning task because they perform the learning activities corresponding to the various instructional steps in a more effective and efficient way. They appear to use this attention and memory capacity to study the text as a whole in depth.

To summarize, one could conclude that the CONTACT-2 strategy was more effective as instructional strategy aimed at conceptual change than the other two conditions (the original CONTACT condition and the control condition No Activation) because students constructed conceptions more accurately representing the relations between the central concepts from the learning tasks and because they achieved higher learning performance scores. Moreover, the effectiveness of the CONTACT-2 strategy appeared not to depend on the degree of conceptual resemblance between the performance test questions and the central concepts from the texts and on the moment of testing.

Conclusions and Discussion

Based upon Ali's (1990) research and the above-mentioned studies by the authors of this chapter (see also Biemans & Simons, 1995, 1996), several conclusions could be drawn.

As described in the previous paragraphs, both the original CONTACT strategy and the revised CONTACT-2 strategy were based upon several influential instructional theories of conceptual change: Taking into account cognitive and instructional conditions formulated by Nussbaum and Novick (1982), Strike and Posner (1985, 1992), Prawat (1989) and other researchers in the field of conceptual change, an activation model consisting of five steps aimed at conceptual change was designed. The studies by Ali (1990) and Biemans and Simons (1995, 1996) provided empirical support for this activation model. To construct correct conceptions (i.e. conceptions that were in accordance with generally accepted scientific views), students appear to need instructional guidance aimed at fostering knowledge-restructuring processes. In this respect, all learning activities corresponding to the various instructional steps seem to play an important role.

To be able to restructure their knowledge, students should first become aware of their preconceptions — they should search for relevant preconceptions in their memory (see also Prawat, 1989). Therefore, instructional strategies should enable students to identify and activate their own prior knowledge. In this respect, Rice et al. (1991) proposed to take a step beyond identification of students' preconceptions about the concepts of interest, in the direction of concurrent characterization of the underlying presuppositions of these ideas (see also Vosniadou, 1994). According to Rice et al. (1991), this could be realized by administering multiple-choice test items, including a description of a problem situation, a multiple-choice question based upon this situation, followed by several possible explanations for the answer selected. The problem situations should be based upon phenomena of which each individual student has some general awareness and common understanding (e.g. weather phenomena) and should require reasoning for the choices made (see also Saxena, 1991). If multiple-choice test items are used to activate students' prior knowledge, answer alternatives should include a set of frequently found preconceptions (see also Becker, 1988).

When students' prior knowledge has been activated, they should compare and contrast their preconceptions with the (new) information from the learning task (see also Hand & Treagust, 1991; Hewson & Hewson, 1984). Students should be given the opportunity to discuss and rationalize similarities and differences between their own conceptions and the information being presented: Explicitly contrasting students' preconceptions with the information from the text is more effective than simply providing scientifically accepted information (see also Maria & McGinitie, 1987). Often, however, merely confronting students with contradictory information is not sufficient to achieve conceptual change. Even when students are aware of existing inconsistencies, they still have the choice between changing their preconceptions and constructing separate conceptions or fitting the new information with their prior knowledge.

When students engage in comparing and contrasting activities (integration and differentiation), real conceptual change is more likely to occur if the plausibility of students' preconceptions decreases and the plausibility of the new conceptions increases. In this respect, Chan (1993) claimed that students' knowledge-processing activities mediate the effects of conflict on conceptual change. Students should actively perform knowledge-building activities to deal with cognitive conflict. In other words, they should treat new information as something that needs to be explained. According to Chan (1993), equivocal findings of previous conflict-based conceptual change approaches could be explained by the fact that the importance of students' constructive learning activities in advancing their knowledge has usually been overlooked. Therefore, students must be actively involved in constructing new conceptions (see also Happs & Mansfield, 1989).

Moreover, conceptual change also requires acceptance of (new) scientific notions (see also Cobern, 1993). An important condition for believing and accepting a new conception (apprehension) is that students recognize its plausibility. They should experience that the new conception enables them to solve problems (and that their preconception does not). Therefore, they should have opportunities to apply, test and evaluate their new conception in an open atmosphere (see also Strike & Posner, 1985, 1992; Watson, 1994). In other words, students must be involved in learning task situations in which incorrect application of unexpected principles may happen. Rather than telling them the right answer, students must be supported in dismantling their own incorrect or incomplete conceptions by confronting them with possible inconsistencies and contradictions entailed by their own conceptions. While resolving the conflicts that arise, students may actively reconstruct the conceptions in question and truly overcome their misconceptions (see also Gang, 1993).

As mentioned above, the learning activities corresponding to the various steps of the CONTACT strategy and the CONTACT-2 strategy appear to be necessary to achieve conceptual change. In other words, the underlying activation model seems to be valid and useful. Additional research on the effectiveness of the activation model, however, is desirable. Additional research is also needed with respect to the negative side-effect found in our first study (see for more details Biemans & Simons, 1995): Students who were guided by the original CONTACT strategy seemed to concentrate on constructing correct conceptions and not on studying the texts as a whole, which resulted in lower learning performance scores on test items that were less directly related to the central concepts from the texts. The learning activities corresponding to the various instructional steps seem to demand considerable information-processing capacity. Consequently, "CONTACT students" seem to lack the information-processing capacity required to study the other information from the learning material in a profound way (and perhaps also the motivation to study this information, which might be seen as less relevant). These findings provide additional evidence for the selective-attention hypothesis (see also Anderson & Pichert, 1978; Goetz et al., 1983; Machiels-Bongaerts, 1993). Based upon our first study, some implications for the design of process-oriented instructional strategies aimed at conceptual change could be formulated. On the one hand, such instructional strategies should support all processes involved in conceptual change and, on the other hand, these strategies should provide a solution for the problem of selective attention.

Therefore, in our second study, the effectiveness of a revised variant of the CONTACT strategy, the so-called CONTACT-2 strategy, was examined (see for more details Biemans & Simons, 1996). The CONTACT-2 strategy was both characterized by adaptations to solve the problem of selective attention and by adaptations to increase the efficiency and flexibility of the original CONTACT strategy. The results of this study showed that students who had been guided by the CONTACT-2 strategy had better conceptions after the training than students from the conditions of CONTACT and No Activation and were able to apply these conceptions in a more adequate way, even after a longer period. The CONTACT-2 strategy also led to the best learning performance both at post-test time and at retention time. Moreover, the selective attention problem had been overcome: Students who had been guided by the CONTACT-2 strategy seemed to have more information-processing capacity left for studying the other information from the learning tasks because they performed the learning activities corresponding to the various instructional steps in a more effective and efficient way. They appeared to use this attention and memory capacity to study the texts as a whole in depth.

During the whole training, students from the CONTACT-2 condition needed less time to finish the sessions than students from the CONTACT condition. Thus, the CONTACT-2 strategy proved to be more efficient than the original CONTACT strategy with respect to time costs as well. Students from the No Activation condition, on the other hand, took less time than students from the CONTACT-2 condition. Both groups of students spent about the same time studying the training texts. Time differences could be explained by the time CONTACT-2 students needed to perform the learning activities corresponding to the steps of the instructional strategy. At the end of the training, these time differences had become much less without affecting differences in learning performance (see also Ali, 1990). Therefore, time-on-task phenomena could not be held responsible for the training effects described above.

To conclude, the adaptations of the CONTACT strategy did indeed result in increased effectiveness, efficiency and flexibility of the strategy, and in an adequate solution to the problem of selective attention. Therefore, the results of this study support the following conclusion with respect to the design of process-oriented instructional strategies aimed at activation of prior knowledge and conceptual change: Instructional designers should both strive for increased efficiency and flexibility of their strategies and try to draw the student's attention to the learning task as a whole and not just to the relations between the central concepts from the learning tasks.

However, with this conclusion, other questions arise. Although the present study showed that it is possible to help fifth- and sixth-graders (primary education) to use their prior knowledge in an active way by means of a process-oriented instructional strategy presented through computer-assisted instruction, it is still unclear, however, what exactly causes the effectiveness of the strategy. A rather complex learning environment was designed, which turned out to be effective in promoting conceptual change. But what are the essential ingredients? Can some instructional steps and measures be skipped? Can stripped variants of the strategy also be made effective? New dismantling studies seem necessary to answer these questions. Of course, other kinds of research are needed too. For instance, studying the generalizability of the instructional strategy to other content domains and other student populations is crucial.

In our view, an additional line of research should be pursued as well. At this point, it should be noted that the CONTACT-2 strategy, like many other instructional strategies aimed at conceptual change, is characterized by a high degree of external control. As had been shown in our second study, a high degree of external control can result in conceptions of a higher quality and in better learning performance, but it may also lead to higher dependence on external support (see also Biemans & Simons, 1992). Dependence on external control can be an undesirable side-effect of an (any) instructional strategy in the longer term: Without external help, students may not be able to initiate and perform the particular learning activities themselves and, thus, to achieve the learning goals (see also Vermunt, 1992). Moreover, designing instructional programmes for all subject matter following a particular instructional strategy such as the CONTACT-2 strategy would be impossible.

Therefore, one could argue that the ultimate goal should be to teach students how to perform the steps of the strategy on their own or, in other words, to teach students how to activate their own preconceptions and how to construct correct conceptions themselves. This seems to require quite another instructional approach: A "learning-to-learn" approach aimed at enhancing self-regulated learning (see also Brown et al., 1989; De Jong, 1992; Jonassen, 1991; Nisbet, 1989; Reeve et al., 1987; Simons & Kluvers, 1994). The results of such training studies should shed some light on the instructional conditions required to teach students how they themselves can initiate and perform learning activities aimed at conceptual change (see Biemans, 1997).

15

Conceptual Change Approaches in Science Education

Reinders Duit

Conceptual Change — A Term with Various Meanings in Science Education

The term "conceptual change" has been used with many meanings in science education research on learning and instruction. Sometimes the term appears to be just another word for "learning". Nevertheless, there seems to be a common core among the most influential approaches, usually called "constructivist", in the research area of science learning and instruction. Constructivist approaches in science education (as well as in mathematics education and in research on learning and instruction in general) share a "view of human knowledge as a process of personal cognitive construction, or invention, undertaken by an individual who is trying, for whatever purpose, to make sense of her social or natural environment" (Taylor, 1993, p. 268). There are many variants of constructivist views and approaches in science education (Good et al., 1993; volumes that provide overviews of constructivist ideas in science and mathematics education are Steffe & Gale, 1995; Tobin, 1993; Treagust, Duit, & Fraser, 1996; substantial critiques of the constructivist view in science education have been raised by Matthews, 1993; and Suchting, 1992; and a review of the critiques is provided by Duit, 1993).

Although there are many variants of meanings given to the term conceptual change there appears to be mainstream agreement that conceptual change has to do with major restructuring of already existing knowledge. Research on students' pre-instructional conceptions in many science domains has shown that these conceptions are very often in stark contrast to the science conceptions to be learned. In other words, that major restructuring of the already existing knowledge is necessary. It is seen as fundamentally different from what may be called "conceptual growth" where only enlargement and enrichment of the already existing is needed. Frequently, there is a reference to Piaget's (1985) distinction between "assimilation" and "accommodation" (cf. Posner et al., 1982), with accommodation denoting conceptual change. There are a number of other distinctions of a similar kind in use. Rumelhart and Norman (1981) distinguish between "accretion" on the one hand and "tuning or schema evolution" and "restructuring or schema creation" on the other. Carey differentiates "enrichment" and "conceptual change" (Carey, 1991) or "weak" and "radical" restructuring (Carey, 1985), Vosniadou (1994) contrasts "theory enrichment" and "theory revision". In science education research frequently there is the distinction between "evolution" and "revolution" in allusion to Kuhn's (1970) terminology (cf. Nussbaum, 1983). There is a tendency to use the term conceptual change for the "revolution" side of the distinction in accordance with the implied major restructuring of the already existing conceptions.

The Conceptual Change Theory

The most influential theory of conceptual change was developed by a group of science educators and philosophers of science at Cornell University (Hewson, 1981; Posner et al., 1982; Strike & Posner, 1985). It has become "very popular and useful" (Pintrich et al., 1993, p. 169) in science education as well as in other fields. The theory has been extensively applied, and with it, also changed (see the review by Hewson & Thorley, 1989).

The Initial Conceptual Change Theory

The four conditions that foster conceptual change are widely known in the lapidary form "dissatisfaction — intelligible — plausible — fruitful"; they may be called the quadriga of conditions of conceptual change.

1. There must be dissatisfaction with current conceptions.
2. A new conception must be intelligible.
3. A new conception must appear initially plausible.
4. A new conception should suggest the possibility of a fruitful research programme.

The initial theory (according to Strike & Posner, 1992, p. 148) provides answers to the question: "How do learners make a transition from one conception, C1, to a successor conception, C2". It deliberately focuses on what has been called a major restructuring of the already existing conceptions. It is based on Piaget's notion of accommodation and on what Kuhn (1970) has called a paradigm shift (i.e. a revolutionary change). The theory establishes analogies between conceptual development in science and in individual learners. The four conditions for conceptual change are derived from the work of philosophers and historians of science, mostly from the work of Kuhn (1970), Lakatos (1970) and Toulmin (1972). The metaphor of the student as scientist in conceptual change theory has been prominent in science education research on students' conceptions in general. Besides others, it has functioned as an attempt to take the students and their thinking seriously (see e.g. Driver's, 1983, idea of the "pupil as scientist", which is similar to Kelly's, 1955, idea of "man-the-scientist"; see also Brewer & Samarapungavan, 1991 and Gauld, 1988). A key metaphor of the theory, conceptual ecology (following Toulmin, 1972) portrays the students' existing conceptual structure as the components of an environmental ecosystem.

Critiques of the Initial Conceptual Change Theory

Linder (1993) discussed "challenges to conceptual change" from the perspective of the phenomenographic approach as developed by Marton (1981, 1986) and his co-workers in Gothenburg. He distinguishes between a "mental model based perspective" and an "experientially based perspective" of conceptions. The first perspective views conceptions as mental representations, i.e. as tangible in head constructs. The latter perspective depicts conceptions as being characterizations of categories of descriptions reflecting person–world relationships. Conceptual change, from the perspective of constructivism, takes place within a person's head. From the phenomenographic perspective, conceptual change is achieved by changing one's relationship with the world. Linder's critique leads to an issue that has been addressed also by other researchers in the field of science education, namely the significance of context in specific conceptions. He points out that it is necessary for students to develop meaningful relationships with the new conceptions in particular contexts. He concludes that less emphasis should be put on:

> efforts to change segments of students' existing repertoires of conceptu-
> alizations and more efforts on enhancing students' capabilities to
> distinguish between conceptualizations in a manner appropriate to some
> specific context — in other words, being able to appreciate the functional
> appropriateness of one, or more, of their conceptions in a particular
> context, making science education into a functional base from which to
> view the world (Linder, 1993, p. 298).

Similar views have been developed by social-constructivist approaches that may be indicated by the situated cognition perspective (cf. Brown et al., 1989; Hennessy, 1993; Lave & Wenger, 1991; Roth, 1995).

Pintrich et al. (1993) have addressed deficiencies of the initial theory of conceptual change by Posner et al. (1982) in an article with the programmatic title "Beyond cold conceptual change — The role of motivational beliefs and classroom contextual factors of conceptual change". The thermal metaphor of "cold" denotes the authors' reservation against overly rational approaches, of "cognition only" models of students' learning. The theory of conceptual change, according to the authors, is too much oriented to rational aspects in two ways. First, it is based on a philosophy of science perspective that is putting major emphasis on rationality, on the significance of logical arguments in the process of conceptual development. More recent developments (than the approaches by Kuhn, Lakatos and Toulmin) in the philosophy of science (e.g. social constructivist approaches like the one by Knorr-Cetina, 1981) have pointed out that manifold "non-rational" issues play a role also. Second, the rational is also overemphasized in the process of conceptual change in individuals from their initial pre-instructional conceptions to the science concepts. The key metaphor of the initial theory of conceptual change, the student as scientist, is undergoing a rigorous discussion (see also Caravita & Halldén, 1994). It is questioned that this metaphor in fact provides valuable analogies for understanding the process of conceptual change. The learning communities in science classrooms and the scientific community are very different, i.e. are operating on the grounds of fundamentally different aims and within fundamentally different institutional conditions. For instance, schools are much more driven by the need to maintain bureaucratic and institutional rather than scholarly norms. O'Laughlin (1992) constructed a similar critique against constructivist approaches in stating that the culture in science classrooms, with its power structures and discourses, are not adequately taken into account. In summarizing this line of critique, conceptual change has to be viewed as a process of bewildering complexity that is dependent on many closely interrelated variables. Conceptual change, the process of conceptual development from students' prior ideas towards science concepts, has to be embedded in a bundle of what may be called "conceptual change supporting conditions".

Among these are motivation, interest and beliefs of learners and teachers, as well as factors of the classroom climate and power structures.

The Revisionist Theory of Conceptual Change

Strike and Posner (1992) have presented a critique of the initial theory of conceptual change that partly comes to quite similar conclusions as the review by Pintrich et al. (1993). Strike and Posner suggest that their initial theory put too much emphasis on the rational, and neglected affective and social issues of conceptual change. They propose a wider range of factors to account for conceptual change. Another important issue of revision concerns students' conceptual ecology. Initially, they neglected the interaction of prior conceptions and the new conceptions. The authors argue now for a developmental and interactionist view of conceptual ecologies. They conclude that their "view of conceptual change must therefore be more dynamic and developmental, emphasizing the shifting patterns of mutual influence between the various dynamic components of an evolving conceptual ecology" (Strike & Posner, 1992, p. 163).

Comments on the Actual View of the Theory of Conceptual Change

The above critiques of the conceptual change theory provide most valuable frameworks for developing more adequate approaches to conceptual change in science instruction, although science educators may doubt whether it is possible to address all the mentioned influencing factors adequately in view of the bewildering complexity of the issue. Here, a remark about the critiques is in order. Conceptual change theory as used in science education is no longer the pure initial theory. Mainstream science educators who refer to the original work, now interpret the theory from a different perspective than their colleagues in the 1980s. Many changes demanded by Pintrich et al. (1993) are already under way, for the constructivist view made it quite clear that conceptual change from students' preconceptions on the content level (e.g. conceptions of heat, energy, combustion, photosynthesis and the like) to science conceptions is not possible on the basis of logical arguments only. It became obvious that not only students' preconceptions of the mentioned content level type are significant determining factors of conceptual changes, but also conceptions of various other kinds, among them conceptions of science (students' philosophy of science ideas), conceptions of teaching and learning (i.e. meta-cognitive conceptions), and also attitudes and emotional beliefs (see also Duit et al., 1996). Conceptual changes at manifold levels are necessary because students and teachers alike hold very limited views of the nature of science (for a review see Lederman, 1992) and meta-cognition (Baird & Northfield, 1992).

Resistances to Change

A key finding of many studies on conceptual change in science education is that change does not come easily, that there are resistances against change to science conceptions. It appears that there are resistances especially in such fields where students' pre-instructional conceptions are deeply rooted in daily life experiences and are continuously supported by such experiences. Conceptions that are based on sense experiences (like the process of seeing, thermal phenomena, conceptions of forces and motions) fall in this category and everyday ways of speaking about natural and technical phenomena. Further, the language used (most available studies have been conducted in Indo-European language with quite similar logical structures) has proven a source of deep-rooted conceptions (Pfundt, 1981). Where conceptions based on sense experiences are concerned, conceptions may not be constructed by the child when confronted with experiences but triggered by innate structures that emerged during evolution (Preece, 1984). Vosniadou and Brewer (1992) introduced the term of "entrenched" belief as something that is deeply embedded in a network of other beliefs. They explicitly go beyond science content and include conceptions such as "ontological beliefs" (i.e. beliefs about fundamental categories and properties of the world) and "epistemological commitments" (i.e. beliefs about what scientific knowledge is and what counts as good scientific theory). Chinn and Brewer (1993) provide a number of examples, both from the history of science and from empirical research on learning science, to illustrate the role of entrenched beliefs as impediments to conceptual change.

Explanations of Resistances to Change

The theory of conceptual change outlined above explicitly or implicitly provides explanations why the observed resistances exist. If a conception is deeply rooted (entrenched in the above meaning of Vosniadou & Brewer, 1992) and has proven successful in most previous life situations there will be no dissatisfaction with this conception. Further, if there is no conception available that is intelligible and plausible from a student's perspective a change is most unlikely. Students are frequently unable to understand the new theory, because their old conceptions provide the interpretation schemata, the goggles so to speak, to look at the new science conceptions. Hence, the new conceptions do not become intelligible and plausible to students. It has to be noted that the condition of "intelligible" does not "guarantee" conceptual change. There are several cases in the literature where students understand a new theory but do not believe it (e.g. Jung, 1993).

Another important issue when understanding of the new conceptions is concerned (i.e. when the condition of "intelligible" is to be addressed) is the importance of sufficient "background knowledge" (Chinn & Brewer, 1993; Schumacher et al., 1993; Strike & Posner, 1985). Without a certain amount of background knowledge the arguments in favour of the new conceptions may not be understood. It becomes obvious that there is a certain dilemma here with similarities to Bereiter's (1985) learning paradox. The new conception becomes understandable only if there is already some knowledge about that conception available.

Schumacher et al. (1993) extensively discuss motivational factors that impede conceptual change. For instance, they claim, that "if a misconception is held in an area where students have little interest, they will be unlikely to invest the cognitive resources" (Schumacher et al., 1993, p. 4). In other words, dissatisfaction substantially depends also on affective features. These authors review research on resistances to change in several domains such as studies on human judgement and decision making, psychotherapy and attitude change. They conclude that resistance to change as found in science misconceptions appears to be a very common trait of human behaviour: There usually are important benefits to having stable conceptions, beliefs or attitudes. These conceptions, beliefs and attitudes have been formed by the individual in processes of adaptation to life world experiences and usually provide valuable frames for behaviour. For this reason, Schumacher et al. (1993) propose to carefully investigate the context in which students' conceptions arise and provide beneficial support of behaviour.

Chi et al. (1994) developed a theory of conceptual change for learning science concepts. It draws on the assumption that conceptual change occurs when a concept has to be reassigned to an ontologically distinct category. They distinguish three "trees" of categories: "matter" (or things), "processes" and "mental states". They provide a number of examples across the sciences where learning of key concepts includes changes of ontological categories. They hold that the most difficult concepts to be learned require a change of ontological category. There is no doubt that, in fact very often, when students have severe difficulties in accepting science concepts, a change of an ontological category is necessary. The physics concept of force, for instance, falls into the category of relations between objects (namely interactions) and not into the category of properties of things as in daily life. Here, force is usually seen as something that strong humans and animals possess. Chi et al., therefore, point to important barriers of learning science concepts but their present theory is limited (Duit, 1995). First, their choice of categories is somewhat arbitrary. The ontological change in case of the concept of force (see above) is in need of a more elaborated set of categories than the three categories as used, namely the change from a property of objects to relations between objects. Second, learning of key science concepts very often is not adequately described by such changes from one category to another. In case of heat concepts, for instance, the undifferentiated heat concept of daily life has to be differentiated and, so to speak, unfolded into the concepts of temperature, heat energy, internal energy and entropy. The naive everyday concept of heat includes facets of all the aspects indicated by the mentioned physics heat concepts (Kesidou et al., 1995). Third, Chi el al. argue on the level of what Pintrich et al. (1993) have called "cold" conceptual change, affective issues are not regarded. Fourth, the theory presents only a syntactic not a semantic explanation of conceptual change (Vosniadou, 1994). Therefore, the perspective of entrenched beliefs in the above meaning appears to be a more inclusive position because it includes not only ontological changes of the type Chi et al. discuss, but also changes of a broader nature.

Resistances to Empirical Evidence

There are many studies available in the domain of students' science conceptions which indicate that counter-evidence does not necessarily change students' point of view as is explicitly or implicitly assumed in many teaching and learning approaches that emphasize the cognitive conflict. A paradigmatic example stems from a study by Tiberghien (1980). A 12-year-old girl is asked to find out if an ice-block wrapped in aluminium foil will melt faster than an ice-block wrapped in wool. The girl believes that the ice-block wrapped in wool will melt first, because, wool is warm and therefore will give heat to the ice. Nature does not care about the girl's conception, the ice-block wrapped in aluminium foil melts first. This empirical evidence does not shake her initial conception at all. She invents a number of protective arguments in favour of her idea.

Chinn and Brewer (1993) provide a review of the role of anomalous data in knowledge acquisition, especially in science. They describe seven ways students deal with discrepant evidence.

1. Ignoring anomalous data
2. Rejecting anomalous data
3. Excluding anomalous data
4. Holding anomalous data in abeyance
5. Reinterpreting anomalous data
6. Peripheral theory change
7. Theory change

They also discuss conditions under which the kind of dealing with anomalous data may occur and identify factors that influence how people respond to anomalous data. These factors are:

Characteristics of prior knowledge

1. Entrenchment of the prior theory
2. Ontological beliefs
3. Epistemological commitments
4. Background knowledge

Characteristics of the new theory

1. Availability of a plausible alternative theory
2. Quality of the alternative theory

Characteristics of the anomalous data

1. Credibility
2. Ambiguity
3. Multiple data

Processing strategies

1. Deep processing

On the basis of this list, Chinn and Brewer draw consequences for promoting conceptual change in science teaching and learning. These consequences comprise most of the issues raised in the considerations of conceptual change outlined above. They also underscore how complex the process of constructing adequate conceptual change instruction really is.

What Changes in Conceptual Change?

It is somewhat striking that, in the literature on conceptual change, the meaning of the term change is not often explicitly discussed. It appears that in most publications of this kind, change is used as it was in the initial theory of conceptual change, i.e. as transition from one conception, C1, to another conception, C2 (Strike & Posner, 1992, p. 148). But what happens to the old conception C1? More traditionally-oriented approaches claimed that the conceptions have to be extinguished and replaced by the new conceptions. Constructivist approaches reject the replacement idea on the basis of an overwhelming set of empirical data from studies on conceptual change.

In fact, it has to be stated that there is no single study listed in the leading bibliographies of research on students' conceptions (Carmichael et al., 1990; Pfundt & Duit, 1994) in which a particular student's conception of the above deep-rooted kind could be completely extinguished and then replaced by a new idea. Most studies show that the old ideas basically stay "alive" in particular contexts and that there is only quite limited success concerning the acceptance of the new ideas. In the majority of studies, the best that was achieved is a "peripheral" conceptual change as described by Chinn and Brewer (1993). During peripheral conceptual change, parts of the initial idea merge with parts of the new idea to form some sort of hybrid idea (Jung, 1993). But the construction of such hybrid ideas does not mean that the old ideas are given up completely. Grandy (1990) provided the following metaphor. Learning, as conceptual change, is not like rearranging the furniture in one's room (wiping out the previous configuration), but like opening up a new room in which one feels uncomfortable and out of place. A return to the familiarity of the old room is likely.

Conceptual change, therefore, is viewed by leading approaches with a constructivist orientation in science education not as exchange but as development of new conceptions that are fruitful, initially in particular contexts; the old conceptions may continue to be valuable in other contexts. What science instruction should then be striving for is not to replace everyday ideas totally by science ideas but to make students aware that in specific contexts, for particular purposes, science conceptions provide a much more fruitful framework than their own conceptions (Jung, 1986). It is also a key aim that the range of contexts in which science ideas are given preference should be continually enlarged. To avoid misunderstandings, it has to be said that among students' ideas there are erroneous pieces that should be corrected. But the majority of key students' science-related conceptions is not of the kind as to allow simple wrong or false categorization. It appears that the sketched view of "situatedness of conceptions" is in accord with the position entertained by the situated-cognition perspective. But this perspective and phenomenological perspectives like Marton's (1986) phenomenography (see above) add a new facet to "classical" constructivist views: Conceptual change is not solely to be seen as "in the head" changes of conceptions, but also as changes of the individual's relation with the world.

Hewson and Hewson (1992) address the issue of context in conceptual change in a slightly different way. They argue that change should be understood as change of status given to a particular conception. They employ the metaphor of an incumbent beaten by the challenger in an election of the mayor. The incumbent loses status, the challenger gains status. In a similar way challenging science conceptions may gain status if instructional attempts were successful. Studies on the issue of status show that it is possible already with students of lower secondary level (about 12-year-old students) to change status, i.e. to lower the status of students' preconceptions and raise the status of the new science conceptions (Hewson & Hennessey, 1992).

Conceptual Change in Science Teaching and Learning

In the following, a brief review of conceptual change approaches in science education is presented. Only the main features of this research will be outlined. More elaborated reviews are provided by Scott et al. (1992), Wandersee et al. (1994) and Duit and Confrey (1996).

A Brief Sketch of the Development of Conceptual Change Research in Science Education

In the middle of the 1970s, research on students' conceptions (some other terms in use are "students' alternative frameworks", and "students' misconceptions") began to bloom worldwide. Initially, the focus was on investigating students' conceptions on the content level, i.e. students' conceptions of key science phenomena, concepts and principles. The development of these conceptions in traditional instructional settings sometimes was also investigated. Critics of that orientation spoke about "misconception hunting" or "butter-flying around the curriculum" (Pines & West, 1986). Studies of this kind are still predominant as the entries in the bibliography of Pfundt and Duit (1994) clearly illustrate. But since the beginning of the 1980s, the number of studies investigating the development of students' conceptions in specifically designed "conceptual change" approaches has considerably increased. There are other remarkable changes regarding the orientation of research in the field under review here (Duit, 1993; Pfundt & Duit, 1994). Initially the focus was almost exclusively on students' conceptions at the content level; now, researchers take into consideration a broad variety of students' and teachers' conceptions. As mentioned already, the constructivist view has been most influential in facilitating these developments.

Characteristics of Constructivist Approaches Towards Conceptual Change

Constructivist approaches usually include a broad spectrum of changes of traditional science instruction. Briefly put, such approaches aim at making science instruction more meaningful for students and allow them to take responsibility for their learning processes. Conceptual change is at the core of these approaches, and is embedded in what has been called "supporting conditions" of conceptual change. Among these supporting conditions are the maintenance of an encouraging classroom climate and student-oriented assessment. From the perspective of conceptual change research, there is a certain difficulty with these more holistic approaches because a large set of variables are changed as compared with traditional approaches. Therefore, it becomes difficult to evaluate the success of these new approaches. In the following, the key characteristics of these approaches will be presented. They comprise the most important "supporting conditions" of conceptual change. Conceptual change strategies in use in science education will be reviewed thereafter. To avoid misunderstandings, it has to be pointed out from the outset that there is nothing really new with constructivist approaches towards conceptual change in science. Most strategies and perspectives are quite well known. What may be called the really new is the attempt to bring together many issues of a student-centred pedagogy under one umbrella view. Furthermore, constructivist approaches are holistic in another sense. Changes of instructional settings are frequently embedded in changes of curricular conditions and teacher education as well (Tobin, 1993). These issues will not be discussed here.

Aims of Instruction

Constructivist approaches usually emphasize the importance of science knowledge for students' present and later lives. In this, constructivist approaches share main concerns with STS approaches (the significance of science for understanding the interplay of Science–Technology–Society) to science education (Yager, 1993). The aim of both approaches is to help students understand the surrounding natural and technical phenomena and its impacts on their lives in a society dominated by technology. The focus is an understanding of science, not the rote learning of definitions and formulas. Another key difference between more traditional and constructivist science instruction is the already mentioned context-dependence of science concepts and theories. It is no longer expected that science knowledge completely replaces everyday knowledge, but that science knowledge allows more fruitful engagement with certain phenomena and processes in specific contexts.

Meta-Knowledge of Science and Meta-Cognition

Meta-knowledge of science (i.e. views of the nature of science concepts and theories) and meta-cognition (views of the learning process) play a double role in constructivist approaches. On the one hand, constructivist science instruction puts emphasis on changing students' views of meta-knowledge and meta-cognition from naive everyday ideas to more adequate ones. On the other hand, they are means to facilitate conceptual change on the content level which, of course, is still a key concern of constructivist science instruction.

Supportive Classroom Climate and Instructional Settings

A large variety of issues may be summarized under the title "supporting conditions of conceptual change". In general, instructional settings are designed to allow students to take responsibility of their learning processes and experience science knowledge as meaningful and significant (compare Pintrich et al., 1993, p. 181). Project-type approaches, more open forms of instruction (e.g. open experimentation; Roth, 1994), and authentic learning activities and learning environments (Roth, 1995) are some labels that may indicate key features of such approaches. Also, ideas of situated and socially-shared cognition (Brown et al., 1989; Hennessy, 1993; Resnick, 1991) count among the significant supporting conditions of conceptual change, for they address the aims of student-centred science instruction outlined above. Taylor and Fraser (1991) developed a "Constructivist Learning Environment Survey" to assess supporting classroom climates in the above sense. The four scales of their instrument reflect key issues that are also pointed out in many other constructivist approaches:

> The *Autonomy* scale measures perceptions of the extent to which there are opportunities for students to exercise meaningful and deliberate control over their learning activities, and think independently of the teacher and other students. The *Prior Knowledge* scale measures perceptions of the extent to which there are opportunities for students meaningfully to integrate their prior knowledge and experiences with their newly constructed knowledge. The *Negotiation* scale measures perceptions of the extent to which there are opportunities for students to interact, negotiate meaning and build consensus. The *Student-Centredness* scale measures perceptions of the extent to which there are opportunities for students to experience learning as a process of creating and resolving personally problematic experiences (Taylor & Fraser, 1991, p. 2).

Assessment

Assessment has many functions in school. Quite frequently, the pedagogical function, i.e. assessment as a means of helping students to learn, is given only scant attention. Constructivist approaches usually differ fundamentally from more traditional ones in this respect. Here, the pedagogical function of assessment among other supporting conditions of conceptual change is given key importance. The metaphor of portfolios (Duschl & Gitomer, 1991; see also Wolf et al., 1991) is frequently used to indicate such assessment techniques. They allow students to show different aspects of their understanding in a way similar to an artist presenting pieces of her or his work in a portfolio.

An Example of a Holistic Constructivist Approach Towards Conceptual Change — The Portfolio Culture

Duschl and Gitomer's (1991) portfolio culture may be taken as paradigmatic for a number of more holistically oriented constructivist approaches in science education. Duschl and Gitomer (1991, p. 848) describe their approach in the following way:

> A portfolio culture is a means of organizing and expressing curriculum and instruction in ways that promote interactions around a collection of work — the portfolio. The label *culture* is meant to convey an image of a classroom learning environment that reflects a comprehensive interplay between teacher, student and curriculum.

Table 1 compares key characteristics of the portfolio science culture with those of traditional science culture. Most characteristics described above are to be found on the right-hand side of Table 1, of course, in some cases with the authors' particular emphases.

Table 1: Contrasting traditional and portfolio cultures in science classrooms (from Duschl & Gitomer, 1991, p. 849)

Traditional Science Culture	Portfolio Science Culture
View of science	
Strict hypothetical-deductive scientific method	Partial scientific method
Logical positivism epistemology	Scientific realism/semantic conception epistemology
Observation/theoretical distinction tenable	Observation/theoretical distinction untenable
Role of learner	
Low student input/non-active image	High student input/non-active image
Scientific meanings received	Scientific meanings negotiated
Low level of reflection	High level of reflection
Use student-developed strategies	Use strategic/principled knowledge
Role of teacher	
Disseminator of scientific knowledge	Crafter of scientific knowledge
Non-participant in construction of scientific knowledge	Participant in construction of scientific knowledge
Strict adherence to prescribed curriculum	Modify and adapt prescribed curriculum
Curriculum goals	
Scientific knowledge	Knowledge about science
What we know	How and why we know
Emphasize fully developed final form explanations	Emphasize knowledge growth and explanation development
Breadth of knowledge	Depth of knowledge
Basic scientific knowledge	Contextualized scientific knowledge
Curriculum units discrete	Curriculum units connected

Pathways from Students' Pre-instructional Conceptions to Science Conceptions

The term conceptual change, as understood in the present chapter, addresses pathways from students' pre-instructional conceptions to the science conceptions, particularly those pathways that need fundamental restructuring of already existing conceptual structures. The basic assumption is the key constructivist idea that construction of new conceptions (learning) is possible only on the basis of the already existing conceptions. Figure 1 presents a classification of pathways that have been used in science-education studies on conceptual change. The first key distinction concerns continuous and discontinuous pathways (see also above).

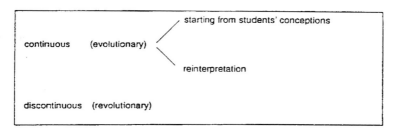

Figure 1: Pathways from students' conceptions towards science conceptions

Continuous Pathways

Continuous pathways try to "avoid" (or bypass) the fundamental restructuring necessary in case of the discontinuous pathways. In the case of "starting from students' conceptions" (Figure 1) the kernel of harmony between the conception of departure (the "anchor", Brown & Clement, 1989) and the target conception is developed step by step. It is not necessary in every case to start from conceptions that students construct when dealing with particular science phenomena and principles. It may also be possible to start from pieces of knowledge in domains where analogies may be drawn to structures or features of the science content in question. In the second case of "reinterpretation" (Jung, 1986), the strategy is a little different. Here, too, resemblances between students' pre-instructional conceptions are the starting point, but they are interpreted in a new way. For example, students of all ages tend to think that whenever a body is moving into a certain direction, a force has to act into the same direction, and therefore pulls the body into this direction (McDermott, 1984). This view is not correct from the Newtonian perspective of classical mechanics. Following the reinterpretation strategy, students are not told that their conception as sketched is wrong. Rather, the teacher helps them to realize that their idea makes good sense from the physics point of view, but in a different way. There is indeed a physics quantity that always points in the direction of the moving body, but this quantity is momentum and not force (Jung, 1986). Another example of the reinterpretation strategy is given by Grayson (1996). Students studying current flow in simple electric circuits usually have the idea that current is consumed when flowing in the circuit. Accordingly, some current is used up in the bulb so that less current returns to the battery than had previously left it. Here, too, students are not told that their idea is wrong. On the contrary, the teacher encourages students' way of thinking and helps them realize that they have something quite correct in mind. Something is indeed "used up" while current is flowing. But this something is energy, transformed into and dispersed as heat. It is obvious that such continuous approaches are in need of very careful reconstruction of the particular science subject-matter structure. Usually such approaches are embedded in very basic changes of more traditionally oriented reconstructions of that kind.

Discontinuous Pathways

In the case of discontinuous pathways, there is a stark contrast between students' conceptions and science conceptions. Cognitive conflict strategies play a key role in all approaches that fall into this category (see the review of such approaches by Scott et al., 1992). There are three primary kinds of cognitive conflict. First, there is the kind of conflict that is created by asking for students' predictions and then contrasting these to experimental results. Second, there is a conflict between the ideas of the students and those of the teacher. Finally, there is a conflict among the beliefs of the students. Cognitive conflict is theorized in Piaget's genetic epistemology where it leads to disequilibrium that demands an interplay between assimilation and accommodation until equilibrium is restored (Dykstra, 1992; Rowell & Dawson, 1985). Festinger's (1962) theory of cognitive dissonance is also used to theorize conceptual change arising from cognitive conflict (Driver & Erickson, 1983). The crucial issue in cognitive conflict strategies is that students need to "see" the conflict. This is very often not the case. What appears to be clearly discrepant from the perspective of a teacher may be viewed only marginally different from the perspectives of the students or not discrepant at all. The above issue of sufficient "background knowledge" (Schumacher et al., 1993) also comes into play here. Students often do not have the means to understand features of the new ideas that are conflicting with their ideas — as seen from the perspective of the teacher. Further, the problems students have in dealing with anomalous data (see the review of Chinn and Brewer's, 1993, work above) point to the difficulties with really bringing their cognitive balance out of equilibrium, so to speak, and to incite conceptual change processes. Students quite frequently appear to have the "strength" to bear conflicts. Much caution is therefore necessary when a cognitive conflict strategy is employed. Vosniadou (1994, p. 66) maintains that there is usually no "sudden shift from one theory to another but a continuous process which happens gradually as different kinds of constraints and particularly those that belong to the framework theory are reinterpreted" (see similar arguments in Caravita & Halldén, 1994).

   It may be interesting to note that discontinuous approaches that are deliberately based on Piagetian stage theory such as the "Learning Cycle" (Lawson et al., 1989) and those that explicitly reject this theory (like Driver's, 1989, "Constructivist Teaching Sequence"; see Figure 2), are only marginally different with regard to addressing conceptual change — because in the very end they are employing the same Piagetian ideas of conceptual change "mechanisms". The learning cycle comprises three phases (Lawson, 1989, pp. 26–27):

Exploration

Students learn through their own actions and reactions in a new situation. They explore new materials with minimal guidance. The new experience should raise questions or complexities that they cannot resolve with their present conceptions or accustomed patterns of reasoning. In other words, it provides the opportunity for students to voice potentially conflicting and at least partially inadequate ideas (misconceptions) that can spark debate and an analysis of the *reasons* for their ideas. Exploration leads to the identification of regularity in a phenomenon ...

Term Introduction

The new term to label the patterns discovered in the exploration stage is introduced.

Concept Application

Students apply the new term and/or reasoning pattern to additional examples. The concept application phase is necessary for some students to recognize the patterns and separate it from its specific contexts and/or to generalize it to other contexts ...

The Learning Cycle and the Constructivist Teaching Sequence share, with many other approaches in use in science education, a period in which students are made familiar with the phenomena in question and a period in which they are made aware of their ideas. At some later stage, the science point of view is brought into debate and there is some sort of negotiation about the values of this view. At the end, a review of the learning pathway is included, which provides students with possibilities to reflect on what they have learned.

As mentioned above, conceptual change teaching and learning usually is embedded in conditions that support conceptual change. Figure 2 provides an example for the Constructivist Teaching Sequence (Scott, 1992; see also Driver & Scott, 1996) of an outline for teaching the particle model. Students are given many opportunities to make their own experiences and to construct their own meaning of the phenomena observed. Another key feature of constructivist approaches also becomes apparent, namely considerations of the nature and range of scientific theory and theory making (see stage B in Figure 2). Students play a simple-rule guessing game here. The teacher writes a number of names at the blackboard following a certain rule (e.g. only names with four letters). Students have to find out the rule via checking their ideas against the evidence. The metaphor of a scientist as a detective is employed in another game in which students are provided with facts of a murder case. They work in groups to find out who the murderer is. They have to check their hypotheses against the evidence provided. In much the same way they are later invited to check their theories of how matter is composed of particles against the evidences as provided in their experiments. Cognitive conflicts play a key role, but are arranged in a cautious way. They are embedded in a process of gradual processing reinterpretations of students' initial ideas towards science views.

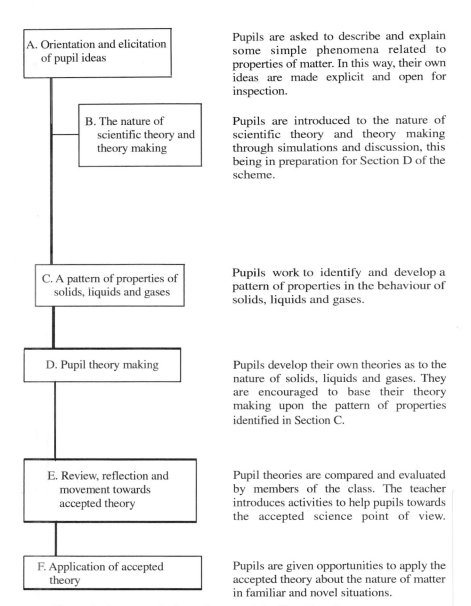

A. Orientation and elicitation of pupil ideas

Pupils are asked to describe and explain some simple phenomena related to properties of matter. In this way, their own ideas are made explicit and open for inspection.

B. The nature of scientific theory and theory making

Pupils are introduced to the nature of scientific theory and theory making through simulations and discussion, this being in preparation for Section D of the scheme.

C. A pattern of properties of solids, liquids and gases

Pupils work to identify and develop a pattern of properties in the behaviour of solids, liquids and gases.

D. Pupil theory making

Pupils develop their own theories as to the nature of solids, liquids and gases. They are encouraged to base their theory making upon the pattern of properties identified in Section C.

E. Review, reflection and movement towards accepted theory

Pupil theories are compared and evaluated by members of the class. The teacher introduces activities to help pupils towards the accepted science point of view.

F. Application of accepted theory

Pupils are given opportunities to apply the accepted theory about the nature of matter in familiar and novel situations.

Figure 2: An example for a Constructivist Teaching Sequence
(from Scott, 1992, p. 205)

To Address or Not to Address Students' Conceptions Explicitly

In most conceptual change approaches, either of the discontinuous or the continuous kind, there is a stage where students are made aware of their conceptions. Walter Jung and his co-workers have developed a very different approach, which falls into the category of continuous pathways. In elementary optics, for example, many deeply rooted alternative conceptions have been found (Jung, 1989). For instance, students do not view the process of seeing a lit object, like a picture on the wall, as light reflected by the picture into the eyes. Rather, students consider seeing in terms of something lying at the picture (namely light) that may be seen when turning the eyes to it. In the optic course, the teacher never speaks about this idea, but tries to arrange a set of adequately designed experiments and arguments to persuade students of the appropriateness of the scientific point of view (Wiesner, 1994). Jung and Wiesner argue against the cognitive conflict strategy because it is too time consuming and may lead students into the wrong direction. Evaluation results show that the continuous pathways approach was significantly better than a traditional approach given to a control group (Wiesner, 1994). These findings point to the importance of conceptual change supporting reconstruction of science subject-matter structures. This is an issue that is given surprisingly little importance in a number of other conceptual change approaches. If analysed from the perspective of the above-mentioned holistic constructivist approaches, however, it becomes obvious that Walter Jung's approach is limited in scope, in that key issues of the above sketched holistic constructivist approaches are not addressed. This approach lacks attempts to support students' abilities to reflect about their own learning, and hence to make them autonomous learners.

Analogies and Conceptual Change

Analogies and their relatives, like metaphors, play a significant role in conceptual change settings. Analogical reasoning is a key process in knowledge acquisition from a constructivist perspective (Glynn et al., 1995). If understanding and learning is possible only on the basis of the already existing conceptions, the already available conceptions have to be scanned for similarities with the newly presented conceptions by the learner. Several studies on conceptual change employ analogies but with varied success. Whereas in some cases analogical reasoning has proven a potent facilitator of conceptual change, this is not the case in other studies (for a review see Duit, 1991). A major reason for failures appears to be that analogical reasoning often cannot take place because the analogies presented to students are understood in a different way by the students than was intended (Duit & Glynn, 1992). Sometimes, not even the analogue domain, i.e. the domain that is the base of analogical reasoning, is familiar to the students to the extent assumed by the presenters of the analogy.

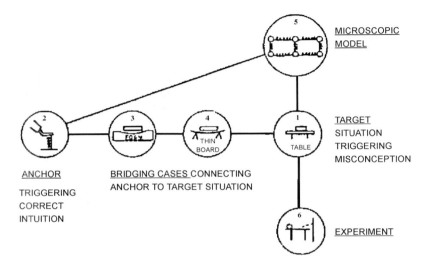

Figure 3: An example for bridging analogies (from Clement, 1987)

The most influential approach of employing analogies in conceptual change settings has been the "bridging analogies" approach of Brown and Clement (1989). It falls into the category of continuous pathways (Figure 1). In Figure 3, an example for the approach is given. The target situation, i.e. the situation to be understood, are the forces acting on a book lying on a table. Students usually have difficulty in understanding that not only does the book act on the table, but also, the table acts on the book (*actio et reactio*). The analogue situation at the left-hand side of Figure 3, called the anchoring situation, intuitively triggers the correct science view for most students. It forms the starting point for a series of sequences of analogical reasoning, so to speak, from one stepping stone to the other. A number of research studies have shown that such a sequence of analogies is successful when it bridges an analogue domain understood by students with the target situation.

Success of Conceptual Change Approaches in Science Education

Providing evidence of success of constructivist approaches is a somewhat difficult matter (Duit & Confrey, 1996). Because of the holistic character of many constructivist approaches to conceptual change, it is difficult to condense the reported results into measures that allow comparisons with traditional approaches. Furthermore, constructivist approaches usually include fundamental restructuring of traditional approaches in many respects. Do the categories for comparison have to come from the traditional approaches or from the new ones? Both are quite different concerning their aims. It appears to be possible only to evaluate these approaches with regard to their own aims, i.e. to investigate whether these approaches achieve their aims or not.

Solomon (1994), in a review of advantages and problems of the contemporary use of constructivism in science education, is rather reserved against constructivist teaching and learning approaches. With regard to the Children's Learning in Science project (Driver, 1989), Solomon admits that much valuable work has been done, but that a final judgement of the success of the teaching and learning methods employed is still not possible.

In a comprehensive review of research on students' conceptions in science Wandersee et al. (1994) analysed 103 intervention studies. They conclude that the wide range of modification studies show varying levels of success. This is true for intervention studies of the confrontation type (the discontinuous pathway type) and of studies that employ analogies. They also address limitations of the nature of the referring studies:

> A brief word of caution about the status of research on conceptual change seems in order. Much of this work is relatively recent in origin and, though promising, is probably best described as "exploratory" in nature. Many of the studies conducted to date have relied on small sample sizes, untested methods, anecdotal records and relatively non-rigorous research designs lacking control group comparisons. Virtually none of the studies has been replicated. However, purely qualitative research continues to improve as research design keeps pace with advances in methods. So, even with the aforementioned caveats in mind, we remain impressed by the relative success some researchers have achieved to date (Wandersee et al., 1994, p. 192).

It appears that this statement adequately portrays the state of the art in the domain of conceptual change teaching and learning strategies in science education. It seems to be valid also on the basis of the other intervention studies available (the recent edition of the bibliography by Pfundt & Duit, 1994, lists about 600 intervention studies of many different kinds).

A meta-analysis of conceptual change approaches in science education included 70 studies investigating intervention studies in science education and in science-related reading education (Guzetti & Glass, 1992). The type of analysis the authors employed only allowed the incorporation of studies that compared a treatment group and a control group. Therefore, major constructivist approaches towards conceptual change, among them the leading ones, such as the Children's Learning in Science (CLIS) project in Leeds (Driver, 1989), were not considered. Nevertheless, the findings show that there is a substantial amount of empirical evidence that challenges students' conceptions in some way and usually results in significantly better outcomes than approaches that do not address students' conceptions explicitly. It appears that this meta-analysis shows that, especially with the theoretical assumptions of conceptual change (Posner et al., 1982), conflict strategies and bridging analogies (Brown & Clement, 1989) are backed up by empirical findings:

> Based on the accumulated evidence from two disciplines [reading and science education is meant here], we have found that instructional interventions designed to offend the intuitive conception were effective in promoting conceptual change. The format of the strategy (e.g. refutational text, bridging analogies, augmented activation activities) seems

irrelevant, providing the nature of the strategy includes cognitive conflict. Despite recent self-criticism of their earlier positions (Strike & Posner, 1992), the genre of instructional strategies described earlier by Strike and Posner (1985) that produces dissatisfaction with current conceptions and shows the scientific conception as intelligible, plausible and applicable, has been effective (Guzetti & Glass, 1992, p. 42).

There is, therefore, good reason for the previously-cited optimistic view of Wandersee et al. (1994). Further close cooperation of research in science education and cognitive science appears to be most promising to investigate both the fine structure of conceptual change processes and the impact of supporting conditions of conceptual change.

References

Preface

Baillargeon, R. (1994). Physical reasoning in young infants: Seeking explanations for impossible events. *British Journal of Developmental Psychology, 12*, 9–33.

Caravita, S., & Halldén, O. (1994). Re-framing the problem of conceptual change. *Learning and Instruction, 4*, 89–111.

Carey, S. (1985). *Conceptual Change in Childhood*. Cambridge, MA: MIT Press.

Carey, S., & Gelman, R. (Eds.), (1991). The Epigenesis of Mind: Essays on Biology and Cognition. Hillsdale, NJ: Erlbaum.

Chi, M.T.H., Slotta, J.D., & de Leeuw, N. (1994). From things to processes: A theory of conceptual change for learning science concepts. *Learning and Instruction, 4*, 27–43.

Chinn, C.A., & Brewer, W.F. (1993). The role of anomalous data in knowledge acquisition: A theoretical framework and implications for science education. *Review of Educational Research, 63*, 1–49.

Collins, A., Brown, J.S., & Newman, S.E. (1989). Cognitive apprenticeship: Teaching the crafts of reading, writing, and mathematics. In L.B. Resnick (Ed.), *Knowing, Learning, and Instruction* (pp. 453–494). Hillsdale, NJ: Erlbaum.

di Sessa, A. (1988). Knowledge in pieces. In G. Forman, & P.B. Pufall (Eds.), *Constructivism in the Computer Age* (pp. 49–70). Hillsdale, NJ: Erlbaum.

di Sessa, A. (1993). Towards an epistemology of physics. *Cognition and Instruction, 10* (2&3), 105–225.

Kuhn, D. (1989). Children and adults as intuitive scientists. *Psychological Review, 96*, 674–689.

Piaget, J. (1950). *The Psychology of Intelligence*. London: Routledge & Kegan Paul.

Pintrich, P.R., Marx, R.W., & Boyle, R.A. (1993). Beyond cold conceptual change: The role of motivational beliefs and classroom contextual factors in the process of conceptual change. *Review of Educational Research, 63*, 167–199.

Posner, G.J., Strike, K.A., Hewson, P.W., & Gertzog, W.A. (1982). Accommodation of a scientific conception: Towards a theory of conceptual change. *Science Education, 66*, 211–217.

Spada, H. (1994). Conceptual change or multiple representations? *Learning and Instruction, 4* (1), 113–116.

Spelke, E.S. (1990). Principles of object perception. *Cognitive Science, 14*, 29–56.

Strike, K.A., & Posner, G. (1982). Conceptual change and science teaching. *European Journal of Science Education, 4*, 231–240.

Vosniadou, S. (1994). Capturing and modeling the process of conceptual change. *Learning and Instruction, 4* (1), 45–69.

Vosniadou, S., & Brewer, W.F. (1992). Mental models of the earth. *Cognitive Psychology, 24*, 535–585.

Vosniadou, S., & Brewer, W.F. (1994). Capturing and modeling the process of conceptual change. *Learning and Instruction, 4*, 45–69.

Vygotski, L.S. (1962). Development of scientific concepts in childhood. In E. Hanfman & G. Vakar (Eds.), *Thought and Language* (pp. 82–118). Cambridge, MA: MIT Press.

Chapter 1

Caramazza, A., McCloskey, M., & Green, B. (1981). Naive beliefs in "sophisticated" subjects: Misconceptions about trajectories of objects. *Cognition, 9* (2), 117–123.

Caravita, S., & Halldén, O. (1994). Re-framing the problem of conceptual change. *Learning and Instruction, 4,* 89–111.

Carey, S. (1985). *Conceptual Change in Childhood.* Cambridge, MA: MIT Press.

Carey, S., & Spelke, E. (1994). Domain-specific knowledge and conceptual change. In L.A. Hirschfeld & S. A. Gelman, (Eds.), *Mapping the Mind: Domain Specificity in Cognition and Culture* (pp. 169–200). New York: Cambridge University Press.

Chi, M.T.H., Feltovitch, P.J., & Glaser, R (1981). Categorisation and representation of physics problems by experts and novices. *Cognitive Science, 5,* 121–152.

Chi, M.T.H., Slotta, J.D., & de Leeuw, (1994) From things to processes: A theory of conceptual change for learning science concepts. *Learning and Instruction, 4,* 27–43.

d'Andrade, R.G. (1989). Cultural cognition. In M. Posner (Ed.), *Foundations of Cognitive Science* (pp. 795–830). Cambridge, MA: MIT Press.

di Sessa, A.A. (1993). Toward an epistemology of physics. *Cognition and Instruction, 10,* 105–225.

Driver, R., & Easley, J (1978). Pupils and paradigms: A review of literature related to concept development in adolescent science students. *Studies in Science Education, 5,* 61–84

Fodor, J. (1983). *Modularity of Mind.* Cambridge, MA: MIT Press.

Gardner, H. (1985). *The Mind's New Science.* New York: Basic Books.

Gelman, R. (1990). First principles organize about relevant data: Number and the animate-inanimate distinction as examples. *Cognitive Science, 14,* 79–106.

Glaser, R., Ferguson, E., & Vosniadou, S. (1996). Cognition and the design of environments for learning: Approaches in this book. In S. Vosniadou, E. De Corte, R. Glaser, & H. Mandl (Eds.), *International Perspectives on the Construction of Technology-Supported Learning Environments* (pp. 13–24). Hillsdale, NJ: Lawrence Erlbaum.

Hirschfeld, L.A., & Gelman, S. (1994) Toward a topography of the mind. In L.A. Hirschfeld & S. Gelman (Eds.), *Mapping the Mind: Domain Specificity in Cognition and Culture* (pp. 3–36). New York, NY: Cambridge University Press.

Kuhn, T. (1970). *The Structure of Scientific Revolutions* (2nd ed.). Chicago: Chicago University Press.

Lakatos, I. (1970). Falsification and the methodology of scientific research programmes. In I. Lakatos & A. Musgrave (Eds.), *Criticism and the Growth of Knowledge* (pp. 91–196). Cambridge, UK: Cambridge University Press.

Larkin, J.H. (1983). The role of problem representation in physics. In D. Gentner & A.L. Stevens (Eds.), *Mental Models* (pp. 75–98). Hillsdale, NJ: Lawrence Erlbaum.

Novak, J.D. (1977a). Epicycles and the homocentric earth: Or what is wrong with stages of cognitive development. *Science Education, 61,* 393–395.

Novak, J.D. (1977b). An alternative to Piagetian psychology for science and mathematics education. *Science Education, 61,* 453–477.

Posner, G.J., Strike, K.A., Hewson, P.W., & Gertzog, W.A. (1982). Accommodation of a scientific conception: Toward a theory of conceptual change. *Science Education, 66,* 211–227.

Quinn, N., & Holland, D. (1987). Introduction. In D. Holland & N. Quinn (Eds.), *Cultural Models in Language and Thought* (pp. 3–40). New York: Cambridge University Press.

Spada, H. (1994). Conceptual change or multiple representations? *Learning and Instruction, 4* (1), 113–116.

Spelke, E.S. (1991). Physical knowledge in infancy: Reflections on Piaget's theory. In S. Carey & R. Gelman (Eds.), *Epigenesis of Mind: Studies in Biology and Cognition.* (pp. 133–170). Hillsdale, NJ: Lawrence Erlbaum.

Strike, K.A., & Posner, G.J. (1985). Conceptual change view of learning and understanding. In L. West & L. Pines (Eds.), *Cognitive Structure and Conceptual Change* (pp. 211–231). Orlando: Academic Press.

Viennot, L. (1973). Spontaneous reasoning in elementary dynamics. *European Journal of Science Education, 1*, 205–221.

Vosniadou, S. (1994). Capturing and modeling the process of conceptual change. *Learning and Instruction, 4*, 45–69.

Vosniadou, S., & Brewer, W.F. (1992). Mental models of the earth: A study of conceptual change in childhood. *Cognitive Psychology, 24*, 535–585.

Vosniadou, S., & Brewer, W.F. (1994). Mental models of the day/night cycle. *Cognitive Science, 18*, 123–183.

Vosniadou, S., & Kempner, L. (1993, April). Mental Models of Heat. Paper presented at the biennial meeting of the Society for Research in Child Development, New Orleans.

Vygotsky, L.S. (1978). *Mind in Society*. Cambridge, MA: Harvard University Press.

Wellman, H.M., & Gelman, S.A. (1992). Cognitive development. Foundational theories of core domains. *Annual Review of Psychology, 43*, 337–375.

Wiser, M., & Carey, S. (1983). When heat and temperature were one. In D. Gentner & A.L. Stevens (Eds.), *Mental Models* (pp. 267–297). Hillsdale, NJ: Erlbaum.

Chapter 2

Backenscheider, A., Shatz, M., & Gelman, S. (1993). Preschooler's ability to distinguish living kinds as a function of regrowth. *Child Development, 64*, 1242–1257.

Baillargeon, R. (1994). Physical reasoning in young infants: Seeking explanations for impossible events. *British Journal of Developmental Psychology, 12*, 9–33.

Baldwin, D., Markman, E., & Melartin, R. (1993). Infants' ability to draw inferences about nonobvious object properties: Evidence from exploratory play. *Child Development, 64*, 711–728.

Barsalou, L. (1987). The instability of graded structure in concepts. In U. Neisser (Ed.), *Concepts and Conceptual Development: Ecological and Intellectual Factors in Categorization* (pp.101–140). New York: Cambridge University Press.

Barsalou, L. (1989). Intraconcept similarity and its implications for interconcept similarity. In. S. Vosniadou & A. Ortony (Eds.), *Similarity and Analogical Reasoning* (pp. 76–121). Cambridge: Cambridge University Press.

Barsalou, L. (1993). Challenging assumptions about concepts. *Cognitive Development, 8*, 169–180.

Berzonsky, M. (1971). The role of familiarity in children's explanations of physical causality. *Child Development, 42*, 705–715.

Bullock, M. (1985). Animism in childhood thinking: A new look at an old question. *Developmental Psychology, 21*, 217–225.

Carey, S. (1985). *Conceptual Change in Childhood*. Cambridge, MA: MIT Press.

Carey, S. (1991). Knowledge acquisition: Enrichment or conceptual change? In S. Carey & R. Gelman (Eds.), *The Epigenesis of Mind: Essays on Biology and Cognition*. Hillsdale, NJ: Erlbaum.

Chi, M. (1992). Conceptual change within and across ontological categories: Examples from learning and discovery in science. In R. Giere (Ed.), *Cognitive Models of Science* (pp.129–187). Minneapolis, MN: University of Minnesota Press.

Dennett, D. (1987) *The Intentional Stance*. Cambridge, MA: MIT Press.

Flavell, J. (1970). Concept development. In P.H. Mussen (Ed.), *Carmichael's Manual of Child Psychology*, Vol. I. New York: Wiley.

Gelman, R. (1990). First principles organize attention to and learning about relevant data: number and the animate-inanimate distinction. *Cognitive Science, 14,* 79–106.

Gelman, R., & Spelke, E. (1981). The development of thoughts about animate and inanimate objects: implications for research on social cognition. In J. Flavell & L. Ross (Eds.), *Social Cognitive Development* (pp.43–66). New York: Cambridge University Press.

Gelman, S. (1988). The development of induction within natural and artifact categories. *Cognitive Psychology, 20,* 65–95.

Gelman, S., & Coley, D. (1990). The importance of knowing a dodo is a bird: Categories and inferences in 2-year-old children. *Developmental Psychology, 26,* 796–804.

Gelman, S., & Kremer, K. (1991). Understanding natural cause: Children's explanations of how objects and their properties originate. *Child Development, 62,* 306–414.

Gelman, S., & Markman, E. (1987). Young children's inductions from natural kinds: The role of categories and appearances. *Child Development, 58,* 1532–1541.

Gelman, S., & Wellman, H. (1991). Insides and essences: Early understandings of the non-obvious. *Cognition, 38,* 213–244.

Inagaki, K. (1990). The effects of raising animals on children's biological knowledge. *British Journal of Developmental Psychology, 8,* 119–129.

Inagaki, K., & Hatano, G. (1991). Constrained person analogy in young children's biological inference. *Cognitive Development, 6,* 219–231.

Jones, S., & Smith, L. (1993). The place of perception in children's concepts. *Cognitive Development, 8,* 113–139.

Keil, F. (1989). *Concepts, Kinds, and Cognitive Development.* Cambridge, MA: MIT Press.

Keil, F. (1991). The emergence of theoretical beliefs as constraints on concepts. In S. Carey, & R. Gelman (Eds.), *The Epigenesis of Mind: Essays on Biology and Cognition* (pp. 237–321). Hillsdale, NJ: Erlbaum.

Keil, F. (1992). The origins of an autonomous biology. In M. Gunnar & M. Maratsos (Eds.), *Minnesota Symposium on Child Psychology* (pp.103–137). Erlbaum.

Kuhn, T. (1982). *Commensurability, Comparability, Communicability.* PSA 1982, Vol. 2 (pp. 669–688). East Lansing: Philosophy of Science Association.

Lamsfuss, S. (1995). Regularity of Movement and the Animate-Iinanimate Distinction. Poster presented at the Biennial meeting of the Society for Research in Child Development, Indianapolis.

Laurandeau, M., & Pinard, A. (1962). *Causal Thinking in the Child.* New York: International University Press.

Looft, W. (1974). Animistic thought in children: Understanding of "living" across its associated attributes. *Journal of Genetic Psychology, 124,* 235–240.

Madole, K. (1992). Infants' Categorization of Objects: The Role of Part Structure and Functional Properties. Unpublished doctoral dissertation, University of Texas at Austin.

Madole, K., Oakes, L., & Cohen, L. (1993). Shake, Rattle, or Roll: Infant Attention to Form Versus Function. Poster presented at the meeting of the Society for Research in Child Development, Seattle.

Madsen, M. (1982). Animism and related tendencies in Hopi children. A replication of Dennis. *Journal of Cross-Cultural Psychology, 13,* 117–124.

Mandler, J. (1992). How to build a baby: II. Conceptual primitives. *Psychological Review, 99* (4), 587–604.

Mandler, J., & McDonough, L. (1993). Concept formation in infancy. *Cognitive Development, 8,* 291–317.

Massey, C., & Gelman, R. (1988). Preschooler's ability to decide whether a photographed unfamiliar object can move itself. *Developmental Psychology, 24,* 307–317.

Medin, D., & Ortony, A. (1989). Psychological essentialism. In S. Vosniadou & A. Ortony (Eds.), *Similarity and Analogical Reasoning* (pp. 179–195). New York: Cambridge University Press.

Medin, D., & Shoben, E. (1988). Context and structure in conceptual combination. *Cognitive Psychology, 20*, 158–190.

Murphy, G., & Medin, D. (1985). The role of theories in conceptual coherence. *Psychological Review, 92* (3), 289–316.

Nelson, K. (1974). Concept, word, and sentences: Interrelations in the acquisition and development. *Psychological Review, 81*, 267–285.

Piaget, J. (1979). *The Child's Conception of the World*. Totowa, NJ: Littlefield, Adams.

Premack, D. (1990). The infant's theory of self-propelled objects. *Cognition, 36*, 1–16.

Richards, D., & Siegler, R. (1984). The effects of task requirements on children's life judgments. *Child Development, 55*, 1687–1696.

Richards, D., & Siegler, R. (1986). Children's understandings of the attributes of life. *Journal of Experimental Child Psychology, 42*, 1–22.

Rosch, E., Mervis, C., Gray, W., Johnson, M., & Boyes-Braem, P. (1976). Basic objects in natural categories. *Cognitive Psychology, 8*, 382–439.

Rosengren, K., Gelman, S., Kalish, C., & McCormick, M. (1991). As time goes by: Children's early understanding of growth in animals. *Child Development, 62*, 1302–1320.

Schwartz, S. (1979). Natural kind terms. *Cognition, 7*, 301–315.

Simon, D., & Keil, F. (1995). An abstract to concrete shift in the development of biological thought: The inside story. *Cognition, 56*, 129–163.

Smith, L., & Heise, D. (1992). Perceptual similarity and conceptual structure. In B. Burns (Ed.), *Percepts, Concepts and Categories* (pp. 233–272). Amsterdam: North-Holland.

Sommers, F. (1971). Structural ontology. *Philosophia, 1*, 21–42.

Spelke, E. (1991). Physical knowledge in infancy: Reflections on Piaget's theory. In S. Carey, & R. Gelman (Eds.), *Epigenesis of Mind: Studies in Biology and Cognition*. Hillsdale, NJ: Erlbaum.

Vygotsky, L. (1934/1962). *Thought and Language*. Cambridge, MA: MIT Press

Chapter 3

Ames, C. (1992). Classrooms: Goals, structures, and student motivation. *Journal of Educational Psychology, 84*, 261–271.

Ball, D. (1993). With an eye on the mathematical horizon: Dilemmas of teaching elementary school mathematics. *Elementary School Journal, 93*, 373–397.

Baltes, M., & Baltes, P. (1986). *The Psychology of Control and Aging*. Hillsdale, NJ: LEA.

Bandura, A. (1986). *Social Foundations of Thought and Action: A Social Cognitive Theory*. Englewood Cliffs, NJ: Prentice–Hall.

Bereiter, C. (1990). Aspects of an educational learning theory. *Review of Educational Research, 60*, 603–624.

Blumenfeld, P. (1992). Classroom learning and motivation: Clarifying and expanding goal theory. *Journal of Educational Psychology, 84*, 272–281.

Blumenfeld, P., Mergendoller, J., & Puro, P. (1992). Translating motivation into thoughtfulness. In H. Marshall (Ed.), *Redefining Learning* (pp. 207–239). Norwood, NJ: Ablex.

Blumenfeld, P.C., Soloway, E., Marx, R.W., Krajcik, J.S., Guzdial, M., & Palincsar, A. (1991). Motivating project-based learning: Sustaining the doing, supporting the learning. *Educational Psychologist, 26*, 369–398.

Borkowski, J., Carr, M., Rellinger, E., & Pressley, M. (1990). Self-regulated cognition: Interdependence of metacognition, attributions, and self-esteem. In B. Jones & L. Idol (Eds.), *Dimensions of Thinking and Cognitive Instruction* (pp. 53–92). Hillsdale, NJ: Erlbaum.

Brophy, J. (1983). Conceptualizing student motivation. *Educational Psychologist, 18*, 200–215.

Chapman, M., Skinner, E.A., & Baltes, P.B. (1990). Interpreting correlations between children's perceived control and cognitive performance: Control, agency, or means-ends beliefs? *Developmental Psychology*, *26*, 246–253.

Chinn, C., & Brewer, W. (1993). The role of anomalous data in knowledge acquisition: A theoretical framework and implications for science instruction. *Review of Educational Research*, *63*, 1–49.

Cobb, P. (1994). Where is the mind? Constructivist and sociocultural perspectives on mathematical development. *Educational Researcher*, *23* (7), 13–20.

Cole, S. (1992). *Making Science: Between Nature and Society*. Cambridge: Harvard University Press.

Confrey, J. (1995). How compatible are radical constructivism, sociocultural approaches, and social constructivism? In L. Steffe & J. Gale (Eds.), *Constructivism in Education* (pp. 185–225). Hillsdale, NJ: Lawrence Erlbaum Associates.

Connell, J.P. (1985). A new multidimensional measure of children's perceptions of control. *Child Development*, *56*, 1018–1041.

Deci, E.L., & Ryan, R. (1985). *Intrinsic Motivation and Self-Determination in Human Behavior*. New York: Plenum Press.

Dweck, C.S., & Elliott, E.S. (1983). Achievement motivation. In E.M. Heatherington, (Ed.), *Handbook of Child Psychology: Vol. 4. Socialization, Personality, and Social Development* (pp. 643–691). New York: John Wiley & Sons.

Dweck, C.S., & Leggett, E.L. (1988). A social-cognitive approach to motivation and personality. *Psychological Review*, *95* (2), 256–273.

Eccles, J. (1983). Expectancies, values and academic behaviors. In J.T. Spence (Ed.), *Achievement and Achievement Motives* (pp. 75–146). San Francisco: Freeman.

Elliott, E., & Dweck, C. (1988). Goals: An approach to motivation and achievement. *Journal of Personality and Social Psychology*, *54*, 5–12.

Fabricius, W. V., & Hagen, J. W. (1984). Use of causal attributions about recall performance to assess metamemory and predict strategic memory behavior in young children. *Developmental Psychology*, *20*, 975–987.

Findley, M., & Cooper, H. (1983). Locus of control and academic achievement: A review of the literature. *Journal of Personality and Social Psychology*, *44*, 419–427.

Gardner, H. (1991). *The Unschooled Mind: How Children Think and How Schools Should Teach*. New York: Basic Books.

Garner, R., Brown, R., Sanders, S., & Menke, D. (1992). "Seductive details" and learning from text. In K.A. Renninger, S. Hidi & A. Krapp (Eds.), *The Role of Interest in Learning and Development* (pp. 239–254). Hillsdale, NJ: LEA.

Graham, S., & Golan, S. (1991). Motivational influences on cognition: Task involvement, ego involvement, and depth of processing. *Journal of Educational Psychology*, *83*, 187–194.

Grolnick, W., & Ryan, R. (1987). Autonomy in children's learning: An experimental and individual difference investigation. *Journal of Personality and Social Psychology*, *52*, 890–898.

Hammer, D. (1994). Epistemological beliefs in introductory physics. *Cognition and Instruction*, *12*, 151–183.

Harter, S. (1981). A new self-report scale of intrinsic versus extrinsic orientation in the classroom: Motivational and informational components. *Developmental Psychology*, *17*, 300–312.

Hidi, S. (1990). Interest and its contribution as a mental resource for learning. *Review of Educational Research*, *60*, 549–571.

Hidi, S., & Anderson, V. (1992). Situational interest and its impact on reading and expository writing. In K.A. Renninger, S. Hidi & A. Krapp (Eds.), *The Role of Interest in Learning and Development* (pp. 215–238). Hillsdale, NJ: LEA.

Hidi, S., Renninger, K.A., & Krapp, A. (1992). The present state of interest research. In K.A. Renninger, S. Hidi & A. Krapp (Eds.), *The Role of Interest in Learning and Development* (pp. 433–446). Hillsdale, NJ: LEA.

Hofer, B., & Pintrich, P.R. (1995). The development of epistemological schemas: Beliefs about knowledge and knowing and their relation to learning. *Review of Educational Research, 67*, 88–140.

King, P.M., & Kitchener, K.S. (1994). *Developing Reflective Judgment: Understanding and Promoting Intellectual Growth and Critical Thinking in Adolescents and Adults*. San Francisco: Jossey-Bass.

Kruglanski, A.W. (1989). *Lay Epistemics and Human Knowledge: Cognitive and Motivational Bases*. New York: Plenum Press.

Kurtz, B.E., & Borkowski, J.G. (1984). Children's metacognition: Exploring relations among knowledge, process, and motivational variables. *Journal of Experimental Child Psychology, 37*, 335–354.

Lefcourt, H. (1976). *Locus of Control: Current Trends in Theory and Research*. Hillsdale, NJ: Erlbaum.

Lepper, M., & Hodell, M. (1989). Intrinsic motivation in the classroom. In C. Ames & R. Ames (Eds.), *Research on Motivation in Education*, Vol. 3 (pp. 73–105). New York: Academic Press.

Malone, T., & Lepper, M. (1987). Making learning fun: A taxonomy of intrinsic motivations for learning. In R. Snow & M. Farr (Eds.), *Aptitude, Learning, and Instruction: Vol. 3. Cognitive and Affective Process Analyses* (pp. 223–253). Hillsdale, NJ: Erlbaum.

Markus, H., & Nurius, P. (1986). Possible selves. *American Psychologist, 41*, 954–969.

Markus, H., & Wurf, E. (1987). The dynamic self-concept: A social psychological perspective. *Annual Review of Psychology, 38*, 299–337.

Meece, J. (1991). The classroom context and children's motivational goals. In M. Maehr & P. Pintrich (Eds.), *Advances in Motivation and Achievement*, Vol. 7 (pp. 261–286). Greenwich, CT: JAI Press.

Meece, J.L., Blumenfeld, P.C., & Hoyle, R.H. (1988). Students' goal orientation and cognitive engagement in classroom activities. *Journal of Educational Psychology, 80*, 514–523.

Nicholls, J. (1984). Achievement motivation: Conceptions of ability, subjective experience, task choice, and performance. *Psychological Review, 91* (3), 328–346.

Nolen, S. (1988). Reasons for studying: Motivational orientations and study strategies. *Cognition and Instruction, 5*, 269–287.

Osborne, R., & Freyberg, P. (1985). *Learning in Science: The Implications of Children's Science*. Auckland: Heinemann.

Paris, S.G., & Oka, E. (1986). Children's reading strategies, metacognition, and motivation. *Developmental Review, 6*, 25–56.

Pintrich, P.R. (1989). The dynamic interplay of student motivation and cognition in the college classroom. In C. Ames & M. Maehr (Eds.). *Advances in Motivation and Achievement: Motivation Enhancing Environments*, Vol. 6. (pp. 117–160). Greenwich, CT: JAI Press.

Pintrich, P.R., & De Groot, E. (1990a). Motivational and self-regulated learning components of classroom academic performance. *Journal of Educational Psychology, 82*, 33–40.

Pintrich, P.R., & De Groot, E. (1990b). Quantitative and Qualitative Perspectives on Student Motivational Beliefs and Self-Regulated Learning. Paper presented at the American Educational Research Association conference, Boston.

Pintrich, P.R., & Garcia, T. (1991). Student goal orientation and self-regulation in the college classroom. In M. Maehr & P.R. Pintrich (Eds.), *Advances in Motivation and Achievement: Goals and Self-Regulatory Processes*, Vol. 7. Greenwich, CT: JAI Press.

Pintrich, P.R., Marx, R., & Boyle, R. (1993a). Beyond cold conceptual change: The role of motivational beliefs and classroom contextual factors in the process of conceptual change. *Review of Educational Research, 63*, 167–199.

Pintrich, P.R., & Schrauben, B. (1992). Students motivational beliefs and their cognitive engagement in classroom academic tasks. In D. Schunk & J. Meece (Eds.), *Student Perceptions in the Classroom: Causes and Consequences.* Hillsdale, NJ: Erlbaum.

Pintrich, P.R., & Schunk, D.H. (1996). *Motivation in the Classroom: Theory, Research, and Applications.* Englewood Cliffs, NJ: Merrill/Prentice-Hall.

Pintrich, P.R., Smith, D., Garcia, T., & McKeachie, W. (1993b). Reliability and predictive validity of the Motivated Strategies for Learning Questionnaire. *Educational and Psychological Measurement, 53,* 801–813.

Pintrich, P.R., Wolters, C., & Baxter, G. (forthcoming). Issues in the assessment of metacognition and self-regulated learning. In G. Schraw & J. Impara (Eds.), *Assessing Metacognition.* Lincoln, NE: The University of Nebraska Press.

Pokay, P., & Blumenfeld, P.C. (1990). Predicting achievement early and late in the semester: The role of motivation and use of learning strategies. *Journal of Educational Psychology, 82,* 41–50.

Qian, G., & Alvermann, D. (1995). Role of epistemological beliefs and learned helplessness in secondary school students' learning science concepts from text. *Journal of Educational Psychology, 87,* 282–292.

Reif, F., & Larkin, J. (1991). Cognition in scientific and everyday domains: Comparison and learning implications. *Journal of Research in Science Teaching, 28,* 733–760.

Renninger, K.A. (1992). Individual interest and development: Implications for theory and practice. In K.A. Renninger, S. Hidi & A. Krapp (Eds.), *The Role of Interest in Learning and Development* (pp. 361–395). Hillsdale, NJ: LEA.

Renninger, K.A., & Wozniak, R.H. (1985). Effect of interest on attentional shift, recognition, and recall in young children. *Developmental Psychology, 21,* 624–632.

Roth, W.-M., & Roychoudhury, A. (1994). Physics students' epistemologies and views about knowing and learning. *Journal of Research in Science Teaching, 31,* 5–30.

Ryan, R., Connell, J., & Deci, E. (1985). A motivational analysis of self-determination and self-regulation in education. In C. Ames & R. Ames (Eds.), *Research on Motivation in Education,* Vol. 2 (pp. 13–51). New York: Academic Press.

Schiefele, U. (1991). Interest, learning, and experience. *Educational Psychologist, 26,* 299–323.

Schiefele, U. (1992). Topic interest and levels of text comprehension. In K.A. Renninger, S. Hidi & A. Krapp (Eds.), *The Role of Interest in Learning and Development* (pp. 151–182). Hillsdale, NJ: LEA.

Schneider, W., Borkowski, J.G., Kurtz, B.E., & Kerwin, K. (1986). Metamemory and motivation: A comparison of strategy use and performance in German and American children. *Journal of Cross-Cultural Psychology, 17,* 315–336.

Schommer, M. (1990). Effects of beliefs about the nature of knowledge on comprehension. *Journal of Educational Psychology, 82,* 498–504.

Schommer, M. (1993). Epistemological development and academic performance among secondary students. *Journal of Educational Psychology, 85,* 406–411.

Schommer, M., Crouse, A., & Rhodes, N. (1992). Epistemological beliefs and mathematical text comprehension: Believing it is simple does not make it so. *Journal of Educational Psychology, 84,* 435–443.

Schommer, M., & Walker, K. (1995). Are epistemological beliefs similar across domains? *Journal of Educational Psychology, 87,* 424–432.

Schunk, D. (1985). Self-efficacy and school learning. *Psychology in the Schools, 22,* 208–223.

Schunk, D. (1989). Social cognitive theory and self-regulated learning. In B. Zimmerman & D. Schunk (Eds.), *Self-Regulated Learning and Academic Achievement: Theory, Research, and Practice* (pp. 83–110). New York: Springer-Verlag.

Schunk, D. (1991). Self-efficacy and academic motivation. *Educational Psychologist, 26,* 207–231.

Schunk, D., & Hanson, A.R. (1985). Peer models: Influence on children's self-efficacy and achievement. *Journal of Educational Psychology, 77*, 313–322.

Shell, D., Murphy, C., & Bruning, R. (1989). Self-efficacy and outcome expectancy mechanisms in reading and writing achievement. *Journal of Educational Psychology, 81*, 91–100.

Skinner, E.A., Chapman, M., & Baltes, P. (1988a). Children's beliefs about control, means-ends, and agency: Developmental differences during middle childhood. *International Journal of Behavioral Development, 11*, 369–388.

Skinner, E.A., Chapman, M., & Baltes, P. (1988b). Control, means-ends, and agency beliefs: A new conceptualization and its measurement during childhood. *Journal of Personality and Social Psychology, 54*, 117–133.

Skinner, E.A., Wellborn, J.G., & Connell, J.P. (1990). What it takes to do well in school and whether I've got it: A process model of perceived control and children's engagement and achievement in school. *Journal of Educational Psychology, 82*, 22–32.

Smith, J., di Sessa, A., & Roschelle, J. (1993). Misconceptions reconceived: A constructivist analysis of knowledge in transition. *Journal of the Learning Sciences, 3*, 115–163.

Steffe, L., & Gale, J. (1995). *Constructivism in Education.* Hillsdale, NJ: Lawrence Erlbaum Associates.

Stipek, D.J., & Weisz, J.R. (1981). Perceived personal control and academic achievement. *Review of Educational Research, 51*, 101–137.

Strike, K.A., & Posner, G.J. (1992). A revisionist theory of conceptual change. In R. Duschl & Hamilton (Eds.), *Philosophy of Science, Cognitive Psychology, and Educational Theory and Practice* (pp. 147–176). Albany, NY: SUNY.

Thagard, P. (1992). *Conceptual Revolutions.* Princeton, NJ: Princeton University Press.

Tobias, S. (1994). Interest, prior knowledge, and learning. *Review of Educational Research, 64*, 37–54.

Vosniadou, S., & Brewer, W. (1994). Mental models of the day/night cycle. *Cognitive Science, 18*, 123–183.

Wade, S. (1992). How interest affects learning from text. In K.A. Renninger, S. Hidi & A. Krapp (Eds.), *The Role of Interest in Learning and Development* (pp. 255–277). Hillsdale, NJ: LEA.

Weed, K., Ryan, E., & Day, J. (1990). Metamemory and attributions as mediators of strategy use and recall. *Journal of Educational Psychology, 82*, 849–855.

Chapter 4

Bakhtin, M.M. (1986). The problems of speech genres. In C. Emerson & M. Holquist (Eds.), *Speech Genres and Other Late Essays* (pp. 60–101). Austin University of Texas Press.

Brumby, M. (1984). Misconceptions about the concept of natural selection by medical biology students. *Science Education, 68*, 493–503.

Bruner, J.S. (1966). *Toward a Theory of Instruction.* Cambridge, MA: Harvard University Press.

Caravita, S., & Halldén, O. (1994). Re-framing the problem of conceptual change. *Learning and Instruction, 4*, 89–111.

Cobb, P. (1986). Contexts, goals, beliefs, and learning mathematics. *Learning of Mathematics, 6* (2), 2–9.

Davis, F. (1974). Stories and sociology. *Urban Life and Culture, 3*, 310–316.

Goodwin, C., & Duranti, A. (1992). Rethinking context: an introduction. In C. Goodwin & A. Duranti (Eds.), *Rethinking Context. Language as an Interactive Phenomenon* (pp. 1–42). New York: Cambridge University Press.

Halldén, O. (1990). Questions asked in common sense contexts and in scientific contexts. In P.L. Lijnse; P. Licht; W. de Vos & A.J. Waarlo (Eds.), *Relating Macroscopic Phenomena to Microscopic Particles* (pp. 119–130). Utrecht: CD-B Press.

Halldén, O. (1993). Learners' conceptions of the subject matter being taught. A case from learning history. In R. Säljö (Ed.), *Learning Discourse: Qualitative Research in Education.* [special issue]. *International Journal of Educational Research, 91,* 317–325.

Halldén, O., Hansson, G., & Skoog, G. (1994). Evolutionary Reasoning in Answers to Two Questions Used to Measure the Development of University Students' Understanding of Evolutionary Theory. Working Paper Series No 4, Department of Education, Stockholm University.

Kahneman, D., & Tversky, A. (1982). On the study of statistical intuitions. In D. Kahneman, P. Slovic & A. Tversky (Eds.), *Judgement Under Uncertainty: Heuristics and Biases* (pp. 493–508). New York: Cambridge University Press.

Linder, C.J. (1993). A challenge to conceptual change. *Science Education, 77,* 293–300.

Norrby, L.-J. (1982). Kemiämnenas Pedagogik: Kunskaper och Pegreppsbildning vid Kemistudiernas Början [The pedagogics of chemistry: knowledge and concept formation in the beginning of studying chemistry]. PU-rapport 1982:2. Stockholm University.

Piaget, J. (1973). *The Child's Conception of the World.* London: Paladin.

Posner, G.J., Strike, K.A., Hewson, P.W., & Gertzog, W.A. (1982). Accommodation of a scientific conception: Toward a theory of conceptual change. *Science Education, 66,* 211–227.

Resnick, L.B. (1987). Learning in school and out. *Educational Researcher, 16* (9), 13–20.

Resnick, L.B. (1991). Shared cognition: Thinking as social practice. In L.B. Resnick; J.M. Levine & S.D. Teasley (Eds.), *Socially Shared Cognition* (pp. 1–20). Washington, DC: American Psychological Association.

Searle, J. (1983). *Intentionality. An Essay in the Philosophy of Mind.* Cambridge: Cambridge University Press.

Solomon, J. (1983). Learning about energy: How pupils think in two domains. *European Journal of Science Education, 5,* 49–59.

Strike, K.A., & Posner, G.J. (1982). Conceptual change and science teaching. *European Journal of Science Education, 4,* 231–240.

Strike, K.A., & Posner, G.J. (1992). A revisionist theory of conceptual change. In R.A. Duschl & R.J. Hamilton (Eds.), *Philosophy of Science, Cognitive Psychology, and Educational Theory and Practice* (pp. 147–176). Albany: State University of New York Press.

Tiberghien, A. (1994). Modeling as a basis for analyzing teaching-learning situations. *Learning and Instruction, 4,* 71–87.

Vosniadou, S. (1994). Capturing and modeling the process of conceptual change. *Learning and Instruction, 4,* 45–69.

Wistedt, I. (1994). Everyday common sense and school mathematics. *European Journal of Psychology of Education, 9,* 139–147.

Wistedt, I. (1999). Reflection, Communication, and Learning Mathematics: A Case Study. *Learning and Instruction, 7,* 123–138.

von Wright, G.H. (1971). *Explanation and Understanding.* London: Routledge and Kegan Paul.

von Wright, G.H. (1979). *Reason, Action, and Experience.* In I. Kohlenberger & Helmut (Eds.), Essays in honor of Raymond Klibanshy. Hamburg: Felix Meiner Verlag.

Chapter 5

Berlin, B., & Kay, P. (1969). *Basic Colour Terms.* Berkeley: University of California Press.

Carpenter, T.P., & Moser, J.M. (1982). The development of addition and subtraction problem solving. In T.P. Carpenter, J.M. Moser & T.A. Romberg (Eds.), *Addition and Subtraction: A Cognitive Perspective* (pp. 10–24). New York: Lawrence Erlbaum.

Carraher, T.N. (1988). Investigando as Relacoes Entre Peso e Volume para Compreender o Conceito de Densidade [Investigations of the relationship between volume and weight and the understanding of the concept of density]. Mestrado em Psicologia, Universidade Federal de Pernambuco, Recife, Brazil. Unpublished Research Report.

Cheng, P.W., & Holyoak, K.J. (1985). Pragmatic reasoning schemas. *Cognitive Psychology, 18*, 293–328.

Chi, M.T.H., Slotta, J.D., & de Leeuw, N. (1994). From things to processes: A theory of conceptual change for learning scientific concepts. *Learning and Instruction, 4*, 27–44.

Desli, D. (1999). Children's Understanding of Intensive Quantities. Department of Child Development and Learning, Institute of Education, University of London. Unpublished PhD Thesis.

Dickson, L. (1989). Area of a rectangle. In D.C. Johnson (Ed.), *Children's Mathematical Frameworks 8–13: A Study of Classroom Teaching*. Windson: NFER Nelson.

Erickson, G., & Tiberghien, A. (1985). Heat and temperature. In R. Driver; E. Guesne & A. Tiberghien (Eds.), *Children's Ideas in Science* (pp. 33–51). Milton Keynes: Open University Press.

Gelman, R., & Gallistel, C.R. (1978). *The Child's Understanding of Number*. Cambridge, MA: Harvard University Press.

Lancy, D.F. (1983). *Cross-cultural Studies in Cognition and Mathematics*. New York: Academic Press.

Lave, J. (1988). *Cognition in Practice*. Cambridge: Cambridge University Press.

Luria, A. (1973). *The Working Brain*. Harmondsworth: Penguin.

Hatano, G. (1997). Learning arithmetic with an abacus. In T. Nunes & P.E. Bryant (Eds.), *Learning and Teaching Mathematics. An International Perspective.* (pp. 209–232). Hove, UK: Psychology Press.

Marton, F., & Neuman, D. (1990). Constructivism, phenomenology, and the origin of arithmetic skills. In L.P. Steffe & T. Wood (Eds.), *Transforming Young Children's Mathematics Education. International Perspectives* (pp. 62–75). Hillsdale, NJ: Lawrence Erlbaum.

Noss, R. (1986). Constructing a conceptual framework for elementary algebra through LOGO programming. *Educational Studies in Mathematics, 17*, 335–357.

Noss, R. (1995). Meaning mathematically with computers. In T. Nunes & P. Bryant (Eds.), *How do Children Learn Mathematics?* (in press) Falmer, UK: Lawrence Erlbaum.

Noss, R. (1997). Meaning mathematically with computers. In. T. Nunes & P.E. Bryant (Eds.), *Learning and Teaching Mathematics. An International Perspective* (pp. 289–314). Hove, UK: Psychology Press.

Nunes, T. (1993). Learning mathematics: Perspectives from everyday life. In R.B. Davis & C.A. Maher (Eds.), *Schools, Mathematics, and the World of Reality* (pp. 61–78). Needham Heights, MA: Allyn and Bacon.

Nunes, T., & Bryant, P.E. (1995). Do situations affect children's understanding of commutativity of multiplication? *Mathematical Cognition*, in press.

Nunes, T., & Bryant, P.E. (1996). *Children Doing Mathematics*. Oxford, UK: Blackwell.

Nunes, T., Light, P., & Mason, J. (1993). Tools for thought: The measurement of length and area. *Learning and Instruction, 3*, 39–54.

Nunes, T., Light, P., Mason, J., & Allerton, M. (1994). Children's Understanding of Area. Institute of Education, Unpublished Research Report.

Nunes, T., & Moreno, C. (1995). What is Five Plus Eight? Deaf Children's Learning of Number Facts. Internal research report, Institute of Education, University of London.

Nunes, T., Schliemann, A.D., & Carraher, D.W. (1993). *Street Mathematics and School Mathematics*. New York: Cambridge University Press.

Piaget, J. (1950). *The Psychology of Intelligence*. London: Routledge and Kegan Paul.

Scribner, S., & Cole, M. (1981). *The Psychology of Literacy*. Cambridge, MA: Harvard University Press.

Vergnaud, G. (1983). Multiplicative structures. In R. Lesh & M. Landau (Eds.), *Acquisition of Mathe-matics Concepts and Processes* (pp. 128–175). London: Academic Press.

Vergnaud, G. (1985). Concepts et schemes dans une theorie operatoire de la representation. *Psychol-ogie Française*, *30*, 245–252.

Vosniadou, S. (1994). Capturing and modeling the process of conceptual change. *Learning and Instruction*, 4, 45–70.

Vygotsky, L.S. (1978). *Mind in Society*. Cambridge, MA: Harvard University Press.

Whorf, B.L. (1956). Science and linguistics. In J.B. Carrol (Ed.). *Language, Thought, and Reality*. Cambridge, MA: MIT Press.

Chapter 6

Andersson, B., Emanuelsson, J., & Zetterqvist, A. (1993a). Naturorienterande ämnen: Materia. Huvudrapport. Den Nationella Utvärderingen av Grundskolan, Våren 1992 [Natural science subjects: Materia. Main report. The national evaluation of the comprehensive school, spring 1992]. Stockholm: Liber.

Andersson, B., Emanuelsson, J., & Zetterqvist, A. (1993b). Naturorienterande ämnen: Ekologi och Människkroppen. Huvudrapport. Den Nationella Utvärderingen av Grundskolan, Våren 1992 [Natural science subjects: Ecology and the human body. Main report. The national evaluation of the comprehensive school, spring 1992]. Stockholm: Liber.

Bakurst, D. (1995). On the social constitution of mind: Bruner, Ilyenkov and the defence of cultural psychology. *Mind, Culture, and Activity*, *2* (3), 158–171.

Barsalou, L. (1992). *Cognitive Psychology*. Hillsdale, NJ: Erlbaum.

Bliss, J. (1989). A common sense theory of motion: A theoretical and empirical approach. In P. Adey; J. Bliss; J. Head & M. Shayer (Eds.), *Adolescent Development and School Science* (pp. 266–272). Lewes: Falmer.

Bliss, J., & Ogborn, J.A. (1993). A common sense theory of motion: Issues of theory and method-ology examined through a pilot study. In P. Black & A. Lucas (Eds.), *Children's Informal Ideas About Science* (pp. 158–172). London: Croom Helm.

Bruner, J. (1986). *Actual Minds, Possible Worlds*. Cambridge, MA: Harvard University Press.

Bruner, J. (1990). *Acts of Meaning*. Cambridge, MA: Harvard University Press.

Bruner, J., Goodnow, J., & Austin, G. (1956). *A Study of Thinking*. New York: Wiley.

Caravita, S., & Halldén, O. (1994). Reframing the problem of conceptual change. *Learning and Instruction*, *4* (1), 89–111.

Chaiklin, S., & Lave., J. (Eds.). (1993). *Understanding Practice. Perspectives on Activity and Context*. Cambridge, MA: Cambridge University Press.

Chi, M., Slotta, J.D., & de Leeuw, N. (1994). From things to processes: A theory of conceptual change for learning science concepts. *Learning and Instruction*, *4* (1), 27–43.

Driver, R., Guesne, E., & Tiberghien, A. (1985). *Children's Ideas in Science*. Milton Keynes: Open University Press.

Edwards, D., & Mercer, N. (1987). *Common Knowledge*. London: Methuen.

Edwards, D., & Potter, J. (1992). *Discursive Psychology*. London: Sage.

Gentner, D., & Stevens, A.L. (Eds.), (1983). *Mental Models*. Hillsdale, NJ: Erlbaum.

Gilbert, J., & Watts, M. (1983). Concepts, misconceptions and alternative conceptions: Changing perspectives in science education. *Studies in Science Education*, *10*, 61–98.

Harré, R., & Gillett, G. (1994). *The Discursive Mind*. London: Sage.

Johnson-Laird, P. (1983). *Mental Models*. Cambridge: Cambridge University Press.

Keller, C., & Keller, J.D. (1993). Thinking and acting with iron. In S. Chaiklin & J. Lave (Eds.), *Understanding Practice. Perspectives on Activity and Context* (pp. 125–143). Cambridge, UK: Cambridge University Press.

Lakoff, G. (1987). *Women, Fire, and Dangerous Things.* Chicago: The University of Chicago Press.

Lave, J. (1988). *Cognition in Practice.* Cambridge, MA: Cambridge University Press.

Lemke, J.L. (1990). *Talking Science: Language, Learning and Values.* Norwood, NJ: Ablex.

Levine, J.M., & Resnick, L.B. (1993). Social foundations of cognition. *Annual Review of Psychology, 44,* 585–612.

McCloskey, M. (1983). Naive theories of motion. In D. Gentner & A.L. Stevens (Eds.), *Mental Models* (pp. 299–324). Hillside, NJ: Lawrence Erlbaum.

Neisser, U. (1967). *Cognitive Psychology.* New York: Appleton-Century-Crofts.

Neisser, U. (1976). *Cognition and Reality.* San Francisco: Freeman.

Pea, R. (1993). Learning scientific concepts through material and social activities: Conversational analysis meets conceptual change. *Educational Psychologist, 28* (3), 265–277.

Pfundt, H., & Duit, R. (1991). *Bibliography: Students' Alternative Frameworks and Science Education* (4th ed.). Kiel: Institute for Science Education.

Resnick, L.B., Levine, J.M., & Teasley, S.D. (Eds.), (1997). *Perspectives on Socially Shared Cognition.* Washington, DC: American Psychological Association.

Resnick, L., Säljö, R., Pontecorvo, C., & Burge, B. (Eds.). (1997). *Discourse, Tools and Reasoning. Essays on Situated Cognition.* New York: Springer-Verlag.

Rogoff, B. (1984). Introduction: Thinking and learning in social context. In B. Rogoff & J. Lave (Eds.). *Everyday Cognition: Its Development in Social Context* (pp. 1–8). Cambridge, MA: Harvard University Press.

Rogoff, B. (1990). *Apprenticeship in Thinking.* New York: Oxford University Press.

Rommetveit, R. (1992). Outlines of a dialogically based social-cognitive approach to human cognition and communication. In A. Heen Wold (Ed.), *The Dialogical Alternative — Towards a Theory of Language and Mind* (pp. 19–44). Oslo: Scandinavian University Press.

Säljö, R. (1994). Minding action. Conceiving of the world versus participating in cultural practices. *Nordisk Pedagogik, 2* (2), 71–80.

Vosniadou, S. (Ed.). (1994). Conceptual change in the physical sciences. *Learning and Instruction, 4* (1). Special issue.

Vosniadou, S. (Ed.). (1994). Introduction. *Learning and Instruction, 4* (1), 3–6.

Vygotsky, L.S. (1986). *Thought and Language.* [A. Kozulin, Trans.] Cambridge, MA: MIT Press.

Wertsch, J. (1985). *Vygotsky and the Social Formation of Mind.* Cambridge, MA: Harvard University Press.

Wertsch, J. (1991). *Voices of the Mind.* Cambridge, MA.: Harvard University Press.

Chapter 7

Ball, T., Farr, J., & Hanson, R.L. (1989). *Political Innovation and Conceptual Change.* Cambridge, UK and New York: Cambridge University Press.

Baron-Cohen, S. (1995). *Mindblindness: An Essay on Autism and Theory of Mind.* Cambridge, MA and London: The MIT Press.

Becker, H.S. (Ed.) (1968). *Institutions and the Person.* Chicago: Aldine.

Becker, H.S., & McCall, M. (Eds.) (1990). *Symbolic Interaction and Cultural Studies.* Chicago: University of Chicago Press.

Berger, P., & Luckmann, T. (1972). *The Social Construction of Reality.* Harmondsworth: Penguin.

Bernstein, B. (1971–1990). *Class, Codes, and Control,* Vols 1–4. London: Routledge & Kegan Paul.

Blau, P. (1964). *Exchange and Power in Social Life*. New York: Wiley.

Bourdieu, P. (1991). *Raisons Pratiques: Sur la Theorie de l'Action*. Paris: Editions du Seuil.

Bourdieu, P. (1994). *Language and Symbolic Power*. Cambridge, UK: Polity Press.

Bourdieu, P., & Passeron, J.-P. (1977). *Reproduction in Education, Society, and Culture*. London: Sage.

Bruner, J. (1987). The transactional self. In J. Bruner & H. Haste (Eds.), *Making Sense: The Child's Construction of the World* (pp. 81–96). London & New York: Methuen.

Burns, B. (Ed.), (1992). *Percepts, Concepts, and Categories: The Representation and Processing of Information*. Amsterdam: North-Holland.

Button, G. (Ed.), (1991). *Ethnomethodology and the Human Sciences*. Cambridge, UK: University of Cambridge University Press.

Comte, A. (1907). *Cours de Philosophie Positive*. Paris: Schleicher.

Cosmides, L., Tooby, J., & Barkow, J. (1992). Introduction: Evolutionary psychology and conceptual integration. In J. Barkow, J. Cosmides & J. Tooby (Eds.), *The Adapted Mind*. Oxford: Oxford University Press.

Davis, K. (1949). *Human Society*. New York: Macmillan.

Deloache, J.S., & Brown, A.L. (1987). The early emergence of planning skills in children. In J. Bruner & H. Haste (Eds.), *Making Sense: The Child's Construction of the World*. (pp. 108–130). London & New York: Methuen.

Durkheim, E. (1951 [1897]). *Suicide*. New York: Free Press.

Durkheim, E. (1956). *Education and Society*. Glencoe, IL: Free Press.

Durkheim, E. (1964). *The Division of Labor*. New York: Free Press.

Durkheim, E., & Mauss, M. (1965 [1915]). *Primitive Classifications*. Chicago: University of Chicago Press.

Feldman, C.F. (1987). Thought from language: The linguistic construction of cognitive representations. In J. Bruner & H. Haste (Eds.), *Making Sense: The Child's Construction of the World* (pp. 131–146). London and New York: Methuen.

Feyerabend, P. (1978). *Against Method: Outline of an Anarchistic Theory of Knowledge*. London: Verso.

Fischer, D.H., Pazzani, M.J., & Langley, P. (Eds.), (1991). *Concept Formation: Knowledge and Experience in Unsupervised Learning*. San Mateo, CA: Morgan Kaufmann.

Fiske, S.T., & Taylor, S.E. (1984). *Social Cognition*. New York: Random House.

Gardner, H. (1991). *The Unschooled Mind: How Children Think and How School Should Teach*. New York: Basic Books.

Garfinkel, H. (1958). Rational properties of scientific and common sense activities. *American Journal of Sociology. 64.*

Garfinkel, H. (1967). *Studies in Ethnomethodology*. Englewood Cliffs, NJ: Prentice-Hall.

Gilbert, J.K., Watts, D.M., & Osborne, R.J. (1985). Eliciting student views using an interview-about-instances technique. In L.H.T. West & A.L. Pines (Eds.), *Cognitive Structure and Conceptual Change* (pp. 11–27). New York/London/Tokyo: Academic Press.

Giroux, H. (1989). *Critical Pedagogy, the State, and Cultural Struggle*. Albany: SUNY Press.

Goffman, E. (1959). *The Presentation of Self in Everyday Life*. Garden City, NY: Doubleday.

Goffman, E. (1967). *Interaction Ritual: Essays on Face-to-face Behavior*. Chicago: Aldine.

Gramsci, A. (1985). *Selections From the Cultural Writings*. London: Lawrence & Wishart.

Hacking, I. (1990). *The Taming of Chance*. Cambridge, UK: Cambridge University Press.

Halldén, O. (1994). Conceptual Change and Contextualization. Paper presented at the Symposium on Conceptual Change, Jena, Germany: Friedrich-Schiller University.

Harré, R. (1972). *The Explanation of Social Behavior*. Totowa, NJ: Rowman & Littlefield.

Homans, G.C. (1961). *Social Behavior*. London: Routledge and Kegan Paul.

Johansson, B., Marton, F., & Svensson, L. (1985). An approach to describing learning as change between qualitatively different conceptions. In H.T. West & A.L. Pines (Eds.), *Cognitive Structure and Conceptual Change* (pp. 233–257). New York / London / Tokyo: Academic Press.

Kalekin-Fishman, D. (1987). Performances and accounts: The social construction of the kindergarten experience. In: P. Adler & P. Adler (Eds.), *Sociological studies of child development*, (pp. 81–104) Vol. 2 .

Kalekin-Fishman, D. (1995). School regulations as a problem for a democratic society. In F. Geyer (Ed.), *Postmodernity, Alienation, and Ethnicity*. Connecticut: Westwood.

Keil, F.C. (1989). *Concepts, Kinds, and Cognitive Development*. Cambridge, MA: MIT Press.

Kelly, G.A. (1955). *The Psychology of Personal Constructs*. Vols 1 & 2. NY: W.W. Norton.

Kornblith, H. (Ed.), (1994). *Naturalizing Epistemology* (2nd ed.). Cambridge, MA and London: MIT Press.

Kroll, J.F., & Deutsch, F.M. (1992). Not just any category: The representation of the self in memory. In B. Burns (Ed.), *Percepts, Concepts, and Categories: The Representation and Processing of Information* (pp. 495–529). Amsterdam: North-Holland.

Kuhn, T.S. (1970). *The Structure of Scientific Revolutions*. Chicago: University of Chicago Press.

Levine, J.M., Resnick, L.B., & Higgins, E.T. (1993). Social foundations of cognition. *Annual Review of Psychology*, *44*, 585–612.

Levy, M. (1963). *Modernization and the Structure of Societies*. NJ: Princeton UIniversity Press.

Lortie, D. (1975). *Schoolteacher*. Chicago: University of Chicago.

Marx, K. (1974 [1857–1858]). *Grundrisse der Kritik der Politischen Oekonomie*. BerlIn Dietz Verlag.

McDowel!, J.H. (1994). *Mind and World*. Cambridge, MA: Harvard University Press.

Mead, G.H. (1934). *Mind, Self, and Society*. Chicago: University of Chicago Press.

Merton, R. (1968). *Social Theory and Social Structure*. NY: The Free Press.

Moore, W.E. (1963). *Man, Time, and Society*. NY: J. Wiley.

Norman, D.A., & Rumelhart, D.E. (1975). *Explorations in Cognition*. San Francisco, CA: W.H. Freeman.

Nunes, T. (1993). Learning mathematics: perspectives from everyday life. In R.B. Davis, & C.A. Maher (Eds.), *Schools, Mathematics, and the World of Reality* (pp. 61–78). Needham Heights, MA: Allyn and Bacon.

Nunes, T., Carraher, D.W., & Schliemann, A.D. (1993). *Street Mathematics and School Mathematics*. New York: Cambridge University Press.

Parsons, T. (1937). *The Structure of Social Action*. New York: McGraw–Hill.

Parsons, T. (1966). *Societies*. Englewood Cliffs, NJ: Prentice-Hall.

Parsons, T. (1977). *Social Systems and the Evolution of Action Theory*. NY: Free Press.

Peacocke, C. (1992). *A Study of Concepts*. Cambridge, MA: MIT Press.

Perkins, D.N., & Salomon, G. (1989). Are cognitive skills context-bound? *Educational Researcher*, *18* (1), 16–25.

Perner, J. (1991). *Understanding the Representational Mind*. Cambridge, MA and London, UK: MIT Press.

Pines, A.L. (1985). Towards a taxonomy of conceptual relations and the implications for the evaluation of cognitive structures. In L.H.T. West & A.L. Pines (Eds.), *Cognitive Structure and Conceptual Change* (pp. 101–116). New York / London / Tokyo: Academic Press.

Plato (n.d.) *The Works of Plato*. (Translated into English with analyses and introductions by B. Jowett) NY: Tudor Publishing Co.

Popkewitz, T. (1991). *A Political Sociology of Educational Reform*. NY: Teachers College Press.

Prigogine, I., & Stengers, I. (1984). *Order Out of Chaos: Man's New Dialogue with Nature*. Toronto: Bantam Books.

Quine, W.V. (1973). *The Roots of Reference*. LaSalle, IL: Open Court.

Salomon, G. (Ed.), (1993). *Distributed Cognitions*. Cambridge, UK: University of Cambridge Press.

Schuetz, A. (1967). *The Problems of Social Reality*, (Ed. and introduced by M. Nathanson). The Hague: Nijhoff.

Skocpol, T. (1979). *States and Social Revolutions*. Cambridge, UK: Cambridge University Press.

Smith, D. (1990). *The Conceptual Practices of Power: A Feminist Sociology of Knowledge*. Boston: Northeastern University Press.

Somers, M.R. (1995). What's political or cultural about political culture and the public sphere? Toward an historical sociology of concept formation. *Sociological Theory, 13* (2), 113–144.

Spencer, H. (1937). *First Principles*. London: Watts.

Spencer, H. (1945). *Education: Intellectual, Moral, Physical*. London: Watts.

Strike, K.A., & Posner, G.J. (1985). A conceptual change view of learning and understanding. In L.H.T. West & A.L. Pines (Eds.), *Cognitive Structure and Conceptual Change* (pp. 211–231). New York/London/Tokyo: Academic Press.

Stryker, S. (1980). *Symbolic Interaction: A Social Structural Version*. Menlo Park: Benjamin/Cummings.

Thagard, P. (1992). *Conceptual Revolutions*. Princeton, NJ: Princeton University Press.

Tilly, C. (Ed.), (1975). *The Formation of Nation States in Western Europe*. Princeton, NJ: Princeton University Press.

Vosniadou, S. (1994). Capturing and modeling the process of conceptual change. *Learning and Instruction, 4*, 45–69.

Voss, J.F., Perkins, D.N., & Siegal, J.W. (Eds.), (1991). *Informal Reasoning and Education*. Hillsdale, NJ: Erlbaum.

Voss, J.F., Wiley, J., & Carretero, M. (1995). Acquiring intellectual skills. *Annual Review of Psychology, 46*, 155–181.

Weber, M. (1947). *The Theory of Social and Economic Organization*, (Ed. with an introduction by T. Parsons). NY: Free Press.

White, R.T. (1985). Interview protocols and dimensions of cognitive structure. In L.H.T. West & A.L. Pines (Eds.), *Cognitive Structure and Conceptual Change* (pp. 51–59). New York / London / Tokyo: Academic Press.

Willis, P. (1977). *Learning to Labour*. Farnborough, UK: Saxon House.

Wittgenstein, L. (1958). *Philosophical Investigations* (translated by G.E.M. Anscombe). NY: Free Press.

Chapter 8

Ajello, A.M., & Bombi, A.S. (1988). Studi Sociali e Conoscenze Economiche. Un Curricolo per la Scuola Elementare [Social studies and economic knowledge. An economics curriculum for elementary school]. La Nuova Italia: Firenze.

Ajello, A.M., Bombi, A.S., Pontecorvo, C., & Zuccermaglio, C. (1986). Children's understanding of agriculture as an economic activity. *European Journal of Psychology of Education, 1*, 67–80.

Ajello, A.M., Bombi, A.S., Pontecorvo, C., & Zuccermaglio, C. (1987). Teaching economics in the primary school: The concepts of work and profit. *International Journal of Behavioral Development, 10*, 51–69.

Berti, A.E. (1991). Capitalism and socialism: How 7th graders understand and misunderstand the information presented in their geography textbooks. *European Journal of Psychology of Education, 6*, 411–421.

Berti, A.E. (1992). Acquisition of the concept of shop profit by third grade children. *Contemporary Educational Psychology, 17*, 1–7.

Berti, A.E. (1993). Fifth graders' ideas on bank functions and interest before and after a lesson on banking. *European Journal of Psychology of Education, 8*, 183–193.

Berti, A.E., & Bombi, A.S. (1981). The development of the concept of money and its value: A longitudinal study. *Child Development, 46,* 77–91.

Berti, A.E., & Bombi, A.S. (1988). *The Child's Construction of Economics.* Cambridge, UK: Cambridge University Press.

Berti, A.E., Bombi, A.S., & De Beni, R. (1986). Acquiring economic notions: Profit. *International Journal of Behavioral Development, 9,* 15–29.

Berti, A.E., Bombi, A.S., & Lis, A. (1982). The child's conceptions about means of production and their owners. *European Journal of Social Psychology, 12,* 221–39.

Berti, A.E., & De Beni, R. (1988). Prerequisites for the concept of profit: Logic and memory. *British Journal of Developmental Psychology, 12,* 221–39.

Caravita, S., & Halldén, O. (1994). Reframing the problem of conceptual change. *Learning and Instruction, 4,* 89–111.

Carey, S. (1985). *Conceptual Change in Childhood.* Cambridge, MA: MIT Press.

Carey, S. (1991). Knowledge acquisition: Enrichment or conceptual change? In S. Carey & R. Gelman (Eds.), *The Epigenesis of Mind. Essays on Biology and Cognition* (pp. 257–291). Hillsdale, NJ: Erlbaum.

Case, R. (1985). *Intellectual Development. Birth to Adulthood.* New York: Academic Press.

Champagne, A., Klopfer, L.E., & Anderson, J.H. (1980). Factors influencing the learning of classical mechanics. *American Journal of Physics, 48,* 1074–1079.

Chi, M., Glaser, R., & Rees, E. (1982). Expertise in problem solving. In R. Sternberg (Ed.), *Advances in the Psychology of Human Intelligence,* Vol. 1. Hillsdale, NJ: Erlbaum.

Chinn, C.A., & Brewer, W.F. (1993). The role of anomalous data in knowledge acquisition: A theoretical framework and implication for science instruction. *Review of Educational Research, 63,* 1–49.

Confrey, J. (1990), A review of the research on student conceptions in mathematics, science and programming. *Review of Research in Education, 16,* 3–56.

Delval, J. (1994). Stages in the child's construction of social knowledge. In M. Carretero & Voss, J.F. (Eds.), *Cognitive and Instructional Processes in History and the Social Sciences* (pp. 77–102), Hillsdale, NJ: Erlbaum.

Eylon, B., & Linn, M.C. (1988) Learning and instruction: An examination of four research perspectives in science education. *Review of Educational Research, 58,* 251–301.

Fisher, K. (1980). A theory of cognitive development: The control and construction of hierarchies of skills. *Psychological Review, 87,* 477–531.

Furnham, A. (1994). Young people's understanding of politics and economics, In M. Carretero & Voss, J.F. (Eds.), *Cognitive and Instructional Processes in History and the Social Studies.* Hillsdale, NJ: Erlbaum.

Furth, H.G. (1980). *The World of Grown-ups.* New York: Elsevier.

Gagné, R.M. (1985). *The Conditions of Learning* (4th ed.). New York: Holt, Rinehart and Winston.

Gardner, H. (1991). *The Unschooled Mind. How Children Think and How School Should Teach.* New York: Basic Books.

Jahoda, G. (1979). The construction of economic reality by some Glaswegian children. *European Journal of Social Psychology, 9,* 115–127.

Jahoda, G. (1981). The development of thinking about economic institution: The bank. *Cahiers de Psychologie Cognitive, 1,* 55–73.

Jahoda, G., & Woerdenbagch, A. (1982). The development of ideas about an economic institution: A cross-national replication. *British Journal of Social Psychology, 21,* 337–338.

Kuhn, T. S. (1970). *The Structure of Scientific Revolution.* Chicago: University of Chicago Press.

Leiser, D., Sevón, G. & Lévy, D. (1990). Children's economic socialization: summarizing the cross-cultural comparison of ten countries. *Journal of Economic Psychology. 11,* 591–614.

McCloskey, M., Washburn, A., & Felch, L. (1983). Intuitive physics: The straight-down belief and its origin. *Journal of Experimental Psychology, Learning, Memory and Cognition.*, *9*, 636–649.

Ng, S.H. (1982). Children's ideas about the bank and shop profit: Developmental stages and influences of cognitive contrast and conflict. *Journal of Economic Psychology*, *4*, 209–221.

Pfundt, H., & Duit, R. (1994). Bibliography. In *Students Alternative Frameworks and Science Education*, 4th ed. Kiel, Germany: Institute for Science Education at the University of Kiel.

Pintrich, P.R., Marx, R.W., & Boyle, R.A. (1993). Beyond cold conceptual change: The role of motivational beliefs and classroom contextual factors in the process of conceptual change. *Review of Educational Research*, *63*, 167–199.

Schug, M.C., & Walstad, W.B. (1991). Teaching and learning economics. In J.P. Shaver (Ed.), *Handbook of Research on Social Studies Teaching and Learning* (pp. 411–419). New York: Macmillan.

Spelke, E.S. (1991). Physical knowledge in infancy: Reflections on Piaget's theory. In S. Carey & R. Gelman (Eds.), *The Epigenesis of Mind. Essays on Biology and Cognition* (pp. 113–169). Hillsdale, NJ: Erlbaum.

Spiro, R.J., Feltovich, P.J., Coulson, R.L., & Anderson, D.K. (1989) Multiple analogies for complex concepts: antidotes for analogy-induced misconception in advanced knowledge acquisition. In S. Vosniadou & A. Ortony (Eds.), *Similarity and Analogical Reasoning*. Cambridge, UK: Cambridge University Press.

Strauss, A. (1952). The development and transformation of monetary meaning in the child. *American Sociological Review*, *17*, 275–286.

Strike, K.A., & Posner, G.J. (1985). A conceptual change view of learning and understanding. In L. West & L. Pines (Eds.), *Cognitive Structure and Conceptual Change*. New York: Academic Press.

Takahashi, K., & Hatano, G. (1994). Understanding the banking business in Japan: Is economic prosperity accompanied by economic literacy? *British Journal of Developmental Psychology*, *12*, 585–590.

Thagard, P. (1992). *Conceptual Revolutions*. Princeton: Princeton University Press.

Vosniadou, S. (1991). Designing curricula for conceptual restructuring: Lesson from the study of knowledge acquisition in astronomy. *Journal of Curriculum Studies*, *23*, 219–237.

Vosniadou, S. (1994). Capturing and modeling the process of conceptual change. *Learning and Instruction*, *4*, 45–69.

Vosniadou, S., & Brewer W.F. (1987). Theories of knowledge restructuring in development. *Review of Educational Research*, *57*, 51–67.

Vosniadou, S, & Brewer, W.F. (1992). Mental models of the Earth: A study of conceptual change in childhood. *Cognitive Psychology*, *24*, 535–585.

Vosniadou, S., & Brewer, W.F. (1994). Mental models of the day/night cycle. *Cognitive Science*, *18*, 123–183.

Chapter 9

Carey, S. (1985). *Conceptual Change in Childhood*. Cambridge, MA: MIT Press.

Carretero, M., Jacott, L., Limón, M., López-Manjón, A., & León, J.A. (1994). Historical knowledge: cognitive and instructional implications. In M. Carretero & J.F. Voss (Eds.), *Cognitive and Instructional Processes in History and the Social Sciences*. Hillsdale, NJ: LEA.

Carretero, M., & Limón, M. (1995). Uses of Evidence in History Experts. Paper presented at the Annual AERA Meeting , San Francisco, USA.

Chi, M.T.H., Glaser, R., & Farr, M.J. (1988). *The Nature of Expertise*. Hillsdale, NJ: LEA.

Chinn, C.A., & Brewer, W.F. (1993). The role of anomalous data in knowledge acquisition: A theoretical framework and implications for science education. *Review of Educational Research*, *63* (1), 1–49.

Dagher, Z.R. (1994). Does the use of analogies contribute to conceptual change? *Science Education, 78* (6), 601–614.

Dreyfus, A., Jungwirth, E., & Eliovitch, R. (1990). Applying the "cognitive conflict" strategy for conceptual change — some implications, difficulties and problems. *Science Education, 74* (5), 555–569.

Klayman, J.K., & Ha, Y. (1987). Confirmation, disconfirmation and information in hypothesis testing. *Psychological Review, 94* (2), 211–228.

Koslowski, B., & Maqueda, M. (1993). What is confirmation bias and when do people actually have it? *Merril Palmer Quarterly, 39* (1), 104–129.

Kuhn, D. (1989). Children and adults as intuitive scientists. *Psychological Review, 96* (4), 674–689.

Kuhn, D. (1993). Connecting scientific and informal reasoning. *Merril Palmer Quarterly, 39* (1), 74–103.

Kuhn, D., Amsel, E., & O'Loughlin, M. (1988). *The Development of Scientific Thinking Skills*. San Diego, CA: Academic Press.

Kuhn, D., Weinstock, M., & Flaton, R. (1994). Historical reasoning as theory-evidence coordination. In M. Carretero & J.F. Voss (Eds.), *Cognitive and Instructional Processes in History and the Social Sciences*. Hillsdale, NJ: LEA.

Limón, M. (1995). *Procesos de Razonamiento en la Solución de Problemas con Contenido Histórico* [Reasoning processes in historical problem solving]. Madrid: Universidad Autónoma.

Limón, M., & Carretero, M. (1998). Evidence evaluation and reasoning abilities in the domain of history: an empirical study. In J.F. Voss & M. Carretero (Eds). *Learning and Reasoning in History*. London: Woburn Press. (252–271)

Limón, M., & Carretero, M. (1997). Conceptual change and anomalous data: A case study in the domain of natural sciences. *European Journal of Psychology of Education, XII*, (2), 213–230.

Mynatt, C.R., Doherty, M.E., & Tweney, D.E. (1977). Confirmation bias in a simulated research environment: An experimental study of scientific inference. *Quarterly Journal of Experimental Psychology, 24*, 326–329.

Piaget, J. (1975). *L'équilibration des Structures Cognitives. Problème Central du Développement*. Paris: P.U.F. English translation [The development of thought: equilibration of cognitive structures]. New York: Viking Press.

Rouet, J.F., Britt, M.A., Mason, R.A. and Perfetti, C.A. (1996). Using multiple sources of evidence to reason about history. *Journal of Educational Psychology, 88* (3), 478–493.

Thagard, P. (1992). *The Structure of Conceptual Revolutions*. Cambridge, MA: MIT Press.

Vosniadou, S. (1991). Conceptual development in astronomy. In S.M. Glynn, R.S. Yeany & B.K. Britton (Eds.), *The Psychology of Learning Science*. Hillsdale, NJ: LEA.

Vosniadou, S. (1994). Capturing and modeling the process of conceptual change. *Learning and Instruction, 4* (1), 45–70.

Vosniadou, S., & Brewer, W.F. (1987). Theories of knowledge restructuring in development. *Review of Educational Research, 57* (1), 51–67.

Voss, J.F., Wiley, J., & Carretero, M. (1995). Acquiring intellectual skills. *Annual Review of Psychology, 46*, 155–181.

Wason, P.C. (1960). On the failure to eliminate hypothesis in a conceptual task. *Quarterly Journal of Experimental Psychology, 12*, 129–140.

Wineburg, S. (1991). Historical problem solving: A study of the cognitive processes used in the evaluation of documentary and pictorial evidence. *Journal of Educational Psychology, 83* (1), 73–87.

Chapter 10

Andersson, B. (1990). Pupils' conceptions of matter and its transformations (age 12–16). *Studies in Science Education, 18,* 53–85.

Chi, M.T.H. (1992). Conceptual change within and across ontological categories: Examples from learning and discovery in science. In R. Giere (Ed.), *Cognitive Models of Science.* Minnesota Studies in the Philosophy of Science. Minneapolis: University of Minnesota Press.

Chi, M.T.H., Glaser, R., & Farr, M. (Eds.), (1988). *The Nature of Expertise.* Hillsdale, NJ: Erlbaum.

Chi, M.T.H., Slotta, J., & Leeuw, W. (1994). From things to processes: A theory of conceptual change for learning science concepts. *Learning and Instruction, 4* (1), 27–43.

Claxton, G. (1991). *Educating the Inquiring Mind. The Challenge for School Science.* London: Harvester.

Dickinson, D.K. (1987). The development of a concept of material kind. *Science Education, 71* (4), 615.

di Sessa, A. (1993). Towards an epistemology of physics. *Cognition and Instruction, 10* (2–3), 105–225.

Engel Clough, E., & Driver, R. (1986). A study of consistency in the use of students' conceptual frameworks across different task contexts. *Science Education, 70* (4), 473–496.

Ericsson, K.A., & Smith, J. (Eds.), (1991). *Toward a General Theory of Expertise.* Cambridge, MA: Cambridge University Press.

Glaser, R. (1992). Expert knowledge and processes of thinking. In D.F. Halpern (Ed.), *Enhancing Thinking Skills in the Sciences and Mathematics.* Hillsdale, NJ: Erlbaum.

Gómez, M.A., Pozo, J.I., & Sanz, A. (1995). Students' ideas on conservation of matter: Effects of expertise and context variables. *Science Education, 79* (1), 77–93.

Hashweh, M. (1988). Descriptive studies of students' conceptions of science. *Journal of Research in Science Teaching, 25,* 121–134.

Nussbaum, J. (1985). The particulate nature of matter in the gaseous phase. In R. Driver; E.Guesne & A. Tiberghien (Eds.), *Children's Ideas in Science.* Milton Keynes, UK: Open University Press.

Pfundt, H., & Duit, R. (1994). *Bibliography: Students' Alternative Frameworks and Science Education.* Fourth Edition. Kiel: Institute for Science Education.

Posner, F.J., Strike, K.A., Hewson, P.W., & Gertzog, W.A. (1982). Accommodation of a scientific conception: Toward a theory of conceptual change. *Science Education, 66* (2), 211–227.

Pozo, J.I., & Carretero, M. (1992). Causal theories and reasoning strategies by experts and novices in Mechanics. In A. Demetriou, M. Shayer & A. Efklides (Eds.), *Neopiagetian Theories of Cognitive Development: Implications and Applications,* London: Routledge Kegan Paul.

Pozo, J.I., & Gómez Crespo, M.A. (1998). *Aprender y enseñar ciencia* Madrid: Morata [To learn and to teach science].

Pozo, J.I., Pérez Echeverría, M.P., Sanz, A., &. Limón, M. (1992). Las ideas de los alumnos sobre la ciencia como teorías implícitas [Students' ideas about science as implicit theories]. *Infancia y Aprendizaje, 57,* 3–22.

Rollnick, M., & Rutherford, M. (1990). African primary school teachers — what ideas do they hold on air and air pressure? *International Journal Science Education, 12* (1), 101–113.

Spada, H. (1994). Conceptual change or multiple representations? *Learning and Instruction, 4* (1), 113–116.

Stavy, R. (1988). Children's conception of gas. *International Journal of Science Education, 10* (5), 533–560.

Vosniadou, S. (1994). Capturing and modeling the process of conceptual change. *Learning and Instruction, 4* (1), 45–69.

Vosniadou, S., & Brewer, W.F. (1992). Mental models of the earth: a study of conceptual change in childhood. *Cognitive Psychology, 24,* 535–585.

Chapter 11

Behr, M., Harel, G., Post, T., & Lesh, R. (1992). Rational number, ratio and proportion. In D.A. Grouws (Ed.), *Handbook of Research on Mathematics Teaching and Learning* (pp. 296–333). New York: Macmillan.

Cobb, P., Yackel, E., & Wood, T. (1992). A constructivist alternative to the representational view of mind in mathematics education. *Journal for Research in Mathematics Education, 23* (1), 2–33.

Gravemeijer, K.P.E. (1994). *Developing Realistic Mathematics Education.* Utrecht: Freudenthal Institute, University of Utrecht.

Davis, R.B. (1989). The culture of mathematics and the culture of schools. *Journal of Mathematical Behavior, 8,* 143–160.

De Corte, E., Greer, B., & Verschaffel, L. (in press). Psychology of mathematics. In D. Berliner & R. Calfee (Eds.), *Handbook of Educational Psychology.* New York: MacMillan.

De Corte, E., & Verschaffel, L. (1985). Beginning first graders' initial representation of arithmetic word problems. *Journal of Mathematical Behavior, 4,* 3–21.

De Corte, E., & Verschaffel, L. (1989). Teaching word problems in the primary school. What research has to say to the teacher. In B. Greer & G. Mulhern (Eds.), *New Developments in Teaching Mathematics* (pp. 85–106). London: Routledge.

Freudenthal, H. (1991). *Revisiting Mathematics Education.* Dordrecht, The Netherlands: Kluwer.

Greer, B. (1993). The modeling perspective on world problems. *Journal of Mathematical Behavior, 12,* 239–250.

Hamers, J.H.M., Sijtsma, K., & Ruijssenaars, A.J.J.M. (1993). *Learning Potential Assessment: Theoretical, Methodological and Practical Issues.* Amsterdam/Lisse: Swets & Zeitlinger.

Kilpatrick, J. (1987). Problem formulating: Where do good problems come from? In A.H. Schoenfeld (Ed.), *Cognitive Science and Mathematics Education* (pp. 123–147). Hillsdale, NJ: Erlbaum.

Nesher, P. (1980). The stereotyped nature of school word problems. *For the Learning of Mathematics, 1,* 41–48.

Nunes, T., Schliemann, A.D., & Carraher, D.W. (1993). *Street Mathematics and School Mathematics.* Cambridge, UK: Cambridge University Press.

Reusser, K. (1988). Problem solving beyond the logic of things: Contextual effects on understanding and solving word problems. *Instructional Science, 17,* 309–338.

Ruijssenaars, A.J.J.M., & Hamers, J.H.M. (1994). Learning potential. In T. Husen & T.N. Postlethwaite (Eds.), *The International Encyclopaedia of Education,* 2nd ed. (pp. 3312–3315). Oxford: Pergamon.

Sälö, R. (1991). Learning and mediation. Fitting reality into a table. *Learning and Instruction, 1,* 261–273.

Schoenfeld, A.H. (1991). On mathematics as sense-making: An informal attack on the unfortunate divorce of formal and informal mathematics. In J.F. Voss, D.N. Perkins & J.W. Segal (Eds.), *Informal Reasoning and Education* (pp. 311–343). Hillsdale, NJ: Erlbaum.

Silver, E.A., Shapiro, L.J., & Deutsch, A. (1993). Sense making and the solution of division problems involving remainders: An examination of middle school students' solution processes and their interpretations of solutions. *Journal for Research in Mathematics Education, 24,* 117–135.

Treffers, A. (1987). *Three Dimensions. A Model of Goals and Theory Description in Mathematics Education.* The Wiskobas project. Dordrecht, The Netherlands: Reidel.

Verschaffel, L., & De Corte, E. (1997a). Word problems: A verhicle for authentic mathematical understanding and problem solving in the primary school? In P. Bryant & T. Nunes (Eds.), *Learning and Teaching Mathematics: An International Perspective.* Hove, UK: Psychology Press.

Verschaffel, L., & De Corte, E. (1997b). Teaching realistic mathematical modelling in the elementary school. A teaching experiment with fifth-graders, *Journal of Research in Mathematics Education*, *28*, 577–601.

Verschaffel, L., De Corte, E., & Lasure, S. (1994). Realistic considerations in mathematical modeling of school arithmetic word problems. *Learning and Instruction*, *4*, 273–294.

Vosniadou, S. (1994). Introduction to the special issue on "Conceptual change in the physical sciences". *Learning and Instruction*, *4*, 3–6.

Vygotsky, L.S. (1962). *Thought and Language*. Cambridge, MA: MIT Press.

Chapter 12

Anderson, R.C., & Pearson, P.D. (1984). A schema-theoretic view of basic processes in reading comprehension. In P.D. Pearson (Ed.), *Handbook of Reading Research* (pp. 255–291). New York, London: Longman.

Baker, L. (1985). How do we know when we don't understand? Standards for evaluating text comprehension. In D.L. Forrest-Pressley, G.E. MacKinnon, & T.G. Waller (Eds.), *Metacognition, Cognition, and Human Performance. Vol 1: Theoretical Perspectives* (pp. 155–205). Orlando, FL: Academic Press.

Beveridge, M. (1985). The development of young children's understanding of the process of evaporation. *British Journal of Educational Psychology*, *55*, 84–90.

Brewer, W.F., & Nakamura, G.V. (1984). The nature and functions of schemas. In R.S. Wyer & T.K. Srull (Eds.), *Handbook of Social Cognition*, Vol. 1 (pp. 119–160). Hillsdale, NJ: Erlbaum.

Brown, J.S., Collins, A., & Duguid, P. (1989). Situated cognition and the culture of learning. *Educational Researcher*, *18* (1), 32–42.

Caravita, S., & Halldén, O. (1994). Re-framing the problem of conceptual change. Learning and Instruction, *4* (1), 89–111.

Carey, S. (1985). *Conceptual Change in Childhood*. Cambridge, MA: MIT Press.

Carey, S. (1991). Knowledge acquisition-enrichment or conceptual change? In S. Carey & R. Gelman (Eds.), *The Epigenesis of Mind: Essays on Biology and Cognition* (pp. 252–292). Hillsdale, NJ: Erlbaum.

Chi, M.T.H. (1992). Conceptual change within and across ontological categories: Examples from learning and discovery science. In R.N. Giere (Ed.), *Cognitive Models of Science* (pp. 129–186). Minnesota studies in the philosophy of science. Minneapolis, MI: University of Minnesota Press.

Chi, M.T.H., Slotta, J.D., & de Leeuw, N. (1994). From things to processes: A theory of conceptual change for learning science concepts. *Learning and Instruction*, *4* (1), 27–43.

Clement, J.J. (1983). A conceptual model discussed by Galileo and used intuitively by physics students. In D. Gentner & A.L. Stevens (Eds.), *Mental Models* (pp. 325–339). Hillsdale, NJ: Erlbaum.

Denis, M. (1982). Images and semantic representations. In J.F. Le Ny & W. Kintsch (Eds.), *Language and Comprehension* (pp. 17–27). Amsterdam: North-Holland.

di Sessa, A. (1988). Knowledge in pieces. In G. Forman & P.B. Pufall (Eds.), *Constructivism in the Computer Age* (pp. 49–70). Hillsdale, NJ: Erlbaum.

di Sessa, A. (1993). Towards an epistemology of physics. *Cognition and Instruction*, *10* (2 & 3), 105–225.

Driver, R., & Easley, J. (1978). Pupils and paradigms: A review of literature related to concept development in adolescent science students. *Studies in Science Education*, *5*, 61–84.

Duit, R. (1994). Conceptual Change Approaches in Science Education. Paper presented at the Symposium on Conceptual Change, University of Jena, Germany.

Duncker, K. (1935). *Zur Psychologie des Produktiven Denkens*. Berlin: Springer.

Gilbert, J. K., & Watts, M. (1983). Concepts, misconceptions, and alternative conceptions: Changing perspectives in science education. *Studies in Science Education, 7*, 107–120.

Glenberg, A.M., Wilkinson, A.C. & Epstein, W. (1982). The illusion of knowing: Failure in the self-asssessment of comprehension. *Memory and Cognition, 10*, 597–602.

Greenspan, S.L. (1986). Semantic flexibility and referential specificity of concrete nouns. *Journal of Memory and Language, 25*, 539–557.

Halldén, O. (1990). Questions asked in common sense contexts and in scientific contexts. In P.L. Lijnse, P. Licht, W. de Vos & A.J. Waarlo (Eds.), *Relating Macroscopic Phenomena to Microscopic Particles* (pp.119–130). Utrecht: CD-B Press.

Johnson-Laird, P.N. (1989). Mental Models. In M.I. Posner (Ed.), *Foundations of Cognitive Science* (pp. 469–499). London: Bradford.

Köhler, W. (1921). *Intelligenzprüfungen an Menschenaffen*. Berlin: Springer–Verlag.

Kuhn, D. (1989). Children and adults as intuitive scientists. *Psychological Review, 96* (4), 674–689.

Larkin, J.H. & Simon, H.A. (1987), Why a diagram is (sometimes) worth ten thousand words. *Cognitive Science, 11*, 65–99.

Mayer, R.E. (1994). Visual aids to knowledge construction: Building mental representations from pictures and words. In W. Schnotz & R.W. Kulhavy (Eds.), *Comprehension of Graphics*. Amsterdam: North-Holland.

McCloskey, M. (1983) Naive theories of motion. In D. Gentner & A.L. Stevens (Eds.), *Mental Models* (pp. 299–324). Hillsdale, NJ: Erlbaum.

Montgomery, H. (1984). Mental models and problem solving: Three challenges to a theory of restructuring and insight. *Scandinavian Journal of Psychology, 29*, 85–94.

Morrow, D.G., Greenspan, S.L., & Bower, G.H. (1987). Accessibility and situation models in narrative comprehension. *Journal of Memory and Language, 26*, 165–187.

Nunes, T. (1993). Learning mathematics: perspectives from everyday life. In R.B. Davis & C.A. Maher (Eds.), *Schools, Mathematics, and the World of Reality* (pp. 61–78). Needham Heights, MA: Allyn & Bacon.

Ohlson, S. (1984a). Restructuring revised — summary and critique of the Gestalt theory of problem solving. *Scandinavian Journal of Psychology, 25*, 65–78.

Ohlson, S. (1984b). Restructuring revised — an information processing theory of restructuring and insight. *Scandinavian Journal of Psychology, 25*, 117–129.

Palmer, S.E. (1978). Fundamental aspects of cognitive representation. In E. Rosch & B.B. Lloyd (Eds), *Cognition and Categorization* (pp. 259–303). Hillsdale, NJ: Erlbaum.

Perrig, W., & Kintsch, W. (1985). Propositional and situational representations of text. *Journal of Memory and Language, 24*, 503–518.

Pfundt, H., & Duit, R. (1991). *Bibliography: Students' Alternative Frameworks and Science Education* (3rd ed.). Kiel, Germany: Institute for Science Education.

Piaget, J. (1950). *The Psychology of Intelligence*. London: Routledge & Kegan Paul.

Piaget, J. (1985). *The Equilibration of Cognitive Structures*. Chicago: University of Chicago Press.

Pintrich, P.R., Marx, R.W., & Boyle, R.A. (1993). Beyond cold conceptual change: The role of motivational beliefs and classroom contextual factors in the process of conceptual change. *Review of Educational Research, 63* (2), 167–199.

Posner, G.J., Strike, K.A., Hewson, P.W., & Gertzog, W.A. (1982). Accommodation of a scientific conception: Toward a theory of conceptual change. *Science Education, 66*, 211–227.

Resnick, L.B., Levine, J.M., & Teasley, S.D. (Eds.) (1991). *Perspectives on Socially Shared Cognition*. Washington, DC: American Psychological Association.

Rowell, J.A., & Dawson, C.J. (1983). Laboratory counter-examples and the growth of understanding in science. *European Journal of Science Education, 5*, 203–215.

Rumelhart, D.E. (1980). Schemata: The building blocks of cognition. In R.J. Spiro, B.C. Bruce & W.F. Brewer (Eds.), *Theoretical Issues in Reading Comprehension* (pp. 33–58). Hillsdale, NJ: Erlbaum.

Rumelhart, D.E., & Norman, D.A. (1978). Accretion, tuning and restructuring: Three modes of learning. In J.W. Cotton & R.L. Klatzky (Eds.), *Semantic Factors in Cognition* (pp. 37–53). Hillsdale, NJ: Erlbaum.

Schnotz, W., Picard, E., & Hron, A. (1993). How do successful and unsuccessful learners use texts and graphics? *Learning and Instruction, 20* (3), 181–199.

Strike, K.A., & Posner, G. (1982). Conceptual change and science teaching. *European Journal of Science Education, 4*, 231–240.

van Dijk, T.A., & Kintsch, W. (1983). *Strategies of Discourse Comprehension*. New York: Academic Press.

Vosniadou, S. (Ed.) (1994a). Conceptual change in the physical sciences. *Learning and Instruction, 4* (1), (Special Issue).

Vosniadou, S. (1994b). Capturing and modeling the process of conceptual change. *Learning and Instruction, 4* (1), 45–69.

Vosniadou, S., & Brewer , W.F. (1987). Theories of knowledge restructuring in development. *Review of Educational Research, 57* (1), 51–67.

Vosniadou, S., & Brewer , W.F. (1992). Mental models of the earth. *Cognitive Psychology, 24* (4), 535–538.

Vosniadou, S., & Brewer , W.F. (1994). Mental models of the day/night cycle. *Cognitive Science, 18*, 123–183.

Vygotski, L.S. (1962). Development of scientific concepts in childhood. In E. Hanfman & G. Vakar (Eds.), *Thought and Language* (pp. 82–118). Cambridge, MA: MIT Press.

Walker, C.H., & Yekovich, F.R. (1984). Script-based inferences: Effects of text and knowledge variables on recognition memory. *Journal of Verbal Learning and Verbal Behavior, 23*, 357–370.

Wertheimer, M. (1925). Über Schlußprozesse im produktiven Denken. In *Drei Abhandlungen zur Gestalttheorie. Erlangen*: Verlag der Philosophischen Akademie.

White, B.Y., & Frederiksen, J.R. (1990). Causal model progressions as a foundation for intelligent learning environments. *Artificial Intelligence, 42*, 99–157.

Chapter 13

Bliss, J., Ogborn, J., & Whitelock, D. (1989). Secondary school pupils' common sense theories of motion. *International Journal of Science Education, 11*, 261–272.

De Kleer, J., & Brown, J.S. (1981). Mental models of physical mechanisms and their acquisition. In J.R. Anderson (Ed.), *Cognitive Skills and Their Acquisition*, Hillsdale, NJ: Erlbaum.

Driver, R., Guesne, E., & Tiberghien, A. (1985). *Children's Ideas in Science*. Milton Keynes, UK: Open University Press.

Gentner, D., & Stevens, A.L. (1983). *Mental Models*. Hillsdale, NJ: Erlbaum.

Glenberg, A.M., & Langston, W.E. (1992). Comprehension of illustrated text: Pictures help to build mental models. *Journal of Memory and Language, 31*, 129–151.

Hegarty, M., & Just, M.A. (1993). Constructing mental models of machines from text and diagrams. *Journal of Memory and Language, 32*, 717–742.

Hegarty, M., Just, M.A., & Morrison, I.R. (1988). Mental models of mechanical systems: Individual differences in qualitative and quantitative reasoning. *Cognitive Psychology, 20*, 191–236.

Johnson-Laird, P.N. (1983). *Mental Models*. Cambridge, UK: Cambridge University Press.

Kieras, D.E., & Bovair, S. (1984). The role of a mental model in learning to use a device. *Cognitive Science, 8*, 255–273.

Lowe, R.K. (1989). Search strategies and inference in the exploration of scientific diagrams. *Educational Psychology, 9*, 27–44.

Lowe, R.K. (1993). Constructing a mental representation from an abstract technical diagram. *Learning and Instruction, 3*, 157–179.

Lowe, R.K. (1994a, June). Background Knowledge and the Construction of a Situational Representation from a Diagram. Paper presented at the Construction of Knowledge in Verbal and Pictorial Environments Conference, Helsinki, Finland.

Lowe, R.K. (1994b). Selectivity in diagrams: Reading beyond the lines. *Educational Psychology, 14*, 467–491.

Lowe, R.K. (1995, August). Supporting Conceptual Change in the Interpretation of Meteorological Diagrams. Paper presented at the 6th European Conference for Research on Learning and Instruction, Nijmegen, Netherlands.

Mayer, R.E., & Gallini, J.K. (1990). When is an illustration worth ten thousand words? *Journal of Educational Psychology, 82*, 715–726.

Osborne, R.J., Bell, B.F., & Gilbert, J.K. (1983). Science teaching and children's views of the world. *European Journal of Science Education, 5*, 1–14.

Payne, S.J. (1991). A descriptive study of mental models. *Behaviour and Information Technology, 10*, 3–21.

Vosniadou, S. (1994). Capturing and modeling the process of conceptual change. *Learning and Instruction, 4*, 45–69.

White, B.Y., & Frederiksen, J.R. (1986). Intelligent tutoring systems based upon qualitative model evolutions. *Proceedings of the Fifth National Conference on Artificial Intelligence* (pp. 313–319), Philadelphia, PA.

Chapter 14

Ali, K.S. (1990). Instructiestrategieën voor het Activeren van Preconcepties [Instructional strategies to activate preconceptions]. Doctoral dissertation. Helmond: Wibro.

Anderson, R.C., & Pichert, J.W. (1978). Recall of previously unrecallable information following a shift in perspective. *Journal of Verbal Learning and Verbal Behavior, 17*, 1–12.

Ausubel, D.P. (1968). *Educational Psychology: A Cognitive View.* New York: Holt, Rinehart & Winston.

Becker, L.A. (1988). Computer-aided misconception-based intelligent tutoring and exercise generation. *Programmed Learning and Educational Technology, 25*, 67–73.

Biemans, H.J.A. (1989). Effecten van een metacognitief trainingsprogramma [Effects of a metacognitive training program]. *Tijdschrift voor Onderwijsresearch, 14*, 286–296.

Biemans, H.J.A. (1994). Activation of preconceptions as part of process-oriented instruction. In F.P.C.M. de Jong & B.H.A.M. van Hout-Wolters (Eds.), *Process-Oriented Instruction and Learning from Text* (pp. 27–36). Amsterdam: VU University Press.

Biemans, H.J.A. (1997). Fostering activation of prior knowledge and conceptual change. Doctoral dissertation. Nijmegen: University of Nijmegen.

Biemans, H.J.A., & Simons, P.R.J. (1992). Learning to use a word processor with concurrent computer-assisted instruction. *Learning and Instruction, 2*, 321–338.

Biemans, H.J.A., & Simons, P.R.J. (1995). How to use preconceptions? The CONTACT strategy dismantled. *European Journal of Psychology of Education, 10*, 243–259.

Biemans, H.J.A., & Simons, P.R.J. (1996). CONTACT-2: A computer-assisted instructional strategy for promoting conceptual change. *Instructional Science, 24*, 157–176.

Brown, D.E. (1992). Using examples and analogies to remediate misconceptions in physics: Factors influencing conceptual change. *Journal of Research in Science Teaching, 29,* 17–34.

Brown, J.S., Collins, A., & Duguid, P. (1989). Situated cognition and the culture of learning. *Educational Researcher, 18,* 32–42.

Chan, C. (1993). Effects of Conflict and Knowledge-Building Approach of Conceptual Change. Doctoral Dissertation. University of Toronto.

Chinn, C.A., & Brewer, W.F. (1993). The role of anomalous data in knowledge acquisition: A theoretical framework and implications for science education. *Review of Educational Research, 63,* 1–49.

Cobern, W.W. (1993, April). World View, Metaphysics, and Epistemology. Paper presented at the Annual Meeting of the National Association for Research in Science Teaching, Atlanta, USA.

De Jong, F.P.C.M. (1992). Zelfstandig Leren — Regulatie van het Leerproces en Leren Reguleren: Een Procesbenadering [Autonomous learning — regulation of the learning process and learning to regulate: a process approach]. Doctoral dissertation. Tilburg: Tilburg University.

De Jong, F.P.C.M., & Simons, P.R.J. (1990). Cognitive and metacognitive processes of self-regulated learning. In J.M. Pieters, P.R.J. Simons, & L. de Leeuw (Eds.), *Research on Computer-Based Instruction* (pp. 81–100). Lisse: Swets & Zeitlinger.

Dochy, F.J.R.C. (1992). Assessment of Prior Knowledge as a Determinant for Future Learning. Doctoral dissertation. Heerlen: Open University.

Duit, R. (1994, September). Conceptual Change Approaches in Science Education. Paper presented at the Symposium on Conceptual Change, Jena, Germany.

Eylon, B., & Linn, M.C. (1988). Learning and instruction: An examination of four research perspectives in science education. *Review of Educational Research, 58,* 251–301.

Gang, S. (1993). On students' preconceptions and a "special self-regulation". *Physics Teacher, 31,* 414–418.

Geddis, A.N. (1991, April). What to do About "Misconceptions": A Paradigm Shift. Paper presented at the Annual Meeting of the American Educational Research Association, Chicago, USA.

Goetz, E.T., Schallert, D.L., Reynolds, R.E., & Radin, D.I. (1983). Reading in perspective: What real cops and pretend burglars look for in a story. *Journal of Educational Psychology, 75,* 500–510.

Gunstone, R.F. (1988, April). Some Long-term Effects of Uninformed Conceptual Change. Paper presented at the Annual Meeting of the American Educational Research Association, New Orleans, USA.

Guzetti, B.J. et al. (1993). Promoting conceptual change in science: A comparative meta-analysis of instructional interventions from reading education and science education. *Reading Research Quarterly, 28,* 116–159.

Hand, B., & Treagust, D.F. (1991). Student achievement and science curriculum development using a constructive framework. *School Science and Mathematics, 91,* 172–176.

Happs, J.C., & Mansfield, H. (1989, March). Students' and Teachers' Perceptions of the Cognitive and Affective Outcomes of Some Lessons in Geometry. Paper presented at the Annual Meeting of the American Educational Research Association, San Francisco, USA.

Hegland, S., & Andre, T. (1992). Helping learners construct knowledge. *Educational Psychology Review, 4,* 223–240.

Hennessey, M.G. (1991). Analysis of Conceptual Change and Status Change in Sixth-Graders' Concepts of Force and Motion. Doctoral Dissertation. University of Wisconsin, Madison.

Hesse, J. (1989). From naive to knowledgeable. *Science Teacher, 56,* 55–58.

Hewson, P.W., & Hewson, M.G.A. (1984). The role of conceptual conflict in conceptual change and the design of science instruction. *Instructional Science, 13,* 1–13.

Jonassen, D.H. (1991). Objectivism versus constructivism: Do we need a new philosophical paradigm? *Educational Technology: Research and Development, 39,* 5–14.

Kelly, J.A. (1993). From Knowing Content to Constructing Knowledge: A Trend Analysis of Secondary Science Education, 1953–1992. Doctoral dissertation. University of North Texas.

Lederman, N.G. (1992). Student' and teachers' conceptions of the nature of science: A review of the research. *Journal of Research in Science Teaching, 29*, 331–359.

Linder, C.J. (1993). A challenge to conceptual change. *Science Education, 77*, 292–300.

Linn, M.C., & Songer, N.B. (1991). Teaching thermodynamics to middle school students: What are appropriate cognitive demands? *Journal of Research in Science Teaching, 28*, 885–918.

Lott, G.W. (1989). Case Studies in Conceptual Change: The Influence of Preconceptions and Aspects of the Task Environment. Doctoral Dissertation. Michigan State University.

Machiels-Bongaerts, M. (1993). Mobilizing Prior Knowledge in Text Processing: The Selective-Attention Hypothesis Versus the Cognitive Set-Point Hypothesis. Doctoral dissertation. Maastricht: University of Maastricht.

Maria, K., & McGinitie, W. (1987). Learning from texts that refute the reader's prior knowledge. *Reading Research and Instruction, 26*, 222–238.

Nisbet, J. (1989, July). Learning to Think — Thinking to Learn: The Curriculum Redefined. Background paper for the International Conference OECD, Paris, France.

Nussbaum, J., & Novick, S. (1982). Alternative frameworks, conceptual conflict and accommodation: Towards a principled teaching strategy. *Instructional Science, 11*, 183–200.

Pfundt, H., & Duit, R. (1994). *Students' Alternative Frameworks and Science Education.* Kiel: University of Kiel.

Pintrich, P.R., Marx, R.W., & Boyle, R.A. (1993). Beyond cold conceptual change: The role of motivational beliefs and classroom contextual factors in the process of conceptual change. *Review of Educational Research, 63*, 167–199.

Prawat, R.S. (1989). Promoting access to knowledge, strategy and disposition in students: A research synthesis. *Review of Educational Research, 59*, 1–41.

Reeve, R.A., Palincsar, A.S., & Brown, A.L. (1987). Everyday and academic thinking: Implications for learning and problem solving. *Journal of Curriculum Studies, 19*, 123–133.

Rice, D.C. et al. (1991, April). The Design and Validation of an Instrument to Identify Preservice Elementary Teachers' Intuitive and School Knowledge of the Concepts of Surface Area/Volume and States of Matter. Paper presented at the Annual Meeting of the National Association for Research in Science Teaching, Lake Geneva, USA.

Roth, K.J. (1985, April). Conceptual Change Learning and Student Processing of Science Texts. Paper presented at the Annual Meeting of the American Educational Research Association, Chicago, USA.

Saxena, A.B. (1991). The understanding of the properties of light by students in India. *International Journal of Science Education, 13*, 283–289.

Schmidt, H.G. (1982). *Activatie van Voorkennis, Intrinsieke Motivatie en de Verwerking van Tekst* [Activation of prior knowledge, intrinsic motivation and text processing]. Apeldoorn: Van Walraven.

Simons, P.R.J., & Kluvers, C. (1994). Tussen verantwoordelijkheid geven en nemen [Between giving and taking responsibility]. *Mesomagazine, 76*, 2–10.

Simons, P.R.J., & Verschaffel, L. (1992). Transfer: onderzoek en onderwijs [Transfer: research and education]. *Tijdschrift voor Onderwijsresearch, 17*, 3–16.

Spiro, R.J., Feltovich, P.J., Jacobson, M.J., & Coulson, R.L. (1991). Cognitive flexibility, constructivism, and hypertext: random access instruction for advanced knowledge acquisition in ill-structured domains. *Educational Technology, 5*, 24–33.

Strike, K.A., & Posner, G.J. (1985). A conceptual change view of learning and understanding. In L.H.T. West & A.L. Pines (Eds.), *Cognitive Structure and Conceptual Change* (pp. 211–231). Orlando: Academic Press.

Strike, K.A., & Posner, G.J. (1992). A revisionist theory of conceptual change. In R. Duschl & R. Hamilton (Eds.), *Philosophy of Science, Cognitive Psychology, and Educational Theory and Practice* (pp. 147–176). Albany, NY: SUNY.

Tergan, S.O., & Oestermeier, U. (1993, August). GELERIAT: A Multifunctional Generative Learning Environment for Promoting Conceptual Change in Elementary Mechanics. Paper presented at the AI-ED 93 World Conference, Edinburgh, Great Britain.

Tirosh, D., & Graeber, A.O. (1990). Evoking cognitive conflict to explore preservice teachers' thinking about division. *Journal for Research in Mathematics Education, 21*, 98–108.

Vermunt, J.D.H.M. (1992). Leerstijlen en Sturen van Leerprocessen in Het Hoger Onderwijs: Naar Procesgerichte Instructie in Zelfstandig Denken [Learning styles and regulation of learning in higher education: towards process-oriented instruction in autonomous thinking]. Doctoral dissertation. Lisse: Swets & Zeitlinger.

Vosniadou, S. (1994). Capturing and modeling the process of conceptual change. *Learning and Instruction, 4*, 45–69.

Voss, J.F. (1987). Learning and transfer in subject-matter learning: A problem-solving model. *International Journal of Educational Research, 11*, 607–622.

Watson, B. (1994). Switch off kids' science misconceptions. *Learning, 22*, 74–76.

Weinert, F.E. (1989). The impact of schooling on cognitive development: One hypothetical assumption, some empirical results, and many theoretical implications. *EARLI News, 8*, 3–7.

Chapter 15

Baird, J.R., & Northfield, J.R. (1992). *Learning from the PEEL Experience*. Melbourne, Australia: Monash University Printing Services.

Bereiter, C. (1985). Toward a solution of the learning paradox. *Review of Educational Research, 55*, 201–226.

Brewer, W.F., & Samarapungavan, A. (1991). Children's theories vs scientific theories. Differences in reasoning or differences in knowledge? In R.R. Hoffman & D.S. Palermo (Eds.), *Cognition and the Symbolic Processes: Applied and Ecological Perspectives* (pp. 209–232). Hillsdale, NJ: Erlbaum.

Brown, D.E., & Clement, J. (1989). Overcoming misconceptions via analogical reasoning: Abstract transfer versus explanatory model construction. *Instructional Science, 18*, 237–261.

Brown, J.S., Collins, & Duguid, P. (1989). Situated cognition and the culture of learning. *Educational Researcher, 18*, (1), 32–42.

Caravita, S., & Halldén, O. (1994). Re-framing the problem of conceptual change. *Learning and Instruction, 4*, 89–111.

Carey, S. (1985). *Conceptual Change in Childhood*. Cambridge, MA: MIT Press.

Carey, S. (1991). Knowledge acquisition: Enrichment or conceptual change? In S. Carey & R. Gelman (Eds.), *The Epigenesis of Mind. Essays on Biology and Cognition* (pp. 257–291). Hillsdale, NJ: Erlbaum.

Carmichael, P., Driver, R., Holding, B., Phillips, I., Twigger, D., & Watts, M. (1990). *Research on Students' Conceptions in Science: A Bibliography*. Leeds, UK: The University of Leeds.

Chi, M.T.H., Slotta, J.D., & de Leeuw, N. (1994). From things to processes: A theory of conceptual change for learning science concepts. *Learning and Instruction, 4*, 27–43.

Chinn, C.A., & Brewer, W.F. (1993). The role of anomalous data in knowledge acquisition: A theoretical framework and implications for science education. *Review of Educational Research, 63*, 1–49.

Clement, J. (1987). Overcoming misconceptions in physics: The role of anchoring intuitions and analogical validity. In J. Novak (Ed.), *Proceedings of the 2nd International Seminar Misconceptions and Educational Strategies*. Vol. III (pp. 84–87). Ithaca, NY: Cornell University Press.

Driver, R. (1983). *The Pupil as Scientist?* Milton Keynes, UK: Open University Press.

Driver, R. (1989). Changing conceptions. In P. Adey (Ed.), *Adolescent Development and School Science* (pp. 79–99). London: Falmer Press.

Driver, R, & Erickson, G. (1983). Theories-in-action: Some theoretical and empirical issues in the study of students' conceptual frameworks in science. *Studies in Science Education, 10*, 37–60

Driver, R., & Scott, P. (1995). Curriculum development as research: A constructivist approach to science curriculum development and teaching. In D. Treagust, R. Duit & B. Fraser (Eds.), *Improving Teaching and Learning in Science and Mathematics* (pp.94–108. New York: Teacher College Press, 1996.

Duit, R. (1991). On the role of analogies, similes and metaphors in learning science. *Science Education, 75*, 649–672.

Duit, R. (1993). Research on students' conceptions — developments and trends. In J. Novak (Ed.), *Proceedings of the Third International Seminar on Misconceptions and Educational Strategies in Science and Mathematics*. Ithaca, NY: Cornell University (distributed electronically).

Duit, R. (1995, August). Constraints on Knowledge Acquisition and Conceptual Change — the Case of Physics. Paper presented at the Symposium "Constraints on knowledge construction and conceptual change: A look across content domains", 6th European Conference for Research on Learning and Instruction: Nijmegen, The Netherlands.

Duit, R., & Confrey, J. (1995). Reorganizing the curriculum and teaching to improve learning in science and mathematics. In D. Treagust, R. Duit, & B. Fraser (Eds.), *Improving Teaching and Learning in Science and Mathematics*. New York: Teacher College Press, 1996.

Duit, R., & Glynn, S. (1992). Analogien und metaphern, brücken zum verständnis im schülerger-echten physikunterricht. In P. Häußler (Ed.), *Physikunterricht und Menschen-bildung* (pp. 223–250). Kiel, Germany: Institute for Science Education at the University of Kiel.

Duit, R., Treagust, D., & Fraser, B. (1995). Research on students' preinstructional conceptions. The driving force for improving teaching and learning in science and mathematics. In D. Treagust, R. Duit & B. Fraser (Eds.), *Improving Teaching and Learning in Science and Mathematics*. New York: Teacher College Press 1996.

Duschl, R.A., & Gitomer, D.H. (1991). Epistemological perspectives on conceptual change: Implications for educational practice. *Journal of Research in Science Teaching, 28*, 839–858.

Dykstra, D. (1992). Studying conceptual change. In R. Duit, F. Goldberg & H. Niedderer (Eds.), *Research in Physics Learning: Theoretical Issues and Empirical Studies* (pp. 40–58). Kiel, Germany: Institute for Science Education at the University of Kiel.

Festinger, L. (1962). *A Theory of Cognitive Dissonance*. Stanford, CA: Stanford University Press.

Gauld, C.F. (1988). The "pupil-as-scientist" metaphor in science education. *Research in Science Education, 18*, 35–41.

Glynn, S., Duit, R., & Thiele, R.(1995). Teaching science with analogies: A strategy for constructing knowledge. In S. Glynn & R. Duit (Eds.), *Learning Science in the Schools: Research Reforming Practice* (pp. 247–273). Mahwah, NJ: Lawrence Erlbaum.

Good, R., Wandersee, J., & St Julien, J. (1993). Cautionary notes on the appeal of the new "Isms" (constructivisms) in science education. In K. Tobin (Ed.), *The Practice of Constructivism in Science Education* (pp. 71–87). Washington, DC: AAAS Press.

Grandy, R.E. (1990, April). On the Strategic Use of History of Science in Education. Paper presented at the annual meeting of the American Educational Research Association, Boston, MA.

Grayson, D. (1995). Improving science and mathematics learning by concept substitution. In D. Treagust, R. Duit & B. Fraser (Eds.), *Improving Teaching and Learning in Science and Mathematics*. New York: Teacher College Press, (pp. 152–161), 1996.

Guzetti, B.J., & Glass, G.V. (1992, April). Promoting Conceptual Change in Science: A Comparative Meta-analysis of Instructional Interventions from Reading Education and Science Education.

Paper presented at the annual meeting of the American Educational Research Association, San Francisco, CA.

Hennessy, S. (1993). Situated cognition and cognitive apprenticeship: Implications for classroom learning. *Studies in Science Education, 22,* 1–41.

Hewson, P.W. (1981). A conceptual change approach to learning science. *European Journal of Science Education, 4,* 383–396.

Hewson, P.W., & Hennessey, M.G. (1992). Making status explicit: A case study of conceptual change. In R. Duit, F. Goldberg & H. Niedderer (Eds.), *Research in Physics Learning: Theoretical Issues and Empirical Studies* (pp. 176–187). Kiel, Germany: Institute for Science Education at the University of Kiel.

Hewson, P.W., & Hewson, M.G. (1992). The status of students' conceptions. In R. Duit, F. Goldberg & H. Niedderer (Eds.), *Research in Physics Learning: Theoretical Issues and Empirical Studies* (pp. 59–73). Kiel, Germany: Institute for Science Education at the University of Kiel.

Hewson, P.W., & Thorley, N.R. (1989). The conditions of conceptual change in the classroom. *International Journal of Science Education, 11,* 541–553.

Jung, W. (1986). Alltagsvorstellungen und das Lernen von Physik und Chemie. *Naturwissenschaften im Unterricht — Physik/Chemie, 34,* (April), 2–6.

Jung, W. (1989). Understanding students' understanding. The case of elementary optics. In J. Novak (Ed.), *Proceedings of the 2nd Int. Seminar "Misconceptions and Educational Strategies in Science and Mathematics",* Vol. III. (pp. 268–277). Ithaca, NY: Cornell University.

Jung, W. (1993). Hilft die Entwicklungspsychologie dem Naturwissenschaftsdidaktiker. In R. Duit & W. Gräber (Eds.), *Kognitive Entwicklung und Lernen der Naturwissenschaften.* Kiel, Germany: Institute for Science Education at the University of Kiel.

Kelly, G.A. (1955). *The Psychology of Personal Constructs.* Vol. 1:2. New York: W.W. Norton.

Kesidou, S., Duit, R., & Glynn, S. (1995). Conceptual development in physics: Students' understanding of heat. In S. Glynn & R. Duit (Eds.), *Learning Science in the Schools: Research Reforming Practice* (pp. 179–198). Mahwah, NJ: Lawrence Erlbaum, 1995.

Knorr-Cetina, K. (1981). *The Manufactor of Knowledge: An Essay on the Constructivist and Contextual Nature of Science.* New York: Pergamon Press.

Kuhn, T. (1970). *The Structure of Scientific Revolutions.* Chicago: University of Chicago Press.

Lakatos, I. (1970). Falsification and the methodology of scientific research. In I. Lakatos & A. Musgrave (Eds.), *Criticism and the Growth of Knowledge* (pp. 91–196). Cambridge, UK: Cambridge University Press.

Lave, J., & Wenger, E. (1991). *Situated Learning: Legitimate Peripheral Participation.* Cambridge, NY: Cambridge University Press.

Lawson, A.E. (1989). Research on advanced reasoning, concept acquisition and a theory of science instruction. In P. Adey (Ed.), *Adolescent Development and School Science* (pp. 11–36). London: Falmer Press.

Lawson, A.E., Abraham, M.R., & Renner, J.W. (1989). A Theory of Instruction: Using the Learning Cycle to Teach Science Concepts and Thinking Skills. NARST Monograph Number One. National Association for Research in Science Teaching.

Lederman, N.G. (1992). Students' and teachers' conceptions of the nature of science: A review of the research. *Journal of Research in Science Teaching, 29,* 331–359.

Linder, C.J. (1993). A challenge to conceptual change. *Science Education, 77,* 293–300.

Marton, F. (1981). Phenomenography — describing conceptions of the world around us. *Instructional Science, 10,* 177–20.

Marton, F. (1986). Phenomenography — a research approach to investigate different understandings of reality. *Journal of Thought, 21,* (3), 28–49.

Matthews, M.R. (1993). Constructivism and science education: Some epistemological problems. *Journal of Science Education and Technology, 1,* 359–370.

McDermott, L.C. (1984). Research on conceptual understanding in mechanics. *Physics Today, 37* (6), 24–32.

Nussbaum, J. (1983). Classroom conceptual change: The lesson to be learned from the history of science. In H. Helm, & J. Novak (Eds.), *Proceedings of the International Seminar "Misconceptions in Science and Mathematics"* (pp. 272–281). Ithaca, NY: Cornell University.

O'Laughlin (1992). Rethinking science education: beyond Piagetian constructivism toward a socio-cultural model of teaching and learning. *Journal of Research in Science Teaching, 29*, 791–820.

Pfundt, H. (1981). Die Diskrepanz zwischen muttersprachlichem und wissenschaftlichem "Weltbild": Ein Problem der Naturwissenschaftsdidaktik. In R. Duit, W. Jung & H. Pfundt (Eds.), *Alltagsvorstellungen und Naturwissenschaftlicher Unterricht* (pp. 114–131). Köln, Germany: Aulis.

Pfundt, H., & Duit, R. (1994). *Bibliography: Students' Alternative Frameworks and Science Education*, 4th ed. Kiel, Germany: Institute for Science Education at the University of Kiel.

Piaget, J. (1985). *The Equilibration of Cognitive Structures*. Chicago: University of Chicago Press.

Pines, L., & West, L. (1986). Conceptual understanding and science learning: An interpretation of research within a sources of knowledge framework. *Science Education, 70*, 583–604.

Pintrich, P.R., Marx, R.W., & Boyle, R.A. (1993). Beyond cold conceptual change: The role of motivational beliefs and classroom contextual factors in the process of conceptual change. *Review of Educational Research, 6*, 167–199.

Posner, G.J., Strike, K.A., Hewson, P.W., & Gertzog, W.A. (1982). Accommodation of a scientific conception: Toward a theory of conceptual change. *Science Education, 66*, 211–227.

Preece, P.F. (1984). Intuitive science: Learned or triggered? *European Journal of Science Education, 6*, 7–10.

Resnick, L.B. (1991). Shared cognition: Thinking as social practice. In L. Resnick, J. Levine & S. Teasley (Eds.), *Perspectives on Socially Shared Cognition* (pp. 1–19). Washington, DC: American Psychological Association.

Roth, W.-M. (1994). Experimenting in a constructivist high school physics laboratory. *Journal of Research in Science Teaching, 31*, 197–223.

Roth, W.-M. (1995). *Authentic School Science: Knowing and Learning in Open-inquiry Laboratories*. Dordrecht, The Netherlands: Kluwer.

Rowell, J.A., & Dawson, C.J. (1985). Equilibrium, conflict and instruction: A new class-oriented perspective. *European Journal of Science Education, 5*, 203–215.

Rumelhart, D.E., & Norman, D.A. (1981). Analogical processes in learning. In J.R. Anderson (Ed.), *Cognitive Skills and Their Acquisition* (pp. 335–359). Hillsdale, NJ: Erlbaum.

Schumacher, G.M., Tice, S., Wen Loi, P., Stein, S., Joyner, C., & Jolton, J. (1993, August). Difficult to Change Knowledge: Explanations and Interventions. Paper presented at the Third International Seminar on Misconceptions and Educational Strategies in Science and Mathematics. Cornell University, Ithaca, USA.

Scott, P. (1992). Conceptual pathways in learning science: A case study of the development of one student's ideas relating to the structure of matter. In R. Duit, F. Goldberg & H. Niedderer (Eds.), *Research in Physics Learning: Theoretical Issues and Empirical Studies* (pp. 203–224). Kiel, Germany: Institute for Science Education at the University of Kiel.

Scott, P., Asoko, H., & Driver, R. (1992). Teaching for conceptual change: A review of strategies. In R. Duit, F. Goldberg & H. Niedderer (Eds.), *Research in Physics Learning: Theoretical Issues and Empirical Studies* (pp. 310–329). Kiel, Germany: Institute for Science Education at the University of Kiel.

Solomon, J. (1994). The rise and fall of constructivism. *Studies in Science Education, 23*, 1–19.

Steffe, L., & Gale, J. (Eds.), (1995). *Constructivism in Education*. Hillsdale, NJ: Erlbaum.

Strike, K., & Posner, G. (1992). A revisionist theory of conceptual change. In R. Duschl & R. Hamilton (Eds.), *Philosophy of Science, Cognitive Psychology, and Educational Theory and Practice* (pp. 147–176). Albany, NY: SUNY.

Strike, K.A., & Posner, G.J. (1985). A conceptual change view of learning and understanding. In L. West & L. Pines (Eds.), *Cognitive Structure and Conceptual Change* (pp. 211–231). Orlando: Academic Press.

Suchting, W.A. (1992). Constructivism deconstructed. *Science and Education*, *3*, 223–254.

Taylor, P., & Fraser, B. (1991, April). Development of an Instrument for Assessing Constructivist Learning Environments. Round table at the annual meeting of the American Educational Research Association, Chicago.

Taylor, P. (1993). Collaborating to reconstruct teaching: The influence of researcher beliefs. In K. Tobin (Ed.), *The Practice of Constructivism in Science Education* (pp. 267–297). Washington, DC: AAAS Press.

Tiberghien, A. (1980). Modes and conditions of learning — an example: The learning of some aspects of the concept of heat. In F. Archenhold, R. Driver, A. Orton & C. Wood-Robinson (Eds.), *Cognitive Development. Research in Science and Mathematics* (pp. 288–309). Leeds, UK: University of Leeds.

Tobin, K. (Ed.), (1993). *The Practice of Constructivism in Science Education*. Washington, DC: AAAS Press.

Toulmin, S. (1972). *Human Understanding: An Inquiry into the Aims of Science*. Princeton, NJ: Princeton University Press.

Treagust, D., Duit, R., & Fraser, B. (Eds.), (1995). *Improving Teaching and Learning in Science and Mathematics*. New York: Teacher College Press.

Vosniadou, S. (1994). Capturing and modeling the process of conceptual change. *Learning and Instruction*, *4*, 45–69.

Vosniadou, S., & Brewer, W.F. (1992). Mental models of the earth: A study of conceptual change in childhood. *Cognitive Psychology*, *24*, 535–585.

Wandersee, J.H., Mintzes, J.J., & Novak, J.D. (1994). Research on alternative conceptions in science. In D. Gabel (Ed.), *Handbook of Research on Science Teaching and Learning* (pp. 177–210). New York: Macmillan Publ.

Wiesner, H. (1994). Ein neuer Optikkurs für die Sekundarstufe I, der sich an Lernschwierig-keiten und Schülervorstellungen orientiert. *Naturwissenschaften im Unterricht — Physik*, *42*, 7–15.

Wolf, D., Bixby, J., Glen III, J., & Gardner, H. (1991). To use their minds well: Investigating new forms of student assessment. In D. Grant (Ed.), *Review of Research in Education* (pp. 31–74). Washington, DC: American Educational Research Association.

Yager, R.E. (1993). Science-Technology-Society as reform. *School Science and Mathematics*, *93*, 145–151.

Author Index

Subject Index

alternative frameworks 3, 60, 271
analogies 264f, 275, 279–281
anomalous data 138f, 141

beliefs 4, 7f, 11f, 92f, 96, 103, 105, 108f, 175, 179, 185, 189, 265–268, 276

categorization 16, 20, 22, 24, 26f, 30f
classroom culture 185f, 189
cognition
  – metacognition 45–48, 105, 200, 202, 205, 250, 254, 266, 272
  – metacognitive awareness 162, 171
  – metacognitive strategies 34–36, 41, 43f, 47
  – situated cognition 83, 85, 89f, 265
cognitive conflict 4, 11, 140, 180, 189, 268, 276f, 279, 282
cognitive development 3–6, 9, 11f, 16, 28, 30, 117
cognitive strategies 34, 36, 41, 43, 47, 49
cognitive tools 78, 81f, 89f, 193, 196f, 200, 207, 209f
computer-assisted instruction 251, 261
concept formation 17, 74, 76
  – economic conceptions 119
conceptual change
  – as integration 4, 6, 163
  – as replacement 5, 10, 163, 171, 270
  – as restructuring 5f, 11, 17, 27f, 87, 116–119, 131f, 140, 154, 194f, 247–250, 258f, 263f, 275, 280
  – as tuning 195, 263
  – levels of conceptional change 60, 64f, 266
context 5, 9–11, 163f, 169, 265, 268, 270, 272, 277
  – cognitive context 54, 60, 62, 64
  – contextualization 54–56, 59–65
  – contextual variables 163
  – cultural context 54, 62, 64
  – situational context 60f, 63
control beliefs 44–46, 49

diagrams 224–227, 229, 245

enrichment 11, 17, 27f, 263
epistemological beliefs 33, 35, 37–39, 41, 45f
experts/expertise 6, 8, 11, 85, 137f, 140, 224

framework theory 6–8, 223–225, 228–231, 244f, 162, 276

goals
  – educational goals 104–106
  – goal orientation 35–38, 40, 42, 46–48

implicit theories 161f
incoherence 200, 202
inconsistency 200–203
instructional practice 107
intentional perspectives 53f
interest 35, 40–42, 46f, 49

knowledge 91–93, 95f, 103, 106, 108–110
  – knowledge about biology 6, 11, 19f, 24, 62f, 161
  – knowledge about chemistry 60, 161f, 165, 167, 169f
  – knowledge about economics 6, 115
  – knowledge about history 137, 140, 154
  – knowledge about mathematics 12, 79
  – functional knowledge 27, 30
  – knowledge acquisition 3, 6–9, 12, 137f, 268, 279
  – prior knowledge activation 247, 251, 255
  – children's knowledge 3, 6, 8f, 17, 21f, 24, 26, 29, 96, 114f, 117f, 122–127, 129–133, 193, 201f, 205 - intuitive knowledge 8, 161f, 167, 169, 171, 195, 245, 280f - organization of knowledge 6, 11f, 16f, 28, 95, 205

learning 7, 9, 12f, 80, 85f, 90, 265–273, 275–277, 279, 281
  – learning how to learn 256